RED TAPE

A John Hope Franklin Center Book

AKHIL GUPTA

RED TAPE

Bureaucracy, Structural Violence, and Poverty in India

Duke University Press   Durham and London   2012

© 2012 Duke University Press

All rights reserved

Printed in the United States of America on
acid-free paper ♾

Designed by Heather Hensley

Typeset in Quadraat by Keystone Typesetting, Inc.

Library of Congress Cataloging-in-Publication Data
appear on the last printed page of this book.

To
Purnima
Always

CONTENTS

ACKNOWLEDGMENTS

The writing of this book has been a long journey. During its gestation period I have acquired many debts that I am happy to acknowledge here. I ask forgiveness from all those people who have contributed in many ways to the arguments in this book but whose valuable inputs I may not remember as I write these acknowledgments. I have presented parts of the book at many venues and have received helpful criticism and comments from a wide variety of scholars all over the world.

My greatest debt goes to the lower-level state officials who allowed me to sit in their offices and travel with them over the course of a year. Although I cannot name them, I want to register their tremendous generosity in having an inquisitive researcher in their midst for such a long time. I learned more from them about government and governance than one can learn from any report or study. Mostly I learned that, however valuable interviews with senior, English-speaking officers of the Indian Administrative Service are to the study of bureaucracy, they can never substitute for observing what happens when a poor, illiterate villager walks into a government office. The data I collected by observing these lower-level officials and by listening to their responses to my interminable questions lie at the heart of the book. Although the book in its final form is more heavily weighted toward the conceptual, my fieldwork thoroughly informs every idea presented here.

This book was written and rewritten several times, and I am grateful to particular institutions for making that possible: I made my first attempts to conceptualize the book in the turret of the beautiful old Smithsonian building in the mall in Washington, where the Woodrow Wilson Center used to be located. I finished a complete draft of the book thanks to a fellowship from the Stanford Humanities Center in 2004–5, for which I am immensely grateful. I wish to thank its then-director, John Bender, for his support. Keith Baker, who subsequently became director, gave me valuable comments on an earlier introduction. After the first draft was finished and reviewed, I wrote a new introduction and then rewrote all the chapters several times. The finished book bears only a passing resemblance to the complete first draft.

Many research assistants contributed to different chapters in the book. At UCLA, I have been fortunate to have the assistance of Anjali Browning, Adam Fish, Jyoti Gulati, Kerry Pusey, and Melanie Sie. Aaron David Shaw supplied superb assistance while I wrote the critical new chapters on forms of state writing at the Stanford Humanities Center. At Stanford, I was also fortunate to get the help of Lalaie Ameeriar, Yoon-Jung Lee, and Manishita Dass as research assistants.

The first chapter benefited greatly from the inputs of several people. I wish to thank in particular Matthew Kohrman for his insightful comments and Miriam Ticktin for her comments and references; the audience at a lecture in Melbourne, where I tried out an early version of the introduction; and Cris Shore and Veronica Strang, among others, after a presentation at Auckland. I received many useful comments at the University of California, Irvine, including those from my discussant, Susan Greenhalgh, and from Karen Leonard, Kaushik Sunderrajan, Tom Boellstorff, and Mei Zhan. The very first version of this chapter was presented at a Center for India and South Asia (CISA) lecture at UCLA, and I am grateful to all those who attended for their questions and queries. In this regard I want to specially thank Sherry Ortner for the encouragement she gave me on hearing that early version. The interest group Mind, Medicine, and Culture read this chapter in an almost final form and gave me many good ideas and suggestions. I am grateful to Linda Garro and Jason Throop for the invitation and to all the participants for their excellent questions. I also presented a version of this chapter at Uppsala University and at the University of Gothenburg, and I am grateful to participants there for their incisive comments. In addition, scholars at the Ecole des Hautes Etudes en Sciences Sociales, Marseilles, the National Institute of Advanced Studies, Bangalore, and the Department of Anthropology at the University of Copenhagen made this chapter better with their questions and comments. Finally, I was asked several interesting questions at a presentation at the School of Law Faculty Colloquium at UCLA. The prose and organization of this chapter benefited greatly from comments made by Anjali Browning. Arguments from a small part of chapter 1 appeared in an article published in *Cahiers d'Études Africaines* 51, nos. 2–3 (2011): 415–26.

Chapter 2 benefited immensely from comments made by Gail Kligman, who used it in a class she taught, and by a presentation in the Department of Anthropology at Aarhus University in Denmark.

Chapter 4 was first written for a workshop that Cris Shore and Dieter Haller organized at Goldsmiths College in London. I am grateful to them for the invitation. An earlier version of the chapter was published in their book *Corruption: Anthropological Perspectives*, and in the journal *Ethnography*. I thank participants at presentations at Harvard University, the University of Vienna, the Australian Anthropological Society's Annual Meeting, the University of Lisbon, and Columbia University for their thoughtful responses to this chapter.

Chapter 5 benefited in its conceptualization from Liisa Malkki's input. I first presented this chapter as a keynote address at the inaugural meeting of the annual Stanford Cultural and Social Anthropology graduate student conference, and later at a colloquium in the Department of Anthropology at UCLA. I wish to thank the audiences at both venues for their questions and comments.

An earlier version of chapter 6 has been published in *Democracy: Anthropological Perspectives*, edited by Julia Paley and published by SAR Press in 2007. I wish to thank Virginia Dominguez for her comments after a presentation to the Israeli Anthropological Association. I also want to thank a very special group of people who read this chapter and gave me excellent comments at an early stage: Anjali Arondekar, Paola Bacchetta, Amita Baviskar, Lawrence Cohen, Saba Mahmood, Purnima Mankekar, and Raka Ray. I also received detailed comments from the group at the School of American Research, although I was unable to attend the workshop, and I wish to thank all the participants for their input.

I also wish to thank audiences at the National University of Singapore, Yale University, the University of British Columbia, where I presented the 3d Goel lecture, the University of Melbourne, the University of Texas at Austin, and the University of North Carolina for their insights and critical questions.

An early version of chapter 7 was first presented as a keynote address at the Annual Spring Symposium, "Neoliberalism in South Asia: Culture, Gender and Labor," at the University of Hawai'i in 2004. Earlier versions of this chapter also appeared in print in the journal *Current Anthropology* and as the introduction to the book I edited with Aradhana Sharma, *The Anthropology of the State: A Reader*, published by Blackwell in 2006.

Versions of the epilogue have been presented at the following venues: the Max Planck Institute for Social Anthropology at Halle, Germany; CISA at UCLA; the Azim Premji University in Bangalore; and the University of Texas at Austin. I wish to thank the audiences at all four places for their valuable input.

I want to thank friends and family who looked after me during the years it took to write this book. In particular I want to thank my mother, Meena Gupta, my mother-in-law, Kamla Mankekar, and my sister, Anita Aggarwal, my brother-in-law, Rahul Aggarwal, and my niece Shefali and her husband, Mihir. I owe a great deal to my father, Jwala P. Gupta, who did not live to see the publication of this book. A large circle of friends formed extended kin who kept me going through difficult times, and I cannot thank them enough for their support and encouragement: George Collier, Jane Collier, Veena Dubal, Julia Jaroch, Arun Kumar, Poornima Kumar, Sylvia Yanagisako, and Ethiraj Venkatapathy. At Stanford, where most of this book was written, I want to thank colleagues with whom I worked particularly closely: George Collier, Jane Collier, Jim Ferguson, Miyako Inoue, Sarah Lochlann Jain, Matthew Kohrman, Liisa Malkki, David Palumbo-Liu, Renato Rosaldo Jr., and Sylvia Yanagisako. Last but not least are the wonderful doctoral students whose persistent questions and inquiries helped me in ways I could not have imagined. Their insights are reflected in this text in many ways. I would like to thank my doctoral students at Stanford: Evelyn Alsultany, Lalaie Ameeriar, Christa Amoroux, Nikhil Anand, Ulka Anjaria, Falu Bakrania, Tom Boellstorf, Federico Besserer, Carrie Bramen, Jackie Brown, Ashish Chadha, Jennifer Chertow, Jocelyn Chua, Cari Costanzo, Donna Daniels, Monica DeHart, Nejat Dinc, Maya Dodd, Alnoor Ebrahim, Jack Ferguson, Kelly Freidenfelds, Helen Gremillion, Stefan Helmreich, Aida Hernandez, Francisca James Hernandez, Margaret Karalis, Yoon-Jung Lee, Jana Sequoya Magdalena, Jisha Menon, Kristin Monroe, Donald Moore, Diane Nelson, Laura Nelson, Julia Olson, Sanjeev Pandya, Amit Rai, Shankar Raman, Helle Rytkonen, Josie Saldana, Victoria Sanford, Suzana Sawyer, Alicia Schmidt Camacho, Mukta Sharangpani, Aradhana Sharma, Lok Siu, Doug Smith, Rebecca Stein, Miriam Ticktin, Mridula Udaygiri, and Michel Welmond. I would also like to thank the students at UCLA with whom I have worked so far: Ziad Munif Abu-Rish, Adam Fish, Hanna Garth, Veena Hampapur, Jaeeun Kim, Cassandra Markoe, Janell Rothenberg, Seema Shah, Ellen Sharp, Tristan Sturm, and Meher Varma.

My editor at Duke University Press, Ken Wissoker, has been unstintingly supportive of this project. I am grateful for his patience, and his willingness to wait until the manuscript was ready to be published. The support he has given me goes far beyond his role as editor, and I will always be grateful to him for the gift of friendship. I also wish to thank other members of the amazing staff at Duke University Press: Leigh Barnwell brought the book to print, Lawrence Kenney did the copyediting, and Heather Hensley was responsible for the graphic design. Scott P. Smiley compiled an excellent index, and Melanie Sie meticulously checked the proofs. I am grateful to them both for their labor.

This book might have been finished earlier were it not for my daughter, Deeya, but it would not have been as good without her intervention. She is my best student and one of my better teachers. In the last year, anytime the book was mentioned in her presence, her refrain has been, "I am bored of hearing about *Red Tape*. Why is it taking so long to finish? I have already written several books in this time." I think she too will be relieved to see the book in print.

Finally, I reserve the best part for my partner, Purnima Mankekar. She listened to the ideas as they developed, read many drafts of all the chapters, gave me constant encouragement and comments, and edited some parts of the book. She protected my time when I was writing intensively, and she helped create an atmosphere in which I could think and write by removing all the red tape that got in the way. Without her, this book would not be possible, and I dedicate it to her.

PART ONE **INTRODUCTION**

POVERTY AS BIOPOLITICS 1

Any study of the state in India must try to address one central puzzle.[1] Why has a state whose proclaimed motive is to foster development failed to help the large number of people who still live in dire poverty? Why do regimes whose legitimacy depends upon bettering the lives of the poor continue to allow anywhere from 250 million to 427 million to live below the poverty line?[2] Another way to frame this question is to ask, After more than sixty years of development efforts by the postcolonial state, why do so many of India's citizens continue to be subjected to the cruelties of endemic hunger and malnutrition and to be deprived of such basic necessities as clothing, shelter, clean water, and sanitation?

Despite being the fourth largest economy in the world, India ranks extremely low on the Human Development Index (134th among 182 nation-states, according to the Human Development Report [2009]).[3] The infant mortality rate is around 56 per 1,000 live births (101 per 1,000 live births for the poorest 20 percent of the population);[4] adult illiteracy hovers around 40 percent; about half of children under five suffer from malnutrition; large proportions of the urban population are homeless—fully half of the residents of Mumbai live in slums and other degraded forms of housing, while at least one-third of the population of Kolkata lives in slums—and an unknown number of rural people live in poor or substandard housing.[5] Yet expenditures on health and education in 2007–8 amounted to less than one-tenth of the national budget.[6] One hundred million women are "missing," and sex ratios are declining even in areas of India such as the South, where they have not been historically unfavorable to women (Sen 1999: 104–7).

One could argue that the high poverty rates and poor social development indices are merely a residual feature of Nehruvian economic policies that muddled along not knowing whether the nation-state was capitalist or socialist and consequently delivering anemic results, which were famously christened by the economist Raj Krishna as "the Hindu rate of growth." Now that India has settled into a period of liberalization, the GDP growth rate has shot up (over 9 percent from 2005 to 2007, followed by a mild dip in the recession years of 2008 and 2009 (IMF 2009), and between 6 and 8 percent in the past two decades), and there have been sharp reductions in the number of people living below the poverty line (from just a bit more than 50 percent in 1977–78 to less than 23 percent in 2004–5). Given this improvement, does not continuing the emphasis on poverty, rather than on the considerable achievements that have been made in other spheres, simply perpetuate the clichéd image of India as a poverty-stricken land? Should one not instead focus on the positive side of development, on the immense progress the state has engineered, and consider chronic poverty to be a colonial legacy and an intractable problem that the postcolonial state has done its best to eradicate? Rather than dismiss such objections, I acknowledge that there is much truth to them. However, for reasons that will become evident in this book, I insist that the life-denying consequences of chronic poverty, far from receiving too much attention, have in fact largely disappeared from public discussion. More important, despite the rhetorical importance given to the eradication of poverty in government policy pronouncements, the scandal of the state lies in its failure to acknowledge that condemning an estimated 250–450 million people to a premature and untimely death constitutes a crisis of grave proportions.[7]

If there was a natural disaster—a famine or an earthquake—in which thousands of people died and many others were displaced from their homes and separated from their families, food sources, or places of employment, there is little doubt it would be considered a dire national crisis requiring massive state intervention to aid in relief and rehabilitation. Now suppose a scenario like the one I describe here actually unfolded. A disaster of this magnitude occurs not once but annually. The consensus among elites both within and outside the state is that such disasters are inevitable and that relief efforts cannot of necessity aid all those who are affected. Some experts suggest that the best thing the state can do to improve the conditions of the poor is to concentrate on facilitating the rapid growth of the economy so that the victims can at least find employment and help to better their lives. How would we react to such a solution? Would we not find such a state of affairs to be appalling and perhaps even outrageous?

Yet this is precisely the situation in postcolonial India. Using a very crude calculation, I estimate that the number of "excess deaths"—the number of people missing from the population because of malnutrition and morbidity —is approximately 140 million.[8] This translates to over 2 million untimely deaths annually, a figure that overshadows the loss of human life resulting from all natural disasters globally. In the decade between 1991 and 2000 the annual global death toll owing to natural disasters, technological mishaps, and human conflict totaled just over 300,000 (Calhoun 2004: 382). Nevertheless, the system of checks and balances composed of the free press and the democratic, multiparty, competitive political system that, as Amartya Sen (1999: 180–82) claims, has been so effective in sounding the alarm of impending famine, drought, or natural disaster has failed to mobilize state and private resources to prevent a disaster of these proportions.[9]

I am concerned, in other words, with what should be considered exceptional, a tragedy and a disgrace, but is not: the invisible forms of violence that result in the deaths of millions of the poor, especially women, girls, lower-caste people, and indigenous people. What makes such violence invisible? How does one think about not only deliberate acts of violence such as police brutality, but also political, administrative, and judicial action or inaction that prevents poor people from making a living, obtaining medical aid, and securing such necessities of life as food, clothing, shelter, and sanitation? Why is faster, more effective state intervention not forthcoming to relieve the suffering of millions of the poorest and most disempowered?[10] How does one describe violence in the absence of events like communal riots, or the displacement of people by dams and other spectacular development projects, or police or army brutality? What are the juridical and social conditions that make the violence of such exceptional poverty normal? Most important, how is violence like this taken for granted in the routinized practices of state institutions such that it disappears from view and cannot be thematized as violence at all?[11]

Engaging the work of Michel Foucault and Giorgio Agamben, I argue that extreme poverty should be theorized as a direct and culpable form of killing made possible by state policies and practices rather than as an inevitable situation in which the poor are merely "allowed to die" or "exposed to death." Seeing the death of the poor as a form of thanatopolitics enables several important interventions. First, it draws attention to the fact that such deaths are not inevitable: far from it, despite being preventable they are not prevented. This is where the contrast with natural disasters is so clear: if the poor were equated to victims of a natural disaster, the urgency displayed in ameliorating their situation and the scale of intervention employed would be of a completely different magnitude. Similarly, if one compares the complacency toward endemic poverty with the impatience displayed toward impediments to growth and accumulation, the disparity is striking. How does one account for the enormous gap between the Indian state's indifferent response to poverty on the one hand and its much more proactive responses to natural disaster and liberalization on the other?

The usual answer to this question is that it must be because the poor are excluded from national projects of development, democratic politics, and cultural citizenship. Agamben suggests that exclusion is the basis for violence in states of exception. For example, the killing of Jews, homosexuals, and gypsies in Nazi Germany was possible because they had been legally excluded from the German state and reduced to "bare life." Contra Agamben (this is my second major point), the paradox of the violence of poverty in India is that the poor are killed despite their inclusion in projects of national sovereignty and despite their centrality to democratic politics and state legitimacy.[12]

I am not blaming bureaucratic attitudes for such perverse outcomes. Without doubt state officials who are uncaring or indifferent to extreme poverty and are interested merely in advancing their own fortunes and careers do exist.[13] However, even if all state officials were sincerely devoted to the task of eradicating poverty, the question is whether the procedures of the bureaucracy would end up subverting even their best intentions. I draw upon a theme first articulated by Michael Herzfeld (1993) in which state bureaucracies are considered to be machines for "the social production of indifference," and the idea proposed by Arthur Kleinman, Veena Das, and Margaret Lock that "bureaucratic responses to social violence intensify suffering" (1997: x); but I modify those lines of reasoning in this book. I argue (this is my third major point) that bureaucratic action repeatedly and systematically produces arbitrary outcomes in its provision of care. While indifference does indeed play an important role in this story, the indifference to arbitrary outcomes is central.

To illustrate and develop these theoretical points, I begin with an extended description of an event that took place during my fieldwork. I choose this event not because it exemplifies what I argue below about the systematic production of arbitrariness but because it is a good example of the kind of antipoverty activities engaged in by the state in India. My description of a development camp has to be put in the context of other prominent recent studies of the camp as an archetypal space created by modern states.

Drawing upon the history of Nazi concentration camps, Agamben writes, "The camp is the nomos of the modern" (2000: 36).[14] In stating this, Agamben effectively extends the space of the camp, via detention centers for immigrants at airports and sports stadiums, to any space where the state of exception is materialized (1998: 174). Although in Agamben's work the camp is closely connected to thanatopolitics and the state of exception, others have investigated camps of different kinds where the utility of Agamben's insights can be broadened and questioned. Lawrence Cohen's (2004) notion of "operability" links forced sterilizations during the Emergency in India in 1975–77 with eye camps and other sites of mass operations.[15] His work demonstrates the continuities in biopolitical processes between the period of emergency and normal times, which underlines one of Agamben's key arguments, while at the same time highlighting the intimate connection between care and repression. Similarly, Ananya Vajpeyi's (2007) discussion of internally displaced people points out how, although state violence is often responsible for forcibly evicting people from their homeland and from their homes, refugee and relief camps set up by nongovernmental agencies and aid organizations slowly restore their rights as citizens.[16] The camp, therefore, is not only a space where citizens are stripped of their rights and rendered into bare life, as Agamben argues, but also potentially a place from which the painstaking restoration of those rights becomes feasible. Didier Fassin (2005) carefully distinguishes camps in contemporary France set up for refugees from their counterparts in the Nazi era. However, he points out that in both cases the political life of citizens in the polis was built on the exclusions practiced through the construction of bare life in the camps. As a final example, I turn to Veena Das's (2007) sensitive portrayal of "resettlement colonies," so named because their inhabitants are former slum dwellers who have been forcibly removed from their homes by state agencies. Das shows how the residents of these colonies experience the state of exception repeatedly through communal riots in which the police openly side with the majority religious community. Das's concern is with how people construct a semblance of normality after such riots, how they go on living with neighbors who they know are the murderers of their family and friends. Here, the resettlement colony itself becomes a camp where the state of exception is actually the norm. Thus, there are many types of camps whose specificity is important and whose form does not simply reproduce the Nazi death camp.[17] The camp I describe is a so-called development camp, one whose register is both tragic and farcical at the same time.[18]

Camp

One hot April morning, as I was sitting in the office of Satendra Malik, the Block Development Officer (BDO) of Mandi, a man walked in to inquire about a camp that was to be held there the following week for providing pensions to indigent, elderly people. The BDO did not know about it and was alarmed to learn of plans for holding such a big event at his office. However, experience and good sense taught him to ask his staff if they had received a message about the camp. When the BDO asked two of his senior staff about it, they did not recollect having seen any notice. The two officials then went to the inner office to search for the notice. When they did not come out for several minutes, the BDO himself went in and some minutes later emerged with the notice in his hand.

The notice took the form of a letter written by the Subdistrict Magistrate (SDM) to the head of the Land Records Office (Tehsildar) informing him of the date at which a camp for elderly pensioners was to be held at each of the four blocks in the subdistrict (tehsil). The SDM had scheduled the meeting for Mandi Block the following week.

Malik turned to me and complained loudly that, as usual, the date had been set without consulting him first. He had already scheduled a meeting of his field staff on that very same day and now would have to reschedule. "Just wait and see," Malik grumbled, "next there will be a notice from the District Magistrate [DM] saying that he has called a meeting on the twenty-first, which will have been set, naturally, without consulting the SDM."

Malik failed to understand why they were scheduling the camp in his office. His staff had nothing to do with the camp except to certify the eligibility of applicants. They were involved in neither the processing of the paperwork nor disbursing the money to beneficiaries.

The notice Malik retrieved clarified the conditions for eligibility: the beneficiary had to be at least sixty years old, own less than one and a half acres of land, and have no adult son (balig ladka na ho) who could look after the beneficiary. The pension amounted to Rs. 100 a month and would be paid directly to the beneficiaries by the Social Welfare office at the district headquarters.[19]

Malik sprang into action and immediately dictated two letters. They were addressed to subordinate officials who maintained the Economic Registers and Family Registers. The letters urged both sets of officials to be present at the camp the following week with their respective registers. Malik delegated responsibility for delivering each of the two letters to a different individual in his office.

After a short while, the official who had been delegated the task of delivering the second letter entered Malik's office to consult him about something else. When Malik inquired about his progress in delivering the letter, the official said he had given the letter to the clerk to dispatch (a record of all incoming and outgoing correspondence has to be made), and the clerk had not yet returned the letter to him. However, he had informed some officials verbally about the camp.

Malik grew so visibly angry as he heard this that he could not contain his fury. "There are two ways to work," he said. "One is to follow the book and satisfy the minimum requirements and the other is to put some effort into your job, to put your heart into it (dil lagā ke kām karo). I had asked you to do this with some urgency, to put your heart into it. However, you have failed to do even this. I acted promptly to not give anyone an excuse to not show up for the camp. But you are just sitting on the letter."

The theoretical importance of this detailed ethnography of the chaotic preparations for a big state event will soon be clear. Of significance here is the sheer contingency underlying the workings of a supposedly highly rationalized, bureaucratic state. First, Malik was fortunate that a citizen's inquiry led him to discover, a week before it was scheduled to occur, that he was to help organize a big event. Second, the junior official who followed regulations and thereby delayed getting the message out might have further jeopardized the event if the relevant officials were not present. The event was thus configured by fortuitous acts of chance and potentially jeopardized by rule-following bureaucratic behavior. Can this tell us something about the provisioning of welfare and about bureaucracy's relations with the poor more generally?

I missed the camp in Malik's office, but I attended another one of the four camps scheduled in the subdistrict. The camp I attended was to begin at 10:30 A.M., but the government medical doctor whose presence was essential did not show up until 12:30 P.M., and the tehsildar arrived even later still. I was soon to learn that, as a rule, the rank of an official was inversely related to punctuality. This was a way not only of signaling how busy the superior officer was but also of discounting the importance of the time of junior officials and clients. That hundreds of elderly, indigent people would have to wait outside in the heat of early summer was not a factor that influenced the actions of any official, high or low.

The doctor was a man of around forty-five, short, with a small paunch and the obsequious, yet officious, manner of one who had served too long in government jobs in out-of-the-way places. On arriving, the doctor requested that a room be set up especially for him, preferably near a window facing the outside of the building. That way he could estimate the age of applicants by looking at them through the window as they passed by.

Since we were waiting for the tehsildar to arrive, I took the opportunity to ask the doctor a few questions. From my experience in doing a rudimentary census in a village I knew that estimating people's ages was no easy matter. Most villagers did not seem to attach a great deal of importance to exact ages (birthdays, for example, were neither remembered nor celebrated), and it was nearly impossible to narrow down an adult's age with any degree of confidence below a variance of five years. I asked the doctor, "How can you tell how old someone really is?" He answered without hesitation, "I can tell just by looking at people." He then proceeded to guess my age to within two years. I was quite impressed with his skill, but the events that followed caused my skepticism to return.

Shortly afterward, a jeep drove into the compound of the block office, and the tehsildar walked in. He quickly took charge of organizing the structure of the camp, telling the doctor that the two of them should sit side by side. That way the doctor could give him the age certificates, and he could approve the applications right away. They set up in the large hall outside. The bare floor was packed with people, most of them prospective applicants accompanied by younger relatives or village headmen. The desks were set up in an L-shape, the doctor occupying the smaller side and the tehsildar the middle of the big table. The tehsildar took out a big stack of application forms and placed them under his desk, out of sight of the applicants and their helpers. While he was busy talking, someone reached under the table and pulled out a whole bunch of applications. Another man tried to follow suit, but the tehsildar caught him in the act and demanded that he first produce the intended beneficiary before he received a form. "Don't waste forms," he said sternly.

The tehsildar then announced in a loud voice that headmen had to certify how many children the applicant had and how much land she or he owned. A large crowd started milling around the desk, and the noise level rose to a crescendo. The doctor started estimating ages, making his notes on the front of each application. He deliberately wrote his estimates of the applicant's age in English so that they could not understand and perhaps challenge what he had written. On the basis of the estimated age and other questions he asked, the tehsildar then decided whether to grant a pension to the applicant. Without revealing if a favorable decision had been made, he told each applicant, "Go away now. Your work is done." The applicants left without knowing if their long wait had been successful and if they were being recommended for a pension.

Echoing the eligibility criteria, the tehsildar asked each applicant the same three questions: "How old are you? Do you have any children? How much land do you have?" A person who replied that she was over sixty, did not have any adult sons, and owned less than one and a half acres of land, was eligible for the scheme. He jokingly told several applicants that they did not look a day older than he did, implying that they should not qualify for the scheme. He asked a man who clearly did not look old enough to be eligible, "How old are you?" and the man replied, "I must be fifty-five or so." The tehsildar looked at me with amusement and said, "When he himself is saying that his age is fifty-five, how can we certify him for this scheme?" He told the doctor to be more vigilant since the government had very strict age guidelines for the program. "I can tell that this man is not sixty and yet you have certified him to be so," he complained. Then he handed the application back to the doctor to amend. He then turned to the applicant and said, "Come back again next year, and you may qualify then. Now go." This case illustrates the indiscriminate nature of the process of selecting supposedly qualified applicants. It depended on both the doctor's guess and the tehsildar's ability to catch someone lying by asking three short questions. It was almost certain that the applicants and headmen knew little about the eligibility criteria for the scheme and that information about eligibility was being passed around outside the building through rumor and speculation. Nothing else could explain why the applicant in the incident described above had stated his age as being less than the minimum required for the scheme.

From time to time the tehsildar would yell for the area in front of his desk to be cleared. "Get away!" he would shout at the top of his voice. "Get away from my desk. I will call you when your application comes to the top of my stack." The crowd would back off, but within a couple of minutes the initial conditions were restored. An old man whose name had just been announced by the tehsildar fought his way to the front of the mass of people crowding the desk. By the time he reached the front, however, the tehsildar had already put his application away, assuming he was not there. The chaos of the room contributed in no small way to the randomness of the decisions. Qualified people like this old man were being turned down not because the tehsildar was deliberately callous or uncaring, but because the pressure of accomplishing things meant that decisions had to be made quickly.

The doctor turned back one of the first few applications he received for lack of a photograph. He told the applicant, "Go back and get a photograph and only then can something be done about your application." The man who had submitted the application pleaded that it was hard to get photographs in the village (*aap to jaante hee hain, babuji, dehat may to aise hee hota hain*). Fortunately, the tehsildar intervened to say it was okay to accept an application as long as a photograph was appended to it eventually. Once again, differences between officials on how to interpret the rules of eligibility—Did the form have to be fully completed before submission or before the disbursement of funds?—made for completely different outcomes for applicants. Someone whose application was declared incomplete by the doctor could be considered eligible by the tehsildar's interpretation.

At one point when the tehsildar shouted at the people gathered in front of his desk to disperse, one man refused to move. The tehsildar asked him loudly and rather brusquely, "Who are you? Why are you standing here?" (*Aap kaun hain? Kyon khaday hain yahaan?*). He replied, rather defiantly, "I am a man" (*Main aadmi hoon*). The tehsildar, not used to being answered in this way, replied in a quieter tone, "I can see that you are a man. But are you a land records official [*patwari*] a headman [*pradhan*], or what?" "I am a headman," he replied. "So say that," said the tehsildar, much more mildly. "What are you trying to get done here?" The headman handed him an application. The tehsildar took a quick look at it and then told him to go and stand in the queue for the doctor's signature. "After that, bring the application to me," he said. It struck me as particularly interesting that the headman chose to respond to the tehsildar's initial challenge not by affirming his privileged bureaucratic role as a headman, but by declaring his rights as a human being (*Aadmi* connotes both "man" and the generic category of "human").[20] The context makes it clear that the man was asserting not just his rights as a human, but also the more specific claims of citizenship, of membership in the national community. He was asserting his right, as a citizen, to be treated with respect by the bureaucrat.[21]

As the tehsildar processed one form after another in which elderly applicants denied having any children, he grew increasingly doubtful of their veracity. "Our population is growing so rapidly," he observed wryly, "and all these people claim to have no children. I find that rather hard to believe, don't you?" Although headmen were supposed to endorse the applicants' statements about the amount of land they owned and the number of adult children they had, it was up to the land records official to check the truth of those statements. In a resigned tone, the tehsildar said that the land records officials probably did not bother to verify the facts independently. What appeared to bother the tehsildar most about the fraudulent applications was that they undermined state authority by putting into question the state's right to adjudicate who deserved to receive a pension and who did not. On the other hand, for many poor, rural people who were there, the entire exercise of figuring out a person's exact age must have appeared largely irrelevant, and the criteria for eligibility cooked up by a bureaucrat sitting in a central office superfluous. After about an hour and a half of intense work during which applications were rapidly processed, the morning's frenzy finally subsided. Work stopped temporarily when the officials took a tea break. During the break I stepped outside the building and saw approximately three hundred people sitting there.

The whole camp wound up soon thereafter. I wondered how many of the poorest villagers had even heard about this program since it did not appear to have been well publicized. Even if they had learned of it, how many elderly people would have been healthy enough to travel to the block office or would have had the money to take public transportation to get there? These issues did not concern the officials organizing the event. The number of people who showed up overwhelmed them, and they were doing their best to process the applications.

I offer this example to give a sense of how development programs actually unfold at the sites where poor rural clients encounter state agencies and bureaucrats. Several features of this vignette illustrate the most important aspects of a theory of the state I will develop here. First, I note that in organizing these camps for the elderly, the state, far from being indifferent to the plight of the poor, displayed great care for a segment of the population that was unproductive in an economic sense.[22] In other words, it would be hard to explain this investment in terms of its economic rationality or political payoff. Second, I want to emphasize the role of contingency in the making of this event. The camp may very well be the model of disciplinary rationality, but its production in this case depended on a number of fortuitous accidents. Paying attention to processes within the state—for example, procedures of planning and implementation, communication or lack thereof across hierarchies, the rule-following actions of particular officials—opens up possibilities of interpretation different from those we might posit were we to look only at finished outcomes, in this case, the camp as an event. The chaotic conditions before and during the camp underscore that one should not confuse the spectacle of disciplinary power with its operation. One of the arguments I make in this book is that operating within that reified entity, the state, leads to misinterpretations of bureaucratic processes and social outcomes that have serious consequences for both scholarship and policy.

I have replaced the notion that bureaucracies represent the rationalization of power in a disciplinary society with a very different picture—one in which the entire process is shot through with contingency and barely controlled chaos. My interest lies in explaining what I referred to above as the production of arbitrariness. In the midst of this chaos, the allegedly rational apparatus of the state makes crucial decisions such as whether a poor person should receive what may be lifesaving aid. However, the procedural bases for these decisions were far from rational. The rational side of bureaucratic process required the enlistment of the services of a medical doctor at the camp. Yet his job consisted of guessing the applicants' age, a task that someone else, someone without his expertise, could have done just as well. Similarly, there was no administrative logic guiding the decision that applications submitted without a photograph should or should not be accepted. Facing the lack of reliable information regarding an applicant's age, landownership, or the number of adult children, officials made decisions on eligibility on the basis of guesswork and contingency. Such arbitrary decisions had no negative consequences for the officials, who were satisfied that they were doing the best under the circumstances; however, for the clients of their programs these decisions mattered a great deal and may have made the difference between life and death, and this becomes central to my theoretical ruminations.

Biopolitics, Bare Life, and Legitimate Violence

One death is a tragedy, a million deaths a statistic.
ATTRIBUTED TO JOSEPH STALIN

The camp for pensioners condensed two features essential to any understanding of the relation between the state in India and the poor.[23] First, that the task of caring for the population is taken seriously by the state and carried out well beyond a utilitarian calculus; second, that despite this approach the poor are exposed to death on an ongoing basis without causing anyone to be alarmed. How is this seemingly contradictory state of affairs to be understood?

One possible answer emerges from the connections Foucault makes between normalization and mortality in his concept of biopower (1990, 2003, 2007).[24] In charting the shift from disciplinary technologies to biopower, Foucault argues that with biopower the control of individual bodies (discipline) is complemented by a focus on the population as a whole. So-called objects like the birthrate and the rate of mortality and morbidity come into a calculus of planning and control. Once the population becomes the target of intervention, its regularities, deviances, anomalies, and peculiarities can be established. For my purposes, the most important point about this argument is that the normal is discovered and established through the statistical analysis of the population. Statistical regularity, in other words, helps establish the prescriptive (2003: 253).

In the Indian case, high rates of poverty, once established as a statistical fact and the normal state of affairs, served to justify and legitimate slow action against poverty on the part of state elites, particularly since there was not much change in rates of poverty in the first five decades after Independence. High rates of poverty are tolerated because, much like any other natural phenomenon, they are seen as part of the landscape. In a very similar vein, Scheper-Hughes introduces the concept of "an average expectable environment of child death" (1992: 20, 273–76) to explain how high infant mortality rates came to be normalized in northeast Brazil. As in the case of the natural cycle of floods and droughts, one can at best cope with such situations by developing adequate mechanisms of temporary relief. This is why any significant reduction in poverty is treated as a cause of great celebration and self-congratulation.

If one were to draw an analogy with India's rates of economic growth in the decades after Independence, the normal rate of around 3.5 percent became so much an established fact that there was consternation only if the economy failed to reach that number. When liberalization was first introduced in the early 1990s, proponents argued that, in order to be effective, a change in policy had to be accompanied by a different mindset that believed that rates of growth of 6–8 percent were possible in India. Promoters of liberalization like P. Chidambaram, who served as finance minister from May 2004 to November 2008, claim that one of its enduring achievements is that the perceived norm has shifted so significantly that these rates of growth are now expected and people ask why India cannot do even better (BBC 2007).

Comparison of such an optimistic discourse with the one applied to acute poverty makes for a striking contrast. Chidambaram himself exemplifies this contrast in an interview he gave to the BBC: "The faster we grow and the more inclusive that growth is, the decline in poverty will be rapid. I'm confident we can wipe out poverty by 2040." The interviewer, incredulous, asks him what he means by "wiping out poverty." Chidambaram replies, "People will have homes, work, food, clothing, access to education and medical care" (BBC 2007).

Keeping the low life expectancies of the very poor in mind, one might well ask why a plan to eradicate poverty that essentially sacrifices an entire generation is considered to be a positive aspiration (and one does not know how much of this will translate into actual achievement). By the time the Indian government plans to wipe out poverty, very few of the poorest people living today will still be alive. Such a statement makes sense to speakers and listeners alike only against a backdrop in which high rates of poverty are taken as normal. In other words, it makes sense as biopolitics. When policymakers establish goals through the norm of high poverty and employ a discourse about the difficulty of reducing poverty in a big, complex country like India, they uncannily echo the justifications used previously for explaining why India could not accelerate economic growth.

As a concept, biopower does not help explain why some people in dire poverty receive help while others do not. Why are some people allowed to die while others are enabled to live? However, this is not to say that biopolitical technologies cannot address such a question. For example, a statistical analysis could reveal that there are significant intraregional variations in poverty rates or considerable intercaste differences, which might lead to specific policy interventions. The bigger criticism of the idea of biopower is that in emphasizing managerial approaches to the population, it fails to address adequately questions of violence. If managing the population perpetrates violence on the poor, how is the form of violence implicit in biopower different from other types of violence? It would be fair to say that the violence implicit in biopower remains undertheorized in Foucault's work.

Agamben introduces an important shift from the Foucauldian idea of biopower by making the distinction between "being killed" as opposed to passively "being allowed to die." The protagonist of *Homo Sacer* and *State of Exception* is the person who can be killed without sacrifice, a person who is expendable. A similar critique is articulated by Achille Mbembe, who points to the lack of engagement with explicit violence that is implicit in the concept of biopower. Mbembe asks, "Is the notion of biopower sufficient to account for the contemporary ways in which the political, under the guise of war, of resistance, or of the fight against terror, makes the murder of the enemy its primary and absolute objective?" (2003: 12).[25] Although the extreme poor are not conceived of as "the enemy" by India's other classes, this critique of biopower enables one to think about the role that violence plays in a situation where the preservation of the self is not dependent upon the death of the other. Are cases in which people deliberately ignore the acute distress of others acts of violence? Can the violence of biopolitics be theorized explicitly outside of a Manichean framework?[26]

The inevitability of the death of the poor attains a different ethical complexion if the violence in such a thanatopolitics is seen as killing rather than simply as allowing to die or exposing to death. Agamben constructs the figure of the *homo sacer* as a person both inside and outside the law, one who can be killed but whose killing does not violate either the law or the legitimacy of the sovereign (1998: 8). Agamben's examples are human guinea pigs for Nazi experiments, eugenics, and euthanasia, but is there a different way to think about thanatopolitics (1998: 136–59)? The extremely poor could be a perfect example of what Agamben means by homo sacer in that their death is not recognized as a violation in any respect: not a violation of a norm, a rule, a law, a constitutional principle, not even perhaps of the idea of justice.[27] Does not providing food, clothing, shelter, and healthcare to someone who is obviously in dire need represent killing? If so, it is important to note that nobody is punished or punishable for taking these lives. Because such deaths are outside the orbit of violation, punishment, and restitution, they represent life that can be killed without being considered a sacrifice— exactly what Agamben means by "sacred life."

However, unlike Foucault, Agamben links this idea of violence against members of a population who are considered *hominis sacri* with a strong notion of sovereignty.[28] It is the sovereign injunction declaring a state of emergency, which positions a certain category of people outside the law and makes them vulnerable to authorized violence. It is only in these conditions that persons can be killed without sacrifice. In other words, Agamben makes a necessary link between the sovereign ban and sacred life, arguing that the sovereign and homo sacer are symmetrical figures, each producing the other.[29] I contend below, however, that it is hard to sustain such an argument for the violence of poverty I am describing in this book.[30]

Useful as Agamben's idea of bare life is for understanding the plight of the very poor in India, the integral connection between the state of exception and the production of bare life is much less persuasive. One reason could be that for Agamben the state of exception depends on a strong theory of sovereignty and a powerfully unified state apparatus (Redfield 2005: 340; Hansen and Stepputat 2006). From Carl Schmitt, Agamben (2005: 1) takes the definition of the sovereign to be the one "who decides on the state of exception." If, by contrast, one considers a situation characterized by fragmented, dispersed, or overlapping sovereignties (Ong 2000), and a state that is pluricentered, multileveled, and decentralized, it becomes much harder to mobilize the theoretical dualisms that characterize Agamben's relationship between the state of exception and bare life.

The poor in India are not excluded from political participation; in fact, as this book demonstrates, they are enthusiastic practitioners of participatory democracy at different levels of politics (Alsop, Krishna, and Sjoblom 2001). Of the two million people elected to various offices by democratic methods in India, the poor constitute a significant number. The failure of the benefits of development to reach them cannot be attributed solely to their exclusion from political community constituted by identities such as nation, religion, or caste (Agamben 1998: 181).[31] On the other hand, despite their inclusion in the national community and the development state, their poverty does not constitute a scandal, and their death does not provoke national soul-searching.[32] Popular sovereignty takes the paradoxical form of inclusion and unspeakable violence; forms of belonging coexist with the production of bare life. What begs explanation in the case of India is the widespread acceptance of the violence being done to the poor at the same time that popular sovereignty is constituted through them.[33]

Who are "the people" through whom popular sovereignty is constructed and who become the object of care in biopolitics? The biopolitical concern with the people presumes a territorial unit whose population is the object of care or exclusion. Foucault distances the idea of security from that of sovereignty in the following manner: "Baldly, at first sight and somewhat schematically, we could say that sovereignty is exercised within the borders of a territory, discipline is exercised on the bodies of individuals, and security is exercised over a whole population" (2007: 11). By "security," Foucault means regulating and managing the risks that affect the population so that negative tendencies do not get out of control. Despite the fact that Foucault's emphasis is not on borders and territory, he still assumes that the population whose risks must be managed is bounded by affective ties and geographical boundaries.[34] The nation-state thus remains the implicit subject of the Foucauldian notion of biopolitics.[35] This is made evident in Foucault's assertion that managing the population is the object of government, which is situated in a particular sociohistorical conjuncture, one marked by the ascent of France and other European states as colonial powers. In that context, the state governed a population that exceeded the borders of the nation. However, despite their occasional concern with large famines, the management of the welfare of the population in the colonies was hardly critical to imperial states.

Is the exercise of sovereignty and the exposure to death in biopolitics implicitly mediated by sodalities such as nationalism?[36] Nationalist affect helps explain why some people become the objects of concern more than others, people whose welfare may be seen as the problem of their own sovereign. This may help explain why poor people who are refugees are so often treated differently from destitute citizens. The responsibility of looking after those who are outside the affective ties of citizenship, even if they share the same territorial space and predicament of livelihood, is often placed on the government of that nation-state to whom those people properly belong. One can ethically distance oneself from the extreme distress of others who are outsiders by blaming their nation-state for its failure to look after its own people (see Daniel 1997), and the suffering of those who are outside our moral community does not matter (Morris 1997: 40). Discourses of mismanagement, corruption, poor policies, and divisive politics can be mobilized to blame the governments of other nation-states for their failures to look after their own citizens.[37] By doing so, however, does one not just reaffirm one's respect for the sovereignty of the nation-state and implicitly recognize its right to expose its own citizens to death?[38] The violence of nationalism becomes explicit both through the categories of poor who are deemed appropriate to neglect and through the failure to help those who are not considered part of the national community.

Poverty as Structural Violence

So far, I have been describing the damage done by persistent and endemic poverty as a kind of violence on the poor. However, what justification is there for the use of the term *violence* to describe the injuries caused by poverty? Further, why describe it as structural violence? Even if we accept this term, there remains the question as to why the state should be linked to it. One way to further a careful and critical appreciation of the term *structural violence* is to ask what kind of limitation it imposes on one's analysis and imagination. I shall argue below that structural violence is both necessary and problematic as an analytic category.

When Max Weber defined the state as the institution that has "the monopoly of violence within a given territory," he was not thinking about structural violence. Rather, he employed violence in the usual sense of a direct act of force that causes physical harm to another person. I take the term *structural violence* from a germinal article published by Johan Galtung in the *Journal of Peace Research* in 1969. Galtung's definition of violence takes one far afield from a narrow focus on the somatic.[39] He identifies violence to be any situation in which there is a difference between the potential and actual somatic and mental achievements of people (1969: 168).[40] Put another way, violence occurs in any situation in which some people are unable to achieve their capacities or capabilities to their full potential, and almost certainly if they are unable to do so to the same extent as others.[41]

The reason such violence is considered to be structural is that it is impossible to identify a single actor who commits the violence. Instead, the violence is impersonal, built into the structure of power (1969: 170–71). Far from being intended, violence in this sense does not even have to be caused by a particular agent. What one finds here is a classically structuralist social theory wedded to consequentialism. Galtung's interest is in outcomes, not in processes. Whenever outcomes are unequal, violence is present. In fact, in this way of thinking, any system with less than full equality displays evidence of violence. The absence of violence is an ideal state that is not likely to be achieved in any given social formation. This interest in outcomes, however, has a broad scope, not limited to questions of food, livelihood, and income. Structural violence is a capacious term that encompasses not only the exclusion from entitlements such as food and water, but also the exclusion of certain groups from particular forms of recognition (citizenship rights, equal rights before the law, rights to education, representation, and so on).

Defined in this way, structural violence exists in tension with some central components of the idea of violence used in social analysis. If one asks a question posed by Veena Das, "What exactly is violated by structural violence?," the answer leads in a considerably different direction than the study of other types of violence. According to Das, violence represents a violation of the everyday sociality of life-worlds. That is why her brilliant study of communal riots, *Life and Words*, focuses on the efforts of victims and perpetrators alike to rebuild a semblance of ordinary life after such events; violence of this kind is episodic, an event that flares up and upsets the seemingly settled contours of daily life. Yet Das suggests that disruptive episodes such as riots do more than disturb the continuity of everyday life. They create a profound uncertainty about the ontological foundations of the social, so that people begin to doubt their ability to navigate a social world they thought they knew well.

Structural violence contrasts sharply with this meaning of violence. It is constant rather than episodic, and, far from disrupting actors' understandings of their social worlds, it provides them with a particular kind of situated knowledge with its own epistemic certainties. One of these certainties is that there is very little ability to absorb risk at the same time that one is forced to undertake highly risky activities. The episodic continues to be important for two reasons. Events beyond one's control can spiral into catastrophe: illness, loss of employment, or, for a poor farmer, the failure of the rains can easily result in a loss of life. These events are closely related to the dull compulsions of everyday life: a prolonged period of malnutrition, for example, can make the body vulnerable to the most common diseases. Catastrophic episodes are also important because they force people on all sides to acknowledge the social inequalities that foreshorten the life chances of the poor. Such events, therefore, may offer insights into the inequities of the social system, a form of situated knowledge that is uniquely available to the poor.

The difference between structural violence and direct violence goes further. In its ordinary meaning, violence requires a perpetrator who commits the violent act and a victim who is injured by it. In the case of structural violence, although there is a victim—someone who is injured by the inequities of social arrangements—it is hard to identify a perpetrator. It is not a victimless crime but its opposite: a crime without a criminal. This particular fact raises the question of what makes it different from the destructiveness of a natural disaster—the devastation that a hurricane or an earthquake can cause in the lives of the poor. One does not identify natural disasters as violence except perhaps when one speaks metaphorically of the violence of nature.

Why should the ill effects of structural inequities be termed violence at all? Is there not a danger of conflating two very different phenomena by the use of such a term? I believe that the analytical perils here are very real. However, there is one compelling—perhaps overwhelming—reason to retain a focus on violence: it keeps one's attention on its impact on mortality. Structural violence results in the premature and untimely deaths of people. Violence here is not so much the violation of the everyday but the reduction to bare life, that is, life in its most naked, essential form. The link between structural violence and mortality has been central to the work of Paul Farmer (2005), and my use of the term owes more to Farmer than to Galtung. Like Farmer, I think structural violence is about "the nature and distribution of extreme suffering" (Sen in Farmer 2005: xiii).

What distinguishes such violence from the destruction caused by acts of nature is that these unfortunate outcomes result from the deliberate actions of social agents. One must keep in mind that certain classes of people have a stake in perpetuating a social order in which such extreme suffering is not only tolerated but also taken as normal. All those who benefit from the status quo and do not wish to see it changed then become complicit in this violence against the poor.[42] In a country like India, the perpetrators of violence include not only the elites but also the fast-growing middle class, whose increasing number and greater consumer power are being celebrated by an aggressive global capitalism.[43]

Structural Violence and the State

It is now possible to clarify the connection between the discussion of structural violence and the state. The chief mission of the postcolonial Indian state as an institution is to bring the fruits of development to the nation and therefore to address inequalities in life chances. Why has it been unable to make more of a difference in the lives of the poor? Viewing poverty through the lens of structural violence makes it very difficult to link the state to the poor with a conjunction: the state and poverty. *Poverty* is not a good word to describe such violence because its continued use in projects of charity and aid to the unfortunate inures one to the deformed ethics of statecraft that tolerates and condones such cruelty. In the chapters that follow, I examine the modalities through which violence is exercised without intention, ranging from corruption and modes of literacy and writing to governmental practices.[44] My aim is to elucidate how a grave national crisis becomes unexceptional, a matter of routine administration, a problem largely uncommented upon in the press or in parliament, and nameable only through banalities on the occasions when it is mentioned.

How can one explain persistent poverty and the extremely low position of India on global rankings of human development? One could argue, for instance, that the state in India has never had the resources necessary to eradicate poverty. Alternatively, using a progressivist narrative of history or a triumphalist version of nationalism or both, one could point out that things are getting better by the day. The rapid growth of the Indian economy after liberalization has directly lowered levels of poverty and provided the Indian state with new resources for antipoverty programs. Conversely, one could seek to unmask the benevolent rhetoric of the state to expose its fundamentally violent character and to show the gap between its rhetoric and its actions. Such an exercise would reveal that repeated statements of good intentions by politicians and bureaucrats are cynical ploys to obtain votes and legitimacy, respectively. One could also argue along more classically Marxist lines that the state is a tool for the perpetuation of inequalities, an executive committee of the bourgeoisie and the emerging classes that are tied to the bourgeois order. In this view, the state regulates the sharing of the surplus among the various fractions of the bourgeoisie and ensures that their internal conflicts do not bring down the system for the generation of surplus (Bardhan 1984: 54–68). Finally, one could, borrowing a formulation from Bruno Latour, argue that we have never been postcolonial: poverty has not been eradicated because the state has continued to function much as the colonial one did, and neoliberalism has succeeded only in bringing to India new forms of empire and neocolonialism (Hardt and Negri 2000). Indivar Kamtekar, for instance, has demonstrated quite convincingly that the continuities in administration, justice, and defense across the colonial–postcolonial divide make the colonial state hypothesis more than just a rhetorical flourish (1988).

It would be easy to adopt a cynical perspective on the motivations of state bureaucrats and politicians and blame them for perpetuating structural violence on the poor. Like any other class of people, bureaucrats sometimes fit that image. However, like Malik in my fieldwork example above, many hardworking bureaucrats were often frustrated by their inability to work effectively to bring about real changes in the lives of the poor people who were so often the target of government programs. This is precisely why I wish to argue in this book that no matter how noble the intentions of programs, and no matter how sincere the officials in charge of them, the overt goal of helping the poor is subverted by the very procedures of the bureaucracy.

There is a very specific modality of uncaring operating here that I will further specify. Uncaring indicates not a psychological state of government employees but a constitutive modality of the state. One could hardly accuse the state of inaction toward the poor: it would be difficult to imagine a more extensive set of development interventions in the fields of nutrition, health, education, housing, employment, sanitation, and so forth than those found in India. The Indian state probably outdoes any other poor nation-state in the number and range of its benevolent interventions. For example, at the time of my fieldwork the staff at the block level was responsible for implementing no fewer than thirty development projects. Given this fact, some programs invariably became more important than others in terms of staff attention and labor.

I have emphasized that it is not the lack of care or a want of attentiveness that result in the neglect and indifference shown to the suffering of poor people by bureaucrats and state elites. State officials and political leaders do not have to be callous or indifferent to the plight of the poor for their actions to have highly negative consequences. At the pension camp, for example, the summary judgments made by the doctor who was guessing the ages of people and by the tehsildar who commented ironically on the rapid growth of the population despite so many people not having children were motivated largely by bureaucratic expediency rather than by indifference or hostility toward the beneficiaries. Without doubt, many beneficiaries would have been worse off without the camp. However, being denied support may well have made the difference between life and death for at least some of the poorest applicants.[45] Importantly, such violence was enacted at the very scene of care.[46] In stressing the intimate connection between violence and caring and in rejecting narratives of the indifference or inattentiveness of the state, I am trying to articulate the ethics and politics of care that is arbitrary in its consequences. I am arguing that such arbitrariness is not itself arbitrary; rather, it is systematically produced by the very mechanisms that are meant to ameliorate social suffering.

What must be explained is not only why government programs aimed at providing nutrition, employment, housing, healthcare, and education to poor people do not succeed in their objectives but also why, when they do succeed, they do so unevenly and erratically. Why, among the universe of needy beneficiaries, do some people manage to receive assistance and others not? This is what I mean by arbitrary outcomes. To my mind, the more analytically perplexing question is why a mechanism—the modern bureaucratic state—that is the hallmark of rational decision making systematically produces such arbitrariness.[47]

In referring to arbitrary outcomes, I do not mean that such phenomena cannot be understood or explained. Nor do I wish to deny that the "social production of indifference" is an important mechanism by which bureaucracies insulate themselves from social suffering (Herzfeld 1993). Nevertheless, it becomes difficult to explain why such indifference generates sharply divergent outcomes for clients who are in similar structural locations. In other words, one would expect that such indifference would operate equally on two clients who have very similar endowments of economic, social, educational, and cultural capital. In Weber's (1968) view, the very distinction between power in a personalistic social world and a modern bureaucratic one is that, in the former, replicability and consistency are neither valued nor produced systematically, whereas in a bureaucracy the person performing the role is (ideally) irrelevant to the outcome. In other words, in a bureaucratic system no matter who occupies an office, the rules governing decision making deliver consistent outcomes.

The production of arbitrariness is not peculiar to Indian bureaucracies but is a feature of any complex bureaucratic organization. Neither are all outcomes arbitrary in the manner I have outlined. Some forms of discrimination are consistent, systematic, and institutionalized. For example, the requirement that any application submitted by a woman to a bureaucratic office contain, for purposes of identification, the name of either her father or her husband, institutionalizes the patriarchal order and normalizes heterosexual marriage.[48] In the first section of this book I argue that the system of corruption functions in just such a manner to discriminate methodically against poor people by raising the rates that people have to pay for services that are nominally free or that are subsidized by the state. Corruption is a systematic form of oppression precisely because it acts uniformly on the population that lacks the income to pay off officials.

I wish to distinguish my position from two other commonly employed explanations for development outcomes that adversely affect the poor. First, I am not arguing that, although development planning and programs are well designed, they founder in their implementation. This position, ubiquitous in the discourse of many middle-class, urban Indians, reproduces both a colonial complaint of the incompetence of the natives and a class bias toward subalterns in the bureaucracy. If the problem is poor implementation, the blame falls inevitably on lower-level officials who, for reasons ranging from corruption to poor training and education, are deemed incapable of implementing the wonderful programs thought up by metropolitan experts. This is one instance in which even those who would normally reify it disaggregate the state, and it is not entirely surprising that one should discover such a move in the context of explaining failure rather than the normal operation of the machinery.

Second, related to this point, I am not arguing that structural violence can be eliminated or greatly attenuated by improving the efficiency of the delivery of state services to the poor. Although there is plenty of room for increased efficiency and although some outcomes might be better if processes were streamlined, the goals of efficiency do not necessarily coincide with the goals of justice. Ascribing inefficiency to lower-level bureaucrats is another way in which subalterns in the bureaucracy are blamed for the failures of development programs.

Finally, although I have made chronic poverty the focus of this examination of the state, I want to underline the importance of writing against an anthropology of abjectness. The people who were the targets of state intervention and benevolent action were not passive or docile victims and did not consider or represent themselves as such.[49] They stood up to officials when they could: for example, the person who answered the tehsildar simply by asserting his dignity to be treated well even if he was an ordinary person. The people I worked with struggled to make things better for themselves; they were inventive and creative in employing whatever means they could to care for their families; they were responsible and committed members of kin networks; and, they contributed to their communities. They were also astute philosophers, people whose unique structural position gave them sharp insights into the injustices of the social system they inhabited. Rather than using the poor as a resource for thinking, I take them as my philosophical and social guides in a process of translation (Rancière 2004).[50] Not only did poor people show up at the offices I studied, but also representations of and by them circulated among officials, and they became the ground for the legitimation of state programs and policies. In other words, there were already complex processes of translation and representation at work in the bureaucratic and democratic imaginary to which poor people were central.

The Field Site

My fieldwork on state antipoverty programs compared the functioning of the Block office, which coordinated the implementation of approximately thirty development programs for an area composed of roughly a hundred villages (a Block in Indian administrative parlance), with the Integrated Child Development Services (ICDS) program, an initiative aimed at improving maternal and child health and welfare. I conducted fieldwork in these two offices in the Mandi subdistrict of Uttar Pradesh (U.P.) for one year. The block office was headed by Malik, the BDO. The twenty employees in the block office worked in a small cluster of buildings just outside the town. Malik had several assistants (ADOs) who specialized in such functions as agriculture, village governance (panchayats), cooperatives, statistics, and industry, service, and business. There were also a couple of junior engineers, one specializing in minor irrigation and one for rural employment schemes. The rest of the staff performed clerical duties.

The goal of the other program I studied, the ICDS, was to provide a set of services that consisted of supplementary nutrition for pregnant women and young children and education, immunizations, and preventive medicine for poor and lower-caste children. The program simultaneously aimed at caring for the population while also investing in the future of the nation through ensuring the health of children and their ability to become productive laborers and citizens. The structure of command of the ICDS bureaucracy at the block level was as follows: a Child Development Project Officer (CDPO) named Asha Agarwal headed it and supervised a clerical staff, which included an account clerk, an employee who handled various other clerical jobs, a peon, and a driver. The CDPO was responsible for overseeing the work of four Supervisors (*Mukhya Sevikas*), eighty-six Anganwadi Workers in the block, and their eighty-six Helpers. The anganwadi workers were responsible for the day-to-day functioning of centers in villages. The anganwadi centers were supposed to operate every day from 9 A.M. to 1 P.M. Since it was not feasible for anganwadi workers to run a center, take care of as many as forty-five children, teach the children, cook food for them, supervise their medical care, and maintain the records all on their own, they were provided with helpers. The helpers' duties included doing all the odd jobs associated with the anganwadi, including rounding up the children to attend the center, cooking when the centers were supplied with food, and cleaning the school. In Mandi, all the helpers, anganwadi workers, and supervisors as well as the CDPO were women; the rest of the office staff were men. The ICDS was the only bureaucracy in the Indian government that was headed and run by women.

The place where I did my research, Mandi, was established as a block in 1961. In 1991 it had a population of just over 130,000 people in eighty-nine villages, of which 42 percent were scheduled caste, the lowest ranks in the caste hierarchy. The modal village size was between 1,000 and 2,000 people. The block-level staff was described as fieldworkers, that is, people whose primary responsibility lay in overseeing work in the field. The block staff played a relatively important role in the relation between the state and the rural population. For many villagers the block staff constituted the state's most regularly visible representatives. However, they were not necessarily the state's most important representatives. That role probably belonged to electricity officials, the police, and the *patwari*, or land records agent.

The block was the bottom end of a complex organizational structure consisting of a subdistrict (tehsil), a district, the regional state, and the federal government, or the Centre. Above the block in the administrative hierarchy was the subdistrict. Mandi subdistrict was somewhat unusual in that it consisted of four blocks, whereas other subdistricts had just two or three. Going further up the hierarchy, there were four subdistricts in Mandi District.[51] The administrative head for the entire district was the District Magistrate (DM), usually a junior official in the Indian Administrative Service (IAS).[52] There was no further level of administration between the sixty-three districts and the provincial state government of U.P.[53] Finally, all the regional governments are organized into a federal union. The constitution mandates a separation of topics over which the Centre, or federal government, has jurisdiction as opposed to areas that are completely under the control of provincial state governments. There are also areas on a joint list in which control is theoretically shared between the Centre and the states. All of this makes for a complex federal structure with some overlapping functions and with legislative, judicial, and administrative functions organized at each level.

Coordination of government functions has to occur not only at different levels (district, regional state, and center), but also within each bureau across these levels. At the local level, there is little coordination of block activities except those under the direct supervision of the BDO. The two offices I studied at the block level, for example, had very little knowledge of one another's activities and no day-to-day contact with one another about their functions, although both were focused on antipoverty activities. A few activities were coordinated at the level of the subdistrict by the SDM, but the chief instrument in this regard was the DM. If there was any coherence to programs and policies at the local level, it was entirely owing to the coordination efforts of the DM. It was not surprising, therefore, that this official embodied state authority and was seen by rural people and lower officials as the center of state power at the local level. This is not to say that the efforts of the DM to lend coherence to the state at the local level were always or even often successful. Calling a meeting of the one hundred most important officials each month was an organizational challenge in itself, but there was no guarantee that the instructions and targets handed out at the meeting would actually be met. Implementation did not refer just to meeting targets: the quality of implementation and the manner in which officials dealt with clients were often as important as, if not more important than, the number of new wells dug or houses constructed.

Given this complex organizational structure, it makes sense to acknowledge partiality as the necessary condition for any study of the state. My fieldwork on these two development bureaucracies focused on the administrative branch of the state as opposed to the judicial or legislative branches. There were inevitably connections across those branches and, in all likelihood, a project that focused exclusively on the courts or local elected officials would have come up with a very different picture of the state. Given my interest in poverty, both of the agencies I studied were welfare agencies in the sense that they provided assets and services to a range of rural clients. If I had studied taxation or revenue collection, or focused on infrastructure by looking at the Electricity Department or the Irrigation Department, or if I had concentrated on state agencies engaged primarily with repressive functions like the police, I might have emerged with a very different view of the state's role in structural violence.

From what I have said above, it might appear that this book is exclusively about the state and poverty at the local level. While such a characterization is not false, it too easily partakes of a misleading understanding of scale. A brief consideration of ICDS makes this clear. Each block in the ICDS program was considered a separate project for the purposes of funding. The program received funding from many sources, including various agencies within the Government of India, multilateral organizations such as UNICEF, and bilateral aid agencies. Projects that received funding from foreign donors were able to purchase larger quantities of food for supplementary nutrition as compared to those blocks that were dependent on the Government of India for their food supplies. Poor children's access to supplementary nutrition was mediated in this way by a complex transnational chain linking to a local program managed by the Government of India.

While it would be true to say that this study of structural violence is based on the state at the local level, this does not mean that I studied the local state. There is a critical difference between those two ideas, and keeping that in mind is essential in the chapters that follow. I contend that a notion of scale that consists of nested hierarchies, so that one level is seen as being encapsulated inside a higher level, is fundamentally mistaken (Ferguson and Gupta 2002). With a concept of nested hierarchies, it makes sense to speak of the local state, which can be contrasted to the regional state or the national state. If, however, the state at the local level is complexly mediated by regional, national, and transnational discourses and practices, of what analytical utility is it to label it the local state? This is why, in thinking of the state's role in perpetuating the violence of poverty, it is never enough to focus entirely on venal local officials, corrupt and brutal police forces, and so forth.

When one considers a federal political structure such as that of India, in which shifts have emerged from a model in which a strong central government was paramount to a system in which regional state governments are much more autonomous, an argument about mediation of levels becomes even more important. For this reason, the historical context of this book is extremely important.

Socialism, Neoliberalism, and the State in India: The Historical Context

This study of the state in India is located at a particularly important historical conjuncture. I began fieldwork for this project just a couple of months after the then–finance minister, Manmohan Singh, had announced a new program for the liberalization of the Indian economy.[54] That decision is now freighted with the extraordinary weight of having initiated the reforms that have enabled the Indian economy to take off into a period of unprecedented growth (but see Kohli 2006 and Virmani 2005 for a different interpretation). At the time that the liberalization program was announced, however, it was seen more as a form of crisis management than as an epochal event. If one listened to ordinary middle-class Indians, the reason the Indian economy faced a foreign exchange crisis was that Rajiv Gandhi had allowed foreign exchange, closely regulated until then, to be expended on the import of consumer goods such as television sets. Foreign exchange reserves had dwindled to the point that they were barely sufficient to pay for the next two weeks of imports, and India was in danger of defaulting on the payments for its foreign debt. Another factor precipitating the crisis was the Gulf War, which caused oil prices to shoot up and India's import bill to skyrocket.

Although the changes initiated in 1991 were not irreversible, further shifts in subsequent years consolidated the direction, if not the pace, of this transition. Cumulatively, these changes have had a dramatic impact on the Indian nation-state, seen most clearly in the completely altered landscape of consumer goods. Other visible changes have been due to the new jobs that are associated with globalization, from call centers and the information technology industry to services in such fields as medicine and finance. These far-reaching transformations have resulted from and have been accompanied by a shift in the role of the state. As a result, forms of structural violence have changed, but so have the prospects of poverty. I explore some of these changes in the epilogue.

To understand the changing relationship between the state and poverty, one has to ask how the state has been remade by the new economic policies initiated in 1991. The answer depends on the sector, level, and branch of the state (Brahmbhatt, Srinivasan, and Murrell 1996; Patnaik 2003). In terms of state branches and levels, the administrative branch was probably affected more than the legislative and the judicial; the federal level of the state probably experienced greater changes than the regional state or local levels; and the industrial and globally influenced service sectors experienced a true transformation as compared to, say, welfare programs or policies aimed at agriculture. Finally, regional states in south India have experienced much faster rates of growth and in all likelihood experienced the forces of globalization wider and deeper than northern states like U.P.[55] If one thinks of changes in state functioning accompanying the rapid growth of the Indian economy, it would be a safe bet that poor people working in the agricultural sector in rural areas of U.P. would be at the opposite end of the spectrum from their urban, South Indian counterparts employed in service industries.

Welfare and subsidy programs were affected by another result of the reforms, which was the cutback of government expenditure in order to reduce the federal fiscal deficit. As a result of the restraining of expenditures, some important programs that provided the poor with a safety net, like the Public Distribution System (PDS) for food grains, experienced budget reductions (Harriss 2009). However, such cutbacks were not implemented across the board. For example, employment development programs such as the Jawahar Rojgaar Yojana (JRY) actually saw large budgetary increases (Echeverri-Gent 1993), whereas during the same period expenditures on public health facilities were scaled back (Jeffery and Jeffery 2009). Furthermore, new types of welfare programs, such as Mahila Samakhya, were introduced that embodied the "enterprise model" of neoliberal reform (see chap. 7) (Sharma and Gupta 2006; Gupta and Sharma 2006). Mahila Samakhya emphasized empowerment and differed from ICDS in that it promised to distribute nothing except knowledge about other government programs (a valuable service that, importantly, is virtually costless).

The remainder of this book sketches a picture of the state in India at the local level at the cusp of what many analysts assume to be a momentous transition. Although my fieldwork was conducted immediately after the announcement of liberalization, at that point none of the changes introduced at the center had yet made any impact on local government or rural life. Since then, two legislative changes have been introduced that have the potential to re-shape rural life. These are the Panchayati Raj legislation and the Freedom of Information Bill. The impact of these legislative changes is as yet unclear; in north India it took several decades for the impact of universal adult suffrage to manifest itself in political life with the success of lower-caste parties and subaltern groups. Similarly, the impact of the reservation of one-third Panchayat seats for women and the right to information from government offices might have effects which become visible only in the long run.

Although liberalization and recently enacted laws may not have had any revolutionary effects for state antipoverty programs at the local level, one gets a different picture by enlarging the historical frame. The enormous expansion of development functions for the state at the local level has been profoundly shaped by postcolonial elites at the center of the administrative and political system (the central state). None of the more than thirty programs being run by the block office, and certainly not the ICDS, had any strong historical precedents in the colonial state.[56] However, recent employment schemes such as the Mahatma Gandhi National Rural Employment Guarantee Act of 2005 may have connections with colonial and precolonial policies of employment on public works projects for purposes of famine relief. Similarly, some of the work of the Irrigation Department in managing canals and digging community tubewells harked back, if not to the colonial state, then to the immediate post-Independence period of community development.[57] Historically, however, these projects were aimed at increasing agricultural productivity, not at poverty reduction as such.

It would have been impossible to construct a similar genealogy, that is, one with colonial connections, for the programs aimed at lower-castes and women. These included schemes to provide free brick (*pucca*) houses for the poorest, to bring community hand-pumps into areas of villages where scheduled castes lived, to enhance subsidies to traditional loan programs for productive investment, to encourage village schools to allow scheduled-caste children to attend by providing subsidies for each child enrolled, to give women priority for some loans, and, through the ICDS, to offer elementary education and vaccination to female children to improve their life chances. If these programs were connected on the one hand to populist politics and the constant effort to obtain the votes of lower-caste groups, they were linked on the other hand to transnational discourses about governmental support to the poorest of the poor, the requirements imposed by international aid agencies for gender equality, and the need to target programs to poor women in particular. However successful these programs have been (and there is much to suggest that they have not had the impact that the resources expended on them might lead one to believe), they have led to a large increase of state personnel at the local level and to a corresponding expansion of the administrative machinery.[58]

The result of this expansion has been a pervasive, sometimes subtle bureaucratization of daily life even for the poorest segments of the population, people who are considered the farthest removed from state bureaucracies. Understanding this process, however, requires a better assessment of the role of government bureaucracies and bureaucrats. Despite an explosion of interest in state institutions, a greater quantity of detailed ethnographic work on bureaucracies is needed to achieve a rich picture of exactly how bureaucracies affect the lives of poor people in towns and villages. My strategy in this book is to focus on three themes to illuminate this connection.

Mechanisms of Structural Violence:
Corruption, Inscription, Governmentality

An ethnography of bureaucracy's relation to poverty is an inherently open-ended project. In terms of themes, bureaus, levels, locations, and methods, there are potentially infinite possibilities in which the state in general and the bureaucracy in particular could be studied. Government bureaucracies are now ubiquitous in the lives of poor Indians, regulating citizens' access to many essential and commonplace goods, from railway tickets to subsidized kerosene.

Since I am specifically concerned with the mechanisms by which the poor come to experience the structural violence perpetrated by the state, I have chosen three broad themes to organize the ethnographic materials: I focus on the themes of corruption, inscription, and governmentality because I see them as being of central importance to scholarship, politics, and policy. My argument is that structural violence is enacted through the everyday practices of bureaucracies, and one therefore needs to look closely at those everyday practices in order to understand why violence coexists with care and why, paradoxically, it is often found in practices of welfare. In the second part of this book I deal with the issue of corruption because it is one of the mechanisms that prevents poor people from getting access to programs that have been set up specifically to benefit them. In part 3, which addresses inscription, I interrogate the writing practices of bureaucracies to ask whether literacy enables bureaucrats to dominate poor people and, if so, how. Part 4 deals with governmentality, contrasting two programs aimed at poor women.

Chapter 2 develops the ideas put forth in this introductory chapter in a different direction. The focus of this introduction has been on poverty and structural violence; the second chapter complements this focus with a more sustained interrogation of the state. Taken together, the two chapters constitute the first part of the book, which is primarily aimed at rethinking the relation between the state and poverty. Chapter 2 makes an argument for the critical importance of disaggregating the state in order to understand the production of arbitrariness. I contend that without theorizing the role played by everyday practices, representations, and narratives in the cultural construction of the state, one cannot appreciate how structural violence against the poor can coexist with political and ideological inclusion. My argument is that the constant reference made to the state as a single, cohesive apparatus makes it impossible to understand the production of arbitrariness vis-à-vis the poor. Instead, paying attention to the everyday practices of specific bureaucracies and to the dissemination and circulation of reified representations of the state is critical to comprehending the nature of bureaucratic interventions in the lives of the poor and the effects of such policies and programs.

When poor villagers in western U.P. spoke about the state, corruption was perhaps the topic they most frequently discussed: indeed, one of the reasons I chose to write about corruption was its centrality to social life. Bureaucratic corruption features prominently in poor people's conversations in towns and villages, and it structures almost all their actions. Part 2 of this book (chapters 3 and 4) is devoted to understanding the relationship between everyday forms of corruption and poverty.

In the scholarship on India, corruption continues to receive very little attention outside a small circle of economists.[59] This is genuinely puzzling because it is hard to think of any domain of social, cultural, and imaginative life in which corruption does not play a prominent role. Why is so little written about corruption in the fields of sociology, anthropology, history, and literary studies? I argue that it is a topic that is extraordinarily productive for all these disciplines: corruption is "good to think with," and it allows for fundamental, transdisciplinary questions to be raised about the connections between structure, action, and affect in social life. Finally, especially where poor people are concerned, corruption is an enormous problem for public policy. One must go beyond the prescriptions of economists to get incentives right in order to address this complex issue. Are there insights that other social scientists and humanists can contribute to help prevent the poor from being further exploited by a system of corruption?

Chapter 3 argues that poor people's understanding of the state is shaped by representations of corruption and the circulation of discourses about corruption. Rural people's relations with the state in India are mediated by their encounters with the local-level officials of particular bureaucracies and by representations of the state that circulate in public culture. By presenting ethnographic vignettes of corruption—the actions of two patwaris, a poor, lower-caste villager's dispute with a headman and the development bureaucracy, and activists in a powerful movement of farmers—I emphasize that what poor citizens really encounter in their daily lives are particular bureaucrats and agencies rather than the state. I argue that neither poor people nor bureaucrats at lower levels of government operate with some vision of a unified state. This is not to say that they are unaware of connections between administrative, legislative, or judicial branches of the state at the local level, as they may appeal to one of these branches to intervene in another. I demonstrate that even the poorest villagers might well be aware of different levels of government and appeal to higher officials when they are stymied by local bureaucrats. Corruption disenfranchises and disempowers the poor and can itself constitute a form of structural violence by making essential goods and services unattainable for the poor. Nevertheless, poor people are not simply victims of corruption but use the various levels of the state to obtain some leverage in dealing with corrupt officials.

Chapter 4 attends to the role of narrative in the cultural construction of the state and the normalization of structural violence on the poor. Since the study of the state has been so dominated by institutional and political economic perspectives, my emphasis on the role of narrative may appear counterintuitive to many readers. However, as chapter 4 demonstrates, narratives, no less than statistics, help construct and represent the state and enable particular modalities of biopolitics. I argue that an essential part of combating acute poverty involves changing the narratives through which structural violence is normalized and hence changing the expectations of what bureaucrats can do and what they can be expected to do. By comparing representations of the state in a popular novel and a well-known ethnography of India, I show how diverse understandings of the state are constructed and disseminated in two dissimilar genres, with their attendant effects on the justification of structural violence and their impacts on subaltern resistance. I argue that effective institutional reform aimed at helping the poor is integrally linked to the reformulation of narratives of the state. Trust, that elusive quality that purportedly marks good relations between states and their citizens, can be produced only by narratives that emphasize that quality and are borne out by the experience of subjects. I am not arguing that states can simply replace narratives of cynicism or skepticism with those of credibility and trust. Rather, I am pointing out that, if institutional reform is to be successful, attention has to be paid to generating new narratives that alter the affective relations between the state and its poorest citizens.[60]

In part 3 I look at another feature of Indian bureaucracies that, politically and culturally, has had enormous consequences for the poor but has received very little scrutiny in the academic literature: the emphasis placed on writing and written materials. The insistence on writing in a context (rural U.P.) in which the overwhelming majority of poor people are illiterate has enormous political consequences, as I explore in chapters 5 and 6. Indian democracy is on the verge of bringing about a fundamental social revolution in north India, as leaders of heretofore subjugated groups with a large, illiterate constituency capture political power through the ballot box. This makes the relations between literacy and power exceedingly complex. What makes it so fascinating theoretically for the study of the state is that it forces scholars to think again about the assumption that literacy by itself makes the poor more empowered and better-informed subjects of the state. It also raises important questions about policy: what does the bureaucratic emphasis on written procedure have to do with questions of accessibility and transparency? How can bureaucracies be better organized to respond to the needs of poor and illiterate clients? Such questions rarely reach the forefront of policy debates: I argue that much more attention needs to be paid to them if one is to understand how structural violence and arbitrariness are produced.

Chapter 5 examines the nature of bureaucratic activity and its relation to writing. I consider distinct forms of bureaucratic writing, including forms and registers, statistics, inspections, and complaints. Writing, in the form of both narratives and statistics, creates certain representations of the state that are powerful not only because government writing is ubiquitous but also because writing is a prime modality of engaging the state. For example, how, specifically, does the requirement that any complaint submitted to a government department must be in written form disadvantage the poor? I argue that the movement and transmission of writing enables many critical functions and properties of the state. For instance, connections across different locales and levels are made possible at the level of everyday practice by the movement of writing within bureaucracies. Typically, the direction of such movements is that statistics, reports, and requisitions travel up the hierarchy and from peripheral offices to central ones; memos, government orders, and money travel in the opposite direction, down. Very often writing is carried by hand by lower officials who travel up the hierarchy to attend meetings or obtain signatures. On the other hand, higher officials travel down to inspect and audit, and they write during and as a consequence of those actions. Writing also travels across different bureaus within a locality and serves an important function in unifying the state at a given level. Even when the function is not so aggregative, writing can be important in coordinating action across agencies. The arbitrariness of state actions can be understood by the poor either through the failure of such coordinating actions or through the mistranslations and misunderstandings that occur when writing moves up and down hierarchies.

One of the most important arguments of chapter 5 is that, theoretically, one makes a big mistake in seeing writing as a by-product of the activity of state officials. I argue instead that writing is constitutive of the state; it is not a substitute for action but is itself a form of action. When state officials talk of doing something, it often means they will draft a document or send a note to a colleague. I argue that interpreting bureaucratic writing in functional terms as being instrumental toward another end is fundamentally mistaken because the vast majority of such writing is not read by anyone, not even by other bureaucrats. One important implication of this for the poor is that writing may not have the importance for the functioning of state institutions that scholars often ascribe to it. By examining inspections and complaints in particular, I find potentially contradictory and sometimes openly conflictual relations between levels or bureaus and between poor clients and bureaucrats.

Chapter 6 attempts to understand the political consequences of the bureaucratic insistence on writing in the context of widespread illiteracy. I argue against the simple idea that writing functions chiefly as a mechanism by which bureaucrats subjugate poor rural peoples who have a low level of functional literacy. The political importance of writing to subaltern peoples is misinterpreted by a strong tendency in academic theorizing to teleological thought, in which the movement from illiteracy to full literacy is seen as a natural or desirable progression of nation-states and civilizations. In light of the examples of civilizations like India and China, where the existence of a small group of literate elites among a largely illiterate population has long been the norm, many of the assumptions of the empowering effects of literacy have to be reexamined. This idea has important implications for the political project of literacy as a means to empower the poor.

In chapter 6 I argue further that subalterns employ three overlapping tactics to contest the power of literate bureaucrats. They educate their children so that they can learn to employ the same tools as bureaucrats and perhaps even secure a state job; they participate actively in the political sphere so that they can put pressure on the bureaucracy without participating in its procedures; and, finally, they mimic state writing by producing counterfeit documents and certificates in order to receive benefits and services. These tactics secure employment, empowerment, and welfare. To briefly consider the second point: the inability to read and write has not prevented subaltern groups from being full and enthusiastic participants in democratic processes. In fact, I argue that new technologies of communication such as television, film, and audiocassettes, which do not depend entirely on the mediation of writing, have helped populist politicians connect with a disenfranchised majority. On the other hand, it appears that bureaucratic processes rely just as much on written documents as they always have; there has been no shift in this regard to accommodate illiterate clients. These contrasting attitudes have led to conflicts between the legislative and administrative branches of the state. Instead of appealing to bureaucratic process to correct wrongs, subaltern groups appeal to politicians to put pressure on bureaucrats. Even within bureaucratic departments the pressure of electoral politics was felt in the form of reservations for lower-caste groups (scheduled castes and other backward castes), and bureaucrats resented having to change what they did because of demands made of them by politicians.

Finally, part 4 explores the connection between bureaucracies and bureaucratization, between the actions of particular agencies of the state and the expansion of processes of government in nongovernmental institutions and realms of social life. The political importance of this theme is growing to the extent that nongovernmental organizations (NGOs) are playing an increasing role in mediating between poor people and a range of actors, including transnational agencies, multilateral institutions, and government agencies. I explore how new modes of governmentality are being put into place through programs like ICDS. Because the subject of theories of the state is so often the nation-state, the transnational dimensions of states are often lost from view. A focus on governmentality also helps one see that states are not the only organizations caring for populations, and that to understand the state one has to position it within a field of other agencies that either compete with the state in the provision of services or complement it by performing functions that it is incapable of doing.

Chapter 7 examines the ICDS program as an example of a classic form of governmentality and compares it to a neoliberal version of governmentality, the Mahila Samakhya program.[61] When the Indian state compared itself to other developing countries, its statistics on mortality and morbidity for infants and young children made its performance look poor by international standards. (These numbers were themselves aggregates of statistics collected from each block and district to obtain data for the whole nation.) The high rates of mortality and morbidity spurred the central government to start a benevolent program like the ICDS. The implementation of this program demonstrates that the affective dimension of state power has as much to do with care as with patrolling, exercising surveillance, and punishment. Thanks to Weber's definition of the state as an organization that exercises a monopoly on violence within its own territory, the stress in scholarship on the state has focused on the repressive aspects of state affect, on its powers to discipline and punish, rather than on its investment in care. The further question that needs to be asked is, why, despite this deep investment in the care of the population, do state actions lead to the death of a massive number of the poor? Could it be that such programs to care for the poor are in place in order to inoculate us from the political possibility that their death should constitute a scandal?

I conclude with a short epilogue that traces the implications of the particular pattern of growth in India for acute poverty. India has seen both rapid growth rates and the persistence of poverty, measured in terms of the absolute numbers of people living below a minimum threshold of nutrition, clothing, housing, healthcare, sanitation, and schooling. In the epilogue I argue that the pattern of growth in India, with its emphasis on services, is unlikely to reduce acute poverty in the foreseeable future. Such an outcome is probable because most of the poor continue to live in rural areas, and in the absence of employment growth in agriculture, rural industries, and the manufacturing sector there is no possibility of employing the vast majority of unemployed and underemployed people in India. Redistributive schemes embodied in welfare programs may ameliorate conditions of acute poverty, but they are unlikely to change the life chances of the majority of poor people unless those people can find gainful employment at a living wage. Lop-sided growth carries with it the danger of perpetuating structural violence on rural peoples and indigenous groups. Although the rhetoric of inclusive growth is central to the legitimation efforts of the current regime, its ability to change the life chances of the poor are small unless there is a fundamental shift in the commitments of the state to the poorest and most disempowered segments of the population.

THE STATE AND THE POLITICS OF POVERTY 2

I want to deconstruct the idea of the state as a unified entity in order to reveal the limitations of conventional theories of the state for addressing violence perpetrated against poor populations in India. I argue that the constant invocation of the state reinforces a discursive and conceptual barrier that obstructs from one's view the varying modalities and techniques that enable bureaucracies to be indifferent to the social suffering of the poor. If, as I proposed in chapter 1, we are to understand the paradoxical relation of different groups of poor people to the state, which simultaneously articulates inclusion and care with arbitrariness and structural violence, then we need to pay close attention to the routinized practices of different branches and levels of the state. I suggest that the failure of Foucault's discussion of biopolitics and of Agamben's concept of the sovereign ban to come to terms with this paradox of inclusion and violence may have to do with the view of the state implicit in their work. Foucault and Agamben draw upon a theory of a strongly unified state apparatus to make their arguments about biopolitics and sovereignty, respectively.

I offer two examples from Foucault's discussion of biopolitics to illustrate how a particular theory of the state undergirds his analysis. Biopolitics as a modality of power depends upon the management of the population. Although Foucault does not explicitly address which level of government is responsible for managing the population, his position regarding the capillarity of power implies that bio-politics does not require centralized control. Foucault's argument for the rise of biopolitics depends on the convergence of diverse institutions in different settings around a particular way of conceptualizing a problem, for which they then seek solutions that involve the control and care of the population. Although nonstate institutions may be significant in some biopolitical regimes, different bureaus, branches, and levels of the state have to be seen as important actors in the formation of any biopolitical regime. Foucault's approach does not help one understand the circumstances that lead to the convergence that produces a biopolitical regime versus situations in which supposed problems in various domains (education, law, criminal justice, health) remain separate. Although Foucault's approach suggests that the management of the population in any biopolitical regime is widely dispersed across institutions, his account of eighteenth-century France implies that bureaucrats and advisors at the central level of the state play the most critical role (Foucault 2007: 55–86).

The second example concerns the fact that Foucault's biopolitical order depends upon the normalizing power of statistics. If one does not critically analyze how those statistics are collected and employed, then the relation-ship between biopower and issues like sovereignty and violence is likely to be misunderstood. How certain social processes come to be statistically repre-sented, and which branches of the bureaucracy and which officials undertake the massive labor of collating and organizing these numbers, can reveal a great deal about the management of the population. This is so because statistics are often linked to what James Scott (1998) has termed legibility, and a detailed statistical record is normally associated with surveillance that is more intensive. However, possessing more detailed statistics does not always correspond to better knowledge about the subject of scrutiny. An analysis of data collection methods, for instance, might very well lead one to conclude that statistics are not very effective as an instrument of biopolitics. Ethnographic observation of how statistical data is collected about subjects, therefore, can serve as an important mechanism for understanding the effec-tiveness of biopolitics.

While doing fieldwork in the village of Alipur I observed how data for the census were collected. I did my own census of every household of Alipur and was interested in finding out if my methods differed from that of census workers. When I asked people what questions census workers had asked them, they expressed surprise that such an exercise had been conducted since none of them recollected meeting a census worker. The mystery was finally cracked when I asked the same question in the house that came first on the main road that led to the village. That farmer told me that the census worker had come to his house and sat on his cot and asked him the names of all the other people in the village, how many members each household had, and so forth. While some information was no doubt collected about village households in this way, the information gained was far from accurate. The biopolitical project of knowing the population to manage it better was deeply compromised by the methods used to collect such data.

The past decade has witnessed an increasing interest in the ethnographic study of the modern state.[1] An important theme running through this literature is that states are not simply functional bureaucratic apparatuses but powerful sites of symbolic and cultural production that are themselves always culturally represented and understood in particular ways (Jessop 1999). It has become possible to speak not only of nations but also of states (Anderson 1991) as being imagined, that is, as entities that are conceptualized and made socially effective through particular imaginative and symbolic devices.[2] However, the articulation of cultural production with biopower and sovereignty is far from settled. Although a few studies have tried to demonstrate how the cultural content of biopolitics and sovereignty matters, the more radical project of showing that these concepts are themselves cultural constructions that have arisen within a distinct social and historical context has yet to be undertaken. The point is that one needs to reflect critically on the assumption of universality implicit in theories of biopolitics and sovereignty. Doing so will enable one to think of alternative conceptualizations and alternative claims to universality (Tsing 2004).

The methodological and epistemological framework I propose parallels the approach pioneered by Philip Abrams. Abrams (1988) recommends suspending belief in the state as an ontological reality that underpins what he calls the "state system," the institutional apparatus and its practices, and the "state idea," the concept that endows the state with its coherence, singularity, and legitimacy. Instead, he directs attention to how the state system and state idea are combined to legitimize rule and domination. Central to this argument is how the idea of the state is mobilized in diverse contexts, and how it is imbricated in state institutions and practices.[3] This conceptualization of the state goes beyond comparing the similarities or differences in functional form between states by emphasizing their historical contexts and conjunctural specificities. At the same time, the dichotomy between the institutional and the conceptual appears to strip the former of its cultural foundations and elides the cultural constitution of the state system. Despite this, Abrams urges one to consider an analytical framework in which functional and institutional approaches to the state can be articulated with cultural and ideological constructions by looking more closely at bureaucratic practices and representations. This is not a matter of balancing different approaches to the study of the state as much as it is a call to see the constitutive connections between political economy, social structure, institutional design, everyday practice, and representation.

Such complexity is precisely what is missing when scholars talk confidently about the state and politicians of the government. In so doing they refer to an entity that has come to be considered merely commonsensical. Yet precisely because it appears to be so self-evident, it behooves one to ask: What exactly is this object, organization, or structure? Where is it to be found? By what mechanisms is its presence revealed? How can one understand it? In response to these questions, I offer some propositions below that attempt to summarize the approach to the state that I am pursuing in this book.[4] This initial theoretical framework constitutes an essential starting point. In subsequent chapters, I unspool these foundational arguments in much greater detail.

In this chapter, I focus on disaggregating the state rather than critically interrogating the category of the poor. Although I often invoke the poor in the discussion that follows, I wish to emphasize that the poor are not a homogeneous group. In fact, a critical and reflexive use of the category of "the poor" enables one to see the diversity of populations so classified as well as the power of state bureaucracies to create an identity based on this category.[5]

Does Foucault's discussion of biopolitics or Agamben's discussion of the sovereign ban necessarily take as its frame of reference a centralized and unitary state? Can breaking down the state into levels, locales, bureaus, and functions offer insight into the production of its indifference to the poor? Does structural violence become more or less likely when the state is decentralized and poorly coordinated? These questions lie in the background to the theoretical propositions advanced in this chapter.

What Is the State?

One of the most striking aspects about references typically made to the state, apart from its purposive nature, is the unitary character of the object being described. The state supposedly decides this and does that; the state speaks with one voice, often the voice of the leader; the state stands for the general good; the state represents the collective interests over those of individual ones, and so forth. Thus, for example, when Agamben (2005: 1) endorses Carl Schmitt's definition of the sovereign as "he who decides on the state of exception," he inadvertently mobilizes a highly unitary state. However, Agamben does not assume that the sovereign is a dictator. On the contrary, he explicitly points out that, in the history of modern Europe, where a state of emergency or exception has been decreed, including Nazi Germany, the leader had been democratically elected and was speaking on behalf of the people, who often widely approved of his actions (2005: 1–31). Agamben operates with a notion of a strong state insofar as he assumes that a decision to declare a state of exception is tantamount to its de facto existence. Agamben does not worry about whether such a decision is effective in creating a state of exception.

Agamben's assumption is not surprising given that, with very few exceptions, most analyses of the state reinforce its unitary and purposive qualities, even when its power is criticized. The state can be described as a repressive force that kills or incarcerates its citizens; it can be a dominating force that constrains the freedom of action or the right of expression of people in civil society; and it can exercise undue control, restricting commerce and capitalist expansion. The state can also be chastised for not looking after the poor and downtrodden or for not regulating the excesses and externalities of capitalist or socialist systems of production resulting in pollution, inequality, poverty, or moral degradation. Even though all of these critiques may differ radically in their evaluations of the state's actions, people with very disparate economic, political, and moral perspectives might still be united in their view of the state as a cohesive, unitary entity.[6]

An ethnographic focus, perhaps more than any other approach, makes evident that the materiality and solidity of the state dissolve under scrutiny. The state consists of congeries of institutions with diversified levels, agencies or bureaus, agendas, functions, and locations. The conventional, widely recognized distinction made in modern nation-states between legislative, judicial, and administrative functions indexes three broad domains of functional specialization. Thinking about the question of the state's location necessitates inquiring about the relationship between the state at the federal level, at the level of regional states, and at the level of the county, municipality, and ward (in India, the district, subdistrict [tehsil], block, village, and ward). Legislative, judicial, and administrative functions may be present at each of these levels. Further, one must inquire into the relation between agencies that regulate different subject areas: departments or bureaus may be responsible for portfolios as diverse as industry, education, defense, policing, medical care, housing, pollution, infrastructure, and the like. If one imagines a three-dimensional grid, each of these portfolios may be subject to legislative, judicial, and administrative action, and each may be found at federal, state, and local levels. Finally, it is imperative to investigate the relations between agencies dealing with external affairs, for example, the military, the diplomatic corps, customs agents, and so forth, some of whose offices and workers may not even reside in the territory of the nation-state they serve, and agencies of the state that function entirely within its territorial borders. What emerges from this depiction of the state is a highly complex array of institutions with multiple functional specializations, modes of operation, levels, and agendas. Attributing organizational unity and purposiveness to such a welter of institutions might defy common sense rather than embody it (see also Gal and Kligman 2000: 20).[7] At the very least, it is clear that the state cannot be taken as a starting point for my analysis. Rather, one needs to take the unity and rationality attributed to the state in scholarly and political discourse as a theoretical and methodological problem to be addressed.

In the conclusion to his famous essay on governmentality Foucault advances an important critique of reducing the state to its functions. He goes on to say, "But the state, doubtless no more today than in the past, does not have this unity, individuality, and rigorous functionality. . . . After all, maybe the state is only a composite reality and a mythicized abstraction whose importance is much less than we think. Maybe. What is important for our modernity, that is to say, for our present, is not then the state's takeover [étatisation] of society, so much as what I would call the 'governmentalization' of the state" (Foucault 2007: 109). While I fully endorse this critique directed against that reified entity—the state—I do not take Foucault's discomfort with a particular conception of the state to be a call for doing away with the problem of the state altogether. Rather, I see it as a reason to start thinking about a different way to conceptualize the state, which is not the same as the question of the "governmentalization" of the state. Part of the problem here is that the reference to "our modernity" and "our present" presumes a shared social experience from which the problem of the governmentalization of the state can be understood. If we do not presume such a shared space, then the problem of the state does not dissolve or disappear as easily as Foucault imagined.

Far from being a unitary organization acting with a singular intention, the state is characterized by various levels that pull in different directions. This is why intention is a poor place to start in thinking about state violence toward the poor. The state is an incoherent agent for the kind of violence I focus on, and even the vocabulary of indifference raises the ghostly specter of an agent who exercises that indifference. However, the point of using the idea of structural violence is precisely to underline how such indifference or violence does not need to be intentionally caused by a particular agent. A disaggregated view of the state makes it possible to open up the black box of unintended outcomes by showing how they are systematically produced by the friction between agendas, bureaus, levels, and spaces that make up the state. A few examples from my fieldwork will illustrate this point.

THREE STORIES

Having previously scheduled a time for an interview, I went looking for the residence of Malik, the Block Development Officer (BDO) of Mandi subdistrict (tehsil). I was told that he lived in an apartment above an elementary school. When I came upon a sign with a thoroughly postcolonial pastiche of a name, "Gandhi Montessori," I climbed the stairs of the building, which was dark and airless, to the top floor. Malik, an elderly man with a shock of silver hair and a hoarse voice that appeared to have reached the end of its useful life, greeted me warmly, served tea, and before long started telling me about the pressures of his job.

There were so many government-sponsored development programs that it was difficult for him to keep on top of them all. He estimated the number of programs he was required to oversee at about thirty.[8] For each program he was given targets for implementation.[9] These numbers were decided from above, without any consultation with implementers like him about their feasibility or desirability. It is true that, like other BDOs, he got a chance to give feedback on how well the programs were working at the monthly meeting at the district headquarters convened by the District Magistrate (DM). However, he said there was little anyone could do about the targets, suggesting that even the DM may have been powerless to influence them. I pressed him for a clarification: "Do you mean that these orders come from the [Uttar Pradesh] state government?" His response was equivocal: "Well, yes, they come from the administration [shaasan se aatein hain]."[10] Since I knew by then that the district administration had substantial leeway in deciding which programs were to be implemented, I asked him why he did not object if the targets were not feasible. He responded, "I usually don't say anything; I just get the work done and show my results. Even if a project is not feasible, I try to do as much as possible. Even if I get only 50 percent done, it is better than nothing. Although what is often sacrificed is quality: I cannot maintain the quality of our programs in the pursuit of numbers."

Targets were set for the whole year and for each month. At the beginning of any given month, the Assistant District Magistrate (ADM) told Malik what percentage of a particular scheme had to be finished by the end of that month. For example, he might be told that 10 percent of the free housing scheme had to be completed in May. Targets were applied to the whole state, ignoring the fact that the disparate conditions in each district required that a mix of programs be used. Despite the considerable development that had been achieved in India, Malik felt that the quality of many of these programs left a lot to be desired. He complained that the people who set targets had little experience in or knowledge of rural areas. People like him who had extensive experience in rural India were not consulted either about the design of programs or about what would be reasonable targets for particular programs. Instead, orders were simply sent from above, and he was told what was to be done.

What stands out here are higher-level officials in the administrative hierarchy making decisions about programs and targets that bear little relevance to realities on the ground; also present, in turn, are subordinates faithfully executing programs on paper but caring little for how well they are implemented. Targets are indeed met, but the ultimate goals of the programs go unfulfilled. Some of the targets coincide with the goals while others do not, but there is little concern with whether they do and why or why not. An indifference to outcomes produces arbitrariness toward the poor people who are the intended beneficiaries of these programs. The rational response of lower-level staff to the discipline of the bureaucracy demands that they pay attention to the targets rather than to the welfare of the people being targeted. This is one of the many ways that procedure rather than ideology operates to prevent services from reaching the poor. Perhaps it would be more accurate to talk about procedure *as* ideology because it is through such procedures that the state comes to be represented and symbolized (see below).

The second story involves Goel, one of the BDO's staff, who had just moved to Mandi from a district in the north. He told me he did not like his new post because there was "too much politics here" and people were not interested in getting things done. There were the usual politics associated with political parties and factions, but in addition bureaucrats like him had to contend with a well-organized, powerful peasant group, the Kisan Union, and "a lot of hooliganism [*goondagardi*]."

Goel's job was to keep statistics on every conceivable subject pertaining to the block. Every month he was required to submit a report summarizing the progress made in the block. The monthly progress reports were supplemented by even more comprehensive quarterly progress reports. The data for these reports were collected at the monthly meeting of village level workers. His job was to compile the information given to him by these workers and to inspect and check those figures. In practice, he took their numbers and simply totaled them up; he had neither the time nor the inclination to verify the accuracy of the data. He showed me the latest quarterly report for the year that had just been approved. It seemed like an enormous exercise, with sixty-two pages of statistics on a host of subjects. He told me that when the block received requests for statistics from a higher official, he was the one who was supposed to answer those letters. The data collected were used in the census and other national statistical surveys.

Goel's complaint about political interference by elected officials makes it clear that even at the local level there is considerable friction between branches of the state, such as the legislature and the administration. However, this example also demonstrates that the routine operations of bureaucracies such as the collection and aggregation of statistics make it possible for officials at different levels and in various branches of government to coordinate their actions. The data collected, aggregated, and distributed across levels of an administrative hierarchy form the shared basis upon which arguments for programs and policies are made.[11] Although the interpretation of such data may vary, it provides a baseline from which agreements can be forged or disagreements voiced. By a process of aggregation, such data can also help construct a broader picture of activity that then makes it possible to attribute actions to a singular agent, the state. This is one way that officials, no less than the public, gain an apprehension of the state as a cohesive entity. Through statistical collation, biopolitics becomes entwined with the representation of the state as singular. Collecting statistics for the sake of compiling them may have more to do with representing the state as singular than with biopolitics because the effectiveness of biopolitics depends on a correspondence be-tween the numbers and the phenomenon being mapped. In order to intervene effectively in reducing population, for example, one would have to measure accurately the number of people in a household, birthrates, longevity, land under cultivation, and so on. For biopolitics, the accuracy of the data does indeed matter, whereas for representing the state as singular, accuracy is not necessarily important but aggregation of the data is critical.

Sharma, an extension worker, added to Goel's complaint about political interference by saying that he encountered problems in his job only if he wanted to get anything accomplished. "The best policy," Sharma said, "is not to do anything. That way, no one can blame you for doing the wrong thing whereas if you go ahead and do something, you are held responsible if it goes wrong." Rather than take Sharma's statement literally, one should interpret it as indicating how difficult it actually was to accomplish something. Sharma proceeded to give an example of the time he took a stack of loan applications to a bank. The official at the branch refused to process the applications on some flimsy pretext. Therefore, Sharma took all the forms, stuck a whole bunch of empty applications in the middle so that it looked like an enormous stack, and then went straight to the DM. Sharma said to the DM, "I've brought all these applications from villagers but the man at the bank refuses to process them." The DM promptly took action against the manager of the state-run bank, and the applications were quickly processed.

This example shows how procedures within a particular bureaucracy prevent officials from accomplishing goals and how even to meet modest and quite legitimate ends officials must manipulate the rules. The emphasis on following rules rather than on achieving results has the effect of preserving bureaucratic order, regardless of its consequences for the clients of those programs. Sharma's appeal to the DM further illustrates that when there are conflicts between officials in different branches of the bureaucracy, it is sometimes possible to petition a higher official to help resolve an impasse. Such appeals, however, are always costly, and there has to be a very good justification for a bureaucrat to risk alienating his peers by approaching a superior officer. As a result, when existing programs fail to help the poor, officials have no incentive to rectify the situation and advocate on behalf of their indigent clients.

The third story concerns Ramnarain, a lower-caste man of the Odh caste whose family had been allotted four acres of wasteland (banjar bhoomi) that formerly belonged to the village commons in Alipur, a village near Mandi where I had previously conducted fieldwork (Gupta 1998). The headman who helped Ramnarain's family obtain the land had taken them to the field and marked out the area allotted to them. Although the land was supposed to be free, some money exchanged hands because the headman claimed that land records officials had to be paid off in order to create and record the new plots.

Several years later Ramnarain discovered that the land they had so assiduously regenerated to fertility had been incorrectly marked by the headman and actually intruded onto the remaining village commons. The land that the headman had marked out for them included more than one acre that officially belonged to plot no. 40, which had been designated the village grazing area. At the same time, some of the land in their plot, plot no. 39, was still lying fallow. Furthermore, the land records erroneously showed that no crops had been grown on either plot for the entire time they owned it. The headman who had allotted the land to Ramnarain's family was now no longer in office, having been replaced by a rival from the opposing faction.

Ramnarain asked the headman of a neighboring village for advice. The headman cautioned him against claiming that he had been cultivating the village commons because that was illegal and would get him into trouble. Yet the headman also insisted that it was important for there to be a record that he had been cultivating plot no. 39 because that would underline his legal claim to the plot. One option would be to exchange the fallow land in plot no. 39 with an equal amount of land that his family had brought under the plow in plot no. 40. That would mean redrawing the plots and would require the help and consent of the headman, who, in turn, would have to declare part of plot no. 40, the village commons, as cultivable land. But when Ramnarain requested the new headman's help he was rebuffed. The headman told him unequivocally that any land transactions he oversaw would first have to favor his supporters. As a result, the only option open to Ramnarain's family was to abandon the acre they were plowing in plot no. 40, despite all the investment in time and money that had gone into it, and shift cultivation entirely within the boundaries of plot no. 39.

Ramnarain next went with some influential people to meet the land records official. He was prepared to spend as much money as was necessary to get the job done, but the land records official said he could not circumvent the new headman. The proposal for redrawing the plots had to come first from the current headman of Ramnarain's village, and the land records official would then do the necessary paperwork. Ramnarain found himself at a dead end: his relations with the new headman were simply not good enough to persuade him to undertake such a politically complex and administratively difficult task.

Ramnarain's story illustrates how subalterns must negotiate with different bureaus and different offices—the office of an elected official (the headman) and of an appointed bureaucrat (the land records official), respectively. To gain entitlement to the land he had been cultivating Ramnarain had to rely on both of these offices to work in concert. However, the interests of the headman lay in reciprocating the favors he had received from his supporters, while the land records official refused to subvert the authority of the headman.

Although bureaucrats and elected officials such as headmen knew they had to work together, they were mutually suspicious of each other. Elected officials like headmen were deeply resentful that they had to pay off bureaucrats to get things done for their clients: this decreased their profit margins and reduced their legitimacy. It also forced them to increase the amount they charged clients in the form of bribes, and the larger sums they received as bribes sowed suspicion among their supporters and clients that they were being greedy, that is, demanding higher sums of money than was justified. In turn, bureaucrats were jealous of elected officials such as headmen who had begun to receive government monies for development programs directly, thereby bypassing the bureaucracy set up for this job. Conflicts between agencies of the state often made it hard for poor people to obtain services, in this case the paperwork to help secure a land purchase. In other instances, as examples in later chapters will demonstrate, conflicts between agencies enabled subalterns to gain a foothold in achieving their goals.

Taken together, these three stories divulge a great deal about the discursive and institutional production of the state and its relation to poverty. An understanding of the state that does not begin with a reified entity may have unexpected implications for the policy and politics of poverty.

Rethinking the State

All claims about the state, as the foregoing illustrates, should be countered with the question, Which state? When analysts refer to the state, do they mean the state at the central or federal level, at the regional level, or at the local level? Which branch of the state are they studying: the administrative, legislative, or judicial? Which particular bureau are they focusing on: the police, the revenue department, the education department, the bureau of worker safety, the electricity department, and so forth? What geographical area is being studied? Finally, what policies, programs, and people do they see as constituting the state? If a theory of the state is to be based upon empirical observation, the kind of theory generated will be determined by criteria such as where and at which level the observations were collected, the particular bureau that was studied, and the policies or programs that were the object of scholarly scrutiny. For instance, very different understandings of the state will emerge from studying federal politics as opposed to studying antipoverty programs at the block level.[12]

Similarly, if one focuses on another feature of the state, for example, the division between the administrative, legislative, and judicial orders, one sees that most studies focus on one or at most two branches of the government.[13] It is important to note this because when one is faced with claims about the state in these studies, one needs to ask whether such claims are true of *all* levels, departments, functions, and programs of the state or only of the ones with which the study is concerned. If the latter, why are those levels, areas, and themes rather than others seen as constituting the state? If one is thinking of the relation between the state and the poor, such a relationship can be illustrated by studying the state at any level of aggregation and by studying any functional area or bureau. However, it makes a difference if one attempts to understand the impact of state policies on the poor by looking at industrial policy at the federal level (where the poor may be invoked as the justification for particular strategies of industrialization but are unlikely to be present) or by looking at welfare policies at the lowest levels (where the poor may be actively involved in shaping and influencing the type of actions taken).

My point is that any understanding of the state is a form of misrecognition. Observing the state at one level or area or bureau cannot provide knowledge of the state by analogy or extension. Rather than see this as a problem, however, I argue that scholars should accept the partiality of their vision as a necessary starting point for analysis. Yet the real danger lies less in the fact that one's understanding of the state is located and partial than in the illegitimate claims often made by analysts as to the completeness and holism of the state.

Scholars, no less than policymakers, are prone to making authoritative pronouncements about the nature of the state, its intentions, its capacities, and its abilities to deliver on its promises, and so forth. I think of such claims to knowledge as illegitimate, not because they intentionally set out to reify the state but because they do so by default. All such statements about the state assume that it is knowable in its fullness, that one can grasp it because its contours are clear, and that its materiality as an institution is beyond doubt. I argue that such epistemological certainty serves to disable particular forms of subaltern politics.

Two implications immediately follow for my understanding of poverty. First, that poor people's knowledge about the state is a form of situated knowledge that one must take seriously, and, although obtained from different sources, it is not more partial or incomplete than that of scholars or policy analysts. Second, one must ask whether forms of managing the population vary from one location, bureau, functional area, and level to another. Rather than take biopolitics as a singular, well-coordinated series of actions generated by that singular entity "the state," one must ask what contradictions and contrasts emerge in the management and optimization of the population across branches of the state.

Why does the holistic concept of the state have such durability? Why do people continue to invoke an entity that cannot be known as such?[14] What is gained by referring to the state instead of to distinct agencies and bureaus? What are the scholarly and political costs—the negative consequences—of reifying the state (Abrams 1988; Taussig 1997)? For example, does such reification make it harder to devise political strategies that empower the poor? Is the only reaction to violence perpetrated upon the poor one of embracing the state in the classic form of extending the liberal, social welfare project or rejecting it altogether in the service of civil society or forms of self-help that may unwittingly participate in a neoliberal governmentality?

Employing the idea of the state is problematic from both a scholarly and a political perspective. From a scholarly perspective it is unacceptable because it gives the illusion of insight by taking for granted what needs to be explained. Scholars of states necessarily have to limit the scope of their study in some way—by concentrating on relations within one or between two of the legislative, administrative, and judicial branches; by focusing on connections between two or more levels, for example, federal and regional state, of a single bureaucracy; or by limiting their attention to elites involved in external and internal affairs, for example, the military's relation to legislators or leaders of political parties. There is no shortage of extremely insightful and productive work *about* particular branches and specific levels of bureaucracies (Sinha 2005). But how analytically sound is it to extrapolate conclusions about the state's relation to the poor from such studies? The issue here does not merely concern the empirical basis upon which generalizations about the state are asserted. Rather, I am drawing attention to the problems caused by presupposing the ontological status of the state as being self-evident rather than taking it up as a focus of analysis.

If this analytical question remained limited to an academic debate, its larger political consequences would be less of a problem. However, theories of the state are centrally involved in public debates about poverty even when the participants do not explicitly employ a specific theory of the state. For example, after market reforms were enacted in India, one very important question centers on what the role of the state should be in poverty alleviation. Are goods such as employment, food, schools, healthcare, and housing best provided by the private sector? Should state relief be limited to the extremely poor? And should it be temporary?

The indiscriminate use of the term *the state* is also problematic because it unwittingly draws the analyst into projects employed by dominant groups and classes to bolster their own rule. As I argue below, reifying the state is an important means of rule and of obtaining consent for rule, which consists of representing that reification as reality. Using the state as a generic analytic category may unintentionally co-opt the analyst into the political task of supporting the status quo. Calls for the state to do more for the poor, as well as criticisms of the state for not doing enough for the impoverished, help reinforce the reality of the state as a unified entity whose actions can make a difference to the lives of the poor. Meanwhile, such views do little to explain why policy decisions by the executive or state elite fail to have the intended results and why there are large discrepancies between intentions and outcomes. Not representing the state as singular may expose a reality that elites have an interest in concealing, namely, that their control of the state apparatus is historically contingent, incomplete, and perhaps even tenuous. Such an acknowledgment opens up new avenues for poor people's politics (see chapter 3).

I am objecting here to the assumption that the state is an object or institution that can be known in its full extent and that this knowledge, in turn, can be utilized for explanatory schemes that purport to answer other questions having to do with the state's capacities, intentions, and actions. In other words, I want to question the ontic status of the state. The state is an interesting object of sociological inquiry precisely because it is a significant and highly consequential social phenomenon: politicians, citizens, courts, bureaucrats, militaries, and legislative bodies might use it to justify their decisions and actions. On occasion branches and levels of the state may act cohesively. For example, one would be justified in saying that the state acted to perpetrate violence on a group of people, as in the pogroms against Muslims in Gujarat in 2002 and the riots of 1984 against Sikhs in Delhi. Leaving aside extraordinary events, the boundary between state and society may actually be constructed through the everyday practices of state offices and representations created by officials (Mitchell 1991b). The commonly held notion of the state, as Mitchell suggests, may be the effect of thousands of humdrum, routinized practices rather than the result of some grand illusion, act of magic, or even a collective national fantasy. However, the opposition Mitchell's claim suggests may in fact overstate the case: instead, one ought to think of the manner in which routinized practices enable such illusions, acts of magic, or fantasies to be created, sustained, and resisted.

Given that the state is really a congeries of institutions, agencies, and agendas at different levels that are not necessarily well connected with each other, the important question to ask is the following: When is the attempt to represent these disparate, conflicting, pluri-centered, and multileveled sets of institutions as singular and coherent actually successful? In other words, by what practices and discourses is the state effectively portrayed as singular and unified to a majority of the population? What conditions allow or enable the state to appear as a commonsensical entity? Particular branches of the bureaucracy may rely on the notion of a unified state in their practices, politicians may invoke the image of a singular state in their speeches, and judicial decisions may both illustrate and depend upon the stature of a unified state for their effectiveness. The everyday actions of bureaus, to the extent that implicitly they invoke a singular state, all help officials and citizens imagine such an entity. The state, therefore, can be seen as a social imaginary that comes into being through practices and discourses. Poor people's discourses of the state in north India sometimes drew parallels with an older imaginary of the king as a protective guardian (mai-baap), but this coexisted with other, less hierarchical, democratic social imaginaries that called upon the state to right historical inequities and forms of discrimination. Even when constructions of a unitary state existed they took multiple forms.

Reifying the state often serves the interest of powerful minorities. One has to recognize that it is most often political leaders and economic elites who attempt to represent the state as purposive, unitary, and cohesive despite the fact that such a condition is rarely realized. The effort to represent the state as a unified actor both to members of the public and to themselves involves a constant ideological struggle. However, it is not only state officials, elected or appointed, who have an interest in representing the state in this manner. Poor people may also represent the state as singular at certain sociohistorical conjunctures. There are times when groups of citizens may represent the state as unified in order to organize in opposition to policies or regimes, to make certain claims, or to argue for limits to government intervention, for instance, with such issues as the separation of church and state and in arguments about privacy. Claims for reservations or quotas in government jobs for lower castes in India can be understood in this manner. In October 2007 poor, landless people demanding land reforms organized a march on Delhi in order to make direct appeals to the state, which they represented very much as a singular and coherent entity (http://news.bbc.co.uk, 28 October 2007). Similarly, political and economic elites may not be united in the project of reifying the state, and diverse fractions of capital or the political class may have an interest in representing the state as fractured and split rather than united and cohesive. When I say that these groups most often have an interest in a stable, unified state, I am referring to periods of relatively settled hegemony rather than to periods of disruption and change in political or economic orders. In such periods of relative stability, preserving the status quo (the rule of law, law and order, a predictable business climate) is usually tied to tightening the hegemonic hold of elite groups.

Such an approach, which inquires into the conditions that allow the state to emerge as a cohesive entity, has several advantages. First, it does not presume the existence of the state as a unified actor and purposive organization. Instead of asking what the state does and what the state is capable of doing, that is, asking questions about state capacity, the approach I am advocating turns the state itself into a focus of investigation. Rather than take the existence of the unified state for granted, it takes the articulations of such a state as a social fact that requires anthropological and sociological explanation. Second, it draws attention to the fact that a great deal of cultural and political work goes into any successful effort to represent a state as singular (see below). Third, it brings issues of representation into the foreground, especially representations engendered through those routinized and repetitive practices that constitute everyday bureaucratic activity. Finally, such signifying practices raise the critical question of the audience for whom such significations are intended to make sense. How representations of the state are understood, by whom, and to what ends are critical issues that have to be attended to in any theory of the state.

In India the rapid expansion of development projects and the incredible growth of the development bureaucracy after Independence constitute an important part of the cultural and political process that helps represent the state to its rural citizens. However, the fact that these efforts manifest through everyday practices that are unsystematic and arbitrary makes representations of a unified state problematic. Studies of representations of the state overwhelmingly have focused on spectacular displays of power and extraordinary events (Cohn 1987b; Navaro-Yashin 2002). Far less consideration has been given to the mundane practices of state agencies. Consequently, such studies have tended to reinforce, perhaps unwittingly, unitary ideas of the state by focusing attention on central leaders and situations in which the state is mobilized around a specific task. Finally, the audience for such representations is understood to be the entire population, and the differential interpretations of magic or fantasy by different segments of the public have rarely been the subject of intensive study.

The discussion so far can be summarized as follows: Rather than taking the unified, coherent state as a point of departure for social analysis, the conjunctural conditions that enable any particular state to be successfully represented as such should be treated as an analytical problem requiring explanation.

I think it would be fair to say that questions of representation have not been central to theories of the state; this is especially true when one thinks of such policy areas as poverty and development. Yet if the preceding argument is accepted, then any discussion of the state must consider the articulation of representations with political economy, institutional design, social structure, and everyday practices.

Poverty as a biopolitical concept owes as much to representations *of* the state as it does to representations *by* the state. The latter point is clear if one takes into consideration that the entire category of poverty emerges from statistical representation. For example, the standard technique of counting the number of people who live below an imaginary income line invented by the state (the poverty line) or the issuing of identity cards to households who qualify as Below Poverty Line (BPL), create and define the category of poverty, which emerges from statistical representations generated by the state. More complex images of the deserving poor, who need aid, versus the undeserving poor, who are a drain on public resources, are then overlaid upon such statistical exercises and are often indistinguishable from them, overdetermining their meaning and semiotic range (Broch-Due 1995). My point is that categories such as the BPL do more than simply construct a class of people as the poor; they also simultaneously help create an image of the state. Representation here is Janus-faced, opening up a classificatory scheme through which the population can be subdivided—the poor, the illiterate, scheduled castes, and so on—for the biopolitical purposes of the state while at the same time representing the state as an entity to the people who are defined by those categories.

My argument diverges from some others that focus on representation in that it emphasizes less the traditional area where scholars tend to look for representations, that is, the public sphere and the media, and instead focuses on the everyday practices of state agencies. The routine operations of bureaucratic agencies have very important signifying functions, and their representational effects should be taken seriously. Such practices, which mediate citizens' contact with state officials and bureaus, may have a greater impact on engendering particular representations of the state than any explicit statement circulating in the public sphere. For example, a major speech by the prime minister about how the government is dedicated to serving the poor by making state institutions more accountable might well be undercut by a poor person's encounter with the bureaucrats in the block office.

Once the link with the signifying functions of everyday practices is established, the problem becomes one of how to cope with plenitude rather than scarcity. Representations of the state seem to be everywhere, and it becomes hard to justify choosing one set of representations over others. The most obvious points of focus are the mass media and mass-mediated public discussion: speeches and interviews given by leaders, debates in parliament, discussions about public policy that take place in the major media, films, television programs, music, the Internet, and so forth (Taylor 1997; Navaro-Yashin 2002). Another, often overlooked source through which the presence of the state is instantiated in people's lives can be seen in what may be called micro-markers. To use a few examples from the United States, micro-markers include commonplace symbols of state power such as seals and signatures on money, FDIC (Federal Deposit Insurance Corporation) logos on bank buildings, and so on. The content and warning labels on packaged foods also indicate the ubiquity of state representation in everyday life. Indeed, so pervasive is the idea that the state will safeguard the health and safety of its citizens that when injury or death occurs through a dangerous product or practice, such as mad cow disease, there is outrage at the state's failure to regulate the product and prevent the harm.[15]

As I mentioned earlier in this book, I will rely chiefly on another source of representations that often escapes the attention of citizens and scholars alike: the everyday practices of state bureaucracies. Poor people in rural India encounter state officials in a number of contexts in the course of their daily life—the state is neither remote nor unapproachable. I contend that the representational efficacy of these encounters in constructing an image of the state far outweighs spectacles and exceptional events.[16]

It is difficult to demonstrate the importance of everyday practices because such practices do not draw attention to themselves and often become the subject of discourse only once their conventions have been violated. For instance, it is only when a person fails to stop when summoned to do so by the flashing lights of a patrol car or when someone jumps a red light that the authority of the local police and state regulation of traffic become visible. People who dutifully follow the rules in stopping at a red light do not thereby discursively thematize the presence of the state in making and enforcing such rules. My interest lies precisely in those mechanisms by which the presence of the state permeates everyday life in ways that go without saying. What are the state effects of such practices? What kind of state is being imagined here, especially when such imaginings constitute an understanding that remains largely under the threshold of discursivity? Rather than focus on those moments when the comforting realities of daily life break down, one should ask how the state maintains the presumably normal state of affairs in which the poor are subjected to such intensive structural violence.

I have demonstrated that a tremendous amount of cultural work goes into representing the state as if it were a singular, purposive entity rather than a set of disparate and loosely connected agencies and bureaus at various locations. But to whom are these representational practices addressed? Specifically, how do they address heterogeneous groups of poor people? As Shore has demonstrated, these questions come to the fore in dealing with emergent formations like the European Union (2000: 1–2).

On the one hand, if the state appears to poor populations to be unitary, it can do so only insofar as poor people perceive this imagined state to be legitimate. On the other hand, it does not follow that legitimacy can be obtained only as long as efforts to forge a state imaginary are successful. Legitimacy is a necessary but not sufficient condition for guaranteeing the effectiveness of representations of the state because it is not an all-or-nothing proposition. For example, a particular branch of the state like the judiciary may enjoy a high degree of legitimacy whereas another branch like the administration may be suspect. Alternatively, one level of the state, such as the central or federal level, may enjoy the confidence of the poor while another level, such as the local level, may be distrusted. Finally, one functional area, such as schooling, may enjoy high confidence among poor citizens whereas another area, such as the police, may not. In all these examples the state cannot be seen as coherent precisely because legitimacy extends to only some bureaucracies at certain levels. Efforts to represent the state as a cohesive actor fail precisely because poor citizens have a clear idea that it is not, in fact, singular and that some branches, bureaus, and levels are more responsive to their needs than others.

Thinking of the state in this way differs fundamentally from the conceptualizations of those who ask whether and under what conditions the state achieves legitimacy (Habermas 1975). In the latter approach the premise that the state is a purposive actor and coherent entity forms the starting point of the analysis, and the question is whether such an actor is able to win the consent of the masses for its rule. By contrast, the approach I am advocating ties the state as an imaginary to the issue of legitimacy: *in order* for the state to be represented as a purposive actor, the work of securing legitimacy must be successful. If the state is a cultural construct, questions of legitimacy are built into its constitution as an object. In such a view, states do not first come to power and then attempt to secure their legitimacy. To the extent that a political party, a junta, or a power bloc can successfully claim to speak for the state, it can do so only if it has secured legitimacy for its rule.

What I am suggesting, therefore, is that successfully representing the state as being unitary to any constituency requires constant and unceasing labor by a hegemonic bloc, which for three reasons is always involved in a cultural struggle to constitute such an imaginary. First, there may be competing political interests, aligned by region, ethnicity, religion, language, gender, sexuality, race, or caste, that are interested in maintaining a disarticulated idea of the state. Such groups may not wish to see any bloc speaking for the state. For example, they may resist supraregional aggregation of authority. Second, there may be very different visions of what the state is, so that one may find several constituencies that are each interested in the state as an imaginary but are not in agreement as to what constitutes such an imaginary. For example, groups demanding rights for poor workers, immigrants, or minorities may each call upon the state for recognition but may also hold a very different idea of the state compared to the idea held by leaders of large corporations. Finally, there might be dissimilar visions of the future that may configure expectations of what the state should be, even though there might be considerable agreement over what the state is at present. In this manner hegemonic blocs constantly struggle to construct the state as an imaginary. For this reason cultural conflicts ought to be seen as being constitutive of the state rather than as an effect of state practices or of state–society relations. Structural violence is always the result of such unequal cultural struggles.

What is the terrain upon which such struggles for imagining the state are waged? The answer that comes most readily to mind is the nation. Much academic and public discussion about the state often centers on the national state. This is important to underline because discussions about the state assume a national space and therefore find it difficult to account for different levels of state institutions that function in distinct geographical settings. What possible reason could there be for including a crèche in Tamil Nadu and an embassy office in Washington, D.C., under the same rubric, the state? If every time one came across the word *state* in academic treatises, one substituted *regional state* rather than *nation-state*, it would become clear that much writing about the state is in fact about the nation-state, not about the state at other levels of aggregation. However, if one means the nation-state, one has to inquire into the relation between forms of imagining the nation and forms of imagining the state, respectively, without assuming the convergence of those imaginaries. The relation between belonging, territory, and bureaucracy becomes extremely important to groups of poor people since it influences the decisions about who can be excluded from the care of the state.

Hegemonic forms of imagining the state are inextricably tied to hegemonic forms of imagining the nation (Nugent 1997). Few people would dispute that the nation is constituted through cultural contestation and that all nations struggle to naturalize themselves as ontological objects. The same arguments hold true for states. Ideas of the nation are often propagated by state organizations and activities, such as state-run schools and development programs like ICDS. States need to be imagined no less than nations, and the task of doing so is no less difficult. Consider for a moment a bureaucracy like the ICDS. Its offices are located in different places within the territory of the nation, and even within a regional state and a district. For its officers no less than for its clients, the unity of this bureaucracy is composed of representations flowing out of forms of repetitive action that involve the movement of people, files, orders, requests, resources, and so forth across geographical locales. The translocality of state institutions, their dispersion in the territory that they administer, perforce makes the state an imagined entity. The biopolitical management of the population, therefore, is inextricably tied to the imaginary institution of the state, and cultural struggles that alter the latter will inevitably change the former as well.

However, there is no reason to think that the processes that enable the state to exist as a social imaginary are restricted to the territorial boundaries of the nation-state. In fact, transnational forces, including most importantly, the interstate system, play a critical role in how the state imaginary is constructed (Chalfin 2006; Gledhill 1999; Meyer 1980; Meyer, Boli, Thomas, and Ramirez 1997). Such systems not only play a critical role in shaping the identity of states (less-developed country, newly industrializing country, and so forth), but also help shape the normative values of a state and the kinds of activities in which it should or should not engage. Moreover, these ideas about states originate not just from other nation-states in the interstate system but from NGOs, transnational corporations, and bodies of international governance that forge treaties and laws (Kapferer 2005; see esp. Chalfin 2006). For example, a state that forcibly displaces people within its borders and arrests them without a trial or that refuses to educate its children is likely to be brought under political and diplomatic pressure within the inter-state system. The legitimacy of such regimes would likely be challenged by organizations from both inside and outside their borders.

Given all this, it may seem surprising that the failure of the state in India to provide medical care and food to its indigent population has attracted so little international criticism. Is this because failing to aid the needy does not breach the rule of law nor violate the norms of citizenship and human rights? Alternatively, is it because the logic of markets privileges the preservation of liberal conceptions of freedoms above all else—so much so that the international community's concern is more with the state's abrogation of individual freedoms than with its neglect of a person's right to live? In sum, the state is constituted of practices and representations that arise from many geographical locales and institutional scales. The biopolitical is intrinsically connected to state imaginaries that are transnational. State and national imaginaries do not always coincide.

Questions of locale and scale lead one to a very important point. Studying the state raises vexing questions about methods that are rarely commented upon explicitly. These questions about methods can be grouped into four main headings: (1) the challenge of translocalism; (2) the challenge of pluricenteredness; (3) the challenge of ubiquity; and (4) the challenge of reification. Any study of the state needs to confront these four challenges simultaneously. The result is not that one obtains a better picture of the whole, a task I have already suggested is impossible. Rather, by explicitly engaging these four issues one gains a better sense of how a particular view of the state is obtained. Together, the four issues force one to think more carefully about how to understand the role of the state in the specific form of violence constituted by acute poverty.

The translocal nature of the state makes it extremely difficult to decide on which level one should concentrate in doing fieldwork. For example, in studying bureaucracies, scholars have to confront the difficulty that any one bureaucracy has offices at various administrative levels. Should one study the block? the subdistrict? the district? the regional state? Or should one study the head offices at the center (federal level)? The answer depends on the question one wishes to ask about the state, but a large range of questions involves several levels at once. If one is doing ethnographic observation at one level, how does one know the effects of simultaneous activities at other levels? As noted above, the impossibility of knowing what is happening at other levels in real time makes the study of the state, like that of other translocal institutions, necessarily partial and incomplete. At the same time, it makes the choice of methods extremely difficult because we have to be very clear as to why we study one level versus another. I chose to study the lowest levels of the administrative hierarchy because that is where I could observe poor rural people coming into contact with state officials. The higher one goes in the bureaucratic hierarchy, the less such interactions are likely to be found. It is also likely that a study of upper levels of administration would have revealed less chaotic conditions of bureaucratic action simply because control was more centralized and focused. For example, at the district level, the DM served as a focal point for the coordination of all development, judicial, and police matters.

The problem of pluricenteredness concerns the relation between branches of the state. Although we might decide to concentrate on one level of the state, say, the headquarters of the subdistrict, how do we link bureaus to one another? I am not referring here to the connections among the legislative, judicial, and administrative branches of the state at the local level. Even if one is studying only one of these branches, say, the administrative branch, how are the connections between the revenue department, the land records offices, the schools and hospitals, the development apparatus, and the police to be made? Does one study specific cases, or follow the daily routines of particular officials as they interact with others, or look for those settings where officials from different bureaus meet? Or do we simply concentrate on one office? The care of the population and structural violence cannot be understood without some comprehension of the complex dynamics that connect these branches of the state to each other. For example, if the landless poor start cultivating the village commons in collusion with the headman, the police might be called in by the headman's opponents to make sure that the landless do not break the law. Each strategy of research yields a different, probably nonoverlapping understanding of structural violence and its relation to the state at the local level. These problems only multiply as one moves to bigger administrative centers since branches of the administration tend to proliferate at higher levels. At such levels, finding the state that is oppressing the poor might present an insurmountable problem.

The third big methodological challenge is presented by the ubiquity of the state. Rather than a paucity of potential sites for research, we are faced with the problem of abundance. Following the argument about the centrality of bureaucratic practices, representations, and micro-markers to the construction of the state, it is hard to think of too many spaces, social or geograph- ical, in which the state is not present. For instance, a strictly institutional analysis of child welfare programs at the local level might assume that the boundary of the state ends with that of the ICDS office. Even here, one would have to ask whether the analysis should remain within the bureaucracy itself or whether one should look at places where nonstate actors and NGOs en- counter state bureaucracies. Can we really understand what transpires in the local ICDS office without knowing how feedback from visiting officials from foreign aid agencies or UNICEF alters the design of the program?

Certainly, Gramscian arguments about hegemony or Althusserian ideas of Ideological State Apparatuses (ISAs) take us far afield from conceptions of the boundaries of bureaucracies. The methodological problem that then arises from the theoretical one concerns the unboundedness of such a theory of the state. Where does the state end? Moreover, if everything is the state, then how does one delimit the object of study? In Althusser's formulation, the ISAs include the system of different churches, public and private schools, the family, the legal system, the political system, including parties, trade unions, press, radio and television, and literature, the arts, sports, and so on. In the face of such an unrestricted domain it is unclear where the specificity of a theory of the state really lies and why one needs such a theory at all. Methodologically, it is also not clear from such a theory of the state where one would begin to observe and understand the state. For example, if the object is to study structural violence enacted upon the poor, from the Althus- serian formulation where would one begin such a study and how would its scope be delimited?

In sum, studying the state raises very difficult methodological challenges: (1) the different institutional scales and geographical locales of state institu- tions or, the problem of translocalism; (2) the existence of multiple bureau- cracies without a center or, the problem of pluricenteredness; and (3) the plenitude of sites where the state can be found or, the problem of ubiquity. The methodological implications these challenges have for the study of bio- politics and structural violence are that different sites or levels of investiga- tion may yield very diverse conclusions regarding how the population is managed and how its care is arranged. However, it also means that one could potentially study such biopolitics and violence at any site or level because there is no privileged site for its production. A final implication of these methodological challenges is that it becomes necessary to study problems of coordination across geographical locales or bureaucracies in order to understand the production of arbitrary outcomes for the beneficiaries of state policies.

The fourth methodological challenge referred to above, namely, the challenge of reification, has to do with the fact that fieldwork on state bureaucracies inevitably draws researchers into complicity with the reification of the state. To the extent that the categories, terminologies, and representations of state officials slip into our analytical vocabulary, we become complicit in perpetuating and legitimating the classificatory schemes used by bureaucrats. For example, poverty as a biopolitical category defined in terms of a line or as an identity created by the BPL cards is a state category that crosses over into analytical work. Once it is taken for granted by researchers, academic discussion tends to center on the accuracy of data collection rather than on a sustained interrogation of the category itself as a form of state simplification (Scott 1998) or a thin description of a complex social reality (Broch-Due 1995). While such analytical schemes do not engender the reification of the state by themselves, they often comprise an essential component in that process (Mitchell 1991b). Second, the practices of writing in bureaucratic offices through which the state is often represented as a cohesive whole are mimicked by forms of academic prose, perhaps even by field notes. In that sense, complicity with reification extends to the form, not just to the content, of scholarly work.

This problem can best be illustrated by an example from one of the two programs I studied: the ICDS program (see chapter 7 for a detailed analysis). At the end of her visit to each child-care center, Asha Agarwal, the head of the ICDS program in Mandi, took out a sheet of paper and a carbon from her files, positioned them on a blank page in the inspection register, and wrote out a short, practiced paragraph that went something like this: "A surprise visit was paid to the Center in Kalan Village on [date and time]. At that time, it was observed that 20 children were present at the Center. Most of the children appeared to know their alphabet and math. The Center was neat and clean. All the registers were found completed as per guidelines. The worker was found to be doing her job satisfactorily."

The first time I accompanied Agarwal on a field trip, she unexpectedly thrust the inspection register in front of me and said, "Now you write something in this." I protested that I really did not know enough; I did not know what to say, and I was not a government employee. However, she would have none of it. "Write whatever you wish," she said matter-of-factly, "but you have to write something." I took the register, closely studied what she had written in Hindi, roughly translated it into English, and then dutifully signed it as she had done. One of the few people who would be able to read an entry in English, she took the register from my hand, read it slowly and deliberately, and then gave it back to me, saying, "You haven't said you are a professor, and you haven't given the name of your university. Put down that it is in America, too." I had little choice but to comply.

Later, back in my room, writing my field notes, I typed, "Visited the Anganwadi Center in Kalan. Reached there at 9:25 A.M. Found 20 children." The only thing I added was a more detailed description of the setting, the teacher, the students, and some self-reflexive comments on the inspection team, of which I was, willy-nilly, a member. It was in this way that my fieldwork participated in my informants' fieldwork. My narratives did not merely build upon the narratives of my informants—stories that I am telling you about the stories they told me. Rather, my stories and theirs overlapped in ways that complicated the difference between data and analysis. Not only did my fieldwork overlap with my informants' fieldwork, we were both engaged in the task of constituting the state through such forms of writing.[17]

My analysis, for this reason, participates in the very processes it attempts to analyze. Recognizing the imbrication of my own narratives and categories in the state is thus the first and most essential step in my analysis of the state. The problem lies not just in the objectification inherent in reification. Rather, the ability to view and represent the state as an object necessarily positions the viewer outside it. Indeed, I am arguing that a position outside the state from which it may be represented as a reified object is unavailable to the analyst. This is a methodological and epistemological challenge as much as a theoretical one. For my purposes it means that one simultaneously has to employ the category of poverty and adopt the metrics of its measurement and be critical of such deployment as well as of the metrics. It is not possible to approach this topic outside of a biopolitical imaginary that is constitutive of not only the Indian state but also the global order of nation-states.[18]

We have to engage the continuities in how rural and subaltern people, state officials, journalists, and academics construct and represent the state. Construct and represent: these are not two separate moments, two distinctive practices, which go into making the state. Rather, they are simultaneous acts that become visible once the state is seen as an effect of cultural practices (Mitchell 1989). The cultural construction and representation of the state are embedded in the everyday practices of fieldwork engaged in by state officials no less than by anthropologists. For this reason the line between discourses of the state and discourses by the state may be a lot fuzzier than analysts have imagined. The discourses of the analyst and the bureaucrat may overlap but so may those of the analyst and poor and subaltern people.[19] In the former case, a record might be created whose political implication is that it enables greater surveillance of the rural poor. However, there is no necessary connection to be made between complicity with bureaucratic representations and politically regressive positions, which may also result from borrowing subaltern categories and discourses. Finally, a strong distinction between bureaucratic and subaltern representations of the state is problematic because of the circulation of ideas and discourses across these domains. The ethical implications that follow from an acknowledgment of the analyst's complicity in projects of the state exert their own pressures on scholarly narratives for accountable positioning and a politics that forsake a pristine space of opposition (Haraway 1988; see chapter 3 for a development of this theme). Hence a special methodological and ethical challenge is created by the inevitability of the overlap between scholarly modes of classification and representation and those generated by state officials themselves—the problem of complicity with reifications of the state. For scholarly work, this means that rather than reject the biopolitical project of classifying the poor altogether, it is instead necessary to implement a critical and reflexive use of this category.

The perspective on the state advanced here brings certain ethical dilemmas and methodological challenges to the forefront. It also brings a particular stance on politics that I now wish to tease out in greater detail (further discussion can be found in chapter 3). Those analysts who see policy prescriptions emerging from their work more often than not have a perspective on policy that is essentially a continuation of the genre of "advice to the prince," that is, recommendations made to state elites who supposedly run the state.[20] Ironically, such analysts sometimes share a view of the state with people on the opposite side: those who attack the state for its failure to do the right thing on behalf of lower classes, subaltern groups, the environment, and so forth. Both groups operate with a reified notion of the state, which is consequential because it helps define what the issues are and at which levels or arenas they should act. Policy advice on combating poverty, for example, rarely incorporates poor people's knowledges or experiences, and the poor themselves are almost never consulted as policy experts about their existential condition and structural position.

What are the political implications of seeing the state as a translocal, multileveled, pluricentered, and ubiquitous phenomenon whose construction is critically dependent on representation and the signifying functions of everyday practice? I suggest that this perspective opens up new tactics for political action and intervention. First, it suggests that we may profitably exploit the contradictions and divergent tensions between multiple agencies, departments, organizations, and levels of the state. Such tactics are keyed to conjunctural possibilities rather than to criticism of or compliance with the state (this point is also further developed in chapter 3). Subaltern people's perspectives, knowledges, and representations could play a significant role for some bureaus at some levels. Second, it indicates that different tactics may be effective and necessary for different levels, agencies, and topics. Intervention at the level of policy formulation may require different tactics by a different group of people than intervention at the lowest levels. An example of such synergistic connections is provided by groups at the federal level in India who fought for greater transparency and decentralization by supporting constitutional amendments such as the Freedom of Information Act and the Panchayati Raj bill that devolved power to local levels of government, respectively. Such actions, although not explicitly motivated by or directed toward combating poverty, may end up helping the implementation of anti-poverty programs. Third, it allows one to see that policy is not made just at the Center and disseminated down the hierarchy to lower levels and peripheral locations. Rather, policy is made at all levels where the meaning of the state is constructed and where the implementation of policy takes place. Policy intervention, therefore, should occur at all of those levels, not just at the top of the bureaucratic hierarchy. New tactics of political intervention are suggested by emphasizing the conjunctural possibilities opened up by the divergent agendas of different organizations and agencies that make up the state at multiple levels. Policy intervention does not take place only at the top levels of bureaucracy but occurs wherever the meaning of programs is being shaped by implementers. As a result, efforts to mitigate structural violence must aim at different levels of the state simultaneously.

Referring to the meaning of states has profound implications for the comparative study of states and especially for the comparative study of poverty eradication programs. Despite the enormous differences in both history and culture that separate the world's various regions, many scholars argue that the institutional forms that nation-states have taken throughout the world are remarkably uniform.[21] But an approach that focuses exclusively on institutional forms, capabilities, and organizational structures misses something critical, namely, what states mean to the people who inhabit them (for example, state officials) or are interpellated by them (as subjects and citizens). Antipoverty programs, for example, look surprisingly similar from one nation-state to another, not least because their global diffusion is facilitated by transnational organizations like the World Bank and the entire global scholarly and policymaking apparatus of development. However, the thin discourse on poverty that pervades these institutions is overwhelmingly concerned with the movement of numbers of people above an imagined line and the delivery of assets and services to the poor, which reveals very little about how poverty is lived and understood by the poor. It also reveals very little about how people understand the role of the state or of particular bureaucracies in perpetuating structural violence or their assumptions about the responsibility of particular branches or levels of the state for ameliorating want.

At a more fundamental level, the ontological (or, rather, ontic) presumption underlying the comparative study of states assumes that they are units of the same kind. Such a judgment presumes an intersubjective agreement about the meaning of states that is cross-cultural, an important issue that is almost never discussed in the comparative analysis of states. If representations are not incidental to institutions but are constitutive of them, the study of everyday practices and of the circulation of the representations that constitute particular states might tell us not just what they mean, but how they mean it, to whom, and under what circumstances.[22] The materiality of files, orders, memos, statistics, reports, petitions, inspections, inaugurations, and transfers, the humdrum routines of bureaucracies and bureaucrats' encounters with citizens: this is the stuff out of which the meanings of states are continually constituted. Such routines are remarkably understudied in contrast to the predominant focus on the machinations of state leaders, shifts in major policies, regime changes, or the class basis of state officials—to name just a few themes that have loomed large in the study of states.

What this implies for the comparative study of poverty and the state is that we should be very cautious in proceeding with a top-down approach, in which the meanings of key terms—the state, the poor, indices of poverty, literacy, and infant mortality—are taken as given and which can then serve as a basis for comparison. Rather, we need to understand how and whether or not in fact the poor are actually constituted in the manner that these categories construct them and how this construction of the poor is enabled through state strategies of classification and enumeration. Comparison between nation-states is only meaningful if the meaning of the state to the poor is roughly similar. If the state means radically different things to poor people in diverse geographical or national contexts, then it does not make sense to juxtapose state policies toward the poor in different nation-states.

Taken together, the preceding arguments enable one to reconfigure the relationship between the state and the poor. The rest of this book demonstrates the value of these propositions through the presentation of ethnographic details that paint a disaggregated view of the state. The portrait drawn in the following pages should help empower scholars to think in new ways about the politics of engaging the state from the perspective of different groups of poor people and to open up the many potential sites and contexts in which the state comes to be represented as united and purposeful to its employees and clients.

Conclusion

Thinking about the relation between the state and poverty requires an interrogation of both of these terms. In chapter 1 I attempted to spell out what I mean by the violence of poverty. In order to do so, I bracketed questions about the state. While it may have at times appeared as if I had accepted a more conventional understanding of the state in that analysis, nothing could be further from the truth. This chapter makes that point clear by specifically interrogating the notion of the state that is so often used in social analysis, political action, and policy debates. The main goal of this chapter has been to lay the theoretical foundation for demonstrating that ideological, political, and categorical inclusion is not enough to prevent extreme forms of structural violence. However, as long as one operates by holding a reified idea of the state, the arguments I make in this book about biopolitics, structural violence, and especially about the production of arbitrariness can make little headway. Why? Because a reified view of the state usually depends on the assumption of a strongly unified apparatus and centralized control even when such an assumption is not explicitly stated.

By contrast, the disaggregated view of the state I am proposing allows one to see contradictions across levels and bureaus in the management and control of the population. This suggests that biopolitics is an internally contradictory, contested project. Biopolitics depends upon the mapping of population to understand regularities and deviances because without such a mapping it is impossible to analyze and optimize the processes that need to be regulated. However, in the cases I am analyzing such a mapping is not available to state officials because processes of enumeration and classification are incomplete and unreliable. Statistical data on the poor are generally unreliable and inadequate, notwithstanding such administrative devices as the requirement to register for BPL status. Even a category such as the poverty line becomes a poor definitional tool because people may move above or below it during the course of a year or perhaps even seasonally (Krishna 2010).

A disaggregated view of the state does not rule out the possibility that the state can appear singular and monolithic to some of its population some of the time. By understanding the conditions in which such an image is successfully constructed, one can gain insight into policy outcomes. Hegemonic blocs wage an interpretive and cultural struggle to construct a relatively stable state imaginary. To the degree that such an effort is successful, it implies not merely the right to rule but also the right to frame the right to rule. Ascendancy in this cultural struggle is meaningful because it frames the conditions that regulate the flow of surplus and shapes the parameters of structural violence. Policy interventions that depend on the power of a singular, reliable state to reinforce them are also affected by the success of claims to legitimacy. In turn, the outcomes of policy reflect back on the state, either underscoring its legitimacy or undermining its solidity.

Finally, the focus on everyday practices, rather than on spectacular displays of state power or unusual and singular events, help one understand how the normal state of affairs is maintained in which intensive violence toward poor populations is taken for granted. I am interested in precisely those conditions that allow all social classes, including the large and formidable state development apparatus, to proceed with normal operations in such a manner as to largely ignore the massive, disproportionate death of the poor. Such a crisis does not disappear as a problem; rather, what is interesting is that the cultural construction of the state is such that it never appears as a problem to which the attention of the development apparatus needs to be directed. Structural violence against the poor, therefore, is constitutive of the state—the perceived normal state of affairs produces death at a massive scale without the suspension of the constitution or the imposition of a state of emergency (Agamben 2005).

PART TWO   **CORRUPTION**

CORRUPTION, POLITICS, AND THE IMAGINED STATE 3

While doing fieldwork in the village of Alipur I was struck by how frequently the theme of corruption cropped up in the everyday conversations of villagers. Most of the stories the men told each other in the evening, when the day's work was done and small groups had gathered at habitual places to shoot the breeze, had to do with corruption (bhrashtaachaar) and the state. Sometimes the discussion dealt with how someone had managed to outwit an official who wanted to collect a bribe; at other times with "the going price" to get an electrical connection for a new tubewell or to obtain a loan to buy a buffalo; at still other times with which official had been transferred or who was likely to be appointed to a certain position and who replaced, with who had willingly helped his caste members or relatives without taking a bribe, and so on. Sections of the penal code were cited and discussed in great detail, the legality of certain actions to circumvent normal procedure was hotly debated, the pronouncements of district officials discussed at length. At times, it seemed as if I had stumbled on a specialized discussion with its own esoteric vocabulary, one to which, as a layperson and outsider, I was not privy.

What is striking about this situation, in retrospect, is the degree to which the state has become implicated in the minute texture of everyday life. North Indian villages are not unique in this respect. I do not invoke this example to tell the charmingly counterintuitive story of cosmopolitan villagers who are better informed than the social scientist about modern institutions such as the national developmental state. At the same time, I am not portraying political sophistication among poor villagers as a strategy of survival, and their knowledge of the state simply as the necessary consequence of a brute struggle for survival against overwhelming odds. Like other people in rural areas, the poor were knowledgeable social actors, and learning more about the state was an invaluable aid to improving one's life chances in the world.

In this part of the book I examine the discourses of corruption in contemporary India. Popular knowledge about the state was intimately tied to discourses of corruption. Although one could theoretically separate knowledge about the state from narratives of corruption, in practice the two were so closely intertwined as to be inseparable.[1] I am especially interested in this relationship because the state is imbricated in the reproduction of the everyday lives of the poor in various ways, especially, but not only, through projects of aid and welfare. Therefore, corruption becomes an especially important site for thinking about structural violence (see Nuijten 2004). Corruption discriminates against all those who do not have the monetary resources to obtain goods and services that are supposed to be provided free or at subsidized prices but that in fact command a market price. It becomes a form of structural violence by placing a value on goods that should be available free from the state and thereby denying some of the poorest people the means to sustain life. Corruption generates the paradox that programs set up in the name of the poor, and whose funding and extension were justified by their potential impact on poverty, deny the poor those very goods and services. Including the poor in the project of sovereignty becomes the alibi that enables the constitutive violence of state antipoverty programs. Routinized practices of retail corruption are one of the ways in which the normal procedures of the bureaucracy result in great structural violence.[2]

The pedagogical functions of the discourse of corruption operated both in the register of informing the poor how to negotiate the demands of the bureaucracy and in letting them know that benefits intended for them would be either denied or channeled to those who were better off. Since I use the term *discourse* quite extensively, it may help to specify what I mean by it and how it is related to two other terms that will crop up repeatedly here and in the next chapter as well: *narrative* and *representation*.[3] Stories about corruption usually had the formal properties of narratives: a central character or subject; a sequence of events that led to a change or reversal of an initial situation; and a causal explanation for the change that culminated in a revelation or lesson (Miller 1990).[4] Narratives of corruption, perhaps more than other narrative forms, rely on happenstance, coincidence, and chance both to serve as explanatory mechanisms and to enhance dramatic value. As used here, the term *discourse* refers to the much broader domain of commentary and meta-narrative structured around a topic such as development, the nation, Gandhism, and corruption, whose regularities and relations can be mapped and studied (Foucault 1982). Finally, I have used *representation* in the narrow sense of re-present, that which is artfully constructed and reconstructed in a textual, audiovisual, or oral medium.

Studying the state ethnographically involves both the analysis of the everyday practices of local bureaucracies and the discursive construction of the state in public culture. Such a formulation, which analytically underlines the importance of everyday practices on one side and of discourses and representations on the other, is not intended to suggest that these are two separate domains.[5] On the contrary, in this book I have emphasized the signifying functions of everyday practices as a central feature. Similarly, one could argue that representations, like speech acts, are themselves practices. However, even such a qualification preserves the basic distinction between the two terms. Only when one sees that practices are configured, enabled, and mediated by discourses and representations does their mutual imbrication become apparent. One could turn this formulation around to say that the production, reception, and repetition of representations are in turn configured and mediated by practices.

Such an approach raises fundamental substantive and methodological questions for the analysis of the state. Substantively, it allows the state to be disaggregated by focusing on different bureaucracies without prejudging their unity or coherence. It also enables one to problematize the relationship between the translocality of the state and the necessarily localized offices, institutions, and practices in which it is instantiated. Methodologically, it raises concerns about how one applies ethnographic methods when the aim is to understand the workings of a translocal institution that is made visible in localized practices. What is the epistemological status of the object of analysis? What is the appropriate mode of gathering data, and what is the relevant scale of analysis? Since the poor are themselves a category created by the state, questions of scale are important not only to understand the state but to understand poverty as well.

An ethnography of the state in a postcolonial context must also come to terms with the legacy of Western scholarship on the state. I argue here that the conventional distinction between state and civil society, on which such a large portion of the scholarship on the state is based, needs to be reexamined.[6] Is it the "imperialism of categories" (Nandy 1990: 69) that allows the particular cultural configuration of state and civil society arising from the specific historical experience of Europe to be naturalized and applied universally? Chatterjee (2004: 27–51) has argued that what is needed is a third term, *political society*, that is understood contradistinctively from civil society to understand the politics of the poor. He feels that the state's relation to the poor cannot be brought into focus within a framework that splits the political field into the state and civil society.

I propose a somewhat different strategy for attacking this problem. Instead of taking the distinction between state and civil society as a point of departure and then analytically mopping up the vast remainder with a third term (*political society*), I propose to employ the discourse of corruption to argue that scholars need to reinterpret what they mean by terms like *the state* and *civil society*. By questioning the utility of this distinction in the Indian context I am not arguing that they are inadequate as descriptors of the entire political field but that one needs to rethink what it is that these terms describe. The discourse of corruption turns out to be a key arena through which the state, citizens, and other organizations and aggregations come to be imagined. Instead of treating corruption as a dysfunctional aspect of state organizations, I see it as a mechanism through which the state itself is discursively constituted. Corruption is an essential lens for understanding the meaning of the state in the Indian context.[7] For example, it helps one comprehend how state violence enacted on the poor is constitutive of its developmental mission.

There is a great need for more, rich ethnographic evidence that documents what lower-level officials actually do in the name of the state.[8] This particularly has implications for the study of poverty since the poor show up much more frequently at the offices of lower-level bureaucrats than they do at higher levels of government. As a rule, the higher up one goes in the bureaucracy, the more likely the poor will appear as representations rather than as clients or supplicants. Although research into the practices of local state officials is necessary, it is not by itself sufficient to comprehend how the relationship between the state and the poor comes to be constructed and represented. This limitation necessitates some reflection on what is possible with data collected in the field. The discourse of corruption, for example, is mediated by local bureaucrats but cannot be understood entirely by staying within the geographically bounded arena of a subdistrict township. For this reason I have combined fieldwork with another practice widely employed by anthropologists, a practice whose importance is often downplayed in discussions of our collective methodological toolkit, namely, the analysis of texts. In particular, I have in mind that widely distributed cultural text, the newspaper (for an early example, see Benedict 1946; Herzfeld 1992a; Bate 2002; Mbembe 1992; Ståhlberg 2002). I have looked at the relationship between the state and the public in English-language and vernacular newspapers in India to understand the role played by the poor in such representations.

The challenge in writing critically about the role of corruption in perpetrating violence on the poor in India is that it can too easily reinforce existing stereotypes of Third World nation-states.[9] Since corruption lends itself rather easily to such stereotypes, I want to note how I proceed to develop a perspective on the state that is explicitly antiorientalist.[10] When notions of corrupt so-called underdeveloped countries are combined with a developmentalist perspective, in which state–society relations in the Third World are seen as reflecting a prior position in the development of the advanced industrial nations, the temptation to compare "them" to "our own past" proves irresistible to many Western scholars.[11] Instead, one needs to ask how one can use the comparative study of Third World political formations to confront the naturalness of concepts that have arisen from the historical experience and cultural context of the West. Focusing on the discursive construction of states and social groups allows one to see that the legacy of Western scholarship on the state has been to universalize a particular cultural construction of state–society relations in which specific notions of statehood and civil society are conjoined.[12] Instead of building on these notions, I ask if one can demonstrate their provincialism in the face of incommensurable cultural and historical contexts (Chakrabarty 2000).[13]

Definitions of corruption in the scholarly literature vary widely, as they do in popular discourse.[14] Most scholarly definitions refer in some way to the misuse of public authority for private gain (Heidenheimer and Johnston 2002: 3–14; Gardiner 2002: 25–40).[15] Such a definition, however, does not incorporate the parallel case of commercial bribery (Husted 1999: 340). Another definition stresses the violation of laws by public officials (Heidenheimer and Johnston 2002: 7–8; Gillespie and Okruhlik 1991: 77). This may be too narrow a view, however, because as Bardhan (1997: 1321) points out, not all instances of corruption are illegal. Moreover, legal codes may be sufficiently complex and crosscutting to make it difficult to determine when they have been violated. Further, legal codes may not overlap with societal norms and may even diverge from them (Gillespie and Okruhlik 1991: 77). Definitional issues are often tied to an understanding of the causes and consequences of corruption, which, in turn, has implications for eliminating corruption (Doig and McIvor 1999; Rose-Ackerman 2006).[16] Some scholars have emphasized the negative consequences of corruption: wasting revenues and resources, holding back economic development, eroding trust in the political system, and supporting unequal access to public goods in contexts of high social inequality (Ades and di Tella 2000; Bardhan and Mookherjee 2005). On the other hand, there has been a revisionist streak in the scholarly literature that points to the positive impact of corruption on economic development as it enables the bypassing of inefficient government mechanisms and lets the market work more efficiently (Bardhan 1997: 1322; Gillespie and Okruhlik 1991: 78–79).[17] As for its impact on the poor specifically, Bardhan (1997: 1336) says, "In general the literature on corruption often overlooks the distributional implications of corruption."[18] Economists have focused largely on the impact of corruption on efficiency and growth and on why some countries have managed to reduce corruption whereas it persists in others (Bardhan 1997).

My goal is not simply to refine prevailing definitions of corruption in the scholarly literature. Instead, I am interested in investigating the wide range of meanings attributed to the term in the context of structural violence. The Hindi term bhrashtaachaar occupies much the same semantic field as corruption.[19] It refers simultaneously to activities that may be illegal, violate societal norms (themselves not singular), or meet with moral disapproval. With its invocation of right behavior, bhrashtaachaar also invokes the moral obligation of ruling elites and upper classes to look after the poor and indigent. The ability of the term to slip between significations has given it widespread currency in public discourse. Actions can be described as corrupt because they fail to meet one or more standards of legal, social, or moral purity (de Sardan 1999). Poor people's denunciations of corruption are very often densely inflected with class intensities.

Corruption may also be such a fecund signifier because it serves as a site for debates prompted by conflicting systems of moral and ethical behavior. Any discussion of corruption necessarily assumes a standard of morally appropriate behavior against which corrupt actions are measured. However, what scale does one employ to determine what is morally right? In most cases, the scale used is the one embedded in legal definitions of corruption. When an action is judged as being corrupt, it is usually concerned with the illegal extraction of rents. Additionally, practices like nepotism, while legal in many political contexts, may nonetheless be deemed morally unacceptable.[20] Legal definitions of corruption can be helpful in attacking practices that work against the poor, but there is no inherent bias in such definitions toward social justice.

Whether they like it or not, when social scientists employ a definition of corruption they participate in this normative enterprise (Robertson 2006: 8–9). Often such a view of corruption is built on the model of the Weberian bureaucrat, that is, the role-fulfilling, disinterested professional occupying a particular location in an organizational structure based solely on professional competence and merit. But is such an individual not as much a figment of a modern imagination as his or her imagined contrast, the role-blurring, unprofessional person who has gained his or her position through hereditary means, political connections, or other morally dubious methods, like buying a public office? Although modern imaginations sometimes appear commonsensical or quotidian, in fact there is an important element of fantasy and Othering present even in the most banal representations of "traditional" peoples, practices, and societies. For this, the Other need not be explicitly present in the discussion, but merely an absent presence at the opposite pole of modernity.[21] Thus, where modern bureaucracies are concerned, even when an unambiguous legal mechanism exists to determine corruption, if there is no widespread social agreement about which scale is to be used to judge correct ethical behavior, the social judgment of corruption can often be contentious and fractured. Judgments about what kind of behavior is corrupt do not simply diverge along class lines; even from the perspective of the poor no single viewpoint exists by which behavior is judged corrupt.[22]

This will become clearer from the series of vignettes that follow. Collectively, they give a sense of the local-level functioning of the state and the relationship that rural people have to state institutions. I begin by considering the everyday interactions of poor villagers and officials with state bureaucracies, which are, to my way of thinking, the most important ingredient in constructions of the state. The section that follows considers the theme of representations of the state in public culture, particularly newspapers. Finally, I attempt to demonstrate how everyday encounters between poor people and the state come together with representations in the mass media. The conclusion systematically draws out the larger theoretical issues raised in the chapter, in particular its implications for structural violence and poverty.

Encountering the State

The majority of Indian citizens and especially the poor encounter the state in their relationships with government bureaucracies at the lowest levels of administration. In addition to being promulgated by the mass media, representations of the state are effected through the public practices of government institutions and agents. In Mandi, the administrative center closest to Alipur, the offices of the various government bureaucracies themselves served as sites where important information about the state was exchanged and opinions about policies and officials forged. Typically, large numbers of people clustered in small groups on the grounds of the local courts, the DM's office, the hospital, or the police station, animatedly discussing and debating the latest news. It was in places like these, as much as in the mass media, that villagers interacted with each other and with residents of the nearby towns and that corruption was discussed and debated.

A close look at these settings, therefore, affords one a sense of the texture of relations between state officials and clients at the local level. Here I draw on three cases that together present a range of relationships between state officials and rural peoples. The first concerns a pair of state officials who occupy low but important rungs in the bureaucratic hierarchy and who successfully exploit the inexperience of two poor rural men. The second case concerns a lower-caste man's partially successful actions to protect himself from the threats of a powerful headman who has allies in the bureaucracy by appealing to a higher official.[23] The third example draws on a series of actions conducted by the Bharatiya Kisan Union, or BKU (Indian Peasant Union), a grass-roots farmers' movement that, for a decade beginning in the mideighties, often struck terror in the hearts of local state officials. Because they give a concrete shape and form to what would otherwise be an abstraction (the state), these everyday encounters provide one of the critical components through which the state comes to be constructed.

Small but prosperous, Mandi houses the lowest ends of the enormous state and central bureaucracy.[24] Most of the important officials of the district, including those whose offices are in Mandi, prefer to live in another, bigger town that serves as the district headquarters. Part of the reason is that rental accommodation is hard to come by in Mandi (as I discovered to my frustration); equally important, living in the district headquarters enables them to stay in closer touch with their superior officers.

Sharmaji was a *patwari*, an official who keeps the land records of approximately five to six villages, or about five thousand plots, lying on the outskirts of Mandi. The patwari is responsible for registering land records, for physically measuring land areas to enter them in the records, and for evaluating the quality of land. The patwari also keeps a record of deaths in the event of a dispute among the heirs about property or, if the need arises, to divide it up at some point. There are a number of officials above the patwari whose main, if not sole, duty is to deal with land records. On average, there are about two such officials for each village. Astonishing as this kind of bureaucratic sprawl might appear, it must not be forgotten that land is the principal means of production in this setting.

Sharmaji lived in a small, inconspicuous house deep in the old part of town. Although I was confused at first, I eventually identified which turns in the narrow, winding lanes would lead me there. The lower part of the house consisted of two rooms and a small, enclosed courtyard. One of those rooms had a large door that opened onto the street. This room functioned as Sharmaji's office, and it was there he was usually to be found, surrounded by clients, sycophants, and colleagues. Two men in particular were usually by his side. One of them, Verma, himself a patwari of Sharmaji's natal village (and therefore a colleague) was clearly in an inferior position. He functioned as Sharmaji's alter ego, filling in his ledgers for him, sometimes acting as a front and sometimes as a mediator in complex negotiations over how much money it would take to "get a job done," and generally behaving as a confidant and consultant who helped Sharmaji identify the best strategy for circumventing the administrative and legal constraints on the transfer of land titles. The other person worked as a full-time man Friday who did various odd jobs and chores for Sharmaji's official tasks as well as for his household.

Two of the side walls of the office were lined with benches; facing the entrance toward the inner part of the room was a raised platform, barely big enough for three people. It was here Sharmaji sat and held court and kept the land registers for the villages he administered.[25] All those who had business to conduct came to this office. At any given time there were two or three groups of people, each interested in its own transactions, assembled in the tiny room. Sharmaji conversed with all of them at the same time, often switching from one addressee to another in the middle of a sentence. Everyone present joined in the discussion of matters pertaining to others. Sharmaji often punctuated his statements by turning to the others and rhetorically asking, "Have I said anything wrong?" or "Is what I have said true or not?"

Most of the transactions conducted in this office were relatively straightforward: adding or deleting a name on a land title; dividing a plot among brothers; settling a fight over disputed farmland. Since plots were separated from each other not by fences or other physical barriers but by small embankments made by the farmers themselves, one established a claim to a piece of land by plowing it. Farmers with predatory intentions slowly started plowing just a few inches beyond their boundary each season so that within a short while they could effectively capture a few feet of their neighbors' territory. If a neighbor wanted to fight back and reclaim his land, he went to the patwari, who settled the dispute by physically measuring the area with a tape measure. These things cost money, but in most cases the "rates" were well known and fixed.

However open the process of giving bribes and however public the transaction, there was nevertheless a performative aspect that had to be mastered. I will illustrate this with a story of two poor villagers and a botched bribe. One day when I arrived at Sharmaji's house in the middle of the afternoon two young men whose village fell in the jurisdiction of Verma were attempting to add a name to the title of their plot. They were sitting on the near left on one of the side benches. Both were probably in their late teens. Their rubber slippers and unkempt hair clearly marked them as villagers, an impression reinforced by their clothes, which had obviously not been stitched by a tailor, who normally catered to the smart set of town-dwelling young men. They appeared ill at ease and somewhat nervous in Sharmaji's room, an impression they tried hard to dispel by adopting an overconfident tone in their conversation.

Although I never did find out why they wanted to add a name to the land records, I was told that it was in connection with their efforts to obtain fertilizer on a loan for which the land was to serve as collateral. When I arrived on the scene, negotiations seemed to have broken down already: the men had decided that they were not going to rely on Verma's help in getting the paperwork through the various branches of the bureaucracy but would instead do it themselves.

Sharmaji and the others present, some of whom were farmers anxious to get their own work done, first convinced the young men that they would never be able to do it themselves. This was accomplished by aggressively telling them to go ahead and first try to get the job done on their own and that, if all else failed, they could always come back to Sharmaji. "If you don't succeed, I will always be willing to help you," he said. Thereupon one of the farmers present told the young men that Sharmaji was a very well connected person. Without appearing to brag, Sharmaji himself said that when big farmers and important leaders needed to get their work done, they came to him.

Perhaps because they had been previously unaware of his reputation, the two nervous clients seemed to lose all their bravado. They soon started begging for help, saying "Tau [father's elder brother], you know what's best, why should we go running around when you are here?" Sharmaji then requested Verma to help the young men. "Help them get their work done," he kept urging, to which Verma would reply, "I never refused to help them." The two patwaris then went into an adjoining room where they had a short, whispered conference. Sharmaji reappeared and announced loudly that they would have to pay for it. The young men immediately wanted to know how much would be required, to which Sharmaji responded, "You should ask him [Verma] that." Shortly thereafter Verma made a perfectly timed reentrance. The young men repeated the question to him. He said, "Give as much as you like." When they asked the question again, he said, "It is not for me to say. Give whatever amount you want to give."

The two clients then whispered to each other. Finally, one of them broke the impasse by reaching into his shirt pocket and carefully taking out a few folded bills. He handed Rs. 10 to Verma.[26] Sharmaji responded by bursting into raucous laughter and Verma smiled. Sharmaji said to him, "You were right," laughing all the while. Verma said to the young men, "I'll be happy to do your work even for Rs. 10 but first you'll need the signature of the headman of your village, that's the law." Sharmaji told them they did not know anything about the law; it would take more than Rs. 14 just for the cost of the application to add a name to a plot, and the application would have to be backdated by a few months. At the mention of the headman, the young men became dismayed. They explained that relations were not good between them and the headman and that they were in opposite camps. I sensed that Verma had known this all along.

Sharmaji then told the young men they should have first found out "what it cost" to "get a name added to the register" these days. "Go and find out the cost of putting your name in the land register," he told them, "and then give Verma exactly half of that." He immediately turned to one of the farmers present and asked him how much he had paid ten years ago. The man said it had been something like Rs. 150. Then both Sharmaji and Verma got up abruptly and left for lunch.

The young men turned to the other people and asked them if they knew what the appropriate sum was. All of them gave figures ranging from Rs. 130 to 150 but said that their information was dated because that is how much it had cost ten or more years ago. The young men tried to put a good face on the bungled negotiation by suggesting that it would not be a big loss if they did not succeed in their efforts. If they did not get the loan, they would continue to farm as they usually did, that is, without fertilizer.

No one could tell them what the current figure was. Even man Friday, who was still sitting there, refused to answer, saying it was not for him to intervene, that it was all up to Sharmaji and Verma. The practice of bribe giving was not, as the young men learned, simply an economic transaction, but a cultural practice that required a great degree of performative competence. When villagers complained about the corruption of state officials, therefore, they were not just voicing their exclusion from government services because these were costly, although that was no small factor. More important, they were expressing frustration because they lacked the cultural capital required to negotiate deftly for those services.[27]

The entire episode was skillfully managed by Sharmaji and Verma. Although they came away empty-handed from this particular round of negotiations, they knew that the young men would eventually be back and would then have to pay even more than the going rate to get the same job done. Sharmaji appeared in turns as the benefactor and the supplicant pleading with his colleague on behalf of the clients. Verma managed to appear to be willing to do the work. The act of giving the bribe became entirely a gesture of goodwill on the part of the customers rather than a conscious mechanism to grease the wheels. Interestingly, a great deal of importance was attached to not naming a sum.[28] In this case, state officials got the better of a couple of inexperienced clients. Petty officials, however, do not always have their way. In the implementation of development programs, for example, local officials often have to seek out beneficiaries in order to meet targets set by higher authorities. The beneficiaries of these programs can then employ the authority of the upper levels of the bureaucracy to exert some pressure on local officials.

Several houses have been constructed in Alipur under two government programs, the Indira Awaas Yojana and the Nirbal Varg Awaas Yojana (the Indira Housing Program and the Weaker Sections Housing Program, respectively). Both programs are intended to benefit poor people who do not have a brick (pucca) house. The Indira Awaas Yojana was meant for landless harijans (untouchables), whereas the Nirbal Varg Awaas Yojana was for all those who owned less than one acre of land, lacked a brick house, and had an income below a specified limit (defined as Rs. 6,400 for the 1992–93 fiscal year).[29] I was told that one of the beneficiaries was Sripal, so I spoke to him outside his new house. Sripal was a thin, small-boned man, not more than twenty-five years old, who lived in a cluster of low-caste (jatav) homes in the village. When I saw the brick one-room dwelling constructed next to his mother's house, I could not help remarking that it looked quite solid. Sripal immediately dismissed that notion.

Sripal was selected for this program by the village headman, Sher Singh. When his name was approved, the village development worker (VDW) took him to the town, had his photograph taken, and then opened an account in his name at a bank.[30] For the paperwork he was charged Rs. 200. After that, he was given a slip (*parchi*) which entitled him to pick up predetermined quantities of building material from a store designated by the VDW. The money required to get the material transported to the construction site came out of his pocket. The VDW asked him to pay an additional Rs. 500 to get the bricks. Sripal pleaded that he did not have any more money: "Take Rs. 1,000 if you want from the cost of the material [from the portion of the house grant reserved for purchasing materials] but don't ask me to pay you anything."

Sripal claimed this was exactly what the VDW had done, providing him with material worth only Rs. 6,000 out of the Rs. 7,000 allocated to him.[31] Once again he had to fork over the transportation expense to have the bricks delivered from a kiln near the village. Sripal claimed that the bricks given to him were inferior yellow bricks (*peelay eenth*) that had been improperly baked. He also discovered that the cost of labor was supposed to be reimbursed to him. Although he had built the house himself because he was an expert mason, he never received the Rs. 300 allocated for labor costs in the program.

As if this were not enough, Sripal did not receive any material for a door and a window, so it was impossible to live in the new house. No official had come to inspect the work to see if there was anything missing. Sripal complained that those whose job it was to inspect the buildings just sat in their offices and approved the construction because they were the ones who had the authority to create the official record ("They are the ones who have pen and paper" [*kaagaz-kalam unhee kay paas hai*]). Sripal himself was illiterate.[32]

Frustrated about his doorless house, he lodged complaints at the block office and at the bank that lent him the money for construction. Meanwhile, Sher Singh, who had been employing Sripal as a daily laborer on his farm, became angry with Sripal for refusing to come to work one day. Sripal explained that he could not possibly have gone because his relatives had come over that day and to leave them would have been construed as inhospitable. In any case, Sripal said, he could not do any heavy work because he had broken his arm some time ago.

When Sher Singh found out that Sripal had complained about him and the VDW at the block office, he threatened to beat him up so badly that he would never enter the village again. Fearing the worst, Sripal fled from the village and went to live with his in-laws. Despite the threat to his life, Sripal was not daunted in his efforts to seek justice. When he saw that his complaints elicited no response, he approached a lawyer to draft a letter to the DM, the highest administrative authority in the area. This strategy paid off in that a police contingent was sent to the village to investigate. When I asked Sripal to tell me what the letter said, he produced a copy of it for me. "What can I tell you?" he asked. "Read it yourself." The letter alleged that the VDW had failed to supply the necessary material and that because the headman had threatened to beat him up he had been forced to flee the village.

After the police visit Sher Singh made peace with Sripal. Under the auspices of the same program he even hired Sripal to construct a home for another person. In addition, Sher Singh stopped asking Sripal to come to labor on his farm. However, the VDW threatened Sripal with imprisonment unless he paid back Rs. 3,000 toward the cost of completing the house.[33] "One of my relatives is the police chief [*thanedaar*]," he reportedly told Sripal. "If you don't pay up, I'll have you put away in jail." Sitting in front of the empty space that was to be the door to his house, Sripal told me he was resigned to going to jail. "What difference does it make?" he asked. "Living like this is as good as being dead."

Although he was ultimately unsuccessful in his appeals for justice, Sripal's case illustrates that even members of the subaltern classes have a practical knowledge of the multiple levels of state authority. Faced with the depredations of the headman and VDW, Sripal had appealed to the authority of a person three rungs higher in the bureaucratic hierarchy.[34] Because the central and state governments are theoretically committed to protecting scheduled-caste people like Sripal, his complaint regarding the threat to his life was taken quite seriously. Sending the police to the village was a clear warning to Sher Singh that if he dared to harm Sripal physically he would risk retaliation from the repressive arm of the state.

Sripal's experience of pitting one organization of the state against others and of employing the multiple layers of state organizations to his advantage no doubt shaped his construction of the state. At the same time, he appeared defeated in the end by the procedures of a bureaucracy whose rules he could not comprehend. Sripal was among those beneficiaries of development assistance who regretted ever accepting help. He became deeply alienated by the very programs the state employed to legitimate its rule. The implementation of development programs therefore forms a key arena where representations of the state are constituted and where its legitimacy is contested. Sripal's case demonstrates perfectly how violence coexists with care: he was provided with shelter, a necessity he could not afford on his own, but at the same time threatened with being jailed. Other poor people, looking at him, would not be wrong to conclude that it was better not to get assistance from the state, even when it was offered for free and even when what was offered was something they desperately needed and could not afford.

However, the commerce between villagers and state officials was not entirely one way. Richer villagers sometimes had recourse to actions that put local officials on the receiving end of villagers' disaffection with state institutions, as can be seen from some examples concerning the BKU. One of the most frequent complaints of farmers was that they had to pay bribes to officials of the Hydel Department to replace burned transformers. Each transformer typically served five to ten tubewells. A young farmer related a common incident to me. The transformer supplying electricity to his tubewell and those of eleven of his neighbors blew out. So they contributed Rs. 150 each (approximately $10 at exchange rates prevailing then) and took the money to the assistant engineer of the Hydel Department. They told him that their crops were dying for lack of water and that they were in deep trouble. He reportedly said, "What can I do? We don't have the replacement equipment at the present time." Therefore, they gave him the Rs. 1,800 they had pooled and requested him to have the transformer replaced as soon as possible. He took the money and promised them that the job would be done in a few days, as soon as the equipment was in. Being an honest man (that is, true to his word), he had the transformer installed three days later.

When the same situation recurred shortly thereafter, the young man went to the BKU people and requested that they help him get a new transformer. So about fifty of the members climbed on tractors, went straight to the executive engineer's house, and camped on his lawn (a common form of civil disobedience in India is to *gherao* [encircle and prevent movement of] a high official). They refused to move until a new transformer had been installed in the village. The executive engineer promised them he "would send men at once." Sure enough, the linemen came the following day and replaced it.

Not all such incidents ended amicably. The quick response of these officials was owing to the fact that the BKU had established itself as a powerful force in that area, as will be evident from a few examples. In one incident a crowd walked off with six transformers from an electricity station in broad daylight (Aaj 1989a). The farmers no longer feared the police and revenue officials, on occasion arresting the officials, tying them to trees, and making them do sit-ups. They refused to pay electricity dues (up to 60 percent of agricultural sector dues remain unpaid in a nearby district) and forced corrupt officials to return money allegedly taken as bribes. I also heard about an incident in an adjacent village where employees of the electricity board were caught stealing some copper wire from a transformer by irate villagers, who proceeded to beat them up and jail them in a village house.

Obviously, no singular characterization of the nature and content of the interaction of villagers and bureaucrats is possible. In contrast to Sharmaji and Verma, who manipulated their gullible clients, stand the officials who were manhandled by the peasant activists of the BKU. Similarly, just as local officials employed their familiarity with bureaucratic procedures to carry out or obstruct a transaction by maneuvering between levels of the administrative hierarchy, so subaltern people like Sripal demonstrate a practical competence in using the hierarchical nature of state institutions to their own ends. At the local level, the state cannot be experienced as an ontically coherent entity: what one confronts instead is discrete and fragmentary: land records officials, VDWs, the Electricity Board, headmen, the police, the Block Development Office, and so forth. Yet—and it is this seemingly contradictory fact that one must always keep in mind—it is precisely through the practices of such local officials and institutions that a translocal institution like the state comes to be imagined. Although the state appeared no more coherent to the poor than to better-off citizens, poor people's access to state officials and government benefits was limited by their lack of cultural capital.

The encounters with the state described in this section help one discern another point. Officials like Sharmaji, who may very well constitute a majority of state employees occupying positions at the bottom of the bureaucratic pyramid, pose an interesting challenge to Western notions of the boundary between state and society in some obvious ways. The Western historical experience has been built on states that put people in locations distinct from their homes—in offices, cantonments, and courts—to mark their rationalized activity as officeholders in a bureaucratic apparatus. People like Sharmaji collapse this distinction between their roles as public servants and as private citizens not only at the site of their activity but also in their styles of operation.[35] Almost all other similarly placed officials in different branches of the state operate in an analogous manner. One has a better chance of finding them at roadside tea stalls and in their homes than in their offices. Whereas modernization theorists would invariably interpret this as further evidence of the failure of efficient institutions to take root in a Third World context, one might just as easily turn the question around and inquire into the theoretical adequacy (and judgmental character) of these theories. In other words, if officials such as Sharmaji and the VDW are seen as thoroughly blurring the boundaries between state and civil society, it is perhaps because those categories are descriptively inadequate to the lived realities they purport to represent.

Finally, it is useful to draw out the implications of the ethnographic material presented in this section for what it tells one about corruption and the implementation of policy. First, the people described here—Sharmaji, the VDW, the Electricity Board officials—are not unusual or exceptional in the manner in which they conduct their official duties, in their willingness to take bribes, or in their conduct toward different classes of villagers. Second, despite the fact that lower-level officials' earnings from bribes are substantial, it is important to locate them in a larger system of corruption in which their superior officers are firmly implicated (see particularly Wade 1982). In fact, Sharmaji's bosses depend on his considerable ability to maneuver land records for their own transactions, which are several orders of magnitude larger than his dealings. His is a volume business, theirs a high margin one. He helps them satisfy their clients and in the process buys protection and insurance for his own activities.

The latter aspect calls for elaboration. It is often claimed that even well-designed government programs fail in their implementation and that the best of plans founder owing to widespread corruption at the lower levels of the bureaucracy. If this is intended to explain why government programs fail, it is patently inaccurate (as well as being class-biased). For it is clear that lower-level officials are only one link in a chain of corrupt practices that extends to the apex of state organizations and reaches far beyond them to electoral politics (Wade 1982, 1984, 1985). Politicians raise funds through senior bureaucrats for electoral purposes and personal enrichment, senior bureaucrats squeeze this money from their subordinates as well as directly from projects they oversee, and subordinates follow suit. The difference is that whereas higher-level state officials raise large sums from a relatively few people, lower-level officials collect it in small figures and on a daily basis from a very large number of people. This explains why corruption is so much more visible at the lower levels.

The adverse impact of everyday corruption on the poor should not be underestimated. Retail corruption has the effect of raising the price of subsidized goods and putting a price on free goods and services provided by the state on which the poor might otherwise have relied for survival. Everyday corruption is one of the mechanisms that convert the site of care and the provision of state welfare into a form of violence. This violence is constituted by the paradox that corruption engenders, namely, that programs intended to benefit the poor end up denying them the goods and services they need. My point here is that one has to see this result not as the unfortunate consequence of corruption at the lower levels of state bureaucracies but as fundamental to the bureaucratic and political structure. The system of corruption ties the political and administrative branches of the state together in the generation of this perverse outcome.

The system of corruption is not just a brute collection of practices whose most widespread execution occurs at the local level. It is also a discursive field that enables the phenomenon to be labeled, discussed, practiced, decried, and denounced. I turn to an analysis of the discourse of corruption, and especially to its historically and regionally situated character.

Representations of Corruption in Public Culture

Analyzing representations of corruption draws attention to the powerful cultural practices by which the state is symbolically constituted to its employees and to citizens of the nation.[36] Representations of the state are constituted, contested, and transformed in public culture (Appadurai and Breckenridge 1988; Appadurai 1996; Hall 1982). For this reason the analysis of reports in local and national newspapers tells one a great deal about the manner in which the state comes to be imagined.[37] Examining these reports for the manner in which the poor are interpellated provides a good sense of the position of the poor in dominant political ideologies. At the same time, the interpretations that poor people had of these reports also give one a sense of what the state meant to them and how it was perceived.

The importance of the media was brought home to me when, barely two months after Rajiv Gandhi was elected prime minister in late 1984, a higher-caste village elder whose son was a businessman with close connections to the Congress (I) told me, "Rajiv has failed." I was surprised to hear him say this and asked why he thought so. He replied, "Rajiv promised to eradicate corruption in his campaign, but has it happened? He hasn't done anything about it." Although Gandhi had not visited the area around Alipur during his campaign, this man was keenly aware of all of his campaign promises. Like many others in Alipur, he listened nightly to the BBC World Service news broadcast in Hindi as well as to the government controlled national radio (Akaashvaani). He was well informed on international events and often asked me detailed questions regarding contemporary events in the United States and Iran.

Until the advent of satellite television in the mid-1990s, newspapers were perhaps the most important mechanism in public culture for the circulation of discourses on corruption.[38] In the study of translocal phenomena such as the state, newspapers contribute to the raw material necessary for thick description. This should become evident by comparing newspaper reports—

conceptualized as cultural texts and sociohistorical documents—to oral interviews.[39] Since newspaper reports in the vernacular press are often filed by locally resident correspondents, they constitute, as do oral interviews, a certain form of situated knowledge. Obviously, perceiving them as having a privileged relation to the truth of social life is naive. They have much to offer, however, when seen as a major discursive form through which daily life is narrativized and collectivities imagined. The narratives presented in newspapers are sifted through a set of institutional filters, but their representations for that reason alone are not more deeply compromised. Treated with benign neglect by students of contemporary life, they mysteriously metamorphose into invaluable field data once they have yellowed around the edges and fallen apart at the creases.[40] Yet it is not entirely clear by what alchemy time turns the supposedly secondary data of the anthropologist into the primary data of the historian.

Apart from theoretical reasons that may be adduced to support the analysis of newspaper reports, the importance of all vernacular newspapers, whether regional or national dailies, lies in the fact that they carry special sections devoted to local news.[41] These are distributed only in the region to which the news applies. If one picks up the same newspaper in two separate cities in U.P., some of the pages inside will have an entirely different content. News about a particular area, therefore, can be obtained only by subscribing to newspapers within that area. In this restricted sense, newspaper reports about a particular area can be obtained only within the field.[42]

The method of studying the state I advance here relates the discourse of corruption in the vernacular and English-language press to statements made by villagers and state officials. As we shall see, local discourses and practices concerning corruption were intimately linked with the reportage found in vernacular and national newspapers. This point will be demonstrated by first looking at a few examples from the national, English-language press and then mostly at vernacular newspapers.[43]

Corruption as an issue dominated two of the three national elections held in the 1980s. In its summary of the decade, the fortnightly news magazine *India Today* (Chawla 1990: 18) headlined the section on "The '80s: Politics" in the following manner: "The politics of communalism, corruption and separatism dominates an eventful decade."[44] Gandhi's election in November 1984 was fought largely on the slogans of the eradication of corruption and preserving the nation's integrity in the face of separatist threats from militant Sikh nationalists. Precisely because he was initially dubbed "Mr. Clean," the subject of corruption later came to haunt him when his administration came under a cloud for allegedly accepting kickbacks from Bofors, a Swedish small-arms manufacturer. In fact, the Bofors affair became the centerpiece of the opposition's successful effort to overthrow his regime. In the elections of 1989, in which a non-Congress government came to power for only the second time in forty-three years of electoral politics, another Mr. Clean, V. P. Singh, emerged as the leader. He had earlier been unceremoniously booted out of Rajiv Gandhi's cabinet because, as defense minister, he had started an investigation into the Bofors affair. The effect of Bofors was electorally explosive because it became a symbol of corruption at all levels of the state. For example, a conductor on the notoriously inefficient Uttar Pradesh State Roadways bus justified not returning change to me by saying, "If Rajiv Gandhi can take 64 crore in bribes, what is the harm in my taking 64 paise on a ticket?"[45]

The discourse of corruption, however, went far beyond just setting the terms of electoral competition between political parties. It not only helped to define the political but also served to constitute the public that was perceived to be reacting to corruption, especially that part of the public that was most vulnerable and least powerful, the poor. Since this was done largely through the mass media, one needs to pay careful attention to newspapers as cultural texts that offer important clues to the political culture of the period. In a series of major preelection surveys, the widely read metropolitan English daily the Times of India attempted to analyze the political impact of Bofors and set out to establish how the electorate viewed corruption. One of its articles begins by quoting a villager who remarked, "If one [political party, i.e., Congress] is a poisonous snake, the other [opposition party] is a cobra" (Times of India 1989: 1). The report went on to say, "Whether the Congress is in power or the opposition makes no difference to the common man and woman who has to contend with proliferating corruption which affects every sphere of life. . . . Bofors doesn't brush against their lives. The pay-off for a ration card or a job does." The "common man and woman" being represented here is most often a lower-middle-class, urban person, the kind who would use a ration card to get subsidized food from public distribution centers.

The article further elaborated the relationship between the "ordinary citizen" and the state with reference to the role of formal politics and politicians: "In U.P., the majority felt that [increasing corruption] stemmed from the growing corruption in political circles. M. P. Verma, a backward class leader from Gonda pointed out that politicians today are driven by a one-point programme—to capture power at all costs. And the vast sums expended on elections are obtained by unfair means. 'Without corruption there is no politics,' said Aminchand Ajmera, a businessman from Bhopal."

The theme of corruption was prominent in an article on a central government scheme to help the poor in *India Today* (1989); the article pointed out how the resources being allocated by the central government were being misused by the state government in Madhya Pradesh.[46] In this example formal politics was not reduced to competition among political parties, and the bureaucratic apparatus (where payoffs for jobs are given) was not confused with the regime (where the benefits of Bofors presumably went). Instead, the discourse of corruption became a means by which a complex picture of the state was symbolically constructed in public culture.

In addition, I examined the local editions of six Hindi newspapers with varying political orientations most commonly read in the Mandi area: *Aaj, Dainik Jaagran, Amar Ujaala, Hindustan, Rashtriya Sahaara,* and *Jansatta.* There were marked differences between the English-language magazines and newspapers mentioned above, with their urban, educated, middle-class readership, and the vernacular press. The reason lay in the structural location of the national English-language dailies within the core regions, that is, the urban centers of capital, high politics, administration, and education. The vernacular newspapers maintained a richer sense of the different layers of the state because their reportage was necessarily focused on events in disparate localities, which corresponded to lower levels of the state hierarchy. However, they could not ignore events at the higher levels of state (region) and nation. By contrast, metropolitan newspapers focused almost exclusively on large-scale events, with local bureaucracies featuring chiefly in the letters of complaint written by citizens about city services. The vernacular press therefore particularly clearly delineated the multilayered and pluricentric nature of the state.

As opposed to the national Hindi dailies like the *Navbharat Times,* the Hindi newspapers with limited regional circulations, read mostly by the residents of the many small towns and large villages dotting the countryside, were much less prone to reify the state as a monolithic organization with a single chain of command. They made a practice of explicitly naming specific departments of the state bureaucracy. The vernacular press also seemed to pursue stories of corruption with greater zeal than its metropolitan counterpart did.[47]

For example, the daily *Aaj* had headlines like the following: "Police Busy Warming Own Pockets" (1989b),[48] "Plunder in T.B. Hospital" (1989f), and "Farmers Harassed by Land Consolidation Official" (1989d). In none of these reports was the state (*sarkaar*) invoked as a unitary entity. In all of them specific departments were named and very often specific people as well. They also documented in detail exactly what the corrupt practices were. For example, the article on the tuberculosis hospital stated exactly how much money was charged for each step (Rs. 5 for a test, Rs. 10 for the doctor, Rs. 5 for the compounder, and so on) in a treatment that was supposed to be provided free of charge. The article on the land consolidation officer named him and stated how much money he demanded in bribes from specific farmers (also named). Similarly, the news story on the police reported that a specific precinct was extorting money from vehicle owners by threatening to issue bogus citations.

Two features of these reports were especially striking. First, state officials higher up the hierarchy were often depicted as being completely unresponsive to complaints and even complicit with the corrupt practices. "Despite several complaints by citizens to the head of the region, nothing has been done" was a familiar refrain in the reports. For instance, one short report stated that the dealer who had the contract to distribute subsidized rations of sugar and kerosene was selling them on the black market with political protection and the full knowledge of regional supervisors (*Aaj* 1989c). Similarly, another story, "To Get Telephone to Work, Feed Them Sweets" (*Aaj* 1989e), reported that corrupt employees of the telephone department told customers that they could complain as much as they wanted, but unless the telephone workers got their favorite sweetmeats the customers' telephones would not work.[49]

The second noteworthy feature in regional newspaper accounts was their emphasis on and construction of the public. A common discursive practice was to talk of the public (*janata*) that was being openly exploited by the police, or the citizens (*naagarik*) who were harassed by black-marketeering, or the people (*log*) whose clear accusation against the hospital was given voice in the paper, or simple farmers (*bholaay-bhaalaay kisaan*) who were ruthlessly exploited by the land consolidation officer. In all cases, the function of the press appeared to be that of creating a space in which the grievances of the masses could be aired and the common good (*janhit*) pursued.

The press was doing much more than simply airing preexisting grievances. The state constructed here was one that consisted of widely disparate institutions with little or no coordination among them, of multiple levels of authority none of which were accountable to ordinary people, and employees, secure in the knowledge that they could not be fired, who treated citizens with contempt. At the same time, these reports created subjects who were represented as being exploited, powerless, and outraged.[50] What is true for the common person in these reports is even truer for the poor, who, because they lacked cultural and economic resources, were even more likely to be treated with contempt by bureaucrats. I foreground the newspapers' functions in order to draw attention to the rhetorical strategy deployed by the mass media to galvanize into action citizens who expect state institutions to be accountable to them.

Although I have sharply differentiated the English-language and vernacular press in their representations of the state and the construction of subjects, it is essential to bear two caveats in mind. First, if one looks at newspapers from different regions of U.P., and published in other languages (for example, Urdu), wide variations are to be found within the vernacular press.[51] Second, mass media are not the only important source for the circulation of representations of the state in public culture. Police and administration officials repeatedly voice their frustration at their inability to counter "wild stories" and "rumors" that contest and contradict the official version of events. Police officials in an adjoining district are quoted in the *Times of India* (Mitra and Ahmed 1989: 12) as saying, "They go about spreading rumours and we can't fight them effectively. These rumours help gather crowds. And the agitated crowd then turns on the police, provoking a clash." The "bush telegraph" [sic] spreads rumors quickly and convincingly (Mitra 1989).[52] Unlike other technologies of communication, such as newspapers, radio, and television, rumor cannot be controlled by simply clamping down on the source of production (Coombe 1993; Guha 1983; Amin 1984, 1995). Rumor therefore becomes an especially effective vehicle for challenging official accounts, especially when agencies of the state transgress local standards of behavior.

By definition, corruption is a violation of norms and standards of conduct.[53] The other face of a discourse of corruption, therefore, is a discourse of accountability.[54] Herzfeld puts the emphasis in the right place when he says, "Accountability is a socially produced, culturally saturated amalgam of ideas about person, presence, and polity . . . [whose] meaning is culturally specific . . . [and whose] management of personal or collective identity cannot break free of social experience" (1992b: 47). Expectations of right behavior, standards of accountability, and norms of conduct for state officials, in other words, come from social groups as well as from the state.[55] Sometimes these standards and norms converge; more often, they do not. Thus, there are always divergent and conflicting assessments of whether a particular course of action is corrupt, even among a category of subjects like the poor. Subjects' deployments of discourses of corruption are necessarily mediated by their structural location (see below). However, state officials are also multiply positioned within different regimes of power: in consequence, they simultaneously employ and are subject to quite varying discourses of accountability. The manner in which these officials negotiate the tensions inherent in their location in their daily practices both helps to create certain representations of the state and powerfully shapes assessments of it, thereby affecting its legitimacy. In fact, struggles for legitimacy can be interpreted in terms of the effort to construct the state and the public symbolically in a particular manner.

Moreover, if one were to document transformations in the discourse of corruption from colonial times to the present (a project beyond the scope of this chapter), it would be clear that the postcolonial state has itself generated new discourses of accountability (Gould 2007). Actions tolerated or considered legitimate under colonial rule may be classified as corrupt by the rule-making apparatuses of the independent nation-state because an electoral democracy is deemed accountable to the people. The sense of pervasive corruption in a country like India might then itself be a consequence of the changes in the discourse of accountability promulgated by postcolonial nationalists (Parry 2000: 30). In addition, significant changes during the postcolonial period have arisen from the pressures of electoral politics, as evidenced by the Bofors controversy, and from peasant mobilization. In the Mandi region the BKU was very successful in organizing peasants against the state by focusing on the issue of corruption among lower levels of the bureaucracy.[56]

Although there are variations in the discourse of corruption within regions and during the postcolonial era, the end of colonialism constituted a major transition. One of the reasons for this is that nationalist regimes, as opposed to colonial ones, sought popular legitimacy that enabled them to act in the name of the people. They placed new responsibilities on state employees and vested new rights in subjects, who are then constituted as citizens (Gould 2007). The postcolonial state consciously set out to create subject positions unknown during the colonial era: citizenship did not just mark inclusiveness in a territorial domain but indicated a set of rights theoretically invested in subjects who inhabited the nation. However, not all subjects occupied the same unmarked terrain of citizenship. Some, the urban middle classes, were privileged in practice, and others, disadvantaged subjects, were invoked for framing policies intended to eliminate substantive inequalities. Indigenous (tribal) people, the scheduled castes, and the poor became the targets of ambitious programs of social reform and development. This not only led to the rapid increase of bureaucratic positions, but also established a relationship of reciprocal dependence between these marginalized groups and the state. The nationalist project of the state, therefore, was predicated on this gesture of inclusion.

The modernism of the postcolonial nation-state is exemplified by the concept of citizenship enshrined in the Indian constitution, a notion rooted in Enlightenment ideas about the individual. My use of the term *citizens* might seem to hark back to a notion of civil society that I argue against in the rest of the chapter. What I am attempting to stress here, however, is that in a post-colonial context the notion of citizenship arises not out of the bourgeois public sphere but out of the discourses and practices of the modern nation-state. Citizenship is therefore a hybridized subject-position, which has very different resonances in a postcolonial context than it does in places where it is thoroughly imbricated with the emergence of civil society. For groups on the social and economic margins, citizenship was principally about inclusion in the developmental project. Another crucial ingredient of discourses of citizenship in a populist democracy like India has been that state employees are considered accountable to the people of the country. The discourse of corruption, by marking those actions that constitute an infringement of such rights, acts to represent the rights of citizens to themselves. The discourse of accountability opened up by the rhetoric of development and citizenship need not become politically significant. Whether it does or not has to do with the level of organization of the groups that are affected by it.

The role of the BKU further highlights regional variations in the discourse of corruption. At the time of my earliest field research, western U.P., the region where Mandi is located, was the center of very successful agrarian mobilizations led by the class of well-to-do peasants. This movement was first led by Chaudhary Charan Singh, a former prime minister who consistently mounted an attack on the urban bias of state policies. It was then given a new direction by the BKU, led by Mahendar Singh Tikait.[57]

The landowning castes in this region became fairly prosperous, as they were the chief beneficiaries of the green revolution. However, this newfound wealth had yet to be translated into bureaucratic power and cultural capital. In other words, given the central role that state institutions play in rural life, these groups sought to stabilize the conditions for the reproduction of their dominance. Because they perceived the state to be acting against their interests, they deployed the discourse of corruption to undermine the credibility of the state and to attack the manner in which government organizations operated.[58]

The discourse of corruption is central to understanding the relationship between the state and social groups precisely because it plays this dual role of enabling people to construct the state symbolically and to define themselves as citizens. It is through such representations and through the public practices of various government agencies that the state comes to be marked and delineated from other organizations and institutions in social life. The state itself and whatever is construed to stand apart from it—community, polity, society, civil society (Kligman 1990), political society—are all culturally constructed in specific ideological fields. It is hence imperative that one persistently contextualize the construction of the state within particular historical and cultural conjunctures. I have employed the discourse of corruption as a means to demonstrate how the state comes to be imagined in one such historical and cultural context. The discourse of corruption here functions as a diagnostic of the state.

The Imagined State

Banwari, a scheduled caste resident of Ashanwad hamlet, 25 kms. from Jaipur, said, "I haven't seen the vidhan sabha [upper house of parliament] or the Lok Sabha [lower house]. The only part of the government I see is the police station four kms. from my house. And that is corrupt. The police demand bribes and don't register complaints of scheduled caste people like me."
Times of India (13 August 1989)

So far, I have dealt with the practices of local levels of the bureaucracy and the discourses of corruption in public culture. Together the two themes enable a certain construction of the state that meshes the imagined translocal institution with its localized embodiments. The government, in other words, is being constructed in the imagination and everyday practices of ordinary people. This is exactly what corporate culture and nationalism do: they make possible and then naturalize the construction of such nonlocalizable institutions. It then becomes very important to understand the mechanisms, or modalities, which make it possible for the poor to imagine the state. What is the process whereby the reality of translocal entities comes to be experienced?[59]

To answer this question, one must grasp the pivotal role of public culture, which represents one of the most important modalities in the discursive construction of the state. Not everyone imagines the state in quite the same manner. So far, very little research has been done on the relationship between diversely located groups of people and their employment of the media of representation and of varying resources of cultural capital in imagining the state. For example, Ram Singh and his sons are relatively prosperous men from one of the lowest castes (*jatav*) in Alipur. They had acquired a television set as part of the dowry received in the marriage of one of the sons. Ram Singh told me, in a confession born of a mixture of pride and embarrassment, that since the television had arrived their farm work had suffered because instead of irrigating the crop they would all sit down and watch television. (Both the pumpsets used for irrigation and the television set were dependent on erratic and occasional supplies of electricity.) Television was a constant point of reference in Ram Singh's conversation.

I interviewed Ram Singh in the context of the impending elections (the elections took place in December 1989; the conversation dates from late July). He said:

> The public is singing the praises of Rajiv [Gandhi].[60] He is paying really close attention to the needs of poor people [*Bahut gaur kar raha hain*]. Rajiv has been traveling extensively in the rural areas and personally finding out the problems faced by the poor. For this reason, I will definitely support the Congress (I).

> We consider the government that supports us small people as if it were our mother and father [*Usi ko ham maa-baap key samaan maantey hain*]. If it were not for the Congress, no one would pay any attention to the smaller castes [*chotee jaat*]. Not even God looks after us, only the Congress.

At this point, his son intervened: "The Congress is for all the poor, not just for the lower castes. It is exerting itself to the utmost, trying to draw people into [government] jobs [*Bahut jor laga rahen hain, naukri mein khichai kar rahen hain*]."

Ram Singh returned to the discussion: "Although the government has many good schemes, the officials in the middle eat it all [*beech mey sab khaa jaate hain*]. The government is making full efforts to help the poor, but the officials do not allow any of the schemes to reach the poor."

"Doesn't the government know that officials are corrupt?" I asked. "Why doesn't it do anything?"

Ram Singh replied, "It does know a little bit but not everything. The reason is that the voice of the poor does not reach people at the top [*Garibon ki awaaz vahaan tak pahuchti nahin*]. If, for example, the government sets aside four *lakhs* for a scheme, only one *lakh* will actually reach us—the rest will be taken out in the middle."[61]

Ram Singh's position here displays some continuity with an older, hierarchical vision of the state.[62] Typically in such views the ruler appears as benevolent and charitable whereas the local official is seen as corrupt. While this may very well be the case, I think one can adequately explain Ram Singh's outlook by examining contemporary practices rather than the sedimentation of beliefs.[63] One should look at practices of the state that reinforce this outlook. When a complaint of corruption is lodged against a local official, the investigation is always conducted by an official of a higher rank. Higher officials are seen as providing redress for grievances and punishing local officials for corrupt behavior.

Ram Singh's case is a reminder that all constructions of the state have to be situated with respect to the location of the speaker. His position helps one understand why he imagines the state as he does. He is an older, scheduled-caste man whose household owned one of the five televisions in the village, a symbol of upward mobility. Several of his sons were educated, and two of them had obtained relatively good government jobs because of their education.[64] The scheduled castes of this area in general and the *jatavs* in particular had historically supported successive Congress regimes.

The first thing that impresses one about Ram Singh's interpretation of the state is how clearly he understands its composition as an entity with multiple layers and diverse locales and centers. Although the word for regime and state is the same in Hindi (*sarkaar*),[65] Ram Singh maintains a distinction between the regime and the bureaucracy. He sees the regime's good intentions toward the lower castes being frustrated by venal state officials. Ram Singh has a sense that there are several layers of government above the one he has dealt with (the very top personified by Prime Minister Rajiv Gandhi) and that the different levels can exert opposing pulls on policy, specifically those that affect a scheduled-caste person like him. Interestingly, Ram Singh reproduces an apologetics for the failure of policy—the formulation is all right, it is the implementers that are to blame—pervasively found in India's middle classes, delivered by politicians belonging to the regime in power, and reproduced in the work of academics, higher bureaucrats, and sympathetic officials of international agencies.

The second striking fact about Ram Singh's testimony is that apart from his nuanced description of the state as a disaggregated, multilayered institution, his analysis closely parallels a discourse on the state that is disseminated by the mass media and is therefore translocal. Ram Singh's example demonstrates the importance of public culture in the discursive construction of the state: he talks knowledgeably about the public's perception of Rajiv and of Rajiv's itinerary.

His son's perception of the Congress as being "for all the poor" also owes a great deal to mass-mediated sources. So does the elision between poverty and social marginality and exclusion that one finds in the rhetoric used by Ram Singh and his son. The Congress party's efforts on behalf of the poor are effortlessly equated with its efforts on behalf of lower castes. Ram Singh and his family were substantial landholders, and although they belonged to the scheduled caste and lived on the margins of the village and of caste society, they were definitely not poor. In merging their marginal social location with economic backwardness, they were not only echoing official and mass-mediated discourse at that time but also employing a self-representation that was widespread in village society. No matter how affluent they were in prac-tice, villagers went to great lengths to portray themselves as being poor, deliberately wearing old clothes, and carefully hiding their wealth. Such rep-resentations of poverty were not to be taken literally, but they did index the real feelings of the lack of cultural capital and the absence of government services such as schools and hospitals. In the case of lower-caste groups, this lack was compounded by the daily experience of social marginalization.

My suspicion that the close association with Rajiv Gandhi and the expla-nation about the corrupt middle levels of the state were influenced by the impact of television gained force when one of his sons explained,[66] "We are illiterate people whose knowledge would be confined to the village. This way [i.e., by watching television], we learn a little bit about the outside world, about the different parts of India, about how other people live, we get a little more worldly [Kuch duniyaadaari seekh laayten hain]."[67]

In the buildup to the elections, the government-controlled television net-work (Doordarshan) spent most of the nightly newscast following Gandhi on his campaign tours. It was not just the country that was being imagined on television through the representation of its parts, but also the national state through the image of its leader. Ram Singh's words reveal that popular understandings of the state are constituted in a discursive field in which the mass media play a critical role. Ram Singh's understanding of the state could not be deduced entirely from his personal interactions with the bureaucracy; conversely, it is apparent that he is not merely parroting the reports he ob-tains from television and newspapers.[68] Rather, what this example shows is the articulation between hegemonic discourses (necessarily fractured) and the inevitably situated and interested interpretations of subaltern subjects. Ram Singh's everyday experiences lead him to believe that there must be government officials and agencies—whose presence, motives, and actions are represented to him through the mass media—interested in helping peo-ple like him. Only that could explain why his sons have succeeded in obtaining highly prized government jobs despite their neglect by local school-teachers and their ill treatment by local officials. Yet when he talks about the public and with a first-person familiarity about Rajiv's efforts on behalf of the poor, he is drawing on a mass-mediated knowledge of what that upper level of government comprises, who the agents responsible for its actions are, and what kinds of policies and programs they are promoting.

There is no Archimedean point from which to visualize the state, only numerous situated knowledges (Haraway 1988; see also chapter 2). Bureau-crats, for example, imagine it through statistics (Hacking 1982), official reports, and tours (this point is developed further in chapters 5 and 6), whereas citizens do so through newspaper stories, dealings with particular government agencies, the pronouncements of politicians, and so forth. Con-structions of the state vary according to the manner in which actors are positioned.[69] It is therefore important to situate a certain symbolic con-struction of the state with respect to the context in which it is realized. The importance of the mass media should not blind one to the differences that exist in the way diversely situated people imagine the state.[70]

Ram Singh's position as a relatively well-to-do lower-caste person, one whose family has benefited from rules regarding employment quotas for scheduled castes, explains his support for the higher echelons of govern-ment. At the same time, his interaction with local officials has taught him that they, like the powerful men in the villages, have little or no sympathy for lower-caste people like him. Therefore, he has a keen sense of the differences among the levels of the state. On the other hand, if he seems to share with the middle class a particular view of the failure of government programs, it is the result of the convergence of what he has learned from his everyday encoun-ters with the state with what he has discerned, as his son indicates, from the mass media. The Congress party's rhetoric about being the party of the poor obviously resonates with Ram Singh's experience; that is why he calls the Congress government his guardians (maa-baap) and blames the officials in the middle for not following through with government programs. Ram Singh's view of the state is shaped both by his encounters with local officials and by the translocal imagining of the state made possible by viewing television.

Conclusion

I have focused on discourses of corruption in public culture and villagers' everyday encounters with local government institutions in order to under-stand the state's relation to the poor in contemporary India. Such a study raises a large number of complex conceptual and methodological problems, of which I have attempted to explore those that I consider central to any understanding of state institutions and practices.

The first problem has to do with the reification inherent in unitary descriptions of the state.[71] When one analyzes the manner in which villagers and officials encounter the state, it becomes clear that it must be conceptualized in terms far more decentralized and disaggregated than has been the case so far. Rather than take the notion of the state as a point of departure, we should leave open the analytical question as to the conditions under which the state does operate as a cohesive and unitary whole (this point is extensively developed in chapter 2). All the ethnographic data presented in this chapter—the cases of Sharmaji, Sripal, Ram Singh, and the BKU and the reports from the vernacular press—point to a recognition of multiple agencies, organizations, levels, agendas, and centers that resists straightforward analytical closure.[72] The fact that poor people in India deal with particular state agencies, bureaucrats, and offices and not with "the state" as such has implications for everything from the design of programs to collective action.

The second major problem addressed in this chapter concerns the translocality of state institutions. I have argued that any analysis of the state requires one to conceptualize a space that is constituted by the intersection of local, regional, national, and transnational phenomena. Bringing the analysis of public culture together with the study of the everyday practices of lower levels of the bureaucracy helps one understand how the reality of translocal entities comes to be felt by villagers and officials. Poor people's relation to the state is therefore not entirely mediated by the nation but also by a transnational developmental discursive field in which concerns about poverty, women, indigenous people, and the environment are important.[73] This fact complicates the causal connection that Agamben makes between sovereign action and bare life (see chapter 1). Where sovereignty itself is transnationally constructed, the production of bare life can never be reduced to the actions of the leaders of the national state. Although much of the discussion proceeds as if the only entity responsible for eradicating poverty is the nation-state and as if the continuing presence of the poor can be explained by the incompetence and corruption of their government or by the lack of will displayed by self-serving rulers, the transnational constitution of sovereignty fundamentally contradicts such a position.

The third important argument advanced in this chapter has to do with the discursive construction of the state. Bringing the question of representation into the foreground allows one to see the modalities by which the state comes to be imagined.[74] The discourse of corruption and accountability together constitute one mechanism through which the Indian state came to be discursively constructed in public culture. It must be kept in mind that the discourse of corruption varies a great deal from one country to another, dependent as it is on distinct historical trajectories and the specific grammars of public culture.[75] Taking the international context of nation-states into account, however, brings their substantial similarities into sharp relief. If a state is to legitimately represent a nation in the international system of nation-states, it has to conform at least minimally to the requirements of a modern nation-state. The tension between legitimacy in the interstate system and autonomy and sovereignty is intensifying for nation-states with the continued movement toward an increasingly transnational public sphere. The accelerating circulation of cultural products—television and radio programs, news, films, videos, audio recordings, books, fashions—has been predicated on gigantic shifts in multinational capital. When this is tied to the reduction of trade barriers, the synchronization of global markets from trade to commodities, offshore production, and the restructuring of markets (exemplified by the European Union), a pattern of extensive crisscrossing emerges (Appadurai 1996). These complex cultural and ideological interconnections reveal that discourses of corruption and hence of accountability are from the very beginning articulated in a field formed by the intersection of many transnational forces. In short, to understand how discourses of corruption symbolically construct the state, one must inspect phenomena whose boundaries do not coincide with those of the nation-state. At the same time, however, these discourses do not operate homogeneously across the world. Rather, they articulate with distinctive historical trajectories to form unique hybridizations and creolizations in different settings (Gupta and Ferguson 1997).[76] In the Indian case, it could be argued that interparty competition in electoral politics, and urban, middle-class political activism has done more to put corruption and clean governance on the public agenda than pressure from the World Bank or Transparency International.[77] Although the poor play a central role in such discourses, regime change by itself is insufficient to alter the conditions that give rise to chronic poverty.

The fourth significant point, which attends to the historical and cultural specificity of constructions of the state, has to do with vigilance toward the imperialism of the Western conceptual apparatus. Rather than begin with the notions of state and civil society that were forged on the anvil of European history, I focus on the modalities that enable the state (and, simultaneously, that which is not the state) to be discursively constructed in a particular cultural and historical conjuncture. By looking at everyday practices, including practices of representation, and the representations of state practice in public culture one arrives at a historically specific and ideologically constructed understanding of the state. Such an analysis simultaneously considers those other groupings and institutions that are imagined in the processes of contestation, negotiation, and collaboration with the state. There is no reason to assume that there is or should be a unitary entity that stands apart from and in opposition to the state, one that is mutually exclusive and jointly exhaustive of the social space. What I have tried to emphasize is that the very same processes that enable one to construct the state help one to imagine these other social groupings—citizens, communities (Chatterjee 1990), social groups (Bourdieu 1985), coalitions, classes, interest groups, civil society, polity, ethnic groups, subnational groups, political parties, trade unions, and farmers' organizations (see especially Taylor 2004). For the purposes of my argument, assembling these groups into some overarching relation is unnecessary. In contemporary discourses of corruption, the term "civil society" is used to refer to a group of mostly urban, middle-class activists who have rallied around the figure of the Gandhian social reformer Anna Hazare. However, it is not clear how broad a base of support these activists have, as has been repeatedly pointed out by politicians who challenge their legitimacy on the grounds that they would never be elected, suggesting that they lack popular support. Chatterjee (2004), as noted earlier, explicitly rejects the idea of civil society, arguing instead for the analytical utility of the contrasting concept of political society.

One of the social groups that has been constructed in relation to the state in India is that of the poor. However, the category of the poor as a social class has gone through multiple mutations. If one adopted a rough chronology, in the period immediately after Independence poverty was mostly seen as a rural phenomenon. Such a view of the countryside had a long antecedent in nationalist thought, in which the role of colonialism in creating an impoverished countryside was politically central. After the green revolution created a class of rich peasants who formed the backbone of farmers' movements against the state, the emphasis in identifying the poor shifted to the social margins, that is, to the lowest castes and indigenous peoples. In addition to a renewed emphasis on job reservations, the state initiated new development policies targeting scheduled castes and tribes. Starting in 1989 the government's decision to implement the recommendations of the Mandal Commission and expand the quota of job reservations led to judicial and bureaucratic theories of "the creamy layer," that is, to a sociology of differentiation in which better-off sections of the lowest castes were separated from the truly poor sections within these socially marginalized groups. This movement, in turn, led to a return to identification of the poor through primarily economic criteria. The government then introduced a new classification, one that makes a household a card-carrying member of the class of the poor by issuing Below Poverty Line (BPL) cards. I argue that threading the specific conjunctures that have given rise to a new category of the poor as those who have BPL cards through a theory of civil society is theoretically unnecessary and analytically ineffectual.

The final question addressed in this chapter is about political action and activism, concerns that should be included in the field of applied anthropology. In the context of the state, the dichotomy of collaboration and resistance is unhelpful in thinking of strategies for political struggle. The reason is that such a gross bifurcation does not allow one to take advantage of the fact that the state is a formation that, as Stuart Hall puts it, "condenses" contradictions (Poulantzas 1973; Hall 1981, 1986a, 1986b). It also hides from view the fact that there is no position strictly outside or inside the state because what is being contested is the terrain of the ideological field. Any struggle against currently hegemonic configurations of power and domination involves a cultural struggle, what Gramsci has called the "war of position." What is at stake is nothing less than a transformation in the manner in which the state comes to be constructed. It is a struggle that problematizes the historical divide between those who choose to do political work within the state and those who work outside it, because the cultural construction of the state in public culture can result from and affect both in equal measure.

By pointing out that advocates of applied work and those who favor activist intervention may sometimes unintentionally have in common the project of reifying the state and then locating themselves with respect to that totality (the one inside, the other outside), I intend neither to equate different modes of engagement nor to belittle the often politically sophisticated understandings that practitioners bring to their activities. All I wish to emphasize is that one's theory of the state does greatly matter in formulating strategies for political action. Just as Gramsci's notion of hegemony led him to believe that 1917 may have been the last European example of vanguardism, what he called the "war of maneuver," so my analysis of the state leads to the conclusion that we can attempt to exploit the contradictory processes that go into constituting it. These contradictions address not only the divergent pulls exerted by the multiple agencies, departments, organizations, levels, and agendas of the state but also the contested terrain of public representation. If it is precisely in these practices of historical narrative and statistical abstraction, in equal parts thin fiction and brute fact, that the phenomenon of state fetishism emerges, then one must remember how unstable and fragile this self-representation is and how it could always be otherwise. For example, I have shown how the discourse of corruption helps construct the state; yet at the same time it can potentially empower citizens by marking those activities that infringe on their rights.

One way to think about strategies of political action, about such dichotomies as applied/activist, inside/outside, policy analysis/class struggle, and developmentalism/revolution, is to draw an initial distinction between entitlement and empowerment.[78] The machinery of development, with its elaborate yet repetitive logic, focuses on the goal of delivering entitlements. As Ferguson (1994) has argued, it does so in fact only to remove all discussion of empowerment from the discursive horizon. Yet the two are not mutually exclusive. And it is here that seizing on the fissures and ruptures, the contradictions in the policies, programs, institutions, and discourses of the state allows people to create possibilities for political action and activism.[79] I see critical reflection on the discourse of development not as a moment of arrival but as a point of departure for political action. Even as we begin to see that we need, as Arturo Escobar (1992) has felicitously put it, alternatives to development, not development alternatives, we must learn not to scoff at a plebeian politics of opportunism, strategies that are alive to the conjunctural possibilities of the moment. John Maynard Keynes served to remind economists and utopians that "in the long run we are all dead."[80] The poor, I might add, live only half as long.

In emphasizing the discursive construction of the state through nationally and transnationally hegemonic discourses of corruption, I wish to undermine the relentless systematicity of structural violence. Bringing down the system of which the state is a part is not the only politics possible and certainly not one that will bring any solace to the poor in the near future—the only future that matters to them. Corruption disadvantages poor people by limiting their access to free and subsidized state services and thereby serves to exclude them from the very programs that are set up for their benefit. Poor people, by definition, do not have the monetary capital to pay for essential goods and services. However, like the two clients of the land records official, they sometimes lack the cultural capital to negotiate for services. Like Sripal, they may lack the educational capital to deal with literate bureaucrats. Unlike rich farmers, they may lack the social capital of networks among bureaucrats, politicians, and judges. At the same time, corruption also reinforces the idea that the legitimacy of the state depends upon its efforts to help the poor. This is the constitutive contradiction of the developmental state: it excludes the people on whom popular sovereignty rests. Corruption is a central aspect of those routine operations of the bureaucracy that enable the very gestures of inclusion to produce an outcome that is its opposite. This is why inclusion in the national, developmental project can coexist with unspeakable violence, with the production of bare life.

I want to examine the centrality of narratives of corruption to the understandings of the state held not only by citizens but also by state officials. Stories of corruption form a distinctive genre—a socially critical one—in contemporary India, and I am interested in tracking the circulation of these stories in a wider arena through such forms as novels and ethnographies.[1] What role do such stories play in biopolitics? Whereas much attention has been showered on statistics as the critical modality of biopolitics, the intimate relation between statistics and narrative in enabling biopolitics has been largely overlooked. Narrative is an essential element of governmentality, and no project of political transformation, resistance, or reform is possible without changing narratives of rule, morality, and subjectivity. For example, changing the patterns of structural violence that create endemic poverty requires changing the narratives through which such violence is normalized and justified. Narratives of corruption are an essential component of the normalization of such violence and as such contain elements of justification and of subaltern contestation and reinterpretation. Nowhere is the importance of corruption narratives in projects of rule more apparent than in the single episode of the imposition of a nation-wide state of exception in India during the Emergency of 1975–77. The Emergency was justified by the need to crack down on widespread cor-

ruption. Humorous narratives of an uncorrupt state became the most powerful ideological support for the state of exception.[2]

Doing fieldwork in a small village in north India, I heard stories about
corruption more often than almost any other genre of folklore.[3] I became
convinced that scholars of contemporary India who ignored stories of corruption missed something tremendously important in social life, something
whose implications for poverty were potentially enormous.[4] It is not often
that social scientists tackle a colorful topic like corruption, and it seems
rather a waste to lose the very qualities of imaginative narration that make
corruption such a fascinating subject. Yet this is precisely the fate of corruption studies. I do not mean this frivolously; what I propose is that we researchers take seriously the hold that corruption has on the popular imagination as a Durkheimian social fact. The comedian Jaspal Bhatti has made a
career out of jokes about corruption, even creating a popular series on Indian
television around the theme.[5]

I argue, first, that the phenomena of corruption cannot be grasped apart
from narratives of corruption, and, second, that narratives of corruption are
inextricably linked to the violence of poverty.[6] In making this argument, I
point to the repertoire of stories that surround corrupt actions. In a culture
with a rich tradition of oral storytelling, perhaps one reason stories about
corruption are the most popular of the everyday narrative arts is that the
actual exchange of money and favors is sometimes secret and illicit.[7] The
experience of corruption on the part of all parties involved occurs in a field
overdetermined by stories about such acts, stories whose reiterability enables
the participants in that particular social drama to make sense of their actions.[8] This reflexive reiteration of actions and their narratives makes the
analysis of corruption inherently complex as a social phenomenon.[9]

The approach I advocate here reinvests corruption with its rightful cha-
risma. In policy and academic circles, the presence of widespread corruption
is often taken as an indication that bureaucratic incentives have not been set
properly, so that state officials are tempted to appropriate public resources
for private ends. This insight may be true enough, but it fails to engage the
sociological imagination.[10] Such an approach does not help explain what
makes corruption such a significant social phenomenon. For instance, looking at rural India, a structural functionalist might plausibly argue that similarities in the experiences of corruption, and the circulation of common
narratives about it, serve as an important means of social cohesion. But why
is corruption the subject of so many stories and such intense discursive
production?[11] Why are rural people in north India, the poor above all, so

fascinated by corruption?[12] Why do they talk about it so much? and why does it occupy their imaginations to such an extent? One would expect that the rich, engrossing narratives of corruption, as a subject of incessant public discussion and debate and as an object of social analysis, have been exhaustively studied. However, this is not the case: in the scholarly work on India there has been remarkably little written about narratives of corruption.[13] Furthermore, the implications of these narratives for poverty have drawn almost no comment at all.

As a form of storytelling, corruption's narrative structures are remarkably rich and resilient and depend on some time-tested recipes. It is not entirely surprising that stories of corruption in rural India sometimes employ idioms and analogies from Hindu religious epics. After all, corruption narratives are steeped in many of the qualities of epic stories: heroism, debasement, the fall of humans from the path of virtue, resoluteness, the overcoming of impossible odds and the making of superhuman sacrifices, and the providential actions of an unknowable deity, which could be anyone from the chief minister to the district magistrate. The last type of action is important for the elements of patronage that are often involved in relations between rulers and their subaltern subjects.

Although such qualities emphasize movement within the narrative, one can think of other ways in which corruption narratives travel. To put it straightforwardly: narratives move their readers, and narratives themselves move or circulate. Stories of corruption are saturated with emotion: disgust, anger, and frustration at corrupt officials or organizations; happiness at having cleverly beaten the system or satisfaction at getting a job accomplished; and humor, sarcasm, and irony can be effective techniques for coping with the absurdities of bureaucratic process.[14] These registers of emotion are embedded in the narratives and actions of state officials themselves, not just of citizens and subjects. Affect needs to be seen as one of the constitutive conditions of state formation, as Stoler (2004) has so persuasively argued.[15]

Narratives of corruption themselves travel in time and space. All of us are acutely aware of the transnational migration of corruption narratives through calls for economic reform and good governance, prescribed by powerful nation-states, multilateral institutions like the World Bank, IMF, and so on, and transnational NGOs like Transparency International, whose slogan is "Ten years fighting corruption" (Harrison 2006). As I point out later in this chapter, corruption narratives also travel within nation-states, villages, and districts through forms of oral storytelling, novels, and newspaper reports (as detailed in chapter 3). Finally, lest we forget our own role as academics in the production and dissemination of corruption narratives, I include a leading anthropologist whose work has traveled widely. How does the movement of narratives of corruption in these various domains affect poor people?

In my analysis I want to trace the analytical and ideological work performed by stories of corruption.[16] In India narratives of corruption become a pivotal mode for enabling rural citizens and bureaucrats to imagine the state as a translocal and multileveled organization. Analyzing stories of corruption gives us insights into how poor people construe which state actions are legitimate and how ideas of the rights of citizens and subjects are constituted (see chapter 3).[17] Put simply, corruption and the narratives that surround it are central to the understandings poor people have of the state. This is why I argue that no scholarly interpretation of the Indian state can afford to ignore narratives of corruption.

In this chapter I triangulate some of my fieldwork data, a prize-winning novel written by an official of the U.P. state government, and the work of one of the major social anthropologists of India, F. G. Bailey. Such a strategy allows me to juxtapose material gathered by participant-observation with representations of the state found in realist fiction and the anthropological representations of a classic ethnography. Although Steinmetz (1992: 506) makes a distinction between social and literary narratives, he acknowledges that the "boundaries between the two are obviously fluid and contested." My juxtaposition of novel and ethnography illuminates this fluid and contested boundary. My fieldwork, conducted over forty years after the ethnography and the novel were published, is in no way intended to be a comparative exercise. However, the continuities and discontinuities between my observations and those texts offer some insight into the role narratives of corruption play in the constitution of states.

Engineering Development

One day, soon after starting my fieldwork, I went to the block office of Mandi Subdistrict (tehsil), one of the offices where I conducted participant-observation. I met two young men there named Das and Chowdhury, both of whom were employed as engineers by different offices of Mandi District. Das's task was inspecting all the work that was done with funds allocated by the Jawahar Rojgaar Yojana (JRY, Jawahar Employment Scheme). He had the job of functioning, de facto, as an anticorruption officer, even though that was not his primary job description.

The JRY, named after India's first prime minister, Jawaharlal Nehru, began in 1989 by combining and streamlining all existing employment programs into one.[18] It soon became the largest government program aimed at rural development, absorbing half of all funds spent on this sector by 1994–95 (Echeverri-Gent 1993). The funds were distributed among the villages of a block according to a formula that depended on the population of the village according to the latest decennial census. Since expenditures under this program were not large enough to boost the rural economy, they aimed to maximize its impact by concentrating on two factors. The first was infrastructure, which had downstream multiplier effects: better village roads and a pond that stayed full during the hot summer months would help agriculture and cattle, respectively. The second goal was to provide employment to poor agricultural laborers, who were often lower caste, during the troughs in the agricultural cycle. The idea was that poor rural households could thus have adequate nutrition during the time when seasonal unemployment was high.

What differentiated the JRY from its predecessors was the mode by which the money was allocated. Instead of being given to the bureaucracy, funds were directly released to village headmen. In a famous statement authorizing this change, former prime minister Rajiv Gandhi had complained that most of the resources for development were being lost because of bureaucratic corruption, so much so that less than 10 percent of the funds reached their intended recipients.[19] The policy of allocating funds directly to headmen dramatically reduced the so-called unofficial incomes of district officials and was the cause of much grumbling and dissatisfaction.

The money for the JRY was supposed to be released in three installments each year. In the year when I was doing fieldwork, only one installment had been released; I was told that the other two tranches were unlikely to be received before the end of the fiscal year. Work sponsored by this scheme included the building of village roads (the most common use), the construction of drains and village ponds, the provision of handpumps for drinking water, and the planting of trees for village afforestation.[20]

The process by which the money was allocated and spent was supposed to work as follows: The village council had to convene a villagewide meeting to decide which development goal should be given top priority. The village council was an elected body consisting of nine members selected from the wards in a village.[21] Elections for the headman and the village council took place at the same time but on different ballots. The deputy headman served as the second in command for all decisions made by the village council. In practice, the councils that were politically split or had a relatively weak headman were more likely to call villagewide meetings and make decisions about programs and beneficiaries at those meetings than councils that were united and controlled by a strong headman. In the latter case, critical decisions were simply taken by the headman in consultation with key members of the village council, and no open meeting was convened.

After the village council had decided which projects to undertake, the junior engineer of the Rural Engineering Service, or JE (RES), prepared an estimate of how much that project would cost. For example, if the village council decided to build a road, the JE would account for the costs of materials, such as bricks and mud, the distance the mud would have to be moved, and so on. Using this estimate, the headman would be given a check from the District Rural Development Authority (DRDA). He would then be responsible for buying the materials and hiring the labor necessary to complete the job. When the work was completed, the JE had to check and approve the work. He then had to send a completion report to the DRDA, which in turn would release the second tranche. Although a JE like Das could hold up the subsequent release of funds, he was under a lot of pressure from higher officials to make sure that all the money that had been allocated under the JRY for the district was actually used. Higher officials wanted to ensure that none of the funds allocated for the program were left unspent and that the financial targets for the program were met.[22]

One official at the block office, decrying the new rules, said that under the old system, when the money came to the district officials, out of Rs. 100 at least Rs. 90 was spent on the program, even if they took Rs. 10 for themselves. "Now," he said, "there is absolutely no accounting for how the money is spent. It is given to the headman, and he can do with it as he pleases. At least under the old system the money was not directly given to the public." The head of the block office voiced similar sentiments. "Even if Rajiv Gandhi was right," he told me, "at least 10 percent of the funds were getting through to their intended recipients. Now not even 5 percent of the funds are used properly."[23]

Das and Chowdhury denounced the JRY because the government had decided to allocate money directly to headmen without making them accountable in any way. They were astonished that no paperwork was required in the scheme. If the headman, with the assent of the village council, decided to build a cobblestone road (kharanjaa), nobody prepared an estimate of how much the road would cost, how much material would be needed, and so forth. Although the JE was supposed to prepare an estimate, the money was usually allocated to headmen without one. This was precisely what was so innovative about this scheme. Realizing that most village headmen were illiterate, the government decided to let them use the money as the village council decided, without burdening them with paperwork. It was felt that requiring headmen to prepare estimates and to do other planning would once again give control of the process to literate bureaucrats. According to Das, the headmen just went ahead and started the work; when the money ran out, they stopped, even if the road was only partially constructed. Das felt that this was as good as throwing away government resources.

One day Das, Chowdhury, and I got into a standard-issue government jeep and headed toward a village where Das had to inspect a road. Das and Chowdhury had requested the village council (*panchayat*) officer, usually known as the secretary, to accompany us. Each secretary was given the responsibility of being the official scribe of village councils in several villages.[24] His job was to attend the council meetings, take minutes, and ensure that the meetings were held according to protocol, that is, that they had a quorum, that rules of conducting an open meeting were followed, and so on. In practice, the secretaries were closely allied to headmen in the villages where they worked. This allowed the headmen and his faction to do what they wanted, and it allowed the secretaries to attend the village council meetings at their discretion and convenience. The only independent check on the work done under the JRY was the inspection conducted by Das and Chowdhury; sometimes a complaint about fraud by villagers would also prompt an official inquiry.

After we had ridden a short distance on a smooth surface, the road ended abruptly, replaced by an extremely bumpy track. It turned out that the construction of that road had been supervised by Chowdhury. He complained that he had asked the district council for funds to improve the road, but the chair of that body did not pay him any heed because he was far too busy bestowing favors on villages that had supported him in his election and villages where he had friends and relatives. Chowdhury explained that the present condition of the dirt road was owing to its inability to withstand the stresses of the rainy season.

We reached the first village where a road had to be inspected. It was inhabited primarily by scheduled castes and Muslims.[25] In western U.P., villages tended to be either multicaste, with a wide range of castes represented, or predominantly single caste. This village was closer to the latter category. When we reached the village Das inquired about the headman and was told he was not in the village. Nobody seemed to know where he was; even his family claimed to have no knowledge of his whereabouts. Das and Chowdhury, along with the secretary, went walking down the village streets looking for the new road. When asked if there had been some road construction recently, villagers appeared not to know but directed Das to two possible locations. The secretary, who was with us and who was supposedly present at the village council meeting when plans for the new road had been discussed, had no clue about its location. However, he did tell us that the village had only four hundred residents and had been allocated Rs. 7,000 in the first installment of the JRY.[26]

We walked along one of the village's main roads until we came to a portion that Das thought might be the new segment. A couple of villagers and a small crowd of children accompanied the officials. To the untrained eye there appeared to be little difference between sections of the narrow street wedged between the brick houses on both sides. An open drain flowed along one side of the road. Das quickly identified the new construction and commented on its deficiencies. The bricks had been laid broadside up, whereas had they been placed on their narrow and deep side the road would have been stronger and the bricks less likely to break. Needless to say, laying them broadside up required fewer bricks and made the road cheaper to build. Both engineers complained about the poor construction. Then we walked back to the headman's house, and Das asked to inspect the register where the headman was supposed to have recorded what he had paid for the construction materials.

People in the headman's household claimed not to know where the register was kept. "Why don't you wait a little?" they said. "He should be back soon." Both engineers knew this ruse only too well. In his most soothing voice Das assured the headman's family that he did not want to look at the registers because he suspected something was wrong but because he wanted to make sure he had inspected the right road. The headman's family again responded by saying they did not know where he kept the register.

Since it was clear that nothing further was to be gained by waiting around, Das and Chowdhury and I jumped into the jeep and headed off to the second village. They asked the secretary to give them directions to the village, but he did not know the way. Das sarcastically inquired how he managed not to know the route to the villages where he was supposed to be recording minutes for meetings of the village council. The secretary replied he knew only the longer route taken by the bus and was unfamiliar with the shortcut we were taking in the jeep. He seemed to imply that Das, as a higher-ranking officer, was not conscious of his privilege in having access to a jeep; if Das had had to spend hours on the bus getting to such an inaccessible place, he might be less judgmental.

A big puddle greeted us at the entrance to the second village. We parked the jeep there, and Das dispatched the secretary to find the headman. He returned a few minutes later, saying that the headman had gone to Mandi for the day. We went through a performance that repeated the essential elements of the previous inspection. Das conducted the inspection without any help from the secretary, who had no idea where the new road in this village had been built. Das and Chowdhury eventually guessed that one of two roads they inspected was the most recently constructed one.

As in the first village, Das asked to see the headman's register only to be stonewalled by his relatives. He then asked to meet the deputy headman and was told that the deputy was not available. Next he requested that one of the members of the village council be introduced to him, but nobody could be located. The secretary did not seem to know personally any of the members of the village council. Ordinarily, secretaries are expected to live near the villages to which they have been assigned. In practice, however, many lower-level government officials continue to reside in their native villages or in the district towns, where schooling opportunities for their children are better, and rarely visit their place of work. When a headman wants to get the secretary's signature on a document, he travels to the town to obtain it.

What Das did learn from the secretary was that Rs. 8,000 had been spent on the road here, and it was much better laid and longer than the road in the previous village we had visited. Das traced the length of the brick road by writing down the names of the people who lived in the houses at each end of the road. When we were leaving, Chowdhury asked the secretary how much of the money allocated for the project had actually been spent on it. The secretary replied, "You have seen it with your own eyes; what can I say?" Chowdhury did not wish to let go: "You must have received something out of all this, some money for chai-paani [refreshments]." The secretary said, "All I get is Rs. 50 here or Rs. 100 there, nothing more than that." "Oh, come, come," Das interjected, "don't tell us that. It doesn't matter how much you make, what matters is how much you think actually gets spent on these things." The secretary remained silent.

One has to interpret the secretary's deferential evasion of Chowdhury's question in the light of changes in the manner in which the JRY was being implemented. Now that the money was being directly allocated to headmen, officials like Das and Chowdhury were being cut out of kickbacks and payments altogether. However, they suspected that secretaries continued to benefit since headmen still needed to get their signatures to verify that decisions and expenditures had been made as reported. Chowdhury's harshness with the secretary has to be interpreted in this light, as arising out of both suspicion and jealousy. The secretary admitted to receiving bribes (euphemistically referred to as money for refreshments) but carefully placed the value of these bribes at such a low level as to not raise any fear of official retribution.

On our way out, Chowdhury commented that villagers no longer displayed any manners; the situation was so bad that they had to ask people even for a drink of water. "The villagers are uneducated, they don't have good manners, and they don't know much about anything," he scoffed. State officials' contempt for villagers appeared to be reciprocated; the villagers seemed to regard them with a great deal of distrust and did not display the warmth toward them that they generally extended to almost any stranger who came there. For example, it would have been customary to greet a stranger, especially an important state official, with an offer of tea and biscuits. At the very least, villagers would have offered them water to drink. To have to ask for a drink of water and not automatically be offered one, as Chowdhury's remark indicates, was an indication that he and other state officials were not welcome. Through their indifference villagers scorned the representatives of the government who claimed to bring the benefits of development to them. None of the men sitting in groups, playing cards, or talking in the center of the village made so much as a move to come near the officials, engage them in conversation, or help them in any way.

That such an attitude was not isolated or unusual was borne out on other occasions and was the subject of commentary by state officials. In another instance, a lower-level official said to me, "Nowadays nobody respects government officials." Had things changed in the years that he had been a government employee? I asked. "Absolutely! When I first joined [government service]," he said, "people used to consider it an honor if I sat down in their house and had tea with them. Now, they will not even offer tea to you unless they feel they have something to gain." I was curious: When did this change occur and why? It was a consequence of villagers' getting more educated, he responded, without the slightest hint of irony: "The more educated a man becomes, the more selfish he gets. It is due to this that villagers no longer have any respect for state officials."[27] Since state officials often derided villagers for their illiteracy and never failed to draw a contrast between their educational credentials and the lack of qualifications of most villagers (see also chapter 5), this unselfconscious reference to the correlation between education and selfishness was very telling. The subtext of this statement was that education had made villagers self-important and had emboldened them to think of themselves as being equal to officials, so that they no longer displayed an appropriately deferential attitude toward officials.

Many of the state officials I interviewed often traced this change of attitude to the period when subsidies first began. They told me that villagers became hostile toward them precisely at the point when the state started emphasizing its developmental role in the provisioning of social welfare rather than its purely infrastructural or repressive role. If this was indeed the case, it is paradoxical that the state appeared to lose legitimacy at precisely that moment when it sought to achieve it by extending its welfare and redistributive functions.[28]

Once we were back in the jeep, Das let the secretary feel the brunt of his fury. "It is obvious that you don't come to these villages at all," he said. "I want to see your diary where you note down all the work that's been done [in these villages]. Bring your records from these two villages to my office tomorrow." The secretary looked quite sheepish and explained that he lived in a village far away, on the other side of the district.[29] After Das had cooled down, he explained that, apart from Chowdhury and him, there were four other pairs of engineers responsible for inspecting work done under the new job scheme. However, the other teams never went on inspection trips because they realized it was just a waste of time. "We are the only ones who regularly conduct these inspections," he said. All they could do was a physical inspection; they could not actually compare the construction to a plan and check if something had been done incorrectly, since no plans for construction needed to be drawn up by village headmen. They could verify that the structure was actually built and did not exist just on paper. However, they could do little else because it was impossible to determine by visual inspection how much money had been spent. In addition, on those few occasions when they did manage to catch a headman for blatant misappropriation of funds, the headman managed to escape punishment by using his political connections. The government required them to do these inspections, but since nothing really came of them they felt it was a waste of gasoline and resources.

State officials like Das and Chowdhury were frustrated in their efforts to check the corruption of headmen under the new scheme of disbursing development resources. Government officials across different levels of the bureaucracy displayed a remarkable unity in their view that the new method of disbursing development revenues was a mistake because headmen had neither the education nor the technical competence or managerial skills to make effective use of resources. However, this reaction was not a disinterested one, as I pointed out above.[30] Stripped of their resource base, development officials were intent on finding fault with the employment program. In addition, once officials like Das and Chowdhury no longer had resources to distribute but became merely instruments of surveillance and discipline, villagers and village officials felt less compelled to act deferentially toward them. Officials like Das and Chowdhury, who were higher up in the development hierarchy, found themselves in the unenviable position of supervising headmen and secretaries of village panchayats who controlled more resources than they did.

In presenting this extended description of the actions and statements of a pair of government officials, my goal has been to stress how much corruption, the suspicion of corruption, and stories of corruption mediate officials' understandings of the state. Officials widely believed that headmen were illegally pocketing funds intended for village development. Indeed, one headman, speaking about the JRY, conceded to me, "This government has been very good for the health of headmen [*sarkaar ney pradhano ki sehat bana dee*]." State officials like Das and Chowdhury were suspicious that headmen were expropriating funds illegally, either by claiming to have spent more than they actually did for things like road construction, or for showing payments to laborers for work that had never been done, or by adding the names of laborers to work sites who had never been employed. Moreover, they were suspicious that headmen were paying off the secretaries of village panchayats to report that they had verified expenditures when they had not. Finally, given the fissures of village society, rival factions who fought for control over democratically elected village councils often spread stories about the corruption of the headman as a way to delegitimize him in the eyes of other villagers and even his supporters. Therefore, the wide circulation of stories of corruption of headmen served its own function in the politics of village life.

I want to draw attention to the fact that I did not describe any incident of bribe taking, or report as an eyewitness on the misuse of funds, or record someone's statements about their abuse of official privilege. The only person who admitted to any corrupt actions was the secretary, but the trifling amounts he claimed to have received as illegal payments could hardly be seized upon as evidence of a crisis of governability in rural India. Despite this lack of hard evidence of any corrupt action, or perhaps because of it, all parties concerned liberally deployed narratives of corruption. This is the social fact that has escaped the attention of economists and other policy analysts.

Narratives of corruption were relatively autonomous of actions because, while such narratives were not manufactured out of thin air (they usually did name people, places, and actions), they were often not eyewitness accounts of corrupt actions. Thus, a broker or a lower-level clerk might gather a large sum of money from a prospective job applicant for a government position, claiming that the money was needed to pay off all the superior officers. This act engenders various narratives about the venality of senior officers. However, in their circulation, the narratives may well be embellished in ways such that they exceed in importance and dramatic value any substantive actions, and whose relations to those actions are never clear-cut. In an insightful article, Parry (2000: 30) stresses this point: "The most solid fact we possess is the *belief* that since Independence the graph of corruption [in India] has curved ever more steeply upwards" (emphasis added).

What is clear is that, divested of resources, development officials consistently employed a story of the misuse of development funds due to the corruption of headmen in complicity with the secretary. Such stories of *corruption, incompetence,* and *mismanagement* attained their force through repetition. I do not see the terms corruption, incompetence, and mismanagement as being interchangeable: an incompetent but honest headman might be criticized by other villagers for lacking initiative but would not be accused of corruption. However, quite often stories of corruption were reinforced by complaints about the incompetence of the headman or by his mismanagement of a project. In fact, although most villagers expected their headman to pocket some of the resources that were supposed to be spent on village development, they were most critical when the amount illegally extracted was so large that the project was severely compromised.[31] Very importantly, stories of corruption were instantiated through inspection trips like the one I have described. Given this narrative of corruption, the half-built, half-baked roads that these engineers saw in the villages were proof that funds had been misappropriated. The inspections reinforced and substantiated a story whose plot was already given. The engineers interpreted the lack of cooperation shown to them by the families of headmen in not surrendering the registers as further evidence that they were trying to hide something, namely, the misuse of government monies. Even the relation between higher officials such as Das and other state employees, such as the secretary, was mediated by the suspicion that the secretary was misappropriating funds.

While narratives of corruption were relatively autonomous of corrupt actions and had their own life and efficacy, they did not function independently of such actions. Any particular action could be inserted into different and sometimes opposing narratives of corruption. For instance, although stories about the corruption of headmen were widely shared among state officials and villagers, there were divergent assessments of whether the JRY program was a success or not. Many villagers and even some state officials were of the opinion that the JRY was at least better than what it had replaced.

The previous programs merely lined the pockets of the officials, who were much more competent in siphoning off most of the funds for themselves. Headmen's lack of familiarity with bureaucratic procedure and their greater accountability to the villagers on whose votes they depended for the next election at least ensured that they spent a larger proportion of the money on the village than officials did. Moreover, since the money was now allocated to each village, funds were not taken, in contravention of the rules, from villages that had no political influence to those that were the homes of powerful politicians.[32] Varying and competing narratives could be mobilized to interpret the actions of headmen.

I heard about a headman who took advantage of the fact that a canal was being dug nearby to get truckloads of gravel delivered to his village for a nominal fee. This relieved the company that was constructing the canal of the responsibility of getting rid of the surplus gravel and secured a cheap source of foundation for the brick road that the headman wanted to construct. He had the road built, then submitted a bill for gravel purchased at market rates from the nearby town and pocketed the difference. This was clearly illegal, and it would normally have triggered an official inquiry for corruption. The person who narrated this story to me was a state official who intended it to be a criticism of the new employment program. Instead, the headman's supporters in the village pointed to his efficiency. He had built a good road by using an opportunity that presented itself—gravel that was almost free—that would certainly have gone to waste if it had been left to a government department to dispose of it. Furthermore, had the road-building project remained in the hands of officials, it might have been several years before the village got a decent road. The state official's narrative of how corruption was endemic to the new program was countered by another narrative that emphasized the benefits of the new program in encouraging village-level initiative in deciding what was necessary and in implementing those goals.

Neither in the state official's criticism nor in the vigorous defense of the headman launched by his supporters were the needs of the poor given priority. One might interpret these competing narratives as exemplifying interelite conflict, with the goal of justifying whether resources were captured by state officials or village elites. However, this conflict did have repercussions for the poor. The fact that the headman was an elected official who had to keep his next term in mind played a critical role in ensuring that resources were directed to people who had helped elect him or were used to recruit new supporters from among poor and lower-caste groups. Although headmen's supporters benefited from these programs even when they were not the poorest groups in the village, I did not find the wholesale diversion of programs away from their targeted recipients. For instance, among Alipur's poor, those who had electorally supported the headman were rewarded with benefits, and those who opposed him, even if they were poorer, failed to get state resources.

Realist Fictions, Anthropological Representations

This section juxtaposes the account of the role played by stories of corruption above with a work of fiction written by a former bureaucrat and a classic ethnography written by a prominent political anthropologist. The novel I look at, *Raag Darbari*, written by Shrilal Shukla, an ex–Indian Administrative Service (IAS) officer, is, in my opinion, one of the richest works of fiction about the postcolonial Indian state.[33] Shukla's novel was conceived as a set of short stories that were episodically connected to each other. He reports that many people in the region who read the novel when it was published saw it as a straightforward and only lightly fictionalized description of life (Shukla 1992: vii). It is this fact, as well as my own reconstruction of the history of rural areas of U.P. through interviews and life histories, which makes me think that there is much to be learned from the novel by treating it as a quasi-ethnographic text.

The second work I wish to examine, in parallel with *Raag Darbari*, is entitled *Politics and Social Change: Orissa in 1959*. Written by one of the foremost anthropologists of politics in India, F. G. Bailey, this ethnographic text, when juxtaposed to the novel, enables one to see how the relation between rural peoples and the state was being portrayed in two very different genres of writing, each of which was committed to realism as a representational practice. When triangulated with these two books, my fieldwork alerted me to dimensions present and recorded, ethnographically and novelistically, four decades ago but not commented on theoretically at the time.

Many similarities between *Raag Darbari* and Bailey's ethnography make them especially productive to read alongside each other. Both portray rural India in the late 1950s. Bailey's title is unusual in that instead of just constructing a timeless picture of a traditional society, as many structural functionalists were wont to do, he is very careful to specify the exact time of his observations. He is acutely aware that the society he is observing is in the process of rapid change, and he is, in fact, providing the reader with an ethnography of how a new form of government—political parties and democratic elections—articulates with existing institutions of village and local politics. The exact dates for the action in *Raag Darbari* are never clearly specified, yet the author's remarks as well as the new state programs that are being introduced into rural U.P. unmistakably define the setting as the late fifties. Both books describe supposedly backward areas: whereas *Raag Darbari* is set in eastern U.P., *Politics and Social Change* describes a village, Bisipara, in that now-infamous parliamentary constituency Kalahandi, whose name is synonymous with famine deaths, the ultimate index of the failure of the development objectives of the postcolonial Indian state. Bailey's book was published in 1963, soon after the events being described in his book had taken place. *Raag Darbari* was published in 1968, won India's most prestigious literary award, the Sahitya Akademi Award, in 1970 and has been a popular book ever since.[34]

Raag Darbari is a work whose insights into the poor, politics, and the state in rural India are without comparison. It is hard for me to think of another novel or ethnography that gives a more sharply etched picture of the large villages and small tehsil towns where the majority of poor rural Indians encounter the state. Shukla was born in 1925 in a village near Lucknow. He served in the U.P. state provincial service and, as noted, in the IAS, being posted mainly around Lucknow. He could draw upon a lifetime of experience and observation in those settings, which form the stage for the novel.

As a representation of rural people's relation to the state, Shukla's novel has circulated widely in north India. The fact that it was written in Hindi immediately gave it a much broader readership base than any work in English, and it was reprinted several times after it won the Sahitya Akademi Award. The movement of this narrative reached entirely different circuits after it was serialized into a TV show, and it then reached a new audience when it was translated into English in 1992 and was marketed by Penguin India, a publishing house that has attained a reputation for quality paperbacks aimed mainly at the English-speaking populations in major metropolitan centers in India and at overseas readers. The book's persistent popularity suggests that the representations of the state found in this narrative are still compelling to contemporary readers. One of the reasons for its continuing popularity is perhaps the fact that most of its readers can identify with its stories of corruption, its cynical perspective on state officials and their actions, and its implicit anger at the system for its unjust treatment of the poor.

The action of the novel takes place in a large village in eastern U.P. called Shivpalganj. *Raag Darbari* means literally "a north Indian classical music composition for the court" and is a well-known composition that attempts to convey musically the magnificence and grandeur of kings and courts. The *raag* being sung refers to the schemes hatched at the *darbar* (or court) of the local leader, Vaidyaji.[35] The connotations of *darbar*, like those of *court*, extend to the representation and display of royal power and glamour. Since this was a period in which democratic representation was supposed to be spreading to villages and local forms of governance regenerated, the title is also a sardonic reflection of the state of affairs in rural India. Vaidyaji is an ayurvedic doctor by profession (the term *vaidya* comes from *Ayurveda* and means "healer" or "doctor"), but his real occupation is to manage the reins of the village farmers' cooperative and the local college and, during the course of the novel, to wrest control of the panchayat.[36]

Vaidyaji goes about consolidating his authority through these institutions with an appearance of supreme detachment, as if he regarded with total contempt the strong-arm tactics he employs to obtain control over village institutions and with a Gandhian phrase ready for every occasion. This statement might appear paradoxical. Vaidyaji maintains the Gandhian political idiom of morality. He thus rhetorically abhors the use of violence or nonconsensual means to achieve political ends. The novel shows how he directs his subordinates to employ violence when necessary for his political success while remaining scrupulously above the fray in his pronouncements. This was a typical posture of many politicians of his era; their hypocrisy is caricatured in the novel. In other words, Vaidyaji is a political type who would be quite familiar to the Indian readers to whom the novel was addressed.

The novel is narrated not through the eyes of a protagonist but from the perspective of many different characters. Its loose plot concerns the arrival in the village of Rangnath, Vaidyaji's nephew (his sister's son), who is pursuing a master's degree in history in the town. Rangnath comes to the healthy environment of the village to recuperate from an unspecified illness.[37] Rangnath is the character whose address is that of the urban, educated readers of the novel. His growing knowledge and disillusionment with village life is richly documented. However, the novel does not sympathize with him; it suggests, rather, that his disgust with the events that unfold demonstrates his lack of connection to the rural world. This lack of knowledge is attributed, at least in part, to the irrelevance of the book knowledge to which he has devoted so much of his life. Shukla paints a picture in which government institutions are integrally involved in all aspects of village life. There is no room for a backward-looking romanticism in the fictional world of Shivpalganj. Anyone who believes that the "real India" lay in its villages, which were models of harmony and cooperation far removed from state power and modern institutions, would be quickly disabused by reading this novel. With a savage wit, Shukla portrays a world in which cynicism is rampant, both about modern institutions and about traditions.

I will focus on representations of corruption and its effects on the poor, particularly during the course of elections, in both the novel and in Bailey's ethnography. In the anthropology of India, one of the most interesting threads in the work of social anthropologists of an earlier generation, who were documenting the effects of modernization, concerned politics and political processes. Scholars produced detailed accounts of elections, the workings of government institutions, and the articulation of local-level bodies of governance such as panchayats with those at higher levels of representation and administration.[38] Much of this work had a developmentalist perspective, and it was conducted in the framework of modernization theory, with the poor as its implicit subject and democratic, industrial society as its telos.

One finds public officials to be ubiquitous in the countryside represented in *Raag Darbari*, and state institutions are intricately woven into the daily routines of poor villagers so that almost no aspect of their life is unaffected by government bureaucracies. Nationalist rhetoric and state development programs also find their way into the nooks and crannies of village life; this is not an idyllic image of rural India, separated from the urban, modern nation by an unbridgeable gulf. If there is a gap that divides them, it is that urban officials and people know very little about rural life, so little that one can characterize this novel as inverting the well-worn axiom concerning rural idiocy. Rural people emerge as the ones wise in the ways of the world, whereas their urban counterparts are depicted as being out of touch and arrogant.

A couple of examples from the novel can help me make the point. The first two episodes of the novel introduce the reader to the workings of the police, establishing the centrality of this key state institution. One of Vaidyaji's opponents in the village received a letter from dacoits, or robbers, asking him to leave Rs. 5,000 in an isolated place. Vaidyaji's son, Ruppan Babu, a student leader who has spent three years trying to pass the exams for the tenth standard, came to the police station to plead for help on behalf of his father's enemy. Ruppan Babu is convinced the letter is a forgery. He mildly and slyly suggests to the subinspector, "Just inquire of your own constables. Perhaps one of them wrote [the letter]." The subinspector rejected that accusation immediately: "No, that couldn't be. My constables are illiterate. Most can't even sign their own names" (Shukla 1992: 10).[39] Having cleared his own men of suspicion, he started talking about "the one topic of conversation for government servants: what government servants used to be like and what they're like now" (Shukla 1992: 11).

Vaidyaji was the manager of the village Cooperative Union, which was the site of an embezzlement. It was rumored that Ram Swarup, an extremely close underling of Vaidyaji's, loaded two trucks with wheat from the cooperative's warehouse that had been stored to be sold as seed to farmers. Everyone assumed that the wheat was being transported to the other warehouse of the cooperative, which was five miles away. Instead, the wheat was taken to the grain market in town and sold for several thousand rupees. Ram Swarup disappeared, and rumors circulated that he had gone to Bombay, but a director of the union reported to Vaidyaji that he had spotted Ram Swarup enjoying a head massage in a neighboring town. Vaidyaji's reaction to the embezzlement was, oddly enough, one of relief. His reasoning was impeccable: "There had never been a case of fraud in our union and so people began to suspect something was wrong. Now we can say we are honest people. There was an embezzlement and we didn't hide it. We admitted it as soon as it happened . . . one thorn has been removed from our flesh" (Shukla 1992: 36). The union then passed a resolution that the government should grant it compensation for the Rs. 8,000 it had lost. Rangnath, Vaidyaji's urban nephew, was uncomprehending: "What's it got to do with the government? The Union Supervisor embezzled the wheat, and you want the government to make it up to you?" (Shukla 1992: 71). Vaidyaji replied, "Who else will give it?" They had informed the police that the supervisor was absconding: "If the government wants our union to survive, and to continue to benefit the people, it will have to pay the compensation. Otherwise this union will collapse" (Shukla 1992: 71). This is a good example of how the poor have to pay the price for corruption that benefits rural elites. Not having subsidized seed for the next harvest may have proven to be no more than an irritation for wealthy farmers, but it probably imposed a high cost for small and marginal farmers, who could not afford to pay high prices for seed grain on the open market.

Village cooperatives, democratic governance in the forms of panchayats, and educational institutions were the three key institutions that were supposed to structurally transform rural India during the first two five-year plans, when the central government relied on institutional reform, rather than new investment, to spur growth in agriculture. Vaidyaji's appeal to the government was based on a shrewd calculation of the importance given to village cooperatives as a central institution of rural development. In fact, the key dramatic moments in *Raag Darbari* are supplied by elections to the village cooperative, the panchayat, and the local college.

Vaidyaji's role in Shivpalganj is perhaps better appreciated by paying closer attention to Bailey's description of the emergence of a new type of political agent with the advent of modern political processes in rural India. Bailey contrasts two villages in Orissa and traces the rise of two types of brokers that emerge. Bisipara is in a backward area of Orissa. It is an isolated village with a strong moral community in which outsiders are distrusted and treated with suspicion. Traditional leaders in Bisipara are quite far removed from the workings and logics of government officers and programs. They have to rely on a broker, a person who knows enough about the ways of bureaucracies to effectively represent the interests of villagers, a person who can "stand up to officials" (Bailey 1963: 58) and who has the right contacts among urban-based politicians and bureaucrats. At the same time, government officials want someone from the village who can get other villagers to become enthusiastic about government programs and perhaps be an early adopter or demonstrator of new schemes. Bailey makes it clear that in a traditional village like Bisipara, a broker gains a lot of power but possesses little legitimacy, being distrusted both by villagers and by officials. The reason is that the broker has to mediate and translate between two moral universes that are incompatible and perhaps even incommensurable. To the extent that such a broker is successful in his job, he often has to live in town, closer to the offices where villagers have to come to get their work done; on the other hand, if such a person no longer resides in the village full-time, he is treated as a person who falls outside the moral community of the village. A broker for a village like Bisipara is a full-service provider, often spending all his time in mediating between villagers and a whole range of government agencies like the administration, police, hospitals, and law courts.

Bailey also presents the contrasting case of Mohanpur, an urban village on the outskirts of Cuttack. In contrast to Bisipara, Mohanpur is an integrated village, one which has no independent political life played out on the village stage since most people who live there are involved in the politics of Cuttack city and Orissa state. A large number of Mohanpur's residents have jobs in Cuttack, and even those who are not employed in the city sell their agricultural output and artisanal production there. However, Bailey argues that Mohanpur is not thereby just a suburb of Cuttack but has its own moral community. Village boundaries and village institutions are jealously guarded from the intrusion of so-called outside politicians (Bailey 1963: 94–95) even though villagers themselves are actively involved in those politics. Given that dozens of Mohanpur's residents are employed in government agencies and bureaucracies, they are well positioned to help when fellow villagers need assistance. Therefore a large number of specialized brokers exist who have specialized knowledge and contacts in particular departments of the bureaucracy; however, precisely because of this there is no need for a full-service broker who would deal with the entire range of government offices.[40]

Shivpalganj, the fictional eastern U.P. village of *Raag Darbari*, is neither an isolated village like Bisipara nor an integrated one like Mohanpur but somewhere in between. In fact, one suspects that behind the choice of Bisipara and Mohanpur as illustrations lies a Durkheimian theory of mechanical and organic solidarity; or perhaps, borrowing from Weber, Bisipara and Mohanpur are ideal types of traditional and modern villages, respectively. It is clear that Bisipara's future will look something like Mohanpur's, and that Mohanpur's future will look something like Cuttack's: the full-service broker will become more functionally specialized, and then he will finally disappear, as the value systems of the traditional village become fully modern. Bailey writes, "The brokers are the people who subvert the integrity of the village community. [*Integrity* here is used in the sense of 'wholeness,' but for a Bisipara villager and for many officials too, the sentence would be just as meaningful if *integrity* were used to mean 'honesty and probity.'] But the brokers are also the people who have transcended the narrow parochialism of village life and have accepted the responsibilities of belonging to a wider community. They are the agents of social change, and they are the means by which Bisipara is becoming integrated into a wider society" (Bailey 1963: 101). By contrast, in Mohanpur the existence of the middle class "is the sign that change has taken place, that the village is no longer a tight world of its own, that village integrity has gone and that parochial horizons have been transcended" (Bailey 1963: 102).

Bailey's typology does not imply which type of broker was better for the poor. One may surmise that people in Mohanpur who lacked cultural capital would find it difficult to seek out a different broker every time they had to deal with a government bureaucracy. On the other hand, since the brokers of Mohanpur were also village residents, they might have been more willing to help a poor coresident without taking large sums of money. By contrast, a professional broker such as the one in Bisipara, whose livelihood depended on this activity, might have charged each client more. If, in addition, Bisipara's broker was upper caste, as is likely, he might have been even less willing to help poor, lower-caste clients. Bailey does not divulge if the two different types of brokers were effective in getting the job done, how much they charged, and who was helped more by their activities, precisely because the different brokers serve to illustrate sociological types in his analysis.

Unlike the middleman of Bisipara, Vaidyaji is a broker who lives in the village and yet mediates between the village and officialdom. However, he does so by controlling all the major village institutions. Unfortunately, the parallel with Bailey's ethnography breaks down on this issue. Readers do not get a detailed analysis of local politics in Bailey since he is primarily concerned with the reception and impact of state-level elections on village life. By contrast, in *Raag Darbari*, one finds that the articulation between state bureaucracies and village institutions animates, or reanimates, village politics. For instance, Vaidyaji suddenly starts to show an interest in the Village Council, work that he had so far regarded as demeaning. His interest is piqued by something he reads in the newspaper, in which the prime minister had reportedly said that " 'village uplift' was only possible on the basis of schools, co-operative committees and village panchayats. . . . Suddenly Vaidyaji realized that he had been working for the village's uplift through the Co-operative Union and the college, and the Village Panchayat was completely out of his hands. 'Aho!' he must have thought, 'That's the reason why Shivpalganj is not being properly uplifted. Why didn't I realize it earlier?' " (Shukla 1992: 104–5). Knowledge of developments outside his village allowed Vaidyaji to realize that a new development initiative would involve the revival of village councils as a cornerstone of government initiatives to bring democracy to the grass roots.

Bailey's archetypical portraits of the isolated (Bisipara) and integrated (Mohanpur) village offer some insights into the articulation of state and national politics with village life. However, Bailey's analysis, while attentive to the structure of political and economic organization, completely leaves out the role of discourses such as nationalism, development, and modernity in mediating among the levels of the political system. For example, Bailey refers at several points to the cynicism with which people in both the villages he studied regarded state and national politics. However, one cannot account for Bailey's observation that people regarded state and national politics with cynicism without understanding, for example, the failure of existing discourses of nationalism and development to address the concerns of rural people in Orissa. In particular, it would have been interesting to find out whether the distribution of cynicism was the same across classes within the village, and whether poor villagers were less hopeful about the fruits of development than were their better-off counterparts.

In *Raag Darbari*, too, one gets a sense that developmentalist and nationalist discourses fail to be owned by the people of Shivpalganj. Vaidyaji himself has a Gandhian saying ready for every illegal act he authorizes or practices. Similarly, leaders and bureaucrats are seen as cynically employing Gandhian discourse for their own ends. This becomes obvious when public officials visit Shivpalganj in the course of making their tours and inspection visits. One reason Shivpalganj was so frequently visited by politicians and officials was that it was close to a town and on the main road: "By this time of the year, a major influx of leaders and servants of the people had already begun. All of them were concerned about the progress of Shivpalganj and as a result they delivered speeches. These speeches were especially interesting for the *gan-jahas* [villagers]. From the very start the speakers set out in the belief that the audience comprised a bunch of idiots, and the audience sat firm in the opinion that the speakers were fools" (Shukla 1992: 55). With this attitude of mutual respect, the villagers listened as every speaker tried to convince them that India was a farming nation, using clever arguments to prove their point, and urging the villagers to grow more food for the progress of the nation. Shukla writes,

> Anything lacking in the speeches was made up for by a publicity campaign. . . . For example, the problem was that India was a farming nation, but farmers refused to produce more grain out of sheer perversity. The solution was to give more speeches to farmers and show them all sorts of attractive pictures. These advised them that if they didn't want to grow more grain for themselves then they should do so for the nation. . . . The farmers were greatly influenced by the combined effect of the speeches and posters, and even the most simple-minded cultivator began to feel that in all likelihood there was some ulterior motive behind the whole campaign. One advertisement . . . showed a healthy farmer with a turban wrapped around his head, earrings and a quilted jacket, cutting a tall crop of wheat with a sickle. A woman was standing behind him, very pleased with herself; she was laughing like an official from the Department of Agriculture. Below and above the picture was written in Hindi and English —"Grow More Grain." (Shukla 1992: 56)[41]

Perhaps nowhere are public officials caricatured more severely than in their predilection for going on tours and in attributing results to their touring, which is also a kind of rural tourism: "An ancient Sanskrit verse explains a point of geography—that is, that the sun doesn't rise depending on where the East is, but where the East is depends on where the sun rises. In the same way senior officials do not go on tour depending on their work, but whenever they go anywhere it automatically becomes an official tour" (Shukla 1992: 159). A "great man" speeding in his car looks at the verdant fields passing by, congratulating himself that his speeches of the previous year had their effect on the winter crop: "[The farmers] had begun to understand all they were told, and they had lost their apprehensions about new ideas. The farmers were becoming progressive, and, in short, the only backward thing about them was that they were still farmers" (Shukla 1992: 160.)[42] He passed by the college and realized that it had been a full forty-eight hours since he had spoken to the country's youth. He ordered the car to turn around so that he could conduct a surprise inspection. As soon as he entered the college, the management declared a holiday so that the students could listen to his speech. He proceeded to tell the students that they were the nation's future, blamed the educational system for turning out clerks, suggested fundamental reform for the educational system in accordance with the recommendations of "thousands of committees," told the youth to farm their fields, drink milk, be prepared to be the next Nehrus and Gandhis, promised to consider the college's problems, ate the dried fruits and nuts and tea that was served to him, and then, the inspection over, set off at high speed in his car (Shukla 1992: 161). State officials are represented as being completely out of touch with the realities of rural life; and what makes this situation even worse is that their ignorance is sanctioned by a smug, supercilious attitude.

However close Shivpalganj might be to the model of Bailey's integrated village, a vast gulf separates village people from state officials. The gap is not due to villagers' lack of familiarity with government bureaucracies and officials. Rather, it is because when officials and villagers do come into contact, they attribute radically different meanings to their exchange. While the work of social anthropologists like Bailey is very insightful about institutional forms, it perhaps too radically separates the sphere of meaning from that of institutional power.

In *Raag Darbari*, one gets a much sharper sense of the misunderstanding and misreading that lie at the heart of state officials' interactions with villagers.[43] State officials are not the only objects of *Raag Darbari*'s sharp satire. The novel is full of examples of villagers bending state institutions to ends they were never intended to serve and diverting public monies into their pockets through various unscrupulous means. In this project, nationalist rhetoric, Gandhism, development discourse, appeals to the public interest, and astrology all come in handy. State planners, high-ranking officials, politicians, village leaders, judges and lawyers, schoolteachers and principals, policemen and criminals, all profess to be committed to national development while pursuing their own enrichment. *Raag Darbari* demonstrates that the rhetorics of nationalism and development attain their power by their ability to be attached to many diverse projects, few of which coincide with the designs of national leaders and planners.

For example, the system of courts, set up to deliver justice, had not been designed with Pandit Radhelal, a character in *Raag Darbari*, in mind. Pandit Radhelal was a professional witness, someone on the border of literacy but with such an innate knowledge of civil and criminal law that he could be counted on to give evidence as a witness without ever being caught lying under cross-examination: "[Pandit Radhelal] too, like the judge, the lawyers, and the clerk of the court, formed an essential link in the legal chain. . . . The moment he stood up in court and swore to tell the truth by God and the Ganga, everyone from the opposing side to the magistrate knew he could only lie. But this knowledge was to no purpose, as judgments are reached not on the basis of knowledge but on the basis of law, and no matter what one might feel about Pandit Radhelal's testimony, the law found it genuine" (Shukla 1992: 67). Like any true professional, Pandit Radhelal had abandoned a general practice to specialize as a witness only in civil cases involving inheritance, but he had trained several disciples who practiced the craft of being a witness whenever the legal system had a need for them (Shukla 1992: 218).

Shukla's portrait of rural India is one that emphasizes the divergence of the meaning of modern institutions from their intended functions. In this regard, his novel differs from those social anthropologists who were investigating the effects of modernization on the Indian countryside. In Shukla's portrayal of rural India, institutions such as courts and cooperatives do not fail to operate as intended because they are novel forms that are modern and Western, too far removed from traditional practices, as anthropologists warned. Rather, they are embraced with great enthusiasm but given entirely new meanings by village elites, who find them to be eminently useful for their own purposes. In Shukla's view, far from helping the poor, these modern institutions reinforce and redouble existing forms of domination. At the same time, it could be asked whether they also open up new possibilities for the empowerment and enfranchisement of the poor.

Conclusion

Although it would be a mistake to attempt to make too close a connection between Shukla's biographical experiences and the characters and plot of *Raag Darbari*, his incomparable insights into the functioning of state institutions in rural India could not have been possible without a lifetime of participant observation in the bureaucracy. More than the work of any social scientist, Shukla's fiction provides astute insights into the everyday practices of state institutions, the interests of various parties involved, the creative employment of nationalist and developmentalist discourse to quite different ends by variously positioned actors, and the texture of how diverse subjects inhabit the state and are interpellated by it. Shukla's portrayal of rural India has few parallels in the ethnographies written by professional anthropologists, especially insofar as the relation between village life and state programs is concerned.

This chapter also contains another implicit critique for the anthropological study of South Asia, from which so much of the classic literature on corruption has arisen. In the fifties Nehru and the Planning Commission pursued a policy of rapid industrial growth, hoping that institutional change in rural areas would unleash forces of productivity. The government pinned its hope on land reform, community development, and village cooperatives as mechanisms that would lead to increased yields without substantial new investments in infrastructure and to the more equitable distribution of income, resulting in the rapid decline of poverty. It is within this context that a whole generation of anthropologists did sophisticated and systematic work on village governance and state institutions, focusing on the new types of political agents who were emerging with the routinization of democratic politics. Bailey's work is part of that movement, but there were a number of other very important anthropologists who did similar studies in different parts of India: Bernard Cohn (1987c), S. C. Dube (1958), Oscar Lewis (1954), Adrian Mayer (1967), D. F. Miller (1965), Ralph Nicholas (1968), Morris Opler and William Rowe (Opler, Rowe, and Stroop 1959) to name just a few. The questions raised by these texts had to do with the introduction of modern institutional forms in rural India. For example, they inquired into the nature of village politics. If village panchayats were to be resurrected as instruments of democracy at the grass roots, and if cooperatives and community development schemes were introduced, what would be their impact on politics in local communities? What were the differential impacts of such schemes? Would they really benefit the poor?[44]

The failure of many of these ambitious schemes of social engineering envisioned as the key to transforming rural India in the Nehruvian vision was often blamed on corruption. Policymakers and scholarly advisors to the government blamed the lack of success of the development enterprise in India on the persistence of allegedly archaic and traditional forms of official behavior in which gift giving was considered legitimate but shaded uncomfortably into bribery. Corruption was often compared to a cancer on the body politic.[45] The anthropologists who studied political processes at the grass roots complicated the pat solutions of many macro-theorists by showing how difficult it was even to define corruption, let alone eliminate it. Corruption was tied up with state legitimacy and distributive fairness but also with local politics; changing incentives for bureaucrats was a necessary but by no means sufficient step for the elimination and redefinition of corruption. For example, was the broker identified by Bailey who mediated between government officials and villagers and collected a fee for his services a part of the corrupt system, or was he a legitimate facilitator, akin to a lawyer who guides his client through the court system? If seen as part of a corrupt system, would poor villagers have been better off without his services? The answer to this question is by no means obvious.

Particularly since the seventies, elections, political parties, and a regular system of democratic political participation have deepened their reach, slowly affecting the lives of poor and lower-caste people in rural India (see chapter 6). This process accelerated after the reformulation of the idea of democratic village governance in the early nineties through a reinvigorated panchayati raj (village councils). The allocation of new financial resources to bodies of village government promises to change the relation of rural citizens to the state and to alter the political balance between castes and classes at the grass roots. The success of political parties of Dalits, or lower-caste groups, like the Bahujan Samaj Party, at the level of regional states is owing to slow-moving but enormously consequential shifts in lower-caste consciousness in the villages (Chandra 2004; Jaffrelot 2003; Michelutti 2002; Wadley 1994).

The theoretical paradigms employed by an earlier generation of anthropologists, with their emphasis on patron–client relations, new types of brokerage, and factional politics generated considerable insights into the dynamics of rural politics, especially in its relation to new state institutions and such procedures as direct democracy. However, political anthropology as a subdiscipline waned in influence and importance. As a result, new studies of changes in rural political institutions in India have lagged behind some of these momentous transformations.[46] With the advent of globalization, new possibilities are being opened up to address the articulation of local politics with changes at national and global scales.

One way to expand the concerns of political anthropology beyond the realm of formal politics is to attend to situations of structural violence, everyday forms of malign neglect, that cause poor people, especially children, women, and lower castes, to die disproportionately from such causes as illness (malaria, tuberculosis, flu), lack of clean water and sanitation, lack of housing, and inadequate nutrition. Although democratic politics and a free press have prevented major famines, as Amartya Sen has argued (1999), they have been much less successful in preventing malign neglect. More people die in India each year from humdrum causes inflicted by the failure of the developmentalist state to provision the poor with basic necessities like food, water, medicine, and housing than if there had been a major famine every ten years. Yet such suffering does not make for headlines; there is no event to report, no story to break, no parliamentary hearings, and usually no government action. An anthropology of politics, in my view, would pay attention to exactly why this kind of unspectacular suffering slips beneath the radar of politicians, academics, journalists, and concerned citizens.

It is not possible to understand such structural violence without having a good grasp on narratives of corruption in contemporary India.[47] Narratives of corruption help shape people's expectations of how bureaucrats will respond to the needs of citizens, of what states can do, and, more important, of what they will do. For example, such narratives may help explain, and may provide justification for, the private appropriation by bureaucrats of resources that are targeted to the poor. Alternatively, they might rationalize the futility of government expenditures on subsidies for food, schooling, and housing for the poor ("It will all go into the pockets of corrupt officials anyway; it will never reach the poor"). Despite his claim that economists are interested mainly in incentives and punishments and his skepticism to approaches emphasizing values, Bardhan (2006: 347) argues that it is important to combat disinformation about official corruption because "nothing perpetuates corruption like exaggerated perceptions of corruption all around."

It is critical that pressure be brought from below to make state institutions more responsive and transparent. However, in order to achieve this end and to accomplish genuine institutional reform, the narratives through which the state is constituted will have to be altered. What this means is that there is a need to mobilize the enormous reservoir of sentiment against everyday forms of corruption that exists all over India, especially among the poorest and most disenfranchised parts of the population.[48] The affective relations between the state and its citizens have to be revalued through new narratives of the state (de Vries 2002).[49] Internationally mobile narratives of efficiency and transparency will simply not accomplish that goal without tapping into meanings that have salience in the everyday lives of common people. The louder and more frequent the calls for transparency, the more likely it will be that, to echo Raag Darbari, even the simple-minded cultivator will suspect that there is some ulterior motive behind the whole thing.

PART THREE   **INSCRIPTION**

The office becomes the location of the desk (the bureau), the clerk and the
file, which is the way the true bureaucracy begins.
—Jack Goody, *The Logic of Writing and the Organization of Society*

This chapter and the next examine the impact of writing as a form
of everyday state action on the poor. My objective is not only to
argue that writing is a key modality by which structural violence is
inflicted on the poor, but also to demonstrate how it functions to
that end. A closer look at forms and contexts of writing yields some
surprising, counterintuitive answers. In this chapter I make an argument for writing's centrality in shaping the state, whereas in the next
I make a case for why writing should not be seen simply as a means
by which scheming bureaucrats take advantage of poor peasants.

Very few scholarly investigations of the modern state have paused
to examine one of its central features: writing (Goody 1968: 1). Bureaucracies are machines for the production of inscriptions. Of all
the activities that go into the daily routines of state officials, writing
is probably the most important. Historians are often grateful to
those anonymous officials who have provided them with the primary
data that constitutes much of our knowledge of "written history."
Goody argues that the formation of bureaucracies is critically dependent on writing because it allows for communication at a dis-

tance, the storage of information in files, and the depersonalizing of interaction (1986: 89–90). However, he carefully delimits the importance of writing: "Writing was not essential to the development of the state but of a certain *type* of state, the bureaucratic one" (Goody 1986: 92; emphasis added).

Forms of bureaucratic writing—routinized, repetitive, and mundane—need the same critical scrutiny in anthropology that they have received from historians and historical sociologists.[1] Perhaps part of the reason bureaucratic writing has received less attention than it deserves is that, as a practice, writing appears familiar, maybe far too familiar, to most academics. We already know what bureaucratic writing involves, since we ourselves practice it and engage with it in a wide variety of contexts. What could possibly be learned by focusing on these modes of textualization? Moreover, why should we pay attention to the forms and practices of writing rather than to its content?

One obvious answer is that writing matters to the poor through its forms and practices, not just through its content. If writing is central to bureaucratic states, it is also often posited as that instrumentality through which bureaucratic domination is exercised over populations. When the population is largely illiterate, this effect appears to be magnified, increasing the scope of exploitation at the hands of bureaucrats, while accentuating the degree of alienation of the poor from the state. I investigate writing's constitutive function in forming and informing the state. I argue that rather than assuming that bureaucratic writing has powerful effects on the poor, one needs to look closely at its forms, the conditions in which bureaucrats write and receive written texts, and the consequences of various types of writing on the poor. I conclude that a broad-brushed dismissal of bureaucratic writing as intrinsically perpetuating structural violence is mistaken and obscures the complexly mediated relationship between forms of writing and structural violence.[2] Agamben's understanding of the production of bare life by sovereign decree points to the production, circulation, and reception of bureaucratic writing, for it is presumed that the sovereign's decision is disseminated through various types of bureaucratic writing. My premise is that if one directs attention to these practices, one might better understand the operation of the sovereign decision and arrive at a more careful appreciation of exactly what relation such a decision has to the production of bare life.

Writing is sometimes seen as a by-product of state activity, as that which merely records actions that state officials have taken. In this view, there is a clear distinction between the activities of bureaucrats, which are seen as primary, and the secondary exercise of recording and commemorating those actions on paper. Writing here primarily serves an archival or mnemonic function, to preserve for later reference, or to recall what happened at an earlier moment in time. We think, for example, of taking minutes or of preparing a list of action points to remind us of the work that was done at a meeting.

Against this conception of writing, I will argue for a perspective that sees the state as constituted through writing.[3] The view I am advocating recognizes that writing is itself one of the main activities of bureaucrats. Even if one thinks of action-oriented departments of the state such as the police, the first thing police officers usually do is to take out their notebooks. They write down the nature of the crime, collect depositions from eyewitnesses if there are any, and note all the relevant information about the crime scene. Whether it is a traffic citation or a report of a homicide or a theft, writing sets in motion a series of other actions, all of which are also recorded during the course of the action or soon after it is concluded. I reflect here on the implications of this fact, particularly for the poor, and ask about the consequences that forms and styles of state writing have for poor people.

If one shifts attention away from action-oriented departments like the police, the first association that comes to mind when thinking about state bureaucracies is paperwork. Why is that so? If bureaucracies are ideal-typical institutional forms whose sole aim is to get things done, producing a paper trail might just as easily be seen as an impediment rather than as a facilitator of action. In fact, much of the common-sense frustration with government inefficiency hinges on the requirements of paperwork imposed by bureaucracies. This is not a feature peculiar to government bureaucracies; doctors complain about the amount of time they spend filling out forms, as do auto mechanics and academics, and similar complaints are voiced by people who are employed by large private corporations.[4]

Therefore, a focus on bureaucratic writing may appear not just reasonable, but indispensable if one is to understand the nature of the modern state, especially in its impact on the poor. What forms does such writing take? What are its functions? How is it compiled, stored, and retrieved? Under what conditions does it occur (see also Riles 2000)? Who writes what, and how does writing travel across bureaucratic hierarchies? Can we usefully see bureaucratic writing itself as a kind of performance? If so, what do such performances mean for the audiences of poor people? What are the affects engendered by bureaucratic writing (Navaro-Yashin 2008)? What is the relation between writing as proof of action on the part of state officials and writing as a form of state action itself? What is the relation between two very different modes of writing: narrative forms, such as letters and memos, and the collection and use of statistics? This topic raises more interesting questions than I can possibly answer here; I will concentrate, therefore, on some issues about the relation between bureaucracies and the poor that loomed large in my fieldwork.

Bureaucratic writing was important to bureaucrats but also to their impoverished rural subjects and clients. Writing was not merely a weapon wielded by powerful bureaucrats to dominate their hapless and often illiterate clients. Bureaucrats themselves often feared receiving written missives from the public. Once a bureaucrat received something in writing, whether a petition from a prospective beneficiary of state programs, a complaint from an aggrieved citizen, or an order from a superior officer, it set in motion actions whose result was always uncertain and hence seldom free of anxiety. For example, as I show below, a written complaint often initiated an inquiry from superior officers; similarly, if a senior officer felt that a subordinate had ignored a written order, the subaltern official often had to face strongly negative consequences. For mostly illiterate, poor rural people, getting involved in forms of writing, forms *and* writing, was something to be feared and avoided at all costs.

State officials in India produce a wide variety of written materials, including orders, circulars, reports, memos, letters, forms, surveys, petitions, complaints, entries in registers, and notes in diaries.[5] While it is not my aim to examine each genre of bureaucratic writing, I will consider some types of collating devices such as files and registers that collect different types of writing under one cover. I will also develop my earlier argument about writing as a constitutive function of the state by examining the relation between writing and state action. I discuss a specific form of bureaucratic writing, namely, the generation and recording of statistics, and the form of writing involved in inspections. In addition, I look at another major genre of bureaucratic writing, the complaint, and consider various types of complaints: those prompted by village feuds, that is, complaints resulting from intra-village rivalries; those filed by members of the public against bureaucrats; and, finally, the most common kind, those occasioned by intra-bureaucratic conflicts.

Forms, Files, and Registers

The prototype of bureaucratic writing is filling out a form. Perhaps more than any other types of writing, forms go together with bureaucracies in the public imagination. A Weberian analysis of a form might emphasize the following features: standardization, replicability, anonymity, and portability (see also Wheeler 1969: 5).[6] By standardizing the information to be collected, the form allows the bureaucrat not only to obtain all the necessary data to make decisions, but also, in theory, to compare the needs of applicants to arrive at a rational decision. The replicability of the form serves the function of enabling the most efficient use of scarce resources. It also enables the applicants to be anonymous because a person's rank or status becomes irrelevant when all forms are exactly alike.[7] Finally, forms are portable both because they encode data that can be translated into statistics (for example, "Of five hundred applications received, 30 percent were from below poverty line (BPL) households"), and because they can be moved up the bureaucratic hierarchy without a lot of contextual information. A higher-level official sitting in Delhi need not know anything about a village in U.P. to read and understand a form submitted by a person from that region.[8] If one may derive from Foucault the suggestion of an inherent affinity between the bio-political and the statistical, then forms are the critical modality by which one is converted into the other.

Forms also enframe and categorize the world.[9] One can study forms for what is excluded from them just as much as for how that which is included is organized. Why are certain things considered irrelevant, and left out of a form? By deliberately excluding what is particular and unique about the circumstances of applicants, do forms end up doing violence to individuals? If so, do the effects of such violence have greater consequences for the poor than for other applicants? Thinking more broadly about the form, one must see it not just as a written document, but also as those routinized performances that have to be enacted before various kinds of bureaucracies.[10] A witness who gives testimony in court, a refugee or asylum seeker who appears before a tribunal, a taxpayer who is audited by the revenue department, all produce performances that are larger, oral versions of the form. The information they have to impart has to be coded and organized into a particular pattern, a form that is recognizable by the court or the bureaucrat. Such performances depend heavily on forms of cultural competence and cultural capital that the poor are less likely to be able to demonstrate than their better-off counterparts.

From the standpoint of the bureaucrat, one of the virtues of the form as a genre of writing is that it can be easily stored, compiled, and organized. Here, one needs to pay attention to the technologies of search and retrieval. In the Indian bureaucracy, the key device for the storing and retrieval of information is the file. The file is the critical unit that organizes bureaucratic life.[11] It is a material object, but it attains a life of its own that often looms larger than that of the people who are supposedly acting on it. What is written in a file or what is missing from it can exert a much greater influence on a decision than the ideas of the person making the decision. People who want to forestall a decision or bureaucrats who wish to teach clients a lesson often collaborate with a lowly office worker to make the file disappear. The wheels of government grind to a halt without a file. If an applicant or dignitary came to visit the top officials in the bureaucracies in which I did my fieldwork, the officer would always call his subordinates and ask them to produce the file. Rarely did they need to mention which file and where it might be found.

The importance of the file was impressed upon me by an officer who said, "If it is not in the file, it does not exist."[12] What exactly does a file contain? Normally, all the paperwork relevant for a particular case is collated into a file. The file for a complaint or a dispute, for example, might consist of the original letter of complaint; the action taken on the original letter by an official to whom the complaint was made; if an investigation was conducted, a report by the concerned officer; and a decision by the superior officer about the action to be taken in light of the investigation. The file usually consisted of pieces of paper, some of which were handwritten and some typed. Typically, the original complaint was handwritten on a nonstandard size of paper. That piece of paper might have notations made by the receiving clerk stating the date and time the correspondence was received by the office and further notations by the officer who acted on it. Copies of the letters or orders that result are included in the file. In contrast to the original correspondence, the investigating officer's report is likely to be typed on a standard size of paper. Finally, the decision might be noted on one of the documents by the superior officer, following which an official letter might be issued signed by that officer and giving details of the decision. The file is a compilation of papers of different sizes and qualities; of annotations often made on original documents by officials; and of copies of outgoing correspondence.[13] These are all bound together by two pieces of string, which go through each page, and the cover of the file. Across the width of the file goes a red tape that keeps anything from falling out. Files are usually stored horizontally one on top of another in metal cabinets that are locked shut to keep out the dust. However, the number of cabinets sometimes does not keep up with the number of files. The excess files are then piled onto any available surface, including the top of cabinets, desks, and so forth.

One can usefully apply Kopytoff's suggestions about the biography of objects to the life history of a file (Kopytoff 1986). After a file is created, a period of intense activity follows during which various pieces of paper are added to the file. For example, a complaint might generate several letters in response, one to the person who filed the complaint, other letters to higher officials for purposes of notification, or orders to subordinate officials to direct them to verify the truth of the complaint or to conduct an inquiry. These procedures, in turn, might generate other reports and memos. After a final decision has been made, the results might be conveyed in terms of a letter to the person who filed the complaint, and copies might be put in the file and sent down the hierarchy to the level at which the complaint was made. Then, the file enters a period of hibernation, collecting dust in the filing cabinet. Depending on the class to which the file belongs—complaint file, file for village x, file for scheduled castes—it might be reactivated, brought back to life by a fresh complaint of the same class and go through a new lease on life before it finds its way back to the metal cabinet.

Files become tremendously important in an administrative system where transfers are frequent. Officials at the higher levels of district administration (district magistrate, subdistrict magistrate) in U.P. were transferred with alarming regularity, often serving less than two years in a single post. As one official explained to me, he was usually faced with a situation in which he had to make decisions even though he had no prior knowledge of the issues, the area, or the people involved. In such circumstances, the file was his best friend. What was in the file determined how he acted, since he had no other basis of knowledge about the case at hand. What was written down and how previous officials had responded to a case in the file were therefore the most important factors determining how a case was decided. Previous officials were likely to have been influenced by local elites who were also the first to befriend new officers. Unless the conflict involved two factions within the local elite, a new official making a judgment based on what was in the file was much more likely to rule in favor of local elites than of poor and subaltern people. Without appearing to be biased in any manner, the emphasis on what was written in a file, therefore, sometimes helped perpetuate structural violence on the poor.

There was also a strong bureaucratic tradition of respecting negative judgments. It was most unusual for an official to overturn a negative decision in a file without very good reasons. Supplicants who had been denied benefits or ruled against in a complaint therefore always found themselves in a disadvantageous position.

I had always taken the expression "to cut through red tape" as a curious metaphorical formulation until I came across files in the lower levels of the U.P. bureaucracy. Only then did I begin to appreciate fully the strong continuities in bureaucratic practice with the colonial era. For example, most forms have to be filled in triplicate (three copies). This was a practice, according to Clanchy (1979: 48), that in the English bureaucracy dates at least to the twelfth century and that was probably bequeathed to Indian government procedure during the colonial era.[14] In fact, there is a strong continuity in practices of writing in offices in the agrarian bureaucracy in India, such as that of the Kanungo and the Patwari, whose functions remain largely unchanged from at least as far back as the Mughal bureaucracy.

Apart from the file, the other objects in which bureaucratic writing was collated were reports and registers. The only reports that the lower-level bureaucrats I worked with prepared were annual reports that had to be passed up the hierarchy. However, the higher one went in the bureaucracy, the more likely he would spend time preparing reports for ministers and the members of the state assembly or for the purposes of publicity and information. Richard Saumarez Smith (1985) makes an important distinction in colonial administration between records and reports. Records referenced rights to land and to revenue and preserved detail about village-level matters; reports, on the other hand, were written in English at the district level by expatriate colonial officials and combined statistical information with records of the customs of the people.

On the other hand, registers were ubiquitous at all levels of bureaucratic practice. One can think of a register as a clutch of forms bound together, since the information that has to be entered between the vertical lines that make up a register is guided by preexisting categories either printed or handwritten on the top of each page. Registers are places where statistics of various sorts are entered. By far the most frequent use of registers is to record attendance, travel plans and itineraries, and other activities of officials. Registers therefore function to regulate and record the details of the daily activities and itineraries of state officials. Agricultural extension workers, for example, might be expected to record the names of the villages they visited, the names of the farmers they contacted, what kinds of information they imparted on their visit, and what actions they took in response to the needs and queries of farmers.

Requiring bureaucrats to enter routine activities in registers was also an important instrument through which state officials exercised surveillance of their subordinates. The supervisor of one of the two offices where I did fieldwork showed me her travel log. In the register, separate columns had been created to record where officials were going, when they expected to be back, whom they had gone to meet, the purpose of the meeting, and the actual time they returned. Officials were required to complete the travel register before leaving their offices. If the supervisor was using the official jeep, she had to record in a different logbook the mileage at the start and end of each trip. Thus it was possible for a higher official to check the mileage in the jeep's logbook against the destination entered in the travel register to ensure that she had indeed traveled where and when she had claimed. Where registers with ready-made columns were not available, they had to be created. The head of one of the offices where I did fieldwork was using up the remainder of the annual budget to purchase ruled registers so that her workers did not have to spend an inordinate amount of their time drawing vertical lines in each of their empty registers.

What does all this paperwork have to do with the main function of these offices, which was to further development? It would be hard to argue that these processes of filling forms and registers and preparing reports more efficiently served poor people or had any direct bearing in improving their lives. However, such a view surely misses the point of bureaucratic activity: if it is not in the official record, an activity might as well not have happened. Poor people provided the context and the pretext for such writing because much of it was devoted to creating numerical representations of them. At the same time, bureaucratic writing also served to exclude the poor from representing themselves both because of its demand for literacy and cultural capital and because of the closed nature of the bureaucratic process. Even if they had been able to read it, poor people could not get access to what was written about them. As my example of the old-age camp in chapter 1 demonstrates, the simple fact of writing numbers in English rendered them inaccessible even to those poor people who were literate in Hindi. However, one also has to recognize that the content of these representations may be of limited interest because what mattered was that representations of the poor provided the ground for various types of conflicts between bureaucrats at different levels and from diverse bureaus. The function of writing in bureaucracies is complex and cannot simply be reduced to its content.

How to Do Things with Writing

The image of the clerk with a pen in his hand is the enduring image of bureaucratic work. Indeed, the main task of state officials is to write. Writing functions to note, to record, and to report. However, it would be a mistake to see writing as that which follows action. It is not as if state officials first conduct meetings, discussions, inspections, observations, and surveys and then write down what transpires in the course of those actions. Rather, writing itself needs to be seen as the central activity of bureaucracies. Writing precedes, accompanies, and follows other actions. It does not merely record what happened but is the main activity that takes place in bureaucratic work. In the Indian case, when a bureaucrat says that he will take care of something, it means he will make the appropriate notations on a file and pass it forward. Alternatively, it may mean he will communicate with a colleague to do the same, perhaps by sending a note or a letter of introduction. This is not unique to government bureaucracies: office work, whether in a large bank or an academic institution, consists largely of making notations on paper or, increasingly, clicks on computer keyboards. Although this is the stereotype of academic work, much of what is accomplished by white-collar workers in any modern bureaucratic institution is done through writing and reading other people's writing. Government bureaucrats are not unique in spending their time filling out forms, writing letters, memos, and reports, reading orders, rules, and regulations, and evaluating peers and subordinates. Nevertheless, even as one acknowledges this fact, writing has an unusually important place in the Indian bureaucracy. Every action involving travel, discussion, inspection, witnessing, and observation has to be accompanied by writing or it might as well not have happened. Writing was not something officials did once they were comfortably seated behind their desks; it was an action that was undertaken everywhere an official went.

An example will help make this point clearer. In an effort to improve its image in rural areas, the U.P. state government had, during the course of my fieldwork, instituted a new program called the Kisan Seva Kendra (Farmers' service center). It ordered all the officials whose jurisdiction overlapped for a group of eight to ten villages to come together to a fixed place once a week from 9:30 A.M. to 5 P.M. The idea behind the program was that if villagers had problems that required action on the part of two or more officials, they would be able to obtain signatures and authorizations in one spot. Since it was widely known that officials rarely went to the villages where they were supposed to work, it was frustrating and time consuming for villagers to track down individual officials in the town, especially since many officials worked out of their homes. Tracking down officials was an impossible task, especially for the poorest villagers, since it required them to miss wage work for the day and spend money to travel into town.

One morning, along with some officials, I took the bus from the town and then had to walk from the metaled road about four kilometers to the village where the Kisan Seva Kendra was to be held. Two of the officials were joking with each other that although they had not yet received written orders requiring them to attend, their department had been informed, and the head of their department had verbally ordered them to be present that day. "We will just sign the attendance register and be on our way," one of them said.

When we reached the village there was some debate as to where the Kisan Seva Kendra was to be convened, some favoring the school as the likely location and others the village council building. As we passed the school on the way in, we saw a few officials sitting in a corner. School was still in session; hundreds of children were sitting on the ground out in the open. Their teachers were huddled in chairs in front of them. Next to them, on the ground, lay two blackboards with various things written on them. The children were busy writing or playing; the teachers were for the most part ignoring them. As we passed one of the two teachers, a young man with a shaven head and a thin ponytail (signifying his status as a Brahmin), one of the officials sarcastically asked how he managed to be teaching while sitting quietly in his chair. When the taunt was repeated, the young teacher snapped back, "Do you keep writing in your files all day in your office?" The official responded that he had other work to do too, not just write in his files. "So do I," said the teacher. "I don't have to be supervising the children all the time."

Interestingly, the teacher had equated writing in files with bureaucratic work. After all, he may have known that the official in question worked in the Irrigation Department and that his designation, like that of many of the other officials there, was that of a fieldworker. Likewise, he took the failure to write all day as evidence of the official's lack of commitment to his job. The teacher justified his own apparent lack of enthusiasm for his job by reminding the bureaucrat of his slack time while fulfilling his professional responsibility.

Once the new members had joined those already assembled, there was much criticism of the secretary, who had so far failed to show up.[15] One official murmured that although the Kisan Seva Kendra had been functioning for a month, the secretary had failed to attend for the previous three weeks. Others voiced the opinion that their presence at the center was worthless if their attendance was not going to be registered. Just then, the secretary appeared. He had barely settled into a chair when he was barraged with questions. Why, asked one of the other officials, had he not submitted reports about any of the previous meetings to higher authorities? The secretary responded that since nothing had happened at any of the previous meetings, there was nothing to report. From a meeting he had attended, the land records official reported that higher officials took the absence of a report as evidence that the Kisan Seva Kendra was not functioning. "It doesn't matter what you write," he told the secretary, "write something and send it up." "But what should I write?" inquired the secretary. "If you tell me what to write, I will go ahead and do it." The land records official then told everyone that he knew another secretary who had sent in four reports, one for each week that the center was supposed to be operating. If the secretary did not file any report, he said, officials higher up would think that nothing is happening here. "If nothing else, let the train run on paper" (aur kuch to nahi, gaadi ko kagaz par he dodaa do).

Without writing, it became much harder to establish that the officials had been present at the Kisan Seva Kendra. Their actions would have come to naught if they were not recorded. Representation was not only an essential accompaniment to action, it functioned as a form of action ("let the train run on paper"). The secretary protested, quite correctly, that even when they attended the Kisan Seva Kendra nothing was accomplished. I spent the entire day at that Kisan Seva Kendra, and only one villager came for help. Most villagers did not even know that such a program was operating; one or two people who came to the school assumed that officials had gathered there for an internal meeting and left them alone.

In this case, writing a report of what had transpired at the Kisan Seva Kendra mattered because it appeared that senior officials saw such a report as proof that the program was being implemented. Would each center be expected to produce a weekly report once the program was off and running with thousands of centers? More important, if such reports were written, would they be read by anyone? The vast majority of bureaucratic writing is never read, even by other bureaucrats whose job it is to monitor subordinates. It is a form of production without a consumer.

What does one make of such excess writing? It has been remarked by many scholars that the prose generated and the statistics collected and reported by modern bureaucracies exceed the needs of the state for purposes of governing and regulation (Appadurai 1993: 316).[16] An argument that focuses on the instrumentality of the state misses the fact that very little of the writing generated and the data gathered by governments is useful and an even smaller percentage of potentially useful information is actually employed for purposes of state. Even if one were to pursue an argument about writing as a form of self-regulation and self-surveillance in a panoptical system, it would be hard to explain the sheer magnitude of what is written by state officials. As long as writing is seen as important only, or mainly, for the functions it performs, as that which accompanies or follows real actions and real decisions, and not as an action in itself, it is hard to understand the proliferation of documents. One has to shift attention away from writing's instrumental function in helping run the government to its constitutive role as that which defines what the state is and what it does.

The proliferation of documents is not a recent phenomenon, one that characterizes modern states. Clanchy has a trenchant observation about the surveys conducted by the English state in the thirteenth century: "Bureaucracy's appetite for information exceeded its capacity to digest it. Making lists was in danger of becoming a substitute for action" (1979: 6).[17] He traces the increasing mass of royal documents to the growing size of the bureaucracy as well as to the fact that such an organization was increasingly stratified and functionally specialized (1979: 46).[18] Such a description appears to cast the bureaucracy of medieval England as a prototype for the division of labor that Durkheim used in his characterization of modern Western societies. However, it leaves open the question as to why it necessarily follows that a stratified, specialized bureaucracy produces more useless writing. For the Indian state, one has to ask additionally what the implications of such useless writing are for structural violence.

Inscribing Numbers

It is easy to overlook statistics when discussing state writing. When we think of writing, we think of its narrative form. Numbers and narrative appear so different from each other that they are more often counterposed than juxtaposed. One speaks of quantitative versus qualitative; complaints about bureaucratic indifference sometimes hinge around being treated like a number.[19] In one famous formulation, a sharp division is postulated between two cultures, one numerate (the culture of sciences and engineering) and the other literate (the culture of humanities).[20] Such a strong contrast, however, belies the degree to which statistics have become part of the prose of the world.

The extent to which statistics have been normalized in our representational practices can be appreciated only when we recognize that the prose form in which we apprehend current events, the news report, fully integrates statistics and narrative. Since much of what is reported in news concerns the state, it is not surprising that, like news reports, state writing tightly interweaves narrative with statistics (Peters 1997: 78). Nowhere is this more apparent than in reports issued by branches of the bureaucracy.[21] However, the textualization of statistics is a pervasive feature of other types of state writing as well and is to be found in forms, registers, orders, letters, regulations, and memos. Inventories and censuses, the oldest forms of state writing, are another important combination of prose and statistics.

I want to draw upon a short example here to illustrate the relation between narrative and statistics. The block development officer (BDO), Malik, was complaining to me that it was very difficult for someone like him who headed an office whose duty was to implement development programs in rural areas to keep on top of each of the more than thirty programs his office had to administer. For each program a target was set for a number of projects or recipients by administrators in the state government (see also chapter 2). Targets were fixed statewide, and the mix of programs was not tailored to individual districts.[22] Although it would reflect well on him if he managed to accomplish 50 percent of what was planned, he always achieved at least 90 percent of the targets set for him. In other cases he exceeded the targeted amount; he proudly told me that he achieved on average 100 percent of his targets.

Malik gave me the example of biogas projects. His office was given the target of initiating fifty such plants in the block, an order which set off a chain of actions. As the BDO, Malik delegated the task to an assistant, who in turn asked the village workers under him to locate suitable recipients. If people were reluctant to set up such plants, they had to be persuaded with other enticements and favors. Once someone agreed to be a recipient, he was registered, and the required paperwork initiated for purchasing equipment for the biogas plant. The location of the plants and their distribution among villages and among castes were guided by statistical categories and requirements, since guidelines about distribution had to be met.[23] These categories and the willingness of potential beneficiaries jointly led to the choice of recipients. Statistics guided the choice of recipients; in turn, once beneficiaries were located they were themselves transformed into a statistic. If the plant did not work, that too was recorded by follow-up visits conducted by the village workers, the block staff, and random visits by senior officials located at the district level.

The field staff knew that, for a complex set of reasons, particular biogas plants did not work after they were set up. However, on its way up the bureaucratic hierarchy such local knowledge was stripped of those narratives and arrived merely as a statistic: "Only 50 percent of the plants were found to be working one year later." When higher officials looked at the numbers and reflected on them, a new set of questions emerged of the following type: Why is the rate of success so low in our district whereas biogas plants operate quite successfully in Meerut District? Why is the percentage of plants working in Block A so different from those in Block B? When such questions arose and explanations were provided by lower-level officials, they marshaled stock narratives that made sense of the anomalous data. Malik provided one such explanation to me: "In Meerut and Muzzafarnagar [districts], biogas plants are doing quite well but here they don't seem to function. The reason lies in the different work cultures in the two places. The cow dung mixture that goes into the plant [as an input] has to be prepared into slurry. Jat women in those districts [the predominant caste group] do the work of stirring the cow dung into slurry. Here, women don't work."[24] These narratives implied that even after the block officials started the plants and made sure that gas was being produced, the plants failed because the owners did not keep up the necessary inputs.

Such a narrative, apart from showing the extent to which programs administered by male bureaucrats to male beneficiaries depend on the agency of women, is already imbued with statistical abstraction in some sense. It employs categorical thinking about the supposed innate qualities of different castes: in this case, Jats in the other districts and Thakurs closer to home. Such a narrative relies on a type of person, with particular qualities and working habits, rather than on actual examples of Jat or Thakur women. The class bias of this program is evident in that Malik does not find it necessary to comment on the work habits of lower-class and lower-caste women, such as Jatavs and Harijans. Rather, he restricts his explanation to the two dominant landowning castes, the Thakurs and the Jats. Explanations similar to these might find their way into official reports, but they are more often to be encountered in oral exchanges between senior and junior officials. Statistics and narrative thus complement each other in making sense of the entries in forms and documents.

There are at least three ways of thinking of the relation between statistics and narrative in state writing. The familiar model is that of the report, in which statistics are embedded in the narrative. Here, a description of programs and policies might be accompanied by descriptive statistics on the number of districts, beneficiaries, and resources. Narrative description here seamlessly blends with statistics written out in words. The prose is often dry and matter-of-fact.

Yet statistics can be present in another role, that of the supplement (Appadurai 1993: 320). Here, statistical tables or their graphical representations punctuate the narrative, which then refers to the tables or figures in the prose. This mode of reading breaks with the left-to-right and top-to-bottom order of reading that is characteristic of languages such as English and

Hindi. Reading such documents requires that one continuously interrupt the flow of sentences to look at the charts and numbers. Most people who work in modern bureaucracies, including academic ones, or who regularly deal with bureaucracies are very familiar with such practices of reading. Sometimes, statistics in reports are also included in an appendix.[25]

Finally, there is the phenomenon of the transformation of narrative into statistics. To take the case of complaints considered earlier, each letter of complaint is in narrative form, giving details of a series of events that transpired. The block office has to submit an annual report in which the number of complaints concerning a program has to be reported to superior officers.[26] As complaints travel up the hierarchy, like Engels's dialectic (1939: 136–46) they transform quality into quantity. The messy details of cases are replaced by the precise factuality of numbers. The function of numbers here is not so much to replace narrative as to represent narrative in a form that makes it easy to compare different programs and areas. The transformation of narrative into statistics reduces the sheer complexity and contingency of any particular case. Factors that might inhibit comparison are turned into a form, that is, a number, that facilitates such comparison.[27]

Another way to think about this is to say that through this transformation into a statistic, the case joins a series of other such cases: the specific and the contingent become part of a type. A problem arises when an office receives a communication that resists easy classification into a type. Complaints, a letter of inquiry, a petition, or a demand for an official inquiry are all recognizable types of communication that can be appropriately classified. However, a type of writing that defies easy categorization creates the problem of where it is to be filed. This is perhaps one of the most important reasons bureaucracies prefer forms. In the absence of a form, the problem of filing writing in its appropriate place becomes enormous. This is not just a matter of narrowly bureaucratic thinking. If something cannot be filed appropriately, it becomes hard to retrieve. Moreover, if it cannot be categorized, can it be counted? and how is the counting to be done? Problems of classification and statistics therefore go hand in hand: both concern the transformation of the many particulars into the few types that can facilitate comparison.[28] The category BPL converts the many facts of someone's material deprivations into a category that can be enumerated and measured. Moreover, it provides a means to equate experiences and histories that are not commensurable and creates a class of people for whom programs are targeted. One of the fallacies of composition that results is that such a classification fails to interrogate why people are in that category, and it fails to appreciate that diverse strategies of poverty alleviation might be needed to address people within the same group.

While several scholars have commented on the transformation of the unruly fecundity of narrative into the "abstract, precise, complete, and cool idiom of number" (Appadurai 1993: 323), few have noticed the manner in which the comparison facilitated by statistics creates narratives of its own. For example, take the ICDS program. Comparing data from different centers in a particular block and from different blocks in a district, an officer might inquire into anomalous results. Why is there such a large discrepancy between blocks in the participation of lower-caste children? Why does one center appear to have especially high participation rates even when no supplementary nutrition is available? Statistical anomalies and statistical variation invite narrative explanation.

Classification and typification are often followed by a process of renarrativization. However, the explanatory narratives that come after statistical representation have a quality very unlike the original ones. As we have seen in the example of the biogas plants, such explanations are generated by officials themselves; they are abstractions in some sense because they are ethnographic generalizations from a kind of knowledge that everyone knows (for example, that Jat women are hardworking as compared to Thakur women); finally, their logic is often justificatory and teleological: they are concerned to shut down further inquiry rather than to open it up. In this manner, numbers generate debate and contention across levels of the bureaucracy (Appadurai 1993: 319–20; Asad 1994: 78).

State officials at all levels of the bureaucracy spent a lot of time generating and recording statistics. But why did the state generate numbers rather than prose? From the earliest known human civilizations there has been an intimate link between the state and processes of enumeration. Much of what is known about the writing of Mesopotamian civilization is that it focused on accounts of state. The Mughal state had elaborate records of taxation, accounting, and land revenue (Richards 1993: 58–93). With the British colonial state came a significant shift in the value placed on numbers, partly owing to the rising importance of statistics for state purposes within Britain itself.[29] Officials of the colonial government feared that without statistical data it would be hard to administer the Indian state because the growth rates of populations, food supplies, and taxes would be impossible to know and the demand for services in the spheres of education, public health, law, and policing would be hard to gauge (Cohn 1987: 242; Appadurai 1993: 219; Asad 1994: 76–77).[30] In the role played by statistics in colonial rule, we see most clearly Asad's contention that "statistics is much more than a matter of representation; it is a tool of political intervention" (1994: 76). Seemingly unimportant bureaucratic decisions about how to classify and collect statistical data about the population led to the rise of what the political theorist Sudipta Kaviraj has called "enumerated communities" (1992b). The use of statistics in this manner allowed for the emergence of ethnic, religious, and linguistic majorities and minorities, which the colonial government utilized for political purposes.[31]

Concentrating entirely on the use of statistics in colonial statecraft might make it easy to forget that enumeration is not merely a tool of political domination but has a productive dimension as well. Arguably, it is precisely the productive aspect of statistics that makes it such an effective tool of domination. The enthusiasm with which enumeration has been taken up by postcolonial states in general, and the Indian state in particular, makes it clear that statistics are now central to the positive goals and means of states and do not merely serve a repressive function. What a state is and what it does cannot be conceived apart from statistics. One of the key functions of postcolonial states has been to increase rates of economic growth and to foster progress and development. Asad points out that "the very concept of progress is in great measure the product of statistical practices. . . . it is inconceivable without the concepts and practices of statistics. 'Progress'—not mere reform—is the political aspiration that the non-European world has acquired from Europe" (1994: 78). As a discipline, statistics today may not hew closely to its original meaning of "the comparative study of states" (Foucault 1991: 96). But transnational governmentality has made the use of statistics to compare states with each other more important than ever before. Statistics have become the measure of good governance. Whether the idea is to gauge the quality of life or the level of corruption, nation-states are constantly measured against each other (Asad 1994: 77–79).

Statistics function as a transnational disciplinary mechanism at the same time they function as an end that states aspire to achieve. The goal of development is not necessarily to have a populace whose lives are rewarding, meaningful, rich, and varied but to have certain rates of growth, to decrease the unemployment rate, or to achieve a GNP per capita that crosses a certain threshold. The aspiration for rich, rewarding life would be dismissed as impractical or without content in most state bureaucracies and among development practitioners because it is hard to measure.[32] One can see the powerfully reductive machinery of development in the measurement and comparison of poverty. The problems of a head-count measure of poverty have been well known for at least one generation of development theorists (Sen 1983). Yet the latest versions of the most widely circulated poverty statistics (the under $1/day and under $2/day figures) continue, despite its many shortcomings as a statistic, to use the head-count measure. There have been efforts to develop a measure that encompasses a wider variety of features of poverty, such as the Human Development Index (HDI).[33] However, despite the commensurability that the HDI provides, it is rarely used in news reports and in intercountry comparisons. In any case, even a comprehensive statistic of poverty such as the HDI does not begin to address the more difficult question of the telos of development.

Snowed in by this "avalanche of numbers" (Hacking 1982), it might be difficult to appreciate the extent to which statistics and narrative continue to be tied together. For example, the Indian census of 1872 was accompanied by an ethnographic survey that fleshed out the statistics by dealing with the characteristics of the social groups recorded in the census (Smith 1985: 167). Bernard Cohn makes a fascinating observation about the reports written by British officials conducting the first census after the uprising of 1857. These reports apparently always included stories about the rumors that were circulating about the colonial state in the region (Cohn 1987a: 239). Such a practice demonstrates the intimate links between the census and rumor as modes of information gathering that serve the state for the purposes of disciplining the population and exercising surveillance over it. It also betrays an anxiety that rumor could undermine the truth that the census revealed and that the knowledge gained by the state from statistics might be ineffective in the face of oppositional subaltern knowledge.[34]

Enumeration is so deeply entrenched as a technique of statecraft that it appears as a neutral technology of government. Asad's emphasis on the inherently political nature of statistics should be a warning sign as to its potential for structural violence. I argued in chapter 1 that the progress being made in reducing a head count of poverty often serves as an alibi for not tackling the problem of chronic poverty more vigorously. The collection of data about individuals, the transformation of those cases into numbers, and their agglomeration and circulation in the bureaucracy enforce commensurability between the lives of poor people. Although forms of classification enable certain insights into systemic patterns of poverty, they may paper over an understanding of the conditions that lead to poverty in different cases and fail to appreciate that diverse strategies of poverty alleviation may be necessary.

Inspections

Enumeration is closely linked to a commonly employed disciplinary mechanism, the inspection. Inspections, conducted by superior officers to check the work of subordinates, are a feature of all levels of the bureaucracy and reinforce the rule-following orientation of Indian government bureaucracies. Inspections are procedures in which the disciplining of subjects and subordinates is carried out. What matters in an inspection is that the subordinate has observed the proper procedure; there is much less emphasis on the results.[35] An entrepreneurial employee who was impatient with bureaucratic process soon learned that getting results was no substitute for doing things the proper way. Inspections often involved tours and sometimes involved physically verifying that there was a correspondence between what had been reported on paper and what existed on the ground. Had the house for which a government subsidy been provided actually been built? Was the day care center really operating? Such on-site visits allowed officials at all levels of the hierarchy to interact with the beneficiaries of government programs, and they were the most visible aspects of bureaucratic work. The state gained visibility not only through the physical assets it helped create (houses, tubewells, village roads and ponds, and so on) but also through inspections of those assets. Inspections took up a great deal of the time and energy of bureaucrats and were a tremendously important part of their working life. However, like the mass of an iceberg that is under water, the greater part of the inspectorial regime was hidden from public view because it involved intra-bureaucratic work. An officer could come to inspect the work of a subordinate in the latter's office, and no member of the public would even know what was going on inside.

As a ritual of state, the inspection's importance cannot be underestimated. An inspection is carried out in many contexts, but I wish to concentrate here on the routine inspection. Although it might appear redundant to characterize an inspection in this manner, there is a difference between an inspection carried out in the everyday, humdrum routine of office and a special investigation triggered by a complaint or an inquiry. The latter may be routinized as well, but it differs from the routine inspection in much the same way a commission of inquiry differs from question hour in parliament. I have presented detailed ethnographic cases of two routine inspections elsewhere in this book. The first example of a routine inspection, in chapter 4, was that of the engineers who were checking road construction as part of a government employment scheme. The work being examined in that inspection had not been done by a state employee but by a representative of the community, the headman. The second instance, to be found in chapter 7, concerns the inspection conducted by the child development project officer (CDPO) of anganwadi workers. This is an example of intra-bureaucratic process, but one which relies to some degree on encounters with nonbureaucrats (to the extent that children are quizzed as part of the inspection or, as in the case of nonfunctioning centers, that neighbors are queried as to when a center was last seen in operation).

Another type of inspection involves the monitoring by state officials of the actions of beneficiaries and not just that of subaltern officials. Tangible goods, as opposed to agricultural loans and subsidies for fertilizer, were often targeted to the poor. Most examples of monitoring of beneficiaries involved the surveillance exercised by state officials on poor clients. For example, it was the duty of the officer in charge of the housing program for poor, lower-caste people, the Indira Awaas Yojana, to inspect the house that had been built with money from the program.[36] The money was released in two or three installments. After the first installment was released, the junior engineer in charge of rural employment schemes (JE-RES) went to inspect the house to make sure the foundation had been laid correctly. Then the engineer went once more to make sure that the roof (lintel) was properly built. The engineer also checked if the house was of the specified size and if it had the correct number of doors and windows. If the house was larger than the sanctioned size, then the government was not responsible if the beneficiary did not have enough money to complete construction or to install doors and windows.[37] On the other hand, if the beneficiary had some extra money he or she could invest it in getting the house plastered and the floor finished because the money allocated was insufficient to complete those tasks.

Like other state actions, inspections prompted government functionaries to write. To better account for what was written and when, I will break down the process into three steps. Writing took place before an inspection in order to prepare the paperwork that higher officials would demand to see during such a process. I have termed processes of writing that took place without knowing whether an inspection would be conducted anticipatory inscription. The work of writing during an inspection helped define what it is that was meant by an inspection. This is one example in which writing is a constitutive modality of state action. Finally, there is the writing that follows an inspection. Typically, the inspecting official prepares a report; in addition, he or she may pose a question or challenge that requires an explanation or a clarification from the official being inspected.

Anticipatory inscription refers not just to what was written when lower-level officials knew about the visit of a senior officer, but also to what was written when such a visit was a possibility. In much the same manner that random checks by the highway patrol operate to inhibit speeding, the inspection's effectiveness as a tool for disciplining lower officials depended on its unpredictability. Since one never knew exactly when a senior officer would decide to conduct an inspection, one always had to be ready. Here, borrowing from a completely different context, I find Jeganathan's (2004: 69–70) idea of "the anticipation of violence" as a constitutive modality of everyday life to be very useful.

The CDPO of Mandi made it a point never to announce in advance when she was going on an inspection visit. However, an anganwadi worker could safely assume that such visits were unlikely at certain times. For example, all the workers knew that the end of the month was a very busy period in the office because the officials there were busy preparing monthly reports. The monthly meeting of all workers in the block took place on the twentieth, and the CDPO was involved in another important meeting on the twenty-fifth. Therefore, even if there was some uncertainty about exactly when the CDPO might arrive for an inspection, most workers knew that the probability that she would tour after the twentieth of the month was extremely low.

Anticipatory inscription for an inspection aimed at producing a text that demonstrated that the official had been doing his or her job well. The type of action instigated by the anticipation of an inspection did not necessarily make officials function more effectively or efficiently, but it did result in the production of documents attesting to their capability. In the example given earlier in this chapter, the officials who showed up for the Kisan Seva Kendra made no secret that they thought the entire exercise a waste of their time. However, once there, they reminded each other repeatedly how they had to make sure they were there on time and did not leave before the designated hour in case a higher official came on a surprise visit. They read the hours mentioned in the government order, saying, "You never know when a higher official might decide to drop in."

What was it that officials wrote in anticipation of an inspection? To start with, they had to note that they were in the office or site where they were supposed to be on any particular day. This meant writing "present" in the attendance registers that were invariably found in all bureaucratic settings. Then, all the routine writing that had to be done had to be completed as early in the day as possible. For example, the anganwadi workers had to make sure they completed the register that recorded which children were present at the center first thing in the morning. As the day progressed, the amount of food prepared and consumed at lunchtime had to be recorded. At the Kisan Seva Kendra, officials were supposed to record all the contacts they had with villagers: who came to the center, what they needed, how their case was disposed of, and so on. In the absence of an inspection, these encounters could then form the basis of a report that the secretary could forward to senior officers.

I went to the anganwadi in Alipur on a Friday, reaching there shortly before noon. About twenty-five children were present, sitting in neat rows. When I went in they all swarmed around me and touched my feet in the traditional mode of greeting elders. The anganwadi worker, Sharmila, was sitting on a stool. She hurriedly fished out another stool for me and cleaned it of bird droppings. The helper then asked me if I had come in a jeep. When I said I had not, Sharmila explained that she had received word from the office in Mandi that the joint director (JD) of the ICDS program was to come on an inspection. The CDPO later told me she had denied Sharmila's application for a leave that day since the JD was in the area and she did not know which project he might suddenly decide to visit. So all the centers located close to the main road were ordered to remain open. We kept waiting for a jeep to show up. Finally, the children were let go when it was past the scheduled time of 1 P.M.

Sharmila asked me if I wanted to look at the inspection register, but I told her I was not there as an official to check on the center. To look at the inspection register was an invitation to make an entry there about how well or poorly the center was operating. All I wanted to do was to visit and observe. She insisted that I look at one of the registers, so I finally reviewed the attendance register. The names of the children had been neatly entered, and whether they had been present on a particular day had been indicated in columns.

Sharmila kept asking me, "What do you want to hear from the children?" This was one of the most common requests during an inspection. Officials could gauge how well and how frequently a center had been operating by checking what the students had learned. When I said that I did not particularly want to hear anything and that she should go ahead and conduct the class as she usually did, she could not believe it. She said, "When officers come, they usually like to hear something. Should I get the children to recite poems for you?" Already embarrassed at being mistaken for a superior officer and having sat through many inspections in which this routine was repeated, I insisted that she not. After some dissuasion, she relented, and the children continued to do what they normally did.

The role of writing during an inspection was even more critical. An inspection, particularly an intra-bureaucratic one, largely consisted of the scrutinizing by senior officials of the writing produced by subordinates.[38] In the process the inspecting officer produced his or her own writing. One of the most important things senior officers did was to scrutinize all the registers that recorded the activities of the subordinates being inspected. They looked at attendance registers to see if the staff had routinely been in the office, leave registers to see if anyone had taken inordinate amounts of leave, and travel registers to see who was away on official business and when, and they compared these registers to ensure that they were consistent. Similarly, they checked to see if the office had met its development targets and if the funds that had been supplied were utilized properly. A detailed inspection was much like an audit and could take several days, but most inspections were shorter and less careful.

Inspecting officials sometimes made their own observations in an inspection register. Such a register then became an archive that the same officials or others like them could check to gain a quick sense of the history of similar observations. For an anganwadi, reading the inspection reports of previous officials who had visited quickly gave one a sense of how present observations might differ from the past. If, for example, an official found an anganwadi that was operating with a good number of students and, after examining the inspection register, discovered that that center had not been operating in the past, he or she could conclude that the performance of the anganwadi worker had improved even if the children did not seem to have learned very much. In another context, the fact that the children did not know very much might well have led to a negative evaluation. Inspecting officials also noted down problems and issues raised by subordinates that needed addressing at a higher level.

Once, when I stopped at the anganwadi office in Mandi, I saw a jeep near the entrance. When I reached the office of the CDPO Asha Agarwal, I found that her customary place behind the desk had been occupied by a man, and she was sitting in one of the chairs opposite normally reserved for visitors. It turned out that her office was being inspected by her boss, who had come on an inspection tour. The symbolic displacement of the head of the office to the chairs normally reserved for supplicants and subordinates made it clear who was doing the inspection and who was being inspected.

Agarwal explained to me her method of conducting inspections. Although the task of the inspection was fairly routinized, there was room for each officer to develop her own distinctive style of conducting an inspection. If Agarwal did not find a center operating on her first visit, she docked the worker's pay for that day and left a written message for the worker requesting an explanation as to why she was not there. Agarwal showed me two examples of letters she had recently written. By the next day she had already heard back from both women. They both explained their absence by saying that their children had suddenly taken ill, the most frequent excuse Agarwal received. Typically, after her initial visit, Agarwal would visit the same center again within a few days. If she found that the center was operating well on both visits, she was satisfied and did not go back for the next few months. If she found continuing problems with it, then she visited it a third time soon after.

The letters of explanation Agarwal received from anganwadi workers are a good example of the writing that ensues as a consequence of the inspection, the last category of writing I consider here. These explanations contain important material and have professional consequences. Early in my fieldwork I attended the monthly meeting of anganwadi workers at the main office in Mandi. A dispute arose at that meeting between the CDPO and one of the workers. The worker complained that the CDPO had come to inspect her center, and when she had found the worker missing and the center not operating she had docked Rs. 150 from her salary. The monthly salary of anganwadi workers was only Rs. 250, so the sum that Agarwal had cut represented most of the worker's monthly salary. "You should have cut Rs. 10 for the day I missed," she said. "There was no reason to have cut so much of my salary." Agarwal hotly disputed this and told the assembly that she had left a paper at the center asking the woman to submit a clarification (*spashtikaran*) explaining why she was not at the center that day. The worker failed to submit this clarification until well after two weeks. Later, in her office, Agarwal showed me a copy of the letter she had written and the response she received. The anganwadi worker claimed to have been absent because her daughter was sick. However, the day on which she said her daughter was sick did not match the day of Agarwal's visit; it was in fact the day after Agarwal had conducted her inspection. Agarwal wanted to know why the worker was absent on the day she went there. She was certain the worker had in fact not gone to the center until two weeks later, found the note, and then written to her with the clarification. She assumed the worker was missing from the center for that entire period and had docked her pay accordingly.

One consequence of an inspection tour is that officials who conduct such tours write about them in a register or in the monthly report they submit to their superiors. Here one can already see the translation from narrative to statistics referred to above: "I went to inspect 6 centers this month; 3 were working well; another 2 were found to be working satisfactorily; and 1 was found to be inactive." Another outcome of inspection tours is that if there is reason to discipline or dismiss a worker or to report on misuse of government monies, the official has to write a letter or report that is then passed up the hierarchy. The type of writing that follows an inspection is thus more often disciplining and reprimanding from one side and pleading and supplicating from the other. If, because of an inspection, a lower official is found to be doing an outstanding job, it is rarely the case that he or she receives official praise in writing. However, successful workers do accumulate symbolic capital because when very senior officials from Lucknow or Delhi come to inspect the work being done under a program, they are steered to these successful projects, especially if they happen to be near a metaled road.

As can be seen from the case of the anganwadi worker who challenged Agarwal publicly about why her salary was docked for two weeks instead of one day, inspections conducted by superior officers sometimes elicited complaints from their subalterns. The inspectorial regime was not intended to operate solely on those poor people who were the targets of development initiatives but permeated the bureaucratic process. However, if, for the moment, one excludes government employees from consideration, inspections largely served to exercise surveillance and discipline over the poor. Inspections and the writing that resulted from them often prompted further writing in the form of complaints.

Complaints

The complaint is a very interesting form because, more than in any other genre it is in the complaint that subaltern resistance and bureaucratic corruption become most visible. Complaints could be filed by members of the public against state officials for not fulfilling their promises or for cheating them of goods they had been authorized to receive. Complaints could also be prompted by conflicts in village life. For example, rivalries between factions often resulted in complaints against headmen. As with inspections, however, the largest subgroup of complaints did not involve members of the public at all. They involved petitions by subordinate officials to higher levels of the state against their immediate bosses. Most such complaints involved the abuse of privilege or ill treatment of a particular employee.[39]

Both inspections and complaints draw attention to conflictual relations within the bureaucracy and between bureaucrats and their clients. A routine inspection may not necessarily be antagonistic and may result even in the appreciation of the work of a subordinate. But the process of conducting the inspection does bring the structural opposition between superior and junior officials into the open, an opposition that might otherwise be concealed by relations of politeness and appropriate deference on the part of the subordinate.

Complaints are a highly important modality through which structural violence against poor people becomes visible. Poor clients usually complain about the nondelivery of goods and services that should have rightfully been granted to them. The appropriation of goods and services intended for extremely poor people by relatively well-off bureaucrats is one of the ways in which structural violence against the poor is perpetrated. Here, the mechanism of exploitation is not the classical Marxist one of the extraction of surplus labor through wage slavery. Rather, it is about the distribution of social surplus. When social surplus is not distributed in the way it is intended, that is, to provide goods and services to extremely poor people for whom it may very well make the difference between life and death, but is instead diverted to enhance the standard of living of government employees, such as bureaucrats, doctors, and engineers, it should be seen as a form of killing rather than simply as another example of the myriad ways in which the poor are exposed to death (see chapter 1). When one combines this fact with the knowledge that written complaints are extremely rare, so rare that for every written complaint about a bureaucrat stealing money and materials that should have gone to a poor person there are several times that number of examples that never come to light, one can appreciate the extent to which the scale of structural violence is likely to be underestimated.

The complaint and the petition represent two opposing modes by which subaltern peoples appeal to those in positions of power. Petitions are written by supplicants who desire to obtain something as a favor. They are pleas to the powerful to grant something that is in their capacity to authorize: a favor, an exception, a special dispensation. By contrast, the complaint is a demand to redress wrongs committed by a person in power. It asserts the complainant's right to due process and, in the case of complaints to government agencies, to his or her rights as a citizen. If any traces of an ideal-typical Weberian bureaucracy are to be found in contexts such as state government in U.P., then its presence can be detected in the complaint. For the complaint is the place where the citizen or the lower-level official faults the higher-level bureaucrat for not fulfilling his or her role. The complaint registers the failure to do what should have been done. Images and ideas of the state found in the complaint register the expectations people have of state agencies and state functionaries. In the form of writing that is the complaint, therefore, one may find potentially important insights into poor and subaltern constructions of the state.

With that in mind, two observations become extremely important: first, that oral complaints are almost meaningless and, conversely, that written complaints are taken with the most extraordinary seriousness by state agencies; and, second, that villagers, for the most part, are extremely reluctant to submit a complaint in writing. Combined, what these observations add up to is that written complaints by poor rural people to state agencies are relatively rare, but when such complaints are received the actions of bureaucrats named in the complaint are invariably subject to unwelcome scrutiny by their superiors.

It might appear strange in a social context in which the poor are largely illiterate that rural government bureaucracies paid so little attention to oral testimony or to mechanisms for converting oral testimony into written form. Yet that was the case. To get something in writing was what officials desired and feared the most. When they wished to initiate action against a lower official or a quasi-government employee like the anganwadi worker or a nongovernment agent like a headman, bureaucrats pleaded with people to send them a complaint in writing. Armed with such a complaint, they could initiate action against the erring party. This is why bureaucrats feared written complaints against themselves. Once such a complaint had been received, it triggered a series of investigations and reprimands from higher officials. Most written complaints were not made directly to the offending party; they were submitted to the official who was their immediate boss or someone even higher up the hierarchy. An investigation invariably followed to determine the truth of the complaint, and the fact of such an investigation itself, no matter what the findings eventually were, involved the official in a flurry of activity to mobilize support against the charges. Important people had to be contacted, resources expended, and favors done to ensure that the result of the investigation did not go against oneself. Complaints were expensive for bureaucrats because they used up material and symbolic resources and because they provided an opening for opponents and enemies within the bureaucracy to sabotage one's career or have a black mark placed in one's service record. It was not surprising that, when faced with oral complaints from villagers about one of their peers, most bureaucrats' instinctive reaction was to dissuade the person from submitting such a complaint in writing.

Poor people were unlikely complainants in the first place because they lacked the cultural capital that empowered them, as villagers, to submit a written complaint against a state official. Even when a person attempted to submit a written complaint, bureaucrats often tried not to register the complaint in the first place; or they attempted to resolve the issues by compromise or threat to such an extent that the petitioner no longer felt compelled to file an official complaint.[40]

If complaints had such an impact, why were most villagers, especially poor people, so reluctant to submit written complaints? This appears especially surprising in a highly litigious society, one in which it was common for a villager, especially someone prominent in local politics like a headman, to be involved in several lawsuits at the same time. Unlike lawsuits, in which the truth of the matter was decided in the courtroom, written complaints against officials involved one in complex procedures of investigation and fact-finding. Many people may have considered filing a complaint against an official to be an exercise in futility because bureaucrats knew the procedures and methods of their administrative bodies and had contacts higher up the hierarchy and so could always manage to escape punishment. By contrast, the petitioner was left vulnerable to retaliation by the officer. Even when it involved complaints against nonofficials like headmen or voluntary workers like the anganwadi workers, poor villagers were extraordinarily reluctant to be entangled in the literate world of bureaucracy, whose procedures were difficult for them to understand. They knew that the outcome of such complaints was unlikely to be in their favor.

What was the nature of the complaints that did find their way into writing? Most involved either acts of corruption or nonperformance of duties by officials. I deal with three classes of complaints here: those made by villagers against other villagers, particularly headmen; complaints by villagers against state officials; and complaints by state officials against other officials, usually their supervising officer. These complaints differ from each other in significant ways, especially since the cultural capital of the people involved and their knowledge of official procedures vary so greatly across the three classes. Of these three classes, the last does not involve the poor directly but may incorporate them into the dispute, as the example I give demonstrates.

VILLAGE FEUDS

When, for example, a peasant felt that his land had been unfairly brought under a neighbor's plow or when an altercation between two parties had resulted in physical injury, the injured party could, and often did, approach the courts for retribution. However, when the case concerned a headman who had pocketed some of the money he received from the government to build a village road, no villager could be identified as the injured party, and there was nothing to be gained from filing a lawsuit. However, one could get the headman into trouble by registering an official complaint, and if the charges against the headman were substantiated, he could be removed and replaced by the district administration. Since village elections were often bitterly contested, the losing side often had an incentive to get the current headman into trouble, both by filing a complaint and thereby embroiling him in bureaucratic paperwork and by sullying his reputation as someone who was under official investigation for corruption. Since everyone knew that charges of petty corruption were unlikely to spur an investigation, the very fact of an official inquiry was sometimes enough to convince people that something substantive lay behind the smokescreen of charges and counter-charges.

Because officials knew few details of the social life in any given village they had to administer, they tended to assume that any charge of corruption against a headman must have to do with village politics. Officials repeatedly told me that most complaints were prompted by rivalry with other political factions in the villages and did not have any substance. Typically, lower-level officials knew a lot more about a village than more senior officials. However, I did not find many officials at the block level, apart from land records officials, who knew the intimate details of the conflicts and alliances of the villages in which they worked. Officials usually had to work closely with the headman to administer many of the programs they were supposed to imple-ment, and unless they had a personal feud with the headman they were extremely reluctant to initiate any action against him.

One day a headman came to Asha Agarwal's office and declared rather grandly, "Your anganwadis have all failed. No one is doing their job." She asked him to be specific: if he had a complaint about a particular anganwadi, she would look into it. He mentioned an anganwadi in his village that was completely nonfunctional. "The worker there doesn't do anything," he com-plained, "and you haven't bothered to check up on her." Agarwal assured him she would look into the matter, saying she would visit the center soon and check things for herself. When he insisted that she come with him that very day she told him she was busy with her work and would come when she had time. Especially since she did not have transportation she could not predict when she would come. In any case, she made it a practice never to announce in advance when she was going for an inspection visit. He said he could arrange for a jeep to come and pick her up if she told him when she was coming. She politely declined his offer.

When Agarwal was able to do so, she went to the headman's village. She found that there were only a handful of students at the center, and, for all practical purposes, it was not functioning. The center was run in the worker's home. When questioned about the lack of children at the center, the anganwadi worker said that one of her own children had smallpox, so the other children had stayed away because of the fear of infection. That did not sound like a lame excuse to Agarwal, so she thought she would wait and check the center again after a while. In the meantime, the headman came back to her office and said, "Did I not tell you the truth?" Agarwal told him she had found things as he had described but that the worker had a genuine difficulty, which she understood. The headman accused her of not answering his question clearly (*golmol baat kar dee*).

After a reasonable time had elapsed, Agarwal visited the center again. Again, she found no students and no functioning center and therefore issued a warning to the anganwadi worker. Shortly thereafter, she went to inspect the center for a third time and again found no students there. This time she decided to fire the woman running it. While she was there, the headman came and asked her not to take action against the anganwadi worker as the center normally functioned quite well. However, Agarwal refused to change her mind. She told the headman, "I acted on your complaint, and three visits have borne out the truth of your complaint. Now you cannot back out, and since your complaint, and my action in response to it, have already been entered in the records, if you withdraw your complaint now, I will ask the DM [district magistrate] to remove you from your post for lodging false complaints against government workers." Hearing this, the headman relented and felt sufficiently threatened to keep quiet.

Although anganwadi workers were not technically government employees and thus could be fired, an elaborate paper trail was necessary to justify the letting go of a worker.[41] For the moment, however, I want to pay closer attention to Agarwal's response to the headman. More than other villagers, the headman was familiar with the procedures of bureaucracy. Yet he too was intimidated by the threat that "lodging a false complaint against a government worker" would result in his dismissal. Agarwal reminded him that his complaint and her actions in response had been "entered in the records," so he could not withdraw his complaint. The power of writing is nowhere more evident than in its ineradicability: a record could not be erased easily. Nor is this a feature peculiar to India or to bureaucracies: that is why the phrase "Let me pencil it in" is so often used to jot down a tentative appointment. The difficulty of altering records explains why bureaucrats felt it was best that a negative evaluation or a complaint against them, however false, not find its way into the record in the first place. What was also fascinating about the incident recounted above was Agarwal's conclusion about the headman's flip-flop. She told me later that what she learned from this episode was that since one could never tell what was going on in the internal politics of villages, one had to take all complaints with a grain of salt. In the absence of detailed knowledge about village politics, bureaucrats adopted a precautionary principle in favor of the status quo. Such a position, in turn, reinforced villagers' beliefs that it was futile to file complaints and that doing so might invite state action against them rather than against the person about whom they were complaining. Above all for poor villagers, complaining about locally powerful people had the dual danger of alienating those who could negatively affect their day-to-day life and of obstructing support from state institutions. Even if state officials were not "pro-landlord" or consciously supporting the dominant castes, their default position of supporting the status quo when confronted with village conflicts had the effect of intensifying structural violence on the poor.

An ex-headman of a village near Alipur told me he had filed a complaint against the new headman. The charges were that the new headman claimed to have built two roads under the Jawahar Rojgaar Yojana (JRY) employment program, one of them fifty-two meters in length and the other fifty-seven meters, but that neither of them had actually been constructed. He also charged the new headman with obtaining false receipts from people of his caste showing he had raised a lot of money to build a community center. On that basis, the headman had obtained matching funds from the JRY to construct the building. But the building already existed as part of the village school, so all he did was to break down part of the building and construct a new brick (pucca) verandah, renaming it a community center. A team headed by an official from the subdistrict came to the village to investigate the complaint. They heard testimony from villagers that was conflicting in every detail, saw that the building supposedly constructed with JRY funds actually existed, as did the roads, and concluded that the complaint against the headman was instigated by village politics (partybaazi). Since the person who had initiated the complaint was in fact a recent loser in the village election, this explanation made eminent sense. Moreover, it accorded only too well with the dominant official interpretation of complaints filed by villagers against headmen.

It might appear easy to verify whether a building already existed or had been recently constructed with government funds. Yet the only people who would have known that fact were village residents or frequent visitors. Although many state officials, apart from the secretary, had visited that village in the course of their routine activities, they came to the village to enact their own functional specializations.[42] Officials like the engineers I described in chapter 4, whose job it was to inspect buildings constructed with government funds, had neither detailed knowledge of each village under their care nor the incentive to acquire such knowledge. When government officials heading an investigating committee came to the village, all they could do was inspect the buildings or roads that were allegedly the site of embezzlement. If the structures existed, the officials usually adopted the precautionary principle and assumed that the headman was right, especially if there was conflicting testimony from villagers. In the absence of any independent source from whom the truth of the charges could be verified, officials usually ruled that the charges against the headman had been instigated by factional politics in the village, most likely by a rival candidate for the headman's position.

In this case, a conflict between two factions and two powerful men masks its effects on the poor. The charge of corruption against the headman for not constructing the building as claimed was important not because it demonstrated that he was corrupt, but because of its implications for the employment of the poor. Part of the funds that the headman had pocketed were supposed to have paid for materials for the new building, but the whole point of the employment program that funded construction was that the larger share was to be used to pay poor laborers. The rival faction who brought the charges against the headman was not materially affected by the diversion of funds, but it had direct consequences for the poorest villagers, who were robbed of a source of income. They were the only people who had a genuine interest in the construction of the building. The inspectorial regime's lack of knowledge about village life had real consequences for the most vulnerable sections of the population. Arbitrariness vis-à-vis the poor in this village was produced by the fact that poor people in another village may have benefited from the same employment program whereas those in this one did not. A corrupt headman could subvert the program and usurp the money intended for them for his own purposes. If such actions were brought to the attention of state officials through a complaint—and such a complaint was unlikely to be lodged by a poor person—it was usually resolved in favor of the headman. In this way state officials became complicit in structural violence against the poor even when they did not explicitly intend to do so.

The situation was quite different, however, when there were complaints filed by citizens against state officials because no ready explanation such as village politics could be marshaled to dismiss the complaint. Such complaints were also interesting because they crossed the state–society divide. One might be inclined to presuppose it was mainly rich villagers or better-off ones who filed complaints against state officials, but such was not always the case. Poor people filed complaints because they were the ones who could least afford to lose out when bureaucrats cheated them of materials or resources. The conflicts between poor people and bureaucrats recorded in complaints demonstrates that the poor are not just passive victims but utilize their rights as citizens to fight back against bureaucratic malfeasance.

In some contexts, the Right-to-Information Act has enabled individual citizens and poor people's organizations to obtain information about how funds allocated for certain projects have been used. For example, if beneficiaries of a program have to be chosen in an open meeting and no such meeting has been held, then a Right-to-Information request can reveal the names of the beneficiaries. On the basis of this information, individuals can file a complaint about the misallocation of funds, for example, if funds reserved for BPL recipients were actually given to non-BPL people.[43]

COMPLAINTS BY PEOPLE AGAINST STATE OFFICIALS

Complaints against state officials had two important features. First, such complaints were usually lodged with a person higher in the bureaucratic hierarchy than the offending official. This happened to be either the immediate boss or a senior bureaucrat several grades above that official. We have seen one such example (see chapter 3) where a lower-caste man complained to the DM about physical threats he had received from a headman in retaliation for a complaint he had lodged about the improper disbursement of funds under the housing program. A politically sensitive charge such as violence against a lower-caste person invited an immediate reaction from the district's highest official. In cases involving a charge of routine corruption or nonperformance of duty, the complaint would be sent back down the hierarchy to the appropriate office. When complaints dealt with the lowest-level staff, they invariably ended up with the BDO.

The second feature of complaints against state officials is the extreme reluctance of most poor villagers to submit a complaint in writing. Such unwillingness was not merely a reflection of the high rates of illiteracy in rural areas, although unfamiliarity with the written word was an important impediment to composing and submitting such complaints. However, as in most contexts marked by what Goody has termed "restricted literacy," there were people, either professional scribes or the formally educated children of relatives or friends, who could write such letters on behalf of the formally illiterate. What truly held people back was the fear that getting involved would somehow make them vulnerable to arbitrary state action, whether in the form of retaliation by the official whom they were complaining about or of a wider web of engagement with higher-level officialdom or agencies such as the police.[44] In other words, cultural and political capital, rather than formal literacy, helped explain the reluctance of poor people to engage the machinery of the bureaucracy.

I was sitting in Malik's office on a hot day in April when an old man, stooped, extremely near-sighted, and wearing dirty clothes, walked in and handed him a piece of paper. Malik quickly glanced at it and then said, "All right, I will look into it." He then handed the sheet over to the JE-RES sitting next to him. The engineer read the letter and repeated what Malik had said. He then noticed something and just as the old man was walking out called him back and asked him to sign the letter. He told him scornfully that he should know they could not accept a complaint without a signature. "Whose name is the house in?" he asked, to which the old man replied that it was in his son's name. He was asked why his son did not come to submit the complaint personally. He said that his son could not spare the time. He was then told that he should ask his son to sign the complaint and then bring it back to them.

Malik and the junior engineer next started questioning the old man aggressively about the number of bricks his son had received and the size of the room they had constructed. I gathered that the letter had charged that his son had been shortchanged on the number of bricks supplied for construction as well as on the money he had received for other construction materials. Malik appeared to get angrier with the man and by now was being openly rude in his tone of voice. "Why did you wait so long to complain?" he snapped. "The house has been incomplete for over a year, why didn't you complain before this time?" The old man explained that he had to come a long way, and on those occasions when he came earlier the BDO had not been in the office. Malik immediately concluded that he was lying. The engineer then asked him why he had not complained when he, the engineer, had gone to the man's village. "I have been there several times," he said, "why didn't you say something to me [then]?" The engineer then told him he would have to wait for an inquiry. But before such an inquiry could be initiated, he needed to come back with a signed letter. At this suggestion, the old man looked defeated; it was clear that the effort of coming back as well as the verbal abuse he had been forced to undergo, was not worth the trouble. After he left, the engineer said that the man was just interested in filing a frivolous complaint: there was nothing wrong with his house. He had been to the village several times and found no problems. When Malik asked the engineer a specific question about the design of the house, the engineer did not remember anything about the complainant's house.

From the very first moment of this exchange it was evident that Malik was unhappy to receive this complaint. However, it took the sharp eye of the junior engineer to find a procedural flaw in the letter, namely, that it had not been signed by the person who had received the housing subsidy. The old man offered to sign the letter himself, but Malik ruled that unacceptable since the recipient of the grant, not his father, had to be the complainant. Both Malik and the engineer were trying their best not to admit the complaint in the first place, for to have done so would have initiated an inquiry that, apart from creating more work for them, might have put their own departmental practices under unwelcome scrutiny. The tone in which they spoke to the old man also underlay the differences in cultural and political capital. Because he was poor, of lower caste, and unfamiliar with bureaucracy, they berated him and questioned him aggressively. They would not have behaved in the same manner if the complainant had been a headman, someone more educated, or a person whom they suspected had connections to politicians or senior bureaucrats. Going to the superior officer to lodge a complaint—in this case, the BDO—did little to help the poor villager, for the BDO was hostile to the complaint from the beginning. He and the junior engineer questioned the legitimacy of the complaint without knowing any of the facts of the case. Perhaps they did not wish to entertain a complaint because they knew that the Indira housing program, under which the house was built, was a politically sensitive scheme aimed at providing the poorest, lower-caste people with homes. Any complaint about corruption on the part of their office would inevitably draw negative attention from senior bureaucrats, politicians, and perhaps even the press. If no complaints filtered up the system, no one would have reason to think there were any problems with either the program or their office.

That same day another man, mild-mannered, diffident, middle-aged, and dressed in dirty clothes, came into the BDO's office to complain that he had not received the subsidy for the cost of labor for digging his tubewell. This program, called the Free Boring Scheme, subsidized some poor people toward the cost of installing a tubewell on their land. Malik and the junior engineer questioned him aggressively as well. "Did you also get an engine?" they asked. "Is the boring working? Is the tubewell in operation?" The answer to all of these questions was affirmative. He was then asked to go to the shop from which he had purchased the engine and get a letter confirming that he had been sold an engine. The man replied, "All the relevant forms have been filled, sir. I am just waiting for the money." Hearing this, Malik switched tactics. He told the man that the officer in charge (junior engineer–minor irrigation) had gone to fix a match for his daughter and was therefore not in the office. "When will he be back?" asked the complainant. Malik replied, "I can't say but he should be back soon. Come back some day when he is here and you should get your money." When the man left I asked how much money was at stake. They usually were granted Rs. 300 to cover the labor costs for the boring, I was told, but the money was handed over only after all the work was finished and it was confirmed that the tubewell was operating.[45]

This case differed from the previous one in that the villager did not bring a formal, written complaint. It was less threatening for the BDO and the junior engineer, and they were less rude and aggressive. Instead of denying him the money outright, they acknowledged that he had a right to it but found an excuse as to why it could not be given to him at that time. Compared to the total cost of a boring, which could reach close to Rs. 10,000, this was a relatively small sum. I later learned that labor costs were rarely reimbursed to the grantees; the staff quietly kept the money. Usually, this did not prove to be a problem because most of the grantees purchased a pump with the subsidy but never used it to operate a tubewell. Instead, they resold the pipes and other equipment they were granted and used the engine for other purposes, like operating a fodder-cutting machine or a power thresher. That is why Malik asked him if the tubewell was operating. If it was not operating there would have been a legitimate reason to deny him the labor subsidy. Since it appeared that this man was actually using the equipment for its intended purpose, they had to find some other reason to delay giving him the money. The official on leave would have filed a leave application, which stated exactly how many days he was going to be away from the office. Although Malik knew when the junior engineer would be back, he deliberately misled the man. Even if the applicant returned, the chances that he would find the junior engineer in the office on any given day were small, as that official had to spend a lot of time in the field. After the applicant came to the office a few times, it was highly likely he would give up the pursuit, as the sum of money was too small to justify the expenditure of time and money entailed in making multiple trips to the block office.

Why would someone so doggedly pursue what appears to be a trivial sum of money? For a poor person who lived on less than one dollar a day, the missing money amounted to a significant proportion of his monthly income. On the other hand, this was a relatively small amount for the bureaucrat. When officials kept the money that was due the beneficiary, it put the welfare of the poor villager into direct conflict with that of the bureaucrat. Once again, the asymmetric consequences of such a conflict need to be kept in mind: what was merely spare change for the officials may very well have meant food for the poor person. Once again, one can see the violent consequences of petty corruption. Officials justified their actions by pointing out that the program was intended to provide a subsidized tubewell, a productive asset that would help the poor person in the foreseeable future. In making sure that the tubewell had reached its destination, they were doing far more for the poor than they would by providing a small cash subsidy.

The importance of writing down a complaint was underlined by an incident in which Asha Agarwal was involved. She told me that half the positions in the anganwadi program were reserved for lower-caste women, but they were well below their quota. Therefore, new vacancies had to be filled with lower-caste women. Although she did not hire any new workers who were higher caste, Agarwal refused to fire a worker who was good at her job simply because a suitable lower-caste woman was available for a position already held by the upper-caste woman. She recounted a case in which some villagers asked her to replace an existing upper-caste worker with a scheduled-caste woman from the village. She refused. She told me that the current worker was a handicapped, upper-caste woman who was one of their model workers. When higher officials came to visit, Agarwal took them to that anganwadi to show them how well the program was functioning. She told the villagers, "First tell me what is lacking in her effort [*uskay kaam mey kami kya hain*]. I can only do something about the case if you have a good reason to complain about her work." She asked them to give her a complaint in writing saying exactly what was wrong with the anganwadi. Predictably, they refused to do that.

Agarwal told me that most hiring decisions in which politicians lobbied for a candidate concerned upper-caste women. She got away by appealing to her inability to hire an upper-caste woman without authorization from higher officials. Therefore, she requested the politicians who were putting pressure on her to submit a written plea to the director of the program to hire someone contrary to the quotas. She knew that no politician would dare write such a letter. That is how she got off the hook.

Here are two disparate examples of the fear of putting complaints in writing. In the first case, villagers were reluctant to file a complaint on false grounds against one of the best workers in the anganwadi program. Not only was such a complaint likely to be dismissed, it would have discredited the people who led the campaign against the anganwadi worker and perhaps even invited official retribution of some kind. In the second case, powerful politicians were afraid to commit to writing that they knowingly violated quotas for lower castes. Such an action might have resulted in negative publicity in the form of newspaper reports or other types of public criticism. Whatever upper-caste politicians might say in private, they did not dare to criticize publicly the policy of quotas for lower-caste people in government jobs.

The reluctance of people to file complaints in writing can be gauged from the fact that the number of complaints was surprisingly low, even for contentious programs like the JRY.[46] The junior clerk for the program told me that in the previous three years they had received a total of two, four, and six complaints, respectively. In the six months after the start of my research, they had received five complaints. Two of them were currently being handled by higher authorities. One of them had already been investigated by a senior officer who had probably filed his report but failed to send them a copy of his decision. Despite the low number of complaints, bureaucrats sometimes voiced frustration about baseless complaints lodged against them. Malik told me he was seeking a transfer from the district because he felt that there was too much political interference in his work. He identified politicians in particular as being responsible for lodging senseless complaints against the administrative staff.

The last example reveals that the comfort level people felt in filing a complaint against a state employee had more to do with power than with literacy, with the cultural capital associated with the knowledge of state procedures rather than educational qualifications. Although the two were often correlated, this was not always the case. The politicians whom Malik was complaining about were not necessarily well educated even if they were literate. But they were confident in their knowledge of government rules and procedures, in contrast to the poor men in the first two examples above. This is perhaps the most important reason why more complaints were not filed against state employees at the lower levels of the bureaucracy. The more powerful the bureaucrat became, the more likely it was that he or she dealt with a small group of social and political elites rather than with the public at large. Here, written complaints from citizens were even more unlikely. However, such officials still had to deal with complaints by the staff they supervised and subaltern members of the bureaucracy who felt they had been treated unfairly.

COMPLAINTS BY STATE OFFICIALS AGAINST OTHER STATE OFFICIALS

By far the largest proportion of complaints against state officials was those filed by their subordinates in the bureaucracy. In a perspective that took the state as a unit opposing civil society, such complaints might disappear from view, as they are internal to the workings of state bureaucracies. However, if we operate with a disaggregated perspective on the state, the relationship between these complaints and those mentioned earlier can be seen more clearly. This is a very interesting genre of complaints because it brings into the open the conflicts and contradictions within bureaucracies. Through these complaints one gets a much richer sense of why bureaucracies work the way they do and how subalterns within the bureaucracy sometimes thwart the plans and intentions of officials at higher levels. Although conflicts within the bureaucracy might not seem to have anything to do with the poor, in fact the poor may play a central role in such conflicts. As we shall see below, subordinates sometimes invoke the poor when charging their superior officer of malfeasance. The legitimacy of a charge of corruption against one's superior officer is enhanced if the resources being diverted were meant for poor, and particularly lower-caste, people.

One feature that complaints in this section share with the types of grievances described above is that, to be effective, they had to be written down. As a genre, complaints within the state share the form of other complaints. The content usually concerns the wrongfulness of the actions of one's immediate boss, and the letter is typically directed to the official who is at least one rung higher in the bureaucratic hierarchy than the boss. Perhaps one of the reasons bureaucrats were more willing to file complaints against superordinate officials is that they knew the rules of procedure and the violations of those rules more intimately than a member of the public would. The fear of retaliation inhibited most officials from filing complaints against their superiors unless the situation was unbearable and doing one's job on a day-to-day basis almost impossible. Although an official who filed a complaint could be sure that his or her job was secure (government officials can be fired only in exceptional circumstances), other types of retaliation were possible: for example, negative annual character reports could prevent or delay future promotions; a leave could be denied, and defying that denial could result in disciplinary action or withholding of a portion of one's pay; and a transfer to a so-called punishment post could force one to live away from one's family if the location was unsafe or did not have good schools for children.[47] So officials who contemplated such an action went ahead with it only when they were desperately seeking to remedy an unviable work environment, and then too only if they had connections with powerful bureaucrats or politicians who would be able to support them during the process. For example, retaliation by one's boss in the form of a punishment posting could be thwarted by the intervention of higher officials or powerful politicians.

Before being promoted to the position of CDPO in Mandi, Asha Agarwal had worked as a supervisor in the anganwadi program in another district. There, she had a run-in with her boss, the CDPO. The storekeeper, in connivance with the CDPO, was shortchanging the anganwadi workers in the supply of food for the supplementary nutrition program. The workers were given ten to fifteen kilograms less food than the fifty kilograms they were supposed to receive. They were then being asked to sign a form that said they had received the full complement of food. Agarwal was also asked to sign to verify that the anganwadi workers had indeed been given the proper amount of supplementary nutrition. Some of the anganwadi workers objected to being shortchanged. Agarwal refused to sign the documents, saying that she felt uncomfortable being complicit in this scheme when the workers disagreed with the practice. She would have agreed to sign had the workers not objected. She told the CDPO that she did not mind looking the other way as long as she was not implicated. Her refusal to go along forced the storekeeper to give the workers the correct amount of supplementary nutrition; this, in turn, emboldened the workers to demand the right amount when they were shortchanged.

The CDPO was very angry with her because of this incident and attempted to make her life as difficult as possible. When Agarwal submitted her touring program for approval, the CDPO kept making excuses, saying, "I'll sign it soon, don't worry. Bring it later; I am busy at this time." Therefore, Agarwal went ahead with her tour program. At the end of the fortnight, the CDPO charged her with absenteeism, saying she had failed to show up at the office when her tour program had not been approved. Agarwal was deemed to be absent without cause, which would have severely affected her career, as it would have counted as a break in service.[48] Furthermore, the CDPO withheld her salary for fifteen days because she was absent from the office.

Such daily harassment continued. One day, the CDPO marked Agarwal absent because she was allegedly two minutes late in reaching the office. The absurdity of this situation can be understood only in the context of a work culture in which people rarely reached the office on time and were routinely late by an hour or more. When Agarwal disputed this act by using as evidence the time on the watches of people in the bank adjacent to compare them with the CDPO's watch, it enraged her boss even more. On another occasion the CDPO refused to give Agarwal casual leave when she had high fever. She had to go to the office of the highest official of the subdistrict, the SDM, who happened to be a friend of her husband, and ask him to intervene. He encouraged her to submit a written complaint, and that is what she did.

Tired of the daily conflict, Agarwal tried to mend fences with the CDPO. She told her she was ready to make an unqualified apology to her in front of the whole office staff if that is what she wanted. She said to the CDPO, "You are older than me and an officer, so I feel it is my duty to apologize to you for any wrong I have committed." However, the CDPO was not willing to accept a verbal apology. She told Agarwal she would be satisfied only when she received such an apology in writing. Agarwal explained to me that she could not possibly make an apology in writing because she had already complained to higher authorities about the CDPO. Agarwal said, "Once you put things into writing, everything changes." A written apology would be tantamount to admitting she had been wrong in filing a complaint in the first place and would have implicated her as the guilty party. She therefore refused to give the CDPO a written apology but asked her to reconsider and accept a verbal apology. The CDPO dismissed Agarwal, saying she was not afraid of any action that Agarwal might attempt against her.

The complaint prompted an inquiry conducted by a senior bureaucrat in the ICDS program. He came to their project office and wanted to know why so many complaints were coming up the hierarchy from that site. He told the staff he would listen to all their complaints, but that they had to speak up then or forever hold their tongue. Agarwal told him everything, and the other people on the staff followed suit. The CDPO had been mistreating several others as well by holding up payments to them. The CDPO complained that her staff did not give her adequate respect. The officer conducting the inquiry then sternly lectured the staff to treat the CDPO with respect. In turn, he asked her to approve all pending payments to the staff within a week. During that week, when members of her staff approached the CDPO to obtain signatures authorizing their payments, she told them to get the signature of the officer who had conducted the inquiry. After being unsuccessful in their quest to get the CDPO to cooperate with them, members of the staff went to the officer who had conducted the inquiry and told him what the CDPO had said. He wrote a note to the DM, who, in turn, suspended the CDPO. Agarwal later learned that the CDPO had given her a bad character report the previous year, but the deputy director of the program had overturned it because he did not believe there were adequate grounds for writing such a report. The next year she might have received another bad character report, but the CDPO was suspended before the time of the year when annual character reports had to be filed. Otherwise, Agarwal said, her promotion would almost certainly have been held up.

This is an interesting case because it demonstrates the struggles that take place within bureaucracies. By paying attention to the contradictions and conflicts within one office, one can see that assumptions about the intentions and actions of the state can paper over what needs to be understood about the dynamics of how states actually function. Much that is written about the capacity and capability of the state misinterprets such dynamics by assuming a unified actor. After all, the capacity of the ICDS office to deliver supplementary nutrition to its workers and thence to the children who were its beneficiaries could be explained only by the conflicts between the CDPO and the storekeeper on the one side, and Agarwal and the anganwadi workers on the other. This was, moreover, a structural conflict, insofar as the interest of the CDPO and the storekeeper in siphoning off food was opposed to the interests of the anganwadi workers. How such conflicts were resolved was critical to how effective the state was in its task of supplying food to poor children (There was another step, namely, how effective the CDPO and supervisors were in preventing the anganwadi workers from siphoning off food for their own use.) Between the outcome—supplementary nutrition for poor children —and the program plan were a series of actors and a number of steps whose dynamic was contingent on various conditions, one of which was intra-bureaucratic process. To talk about these conditions as state capacity would be correct, but it would obscure the fact that there might be very different reasons why state capacity appears to be the same in two cases.

Another important feature of this story is that it demonstrates that even conflict between bureaucrats at different levels incorporates the poor in complex ways. As chapter 7 demonstrates, the anganwadi workers were simultaneously workers and clients of the welfare state. Many anganwadi workers were chosen for the job because they lacked other means of support. Thus, it is significant that Agarwal mobilized two sets of poor people in her complaint against her CDPO. It is worth considering if Agarwal's complaint would have been as effective if the (poor) anganwadi workers were not being cheated and, in turn, if the poor children who were the targets of supplementary nutrition were not being deprived of food. The legitimacy of Agarwal's complaint was underlined by its reference to the poor who were the apparent victims of her boss's malfeasance. This is one example of how intra-bureaucratic conflict actually resulted in a reduction of structural violence insofar as it enabled more supplementary nutrition to reach anganwadi workers and perhaps to the population that suffered the worst consequences of malnutrition: the children who attended the anganwadi.

In addition, this case is fascinating because it shows the strategies bureaucratic subalterns employ to keep a check on their supervisors. A boss in a very hierarchical system like the Indian state could be overbearing, but her power was not completely arbitrary. Agarwal was willing to apologize to her boss because once she crossed swords with her she realized that the CDPO could employ many techniques of retaliation, such as denying her leave, writing a bad character report, and so forth. Would she and the other staff members have been successful in their complaint had higher officials been in favor of the CDPO? Had the CDPO been more skillful in managing her image before her own bosses, it was likely they would have dismissed the complaints coming from below in much the same way that the block-level staff dismissed complaints filed by villagers against headmen. In the absence of firsthand knowledge of work conditions in the office, they would attribute such complaints to politics. Very often the de facto explanation for such conflicts was that honest, that is, noncorruptible, officers were harassed by their staff because they prevented them from engaging in corrupt activities.

Another example of such a case stems from my fieldwork with the supervisor of the seed farm in the village of Alipur, one of the villages in Mandi Block. One man on the staff at the farm, the driver whose job was to operate and maintain the farm's tractor, was disaffected with the supervisor because he thought he did not share enough of the farm's produce with its staff. None of the farm's produce was supposed to be given to the staff, but it was common for the head of the farm to allocate a token of the output to the staff before the total amount of the harvest was officially tallied. When the pea crop was harvested, it was put into sacks that were stored in one room of the farmhouse. Soon after, the supervisor left for a short holiday. When he returned he found that several sacks of peas had been stolen from the room.

Apparently someone on the staff had deliberately left a side door to that room unbolted from the inside when the sacks of peas were being stored there. When the supervisor left town for his vacation, they had sneaked into the room at night, stolen several sacks of peas, and sold them.[49]

After this incident the driver cooked up another scheme to get his supervisor into trouble. He took a tire from the tractor and exchanged it for a worn tire from someone he knew. Then, using the name of the man to whom he had sold the tire as a complainant, he filed a report with the head of the bureaucracy that alleged that the supervisor had sold him a tire from the farm's tractor and pocketed the money. This prompted an official inquiry, and a senior official was sent to investigate the complaint. Having been informed of the inquiry, the supervisor personally went to meet the person who had filed the complaint. When he got there, he asked the man if he knew the supervisor of the farm and if he had bought a tire from him. Not knowing whom he was talking to, the man truthfully stated that he had never met the supervisor. The supervisor introduced himself and asked him why he had filed a false complaint. The man denied having done any such thing. It turned out he had no knowledge of the complaint and that the letter had not been written by him. When the supervisor queried him about who had given him the tire, he stated that it was the driver. Therefore, the supervisor asked him to write a statement saying that he did not know the supervisor and that the supervisor had not sold him the tire. When this evidence along with the man who bought the tire were presented at the inquiry, the supervisor was acquitted of all charges.

The supervisor managed to get back at the driver. The driver took a leave without filing a leave application. Normally, if one of the staff was absent for a short period, say, a day or two, the supervisor would record them as being present in the attendance register. This time the supervisor refused to accommodate the driver and falsely record him as being present when he was in fact away. He threatened the driver that he would consider his absence to constitute a break in service (see Agarwal's case above for a similar threat). In this case, the threat was effective. The driver was terrified he would lose his seniority, and it forced him to acknowledge his role in selling off the tire. More important, he confessed to being involved in the theft of the sacks of peas and named other people on the farm's staff who had collaborated with him.

The seriousness with which written complaints were taken perhaps encouraged their fabrication. Unlike the previous case, in which junior officials complained in order to obtain justice, here the complaint was used to implicate the boss falsely in a scandal. Therefore, one should be wary of an interpretation that celebrates the complaint as a form that enables the subaltern to right wrongs. If the driver had been cleverer in his planning and collaborated with a villager who was willing to make a false statement, he could have placed the supervisor in deep trouble. On the other hand, if one sees this example from the perspective of a higher official sent to investigate the case, it differs little from the previous one. In the absence of better information, the investigating official was just as likely to conclude that both cases were about intra-office politics and hence that the charges were essentially baseless or that both cases were about corrupt officials who were persecuting their subordinates. In this example, the ability to retaliate finally allowed the supervisor to learn the truth behind the complaint and revealed to him the persons involved in the theft of the sacks of peas.

The signature of certain officials was often critical if one wanted to file a complaint. This was confirmed in an incident in which one of his staff came to Malik requesting that he sign a letter. The letter was addressed to the superintendent of police (SP) and complained that the station chief (*thanedar*) of the local police post was not doing his job. Malik refused to sign the letter because he said he was not the appropriate person to complain to the superintendent of police. He asked the subordinate to get the SDM to sign the letter because he was the appropriate official to address the police superintendent.

When that official left, Malik turned to me, sputtering with rage: "What does he think I am, a fool?" He then gave me the full background to this unfolding drama. It turned out that the ADO (panchayats) had been instructed to file a complaint with the police (First Information Report, or FIR) against the headman of a village. He did not wish to do so because the headman had the support of the locally elected official to the state assembly (the Member of the Legislative Assembly, or MLA). Therefore, he was trying to push the responsibility for filing the FIR onto someone else. He asked the head of the local police post to register the complaint, but that official refused to do so because he did not wish to incur the wrath of the elected official. This is why the ADO wanted his boss to complain to the SP that the station chief was not doing his job.

In both of these cases, intra-bureaucratic conflict was caused by the fear of bureaucrats of getting involved in actions against elected officials like headmen or members of the regional state legislature. Here we see how struggles between different branches of the state, the legislative and the executive, result in conflict within the bureaucracy itself. Bureaucrats complained that they had been reduced to becoming servants of politicians, who did not respect them and forced them to indulge in corrupt actions. On the other hand, politicians complained that they could not get anything done because of a recalcitrant and entrenched bureaucracy that was interested only in its own privilege and not in getting results. Even if they were protected from losing their jobs, bureaucrats at the lowest level were most reluctant to cross swords with local politicians, whether they were petty leaders like headmen or more important politicians, such as the local MLA. The poor were central to this struggle among branches of the state: bureaucrats bemoaned the fact that kickbacks to politicians were rising in scale, preventing them from allocating funds to the poor as intended; on the other hand, politicians alleged that bureaucrats selfishly guarded their privileges rather than conscientiously attend to the implementation of programs for the poor. Although the poor were invoked as the reason each group was doing what it did, they seldom benefited from this conflict. Individual poor people could employ the conflict to their benefit, but it would be hard to argue that the poor as a group benefited from it. The conflict was about how the social surplus was to be split among elites—whether the social surplus should go to politicians or bureaucrats. It was not about ensuring that structural violence against the poor would in fact be ameliorated. The poor were invoked in intra-elite struggles but did not necessarily gain from such representation.

The examples presented here manifest that intra-bureaucratic conflicts and the functionality or dysfunctionality of state institutions are not necessarily connected. The ability of junior officials to file complaints against their superior officers did not necessarily make for a state that was more transparent, more accountable, more egalitarian, more rule-oriented, more efficient, or more Weberian in its commitment to process, order, and the duties of office. However, it opened a window on the conflicts and contradictions within bureaucracies that have an enormous impact on what they can accomplish, for whom, and under what circumstances. If such intra-bureaucratic conflicts are ignored, the tendency in academic work to reify state institutions into overly purposeful, unitary, and motivated actors is reinforced. However, this investigation into complaints does open up ideas for forms of intervention on behalf of the poor, using the conflicts within the bureaucracy to the advantage of its dispossessed clients.

Conclusion

I make an argument for the importance of writing in the relationship between states and poor people. Although much of what constitutes the historical archive is the inscription of anonymous bureaucrats in the course of carrying out their routine activities, very few scholars have paid attention to the forms that such writing has taken. My objective is not to do a study of the genres of bureaucratic writing but to see how forms and practices of writing matter to the poor. I argue that if one begins to see writing not just as that which follows bureaucratic action but also as constitutive of such action, it would change how one evaluated the role of inscription. Writing is one of the chief activities of bureaucrats; it is not secondary or subsequent to bureaucratic activity. The mistake in seeing writing as a substitute for action (Clanchy 1979: 6) is that it does not understand that writing is itself a form of action and is perhaps the most important of bureaucratic activities. Interpreting the act of writing as functioning merely to record or commemorate real bureaucratic activity prevents one from seeing that writing is not just a by-product of the routines of state officials but is constitutive of states. To a state official, doing something often means writing down figures and narrative. In the absence of writing, actions are considered incomplete or, as the example of the Kisan Seva Kendra demonstrates, may not be considered to have happened in the first place. A corollary is that the amount and nature of bureaucratic writing far exceeds the functional requirements of administration, internal surveillance, and efficiency: it is an end in itself. Moreover, writing does not function to better serve the poor, increase the efficiency of the state's development efforts, or make bureaucrats more accountable. By itself, the fact that writing is constitutive of the state in India does not necessarily make it complicit with structural violence. Below I argue emphatically against a dominant scholarly and political tendency that sees writing as inherently exploitative in the context of widespread rural illiteracy. However, there are certain features about the contexts and content of writing that may lead to such a result. Therefore, one has to attend carefully to the precise circumstances under which writing collaborates with structural violence.

Once the centrality of writing to state practice is acknowledged, scholars can turn their attention to the different shapes it takes. It is not without reason that bureaucracies are associated with forms. The form is the essence of paperwork that often drives citizens to despair and leads to the disparagement of entrenched bureaucracies. Forms help to enframe and categorize; they are containers for standardization, replicability, anonymity, and portability. Applicants who have filled in forms can be more easily compared to each other, and the information contained therein can be more easily converted into statistics. The standardization enabled by forms also allows writing to be stored and retrieved under appropriate conditions. This is where files and registers prove to be very useful. Finally, reports represent the activities of particular offices or one wing of the state in a form that can be read by consumers, whether they are other officials or the public.

Numbers are perhaps the most common form of state writing. The collection and reporting of data, accounts, and reports rely heavily on statistical information. I have argued for a view of statistics that sees it as being essentially complementary to narrative rather than a substitute for it or a competitive mode of inscription. Statistics classify and help bring individual cases into order through typification. Although narratives transform themselves into statistics as they travel up the bureaucratic hierarchy, the movement is not all one way, as statistical anomalies themselves invite the remobilization of narrative as a mode of explanation. Finally, statistics produce social worlds rather than serving a purely repressive function of surveillance and control, as can be seen in the goals that states set for themselves in terms of growth rates and development indices. I have demonstrated that the seemingly obsessive efforts to enumerate the poor and to measure a nation-state's progress by the numbers of people lifted above the poverty line betray a faulty measurement of poverty. Despite its well-documented problems, counting the number of heads below a poverty line (for example, $1/day) continues to be the yardstick by which rates of poverty are measured, and compared across nation-states. Techniques of enumeration that include people who are poor for very different reasons and poor to very different degrees under a seemingly objective measure can perpetuate structural violence by equating incommensurable experiences of suffering and by offering misleading solutions to chronic poverty. One can see the dangers of such schemas of enumeration in the proliferation of "scalable" schemes for BPL families in India. All of these schemes assume commensurability among the families so classified, although they may not account for the manifold reasons those families are poor and for what needs to be done to pull them out of poverty.

Inspections and complaints are two forms of writing that bring several types of conflicts into the open. Through complaints, one can gain insight into popular and subaltern constructions of the state. There are two opposing ways to interpret complaints: one view sees complaints as arising from the breakdown of normal procedures and functions, whereas the other considers them as functional to the normal operation of bureaucracies. The fact that there were such few complaints and that each written complaint was taken so seriously might suggest a malfunctioning. In other words, only when the routine operation of state bureaucracies breaks down do citizens and subalterns feel compelled to file a complaint. However, as we have seen, there is little relation between how well poor people might feel a program works and the number of complaints that are filed because most people are extremely reluctant to write a letter of complaint. We have also seen examples of how reluctant state officials are to admit a written complaint; furthermore, written complaints are often not registered because of technicalities, for example, the lack of a signature or the absence of an official. On the other hand, complaints can be interpreted as the expression of structural conflicts within bureaucracies and between bureaucrats and impoverished beneficiaries of government programs. The two explanations can be reconciled, for the normal operation of bureaucracies consists precisely in depoliticizing structural conflict. This is done not only through neutral procedural rules but also by habits of deference and other techniques of comportment through which constituents, clients, and subalterns perform their roles in reproducing structural inequalities. The smooth operation of bureaucracies thereby depends not only on Weberian bureaucrats performing their roles, but also on those poor people who are the objects of their intervention performing their structurally given roles. Complaints by poor clients against government officials make visible the structural violence that is normally hidden by such techniques of deferential comportment.

The connections between writing, comportment, and behavior anticipate my exploration below of the relation between the practices of writing documented here and the role played by education and literacy as forms of cultural and symbolic capital. Structural violence is closely connected to asymmetric cultural and symbolic capital but often in surprising ways.

LITERACY, BUREAUCRATIC DOMINATION, AND DEMOCRACY 6

The Indian state may appear no different from other modern bureaucracies in the importance it gives to writing. What makes this emphasis on writing, which borders on an obsession, so significant in the Indian context, however, is that bureaucrats, at least at lower levels, often have to deal with a population of clients who are largely illiterate. The consequences of insistence upon writing in a social context in which literacy is highly stratified have seldom been appreciated in the scholarly literature on states.[1] In such a context, the power of the state is intimately bound to the power of the written word.

I seek to break the chain of causation that leads straight from literacy to domination. If one follows that course of thinking, literacy is considered to be the key that enables bureaucrats to exploit illiterate people. Since there is a very high correlation between poverty and illiteracy—in India most poor adults are illiterate, although not all illiterate people are poor—this diagnosis implies that making poor people literate is central to solving the problem of poverty. The view that literacy can help the poor in ameliorating structural violence and mitigating bureaucratic arbitrariness makes a lot of sense, particularly given bureaucratic demands to submit communications in writing and the proliferation of forms and contexts of bureaucratic writing. Nevertheless, I argue that such a view both overestimates the importance of writing and underestimates the political capacities of the poor. In a democratic context the poor are not simply subjugated by literate elites: they have alternative avenues of political action. I examine some of the strategies employed by the poor to combat the dominance wielded by literate bureaucrats. I argue against the idea that structural violence can be explained by the differential access to literacy between poor villagers and bureaucrats. In the world of well-meaning activists, scholars, and bureaucrats, making poor people literate is seen as a key to the eradication of poverty. I argue, by contrast, that literacy does not have such a central role either to the perpetuation of structural violence or to its amelioration. However, the imbrication of literacy in state functioning does have implications for how exactly one goes about eradicating poverty or mitigating structural violence inflicted on the poor.

While conducting fieldwork I found farmers in U.P. to be very suspicious of my desire to record what they were growing in their fields. I gradually learned they were afraid that by giving me detailed information about their crops they would invite more finely calibrated forms of taxation. At that time, given my position as a student researcher, I dismissed such concerns. To my mind, since I was not a state official there was no good reason to link my writing to projects of state domination. However, villagers' views of the state were perhaps innately Foucauldian; they understood, in a manner I was to appreciate only much later, the intimate link between (state) power and knowledge.

Before dealing with the specific question of bureaucratic writing, I wish to step back for a moment and consider one particular view concerned with writing in anthropological work. Jack Goody, whose pioneering work in this area invites further scholarly attention, famously complained that "social anthropologists have thought of their discipline as being primarily concerned with 'preliterate,' 'primitive,' or 'tribal' societies and have generally looked upon writing (where it existed) simply as an 'intrusive' element. . . . It is clear that even if one's attention is centered only upon village life, there are large areas of the world where the fact of writing and the existence of the book have to be taken into account, even in discussing 'traditional' societies" (Goody 1968: 1, 5).

Around the same time, Claude Lévi-Strauss, the dean of structuralist anthropologists, took the controversial stance that writing had proved to be unimportant to what was perhaps the most important advance made in the history of humanity: the neolithic revolution. Lévi-Strauss argued that writing appeared after the time when humanity had already made its most essential and fundamental discoveries, that is, after the development of agriculture, the domestication of animals, pottery making, and weaving (Lévi-Strauss 1969: 27–28; 1967: 291). Those inventions, he surmised, must have been the result of processes of experimentation over long periods. Therefore, he claimed that the most fundamental human progress could and did take place entirely through the oral transmission of knowledge from generation to generation, without the intervention or employment of writing (Lévi-Strauss 1969: 28). The polemical thrust of Lévi-Strauss's comment was aimed at dismantling the common characterization of nonindustrial peoples in a manner that conjoined the notions of "preliterate," "primitive" and "tribal," treating them as synonyms, as is made evident in the quote from Goody above. Lévi-Strauss's intervention introduced a dissonance between the teleologies of literacy and of social evolution: civilization, he argued, is neither synonymous with writing nor one of its consequences.

Is Lévi-Strauss's understanding of writing too restrictive? In *Of Grammatology*, Derrida forcefully argues that writing in the narrow sense of the term may have been unknown during the neolithic era, but scripts that preceded the alphabet must be seen as a legitimate form of writing as well. To not consider systems of writing that differ from "writing as we know it," Derrida (1976: 129) concludes, is its own form of ethnocentrism.[2]

Not only is the anthropological notion of how we define writing in question, but the close connection between writing and domination has also been a contentious issue. The most extreme version of this thesis holds that writing creates inequality because it separates social groups. Goody, for example, appears to have endorsed such a position when he wrote, "Until recently writing *created* a radical divide between literate and illiterate elements in a population" (Goody 1986: 121; emphasis added). In this case, writing is an agent that divides social classes. Similarly, Lévi-Strauss, not content with demonstrating the irrelevance of writing to the greatest advances of civilization, took the argument even further by connecting writing not only to domination but also to the very notion of progress: "The only phenomena which, always and in all parts of the world, seem to be linked with the appearance of writing . . . is the establishment of hierarchical societies, consisting of masters and slaves, and where one part of the population is made to work for the other part" (Lévi-Strauss 1969: 30). There appears to be a difference between this position and the more emphatic version attributed to Goody above, in that Lévi-Strauss suggested only that writing is correlated to hierarchy but is not its cause. In other words, writing may not explain why social inequalities exist or come to be established in the first place, but it does facilitate or enable the reproduction of those inequalities.

Lévi-Strauss suggested that in modern, post-Enlightenment Western societies, progress is necessarily connected with domination, and writing provides the link between the two. Progress in the modern scientific sense, Lévi-
Strauss maintained, is possible only with the accumulation of knowledge,
which requires writing. His position is most clearly articulated in the following statement: "Starting with the problem of progress, we say that it was
connected with the capitalization or totalization of knowledge. This process
itself only appeared possible after the point at which writing first came into
existence, and writing itself, in the first instance, seemed to be associated in
any permanent way only with societies which were based on the exploitation
of man by man" (Lévi-Strauss 1969: 30–31). Consciously drawing upon Marx
but considerably changing his emphasis on the mode of production, Lévi-
Strauss here seamlessly links progress, knowledge, writing, and domination, without positing that some fundamental transformation occurs specifically with the rise of industrial capitalism.

Such a position was no doubt intended to be a provocation, especially
since the assumed positive relationship between progress, knowledge, and
writing had been so firmly ensconced as to have become a global "common-
sense." However, this presumption runs the risk of arriving at the conclusion
that the absence of exploitation and liberty " 'go hand-in-hand' . . . with
illiteracy" (Derrida 1976: 132). Derrida criticizes Lévi-Strauss's seeming nos-
talgia for what came before modernity, for the small-scale communities in
which "a unanimous people assembled in the self-presence of its speech"
(1976: 134). Derrida traces such a position to Jean Jacques Rousseau, who felt
that "social distance, the dispersion of the neighborhood, is the condition of
oppression, arbitrariness, and vice" (1976: 137; emphasis added). Hierarchy,
he argues, is the result of the scale of social organization rather than of
writing in particular. Moreover, he thinks Lévi-Strauss covertly elided hierarchy with domination and political authority with exploitation (Derrida
1976: 130–31). Derrida's critique allows one to see, for example, the partiality
of Lévi-Strauss's observation that in societies with restricted literacy the
scribe and the usurer are often the same person because the "usurer has thus a
twofold empire over his fellows" (Lévi-Strauss 1967: 291). What Lévi-Strauss
fails to appreciate is that in such conditions of restricted literacy, the opposition to usury is often also led by literate elites, whether they are members of
clerical orders or nationalists or leaders of sectarian or millenarian movements. The relation between writing and domination appears to be much
more variable and open-ended than Lévi-Strauss leads one to believe.

It is through these debates about writing's relation with domination that my analysis of the state comes into focus. In conditions of restricted literacy, writing by state officials for the purposes of bureaucracies attains great importance because it is politically powerful. But do conditions of restricted literacy make bureaucratic writing a mechanism for the enactment of structural violence on the illiterate parts of the population? Lévi-Strauss seems to suggest as much.

Writing in this sense refers to inscription in the form of numbers as well as letters.[3] For example, Goody (1986: 93) pointed to "the close connection between taxation and the census, the numbering of the people and the collection of their 'surplus.' " Similarly, Lévi-Strauss (1969: 30) argued that the first uses of writing were closely connected to power: "It was used for inventories, catalogues, censuses, laws and instructions" (see also Lévi-Strauss 1967: 292–93). By 1279 in England surveys and inventories had become so much a part of crown business that the chief reaction of contemporary chroniclers to the announcement of an ambitious royal survey was weariness (Clanchy 1979: 6). Inventories as a form of bureaucratic writing are critical not just in the daily, mundane activities of states but also in repeated yet irregular activities like wars. From ancient Egypt to the formalized committees called prize commissions set up by the British colonial government (Goody 1986: 93; Hevia 1994) inventories are a central part of the sharing of war booty.

The most important implications of literacy for bureaucracies, however, may not lie in the power it bestows on bureaucrats vis-à-vis the lay population. Rather, it lies in the control it allows higher bureaucrats to exert on lower-placed ones through the extension of authority enabled by the portability of written orders and documents (Green 1981: 367).[4] It has been argued even that written documents facilitate stronger states by preventing fission between territorially distant parts of a state, both because writing makes communication easier and cheaper and because it requires that all state officials have a common written language (Goody 1986: 110–13).[5] In conditions of restricted literacy, bureaucrats might well constitute the major fraction of the literate population; in such situations, literacy helps provide such officials with a community that is not restricted to face-to-face interaction (Goody 1986: 8).

For such reasons it has often been presupposed that literacy is the precondition that allows for solidarity between elites in such sectors as business, government, and politics and the arts and education. Even when literacy is not restricted in the extreme, "the old school tie" has functioned to forge such connections. But one should be wary of arguments that automatically tie forms of cultural capital to group solidarity. Depending on the context, even when the size of the literate elite is small there may be divisions along political lines because their class interests are opposed or because of ethnic, linguistic, or racial antagonisms.[6] For example, the first generation of nationalist elites in India were trained in British schools and colleges and often shared much more in terms of cultural and educational capital with the colonizers than with the illiterate populations they claimed to represent. Thus, rather than merely paying attention to the presence or absence of such writing, one needs to think about the uses to which writing is put in the functions of states, that is, to the forms, contexts, and meanings of state writing and to the various ways in which it is used by bureaucrats and their subjects. Rather than assuming that structural violence is the result of bureaucratic writing, one needs to know when and how the two phenomena are connected.

How are writing, literacy, and orality related? There is a strong presumption in modernist thought that associates writing with rationality and orality with superstition. A story about bird flu that appeared in the *New York Times* illustrates this position perfectly, but the example can be endlessly multiplied: "[Accusations of a witchcraft killing demonstrate] . . . what United Nations and American officials describe as the difficulty of preventing a global human epidemic of bird flu: the disease is most prevalent among poultry and wild birds in impoverished rural areas of Southeast Asia with low levels of literacy, high levels of superstition and very little health care" (Bradsher 2005: A1). The prejudice displayed by the agents of global governance and the West against poor, illiterate people in the Third World in making a link between rationality and literacy might be easy to dismiss. Yet such connections have an enduring legacy in the West. The result is that illiteracy is naturally associated with life-threatening forms of inequality and with structural violence and, conversely, that literacy is associated with the end of forms of severe inequality. How does one begin to break down such associations?

Three important points must be made here. First, in a discussion of literacy, one has to distinguish between the capacity to read and the capacity to write (see below). If one does not think of literacy as a well-defined state of achievement, one can better appreciate the political implications of a gradient of literacy.[7] Following Collins and Blot (2003: 3–4), one should perhaps talk not about literacy (with its universalizing model of a set of techniques and uses of language) but of literacies (as the culturally variable relation between people and texts). The second point follows from the first. If one interrogates the distinction between orality and literacy, it becomes quite clear that this dichotomy does not have the same implications in diverse cultural and historical circumstances. In other words, orality and literacy are not polar opposites.[8] Not only are the connotations of *orality* and *literacy* quite different, but the meaning of such a distinction itself is unstable. Kaviraj (1992b: 28–29) points out that in precolonial India writing was used quite sparingly even by people who were well versed in writing and that this phenomenon has to be explained by the peculiar social configuration of orality and literacy rather than by the presence or absence of writing.

Finally, the entire issue of literacy is rendered much more complex when one considers a social context in which people might speak and write several languages. Here, one must ask how speaking, reading, and writing functions are distributed across languages. Literacy, then, conveys not just the ability to read and write but also the differential ability to read and write a particular language. Tarlo (2003: 77–79) offers the example of people whose ability to negotiate the Delhi bureaucracy's entitlement of house plots is stymied by their lack of knowledge of an archaic English in which official documents are drafted. Here, the ability to read and write Hindi is of little use; it is literacy in English, and a peculiar form of English at that, which is essential. In the context of U.P., English and Hindi are the most important languages since they are the languages of officialdom. However, at the lower levels of administration in U.P., one almost never comes across documents drafted in English. If it appears that I have less to say about the multilingual context of literacy in this chapter, it is because Hindi was really the only language that mattered to the officials and villagers with whom I worked. An ethnography that focuses on higher levels of the bureaucracy or that is conducted in parts of India where Hindi is not the dominant language would have to confront more centrally the problem of literacies in English and the vernacular.

For all these reasons, although I have employed the term *restricted literacy* in the rest of this chapter, I wish to question the transitional and comparative nature of that formulation as found in Goody's work. Restricted literacy does not mean the same thing in different cultural contexts: first, because the distribution of oral and literate functions may be very diverse in societies that have small literate elites; and, second, because it is not an intermediate state on the way from an oral society to a literate one. For this reason I problematize both the category of orality and that of literacy, although I concentrate largely on literacy here. In fact, my argument is that the relationship between literacy and orality is one of radical contingency and that there is no necessary relationship between the ability to read and write and bureaucratic scale, the reliability of communication, democratic participation, or subaltern empowerment.[9] Stated baldly, such an argument appears to fly in the face of the commonsensical idea that literacy, especially in the form of the capacity to write, is the key to efficient administration in complex states and to enabling subalterns to gain freedom from oppression. In challenging the conventional wisdom about the enormous power of literacy, I am also suggesting that, contrary to the conventional view, the attainment of literacy by the poor does not have the magical effect of empowering them and increasing their capacity to resist structural violence.

The remainder of this chapter is dedicated to examining the varying relation between literacy and power more fully, with its attendant implications for structural violence on the poor. I begin my analysis by addressing the relationship between the written and the oral in government bureaucracies. I follow this with a discussion of the bureaucratic fetishism of degrees and documents. Finally, I conclude the chapter looking at strategies employed by subaltern groups to undermine or challenge bureaucratic writing.

The Written and the Oral

For Indian bureaucrats a vast gap separates the written from the oral, and the written is given pride of place. Oral complaints have no bureaucratic or judicial standing; by contrast, written complaints are treated with the utmost seriousness (see chapter 5). From the perspective of the block staff the most important goal was to avoid having a written complaint submitted against them. For instance, on one of my many visits to the Kisan Seva Kendra (see chapter 5) I came across a heated debate between a villager and the officials present. After it was over the villager said he wanted to register a complaint against the functioning of the village council (*Gram Panchayat*). "What is your complaint?" asked one of the officials. He replied that the village council did not hold meetings, that council members were not informed when such meetings did take place, and that there was no public forum where beneficiaries were selected for programs like the Indira Awaas Yojana (as noted earlier, a house-building scheme for indigent people) and other government schemes. The secretary of his village replied that the village council had indeed met. He then stated the dates and said that if the man did not know those dates it was not the council's fault. He also said he had noted down the date at which a meeting had been held to select beneficiaries. The man insisted that his complaint be written down in the register of complaints by villagers.

One of the officials interjected that they could act on his complaint only if he submitted it in writing. Another official reiterated, "Submit it in the form of a petition" (*Ek prastaav ke roop may day deejeeay*). "Why do I need to give it in writing?" insisted the man. "Isn't the purpose of this meeting that people can submit their complaints verbally?" The officials remained firm. Soon afterward, the man left, saying, "I don't want to disturb your meeting any more than necessary. I just wanted to bring this to your attention. Please go on with your meeting." After he left, none of the officials made any effort to note down what he had said.

It was clear that the man who was complaining was educated and that he was a member of the village council, although on the opposing side of the current headman. But even someone well informed like him thought it was largely an internal meeting of officials instead of a context to invite villagers to submit problems and complaints. When he apologized for disturbing their meeting, none of the officials present corrected him by saying that their purpose in being there was to serve the public and act on complaints such as his. They resisted noting down his complaint, knowing full well he would be unlikely to submit it in writing. I later asked the secretary how it was possible for someone on the village council not to find out when a council meeting would convene. He explained that a quorum for a village council meeting was considered met when three of its nine members were present. Usually, the headman called three or four people from his faction on the council to his house for a village council meeting. "If you pass these people talking inside the headman's house, you would not know that it is a village council meeting," volunteered the secretary helpfully. This is why the man was under the erroneous impression that no village council meetings had been called! The secretary had undercut the man's complaint by giving him the exact dates at which such meetings had taken place. The dates had been recorded, were official, and could be used to refute any allegation such as the one raised by the man about the headman's failure to call council meetings to select beneficiaries of government programs.

The preceding decennial census had put the literacy rate for Mandi Block at a mere 29 percent, and this implied not the ability to read a letter or write a petition but merely to sign one's name. Since literacy was highly correlated with poverty, such low rates of literacy might imply that conditions were ripe for bureaucratic elites to dominate the poor, making literacy a key mechanism by which structural violence is perpetuated. However, two factors militate against such a simple reading of power relations. The first is that one needs to situate such restricted literacy in a historical context in which rural peoples have long been accustomed to dealing with state officials. Scribes and other literate intermediaries were widely employed, thereby reducing the importance one might be tempted to give to the imbalance between literate state officials and the largely illiterate population.[10] Second, one must not forget that, in the democratic context of postcolonial India, bureaucrats are answerable to elected officials, some of whom are themselves barely literate. Therefore, the continuing distrust of the oral in bureaucratic procedure is, in some ways, surprising and in need of explanation, rather than a practice one can take for granted. At the very least, one might expect that new bureaucratic initiatives, as opposed to long-standing practices, make room for oral inputs from rural peoples, particularly from those poor, lower-caste people whose rates of literacy are even lower than the average and who have been the clients and target of an emergent populist politics.

One argument in favor of the written is that it is better at preserving and recording events and actions; the oral is transitory and potentially more open to corruption and contradiction. For example, a written complaint can be passed up the hierarchy verbatim, whereas an orally transmitted complaint is likely to have errors of transmission, as each person who passes it upward unconsciously changes or embellishes it to suit his or her own purpose. But written complaints can be lost: a file can be accidentally or deliberately misplaced. Similarly, the veracity of a complaint can be called into question because of a minor factual error: a wrong date or a missing or misstated fact. Small inconsistencies are better tolerated in oral testimony than in written. In Indian bureaucracies written documents are not always chosen as a preferred medium for their ability to preserve the truth of the official record. Tarlo (2003: 74) demonstrates this very convincingly in her discussion of paper truths, "whose status as truths was intrinsically linked to their symbolic value as official papers."[11]

One can also easily imagine a situation in which oral testimonies at the interface of bureaucracies and poor people are converted to written documents when such documents are required for purposes internal to bureaucracies. This is already done in procedures such as the First Information Report (FIR) collected by the police whenever a person comes to report a crime or an attack. Something similar in other offices would allow a poor villager's oral testimony to be converted into a written document: the scribe would move into the government office, and his or her job would be to record oral complaints and petitions.[12] The example of the man who wanted to register a complaint at the Kisan Seva Kendra demonstrates that the opposite situation prevails in most bureaucratic offices. Bureaucrats are not only reluctant to write down oral testimony, but also insist that the person who has a complaint first submit it in writing before they are even willing to consider acting on it. The substance of the complaint is therefore bracketed: however plausible or true such a complaint might be, if it is not in the right form it cannot be admitted.

Why do written documents now appear to have this property of preserving original intent more reliably and of providing stability of meaning as the document is transmitted from one hand to another? Such a position is by no means either universal or self-evident. In other situations of restricted literacy, the oral is sometimes considered more reliable and less prone to error than written documents. For example, oral testimony was considered a better way of arriving at the truth in court proceedings in England until the recounting from memory of records and title deeds was disenfranchised, or "ruled out of court," and written documents were substituted instead (Clanchy 1979: 3). In modern courts all over the world oral testimony by key witnesses still serves as the most important procedure for discerning the truth of the evidence, often supplying the suspense in real-life cases and in the genre of the detective thriller. This may appear surprising given the importance of writing to court procedure and to the significance of documentation, which now refers exclusively to written materials. It is ironic, although not surprising, that even oral testimony, elicited under strict rules, is transcribed verbatim by a court stenographer.[13] What is one to make of the continuing centrality of oral testimony in a bureaucracy densely entangled in a forest of paper?

The question of reliability is the most important one, in terms of evidence and also of transmission.[14] Messick, in his fascinating study on the transmission of the sharia' in Yemen (1993), points out the contrast often made in Islamic "tradition" and "jurisprudence" between writing and oral instruction.[15] Writing is considered an unreliable and error-prone form of disseminating the sharia' as compared to oral transmission from teacher to pupil. The reason follows Socratic thought in that, contrary to modern Western prejudice,[16] it sees the written word as that which makes the text more vulnerable to interpretive play and distortion (1993: 24–26). In the oral transmission of a text the speaker guarantees the reliability of the text: she can be interrogated, and meanings that are unclear or ambiguous can be clarified (1993: 27). By contrast, a written text offers no such possibility: it is open to misinterpretation by people who do not understand it (Plato 1995: 80–81). Messick (1993: 211) summarizes the view dominant in Islamic jurisprudence: "Texts 'loose' in the world are, like jahil individuals, in trouble and troublesome."

At first glance, a position that privileges the oral might appear archaic today, but people express their solidarity with Socrates every time they schedule a personal meeting rather than convey messages by e-mail. I have often heard people justify such a preference by saying that the potential for being misunderstood is greater in e-mail.[17] Take the role of the job interview or the personal lecture in the academic world in the contemporary United States. Given that publishing is so important in research universities, one would expect that a careful evaluation of the written work should be the clearest indication of the quality of a job applicant. However, it is often noted that the quality of a person's mind is judged by how she or he responds to questions in the job interview. Similarly, in the face of increasing pressures to cut the costs of educational services by using taped lectures and computer lessons, academics respond that real learning can take place only in face-to-face interaction with a small group of students in a classroom. Even with advanced students (or especially with them), that is, students who are quite capable of interpreting texts on their own, the importance placed on the oral transmission of knowledge in a small graduate seminar underlines the continuing centrality of the oral in an institutional context that supposedly privileges the written word over everything else.[18]

Legal bureaucracies might appear to be anomalous because of the importance they continue to give to the spoken word. This does not seem to be the case in other branches of the state bureaucracy. But that was not always the case. Bureaucratic procedure was so dependent on the spoken word in twelfth-century England that the term *record* itself meant "to bear oral witness, not to produce a document" (Clanchy 1979: 56). Four knights had to go in person to convey a record to the king's court. Within fifty years the meaning of a record had completely changed to indicate a written document (Clanchy 1979: 56–57). Similarly, Messick (1993: 210) reports that in Yemen, when important papers like the appointment to a judgeship had to be delivered, two witnesses traveled with the document. The reliability of the document depended primarily on a knowledge of the character of the writer; if the author of a text was unknown and unknowable, the text itself became inherently suspect (Messick 1993: 214). If the text had to be transported some distance, its authenticity was attested to by the witnesses, and the reliability of the witnesses depended on their social reputations. Odd as this may sound to modern ears, we have something similar in the contemporary world in the services of the personal courier. Valuable documents are often hand-carried, and this serves the function of ensuring that the document that was handed over at point A is the same as that which was delivered at point B, the only difference being that we do not depend as much on the courier's personal reputation as on that of the company for which she works.[19] Messick (1993:

216) concludes that "official writing," in which the state authorized standardized text through an official and through such marks as notarization and signatures, functioned to replace the personal reputation that guaranteed the authenticity of a text.

Why have bureaucracies and state bureaucracies in particular become so dependent on writing? One answer is that written communications increased the reliability of information, especially in territorially expansive states. In this view, writing allows for stronger bonds between center and periphery and "mitigates the fissive tendencies of large empires" (Goody 1986: 2). Writing also contributes to more efficient administration, as censuses, taxes, trade, and estate agriculture can all be managed much better through written records (Goody 1986: 2). Among the earliest known bureaucratic texts from the Syrian kingdom of Ebla (ca. 2400 BC) are letters, edicts and treaties. Letters not only allowed communication across levels; answers by higher officials to questions posed by lower ones could be referred to in the future for clarification or be cited as precedent in dealing with similar situations (Goody 1986: 96). Kaviraj (1992b: 28–29), however, questions this logic when he says, "The intimate connection so common in European culture between institutions, i.e., the extension in the scale of social practices in time and space, and consigning things to the fixity of writing does not seem to obtain [in India]. Enormous and essential structures of social exchange and communication are entrusted to oral continuity rather than written codification."

Perhaps nowhere is this dynamic more formalized than in modern legal bureaucracies, in which lower courts often wait for the highest court to decide a case and then follow the ruling as precedent. The portability of written communication in the form of scrolls or sheets of paper is a huge advantage in its dissemination. Issues of security and authenticity, however, have continued to be a big problem: documents, precisely because of their portability, are easily stolen or replaced with forged ones. To ensure the security of transmission, effective modes of transporting the inscriptions of bureaucracies developed quickly in the form of postal services (Goody 1986: 96). Even today, the importance given to the security of the mail is evident in that, in most countries, the state can imprison a person for tampering with or opening someone else's mail. A secure postal service is one that can effectively prevent mail from being intercepted and replaced. Other practices, such as notarizing important correspondence and sending copies of a letter to different offices, also help prevent fraud. However, the world of official documents is always shadowed by the counterfeit. As we shall see below, the authenticity of documents has continued to trouble bureaucracies up to the present.

Although I do not attribute a causative role to it, there is little doubt that the rise of written documents is connected to the enforcement of contracts. Written documents enable the rights to ownership and relations of contract to be prosecuted in court, a fact that has consistently worked to the detriment of the unlettered poor. The admissibility of a written document as evidence and the ability to prosecute incorrect or deliberately misleading writing allow for reparations in case of breach of contract. So normalized is the evidentiary property of written documents that it makes it possible to dismiss unenforceable contracts with the phrase, "It is not worth the paper it is written on." However, one should be cautious not to attribute too much importance to the law. There is little doubt that the creation of a specialized legal language designed to reduce ambiguity also helped to increase the importance given to writing. Perhaps more crucial to the importance placed upon writing in bureaucratic states, though, was the spread of commercial transactions that grew exponentially with an expanding capitalist economy and the concomitant commodification of writing itself, enabled by the printing press in the form of manuscripts, books, and newspapers. Far from being considered unreliable because of its openness to divergent interpretations, the written word, as opposed to oral texts, increasingly became identified with precision, clarity, and lack of ambiguity. The identification with precision perhaps encouraged an instrumental view of language as a tool by which one expresses thoughts or ideas. The clarity of language sought by versions of analytic philosophy depended on a prior belief that written communication could achieve a precision of expression not possible with oral speech.

Writing, however, does not now occupy a privileged position only in state bureaucracies. The practice of history, a craft intimately linked with the growth of nationalism and with nation-states as we know them today, casts a suspicious eye upon any evidence that is not backed by written sources. Few self-respecting historians would trust purely oral sources without the backup of written texts to cross-check oral history. Such an operation implicitly sets up a hierarchy of texts in which the written word is seen as more trustworthy, less prone to interpretive error, and more accurate across time and space than oral or recitational forms of speech. Sometimes there is little evidence of the circumstances in which texts were written and who their intended audience was and hence of their rhetorical function in an existing social milieu; nevertheless, written texts, as objects of interpretation, are considered less problematic than oral ones.[20] The interpretive bias in favor of those with cultural capital is thus reinforced by this focus on the written, as poor people everywhere were much less likely than the rich to leave written records.

Even historians of writing have expressed doubts as to the continuing salience and centrality of the written word. The technology of writing, Clanchy surmises, "may be entering its final century" (1979: 8), what with the reassertion of oral modes of communication via televisual technologies and emerging inventions that make visual telephonic communication affordable. Media critics were already proclaiming that radio and the gramophone had introduced a "new age of orality" and that the "age of print" simply represented an interval between two epochs of orality, one before print and an emerging one that would follow it (Kittler 1999: xii). Such views have a strongly teleological cast, progressing from orality toward a world of print and literacy and from there to a new epoch of orality. The shift from one era to the other is marked by displacement. Therefore, scholars have posited the concept of oral residues in literate cultures. For instance, Clanchy (1979: 2) observes that reading aloud, an oral mode of communication, *persisted* for a long time after the advent of literacy (emphasis added). The natural progression implicit in such a statement would see literacy not existing alongside, but replacing, oral communication. An alternative view is presented by Stock in his impressive study of the rise of literacy in eleventh- and twelfth-century Europe. Stock emphasizes not the displacement of oral cultures by literate ones, but the changing relation between them (1983: 3–11).

If one reverses this assumption and sees that in civilizations such as India and China conditions of restricted literacy, not the exceptional states of complete illiteracy and total literacy, have been the rule, then the coexistence of written and oral modes of communication, and especially transmission across these genres, is unsurprising. More important, perhaps, is that the economy of exchange between the written and the oral may operate on different principles. Kaviraj (1992b: 28–29) argues that in traditional India the class of people who jealously guarded their privilege of reading and writing, the Brahmins, nevertheless relied heavily on memory and oral recitation for the transmission and preservation of knowledge. This has more to do with a knowledge tradition in which speech and intonation are closely linked to transcendental knowledge and in which the theory of speech is far better elaborated than an epistemology of writing.[21]

The continuing importance of the written, rather than its displacement, is true even of the second epoch of orality in the West. Witness, for example, the morning programs on U.S. television; one of their regular features is a glance at the headlines of leading newspapers. Rather than see the written in opposition to the oral, one needs to pay attention, historically and in the present, to modes of intertextuality. What moderns may be witnessing is not so much the displacement of the written by the oral, but a new relation of exchange between their respective economies (Stock 1983).

An example from my fieldwork might help make this point clearer. The bureaucrats, all literate, who had gathered for the Kisan Seva Kendra mentioned above were debating a fine point about what uses could be made of the money allocated for this new program. For instance, if they were required to be in a village all day long, could the money be used to buy chairs so that they could sit down comfortably? The secretary replied that the scheme contained no provision for purchasing equipment or for building a space where they could gather. Having said this, he took out a long, cyclostyled sheet of paper from his bag and said, "You can read it for yourself." This was passed around, and, at the request of the others, a land records official agreed to read it aloud for the benefit of everyone present. The government order (GO) was signed by the Chief Secretary of the provincial U.P. state government. It gave detailed instructions as to who was to attend the Kisan Seva Kendra, what its function was supposed to be, and how that function was to be achieved. It listed all the people who were to be present. Some officials, for example, land records officials (*patwaris*), an agriculture development officer (ADO), the secretary, the village development officers, and the auxiliary nurse midwives were expected to be present every Thursday. Linemen from the Electricity Department and representatives of the Irrigation Department were to attend on the first and third Thursdays of the month. Tubewell operators were expected to be at the tubewells at that time. The directive ordered the officials not to waste time but to ensure that the day was spent productively. All the officials were required to attend from 9:30 A.M. to 5 P.M. The order also proposed that a suitable place be found for the centers to operate and advised that a board identifying the center be put up at that site. If a problem could not be solved at the center, the order suggested that the officials present refer the matter to departments higher up the bureaucratic hierarchy.

Several interesting aspects underlie this oral performance. The officials who had gathered at the Kisan Seva Kendra came from different departments of the bureaucracy. The GO, which required them to attend, had been sent to the heads of their respective departments, who had presumably read it and told them what they were expected to do. Apart from the secretary, none of them had actually seen the GO. That was one level at which the written had already been translated into the oral. When the secretary produced the order, it could have been passed from one person to the next, each of whom could have read it silently, for they were all literate and well versed in bureaucratic prose. Yet there was a call for reading it aloud, not merely because such an act speeded up the transmission of the text and therefore was more efficient, but also because oral communication allowed for commentary, discussion, and debate. They could interrupt the person reading, interject comments, voice criticism, and debate various points. Reading aloud created a community of subalternity shaped by the GO: it was highly unlikely that all these lower-level officials from various branches of the bureaucracy would have ever found themselves in the same space. What brought them together, uniting them in this uneasy space of companionship, was an order from above that all of them roundly criticized as a waste of time.

These examples from the Kisan Seva Kendra also demonstrate the directionality of the flow of forms of communication. Both written and oral communications as well as translations from one to the other traveled easily from higher levels of authority to lower ones. It was much more difficult for something in writing to go up the hierarchy, from lower-level bureaucrats or especially from poor, rural peoples. The inability of poor subalterns to send writing up the hierarchy was due to the fear of getting involved with the state rather than due to the unfamiliarity with writing, although familiarity with writing also usually implied a greater knowledge of the world of bureaucracy, which might contribute to a greater willingness to engage the state. State officials like Asha Agarwal, the head of the ICDS program in Mandi Block, were frustrated when they received oral complaints from villagers about day care centers that were not functioning. Such complaints were useless because officials could not act on the basis of oral complaints. When Agarwal tried to persuade villagers to give her a written complaint, they almost never followed through. "The problem," she told me, "is that with government work, unless you have something in writing, you cannot build a case and take any action."[22] Clanchy (1979: 2) argues that trust in writing develops over time and is the result of a "growing familiarity with documents." Here again is a progressivist narrative of total literacy. If one views restricted literacy as a transitional phase from total illiteracy to a condition of universal literacy, then (and perhaps only then) such a formulation makes sense. But if restricted literacy is seen as the normal condition for most people in the history of humankind, then "familiarity with documents" has little correlation with people's trust or distrust of writing.[23] For instance, poor people in rural north India have long been familiar with documents such as deeds of land-ownership. Here, the attitude toward writing is determined not by people's relationship to writing but by their relationship with the state.

Structural violence here is not perpetuated by the writing of state officials. Conversely, neither is the ability to combat structural violence dependent on literacy. Structural violence certainly does articulate with illiteracy, but it does not do so in the manner that most people presume. Poor people are not subject to structural violence because they lack papers or because they lack the ability to read the writing of state officials.[24] They suffer from structural violence because they lack assets, and, more important, they lack the means to acquire assets and access to services that might enable them to survive. Their ability to acquire productive assets through loans and grants distributed by the state, from milch cattle to small pieces of village land, may be facilitated by literacy but are not dependent on it. Whether a poor family gets a sixth of an acre of common land through state redistribution programs aimed at providing land to the landless has more to do with that family's political connections or its capacity to pay the relevant officials for getting supposedly free land than with the ability of one of its members to write a petition or to fill out a form. In the struggle for survival, literacy is often quite helpful, but it is by no means essential.

The Irrational Reverence for Degrees and Documents

Given Weber's characterization of modern state bureaucracies as the embodiment of instrumental rationality, one of the abiding paradoxes I found during my fieldwork was that bureaucrats at all levels in U.P. treated degrees and formal educational qualifications with a reverence that can only be characterized as irrational in its excessiveness and in its lack of connection between means and ends. A parallel phenomenon was to be found in the manner that subaltern peoples treated documents, almost as if they believed them to possess magical powers. Documents embodied and congealed state power. They were invested with the aura of the state and therefore had to be safeguarded in one's possession. Brought out of its hiding place at the appropriate time, a document could produce magical effects for a poor person in the form of a grant or a state-subsidized loan.

One influential explanation for the importance given to educational qualifications in modern bureaucracies is offered by Weber (1968: 1000). Educational achievements and particularly success in competitive examinations serve to create a privileged class in government service, although Weber (1968: 999–1000) points out that such competitions are not limited to bureaucratic structures and are to be found even in professions such as medicine and law.[25] Acquiring a "patent of education" becomes a powerful means of social distinction and creates among bureaucratic circles a meritocratic aura that is a modern analog of the "proof of ancestry" in the feudal world (1968: 1000). The irony inherent in a system that produces an elite from a meritocratic process is not lost on Weber. In his view, what makes modern bureaucracies effective and efficient is that they recruit individuals based on talent, as evidenced by success in competitive examinations, and not on birth or class position. But Weber also appreciates the danger that there is little to prevent such a group from acquiring the trappings of aristocracy, one whose privilege is founded not on birth or landed property but rather on a "patent of education."

Not surprisingly, the bureaucrats I worked with in India unambiguously subscribed to the view that educational qualifications and success in examinations were an index to a person's intelligence and capability. Education represented competence; for the same reason, incompetence was usually explained by a lack of education. These bureaucrats appeared to subscribe to the theory that in the absence of full information about a person's intelligence and abilities, educational qualifications functioned to screen candidates and to signal their abilities to an employer. Even in the absence of any empirical confirmation of a positive correlation between education and competence, such a correlation was widely held to be true among all levels of the bureaucracy. The dismissive attitude bureaucrats adopt in dealing with poor villagers has its roots in their general devaluation of people who are not educated.

For instance, when I first met the two engineers Das and Chowdhury at the block office (see chapter 4), they voiced severe criticism of the staff employed at the office. They had been questioning one of Malik's subordinates about some matter and were dissatisfied with his response. "The problem," said Chowdhury, "is that they are uneducated and don't really know what they are doing." Rather than blaming the individual officer for incompetence, Chowdhury offered a general explanation that connected his poor performance with his educational background. The two engineers then proceeded to strongly criticize Malik, in whose office they were sitting (he had not yet arrived at the office). Talking about the poor quality of the staff, one of them commented that when the head of the block office himself was uneducated, one could not expect much from the staff. The engineer noted that Malik had only a high school education. As an ADO, he used to be an assistant to the BDO and then received a promotion to his current job. The implication was that Malik was not educated enough to justify his status and was not placed in such a position by doing well in a competitive exam. Rather, he had been promoted to his current position by dint of seniority.[26]

As I listened to the engineers I learned that this outburst against the block staff had been provoked by their frustration at an inquiry they were conducting into the activities of a headman. The engineers had prepared a report critical of the headman and needed Malik's signature to corroborate their findings. He had apparently refused to sign, while stating that he was in full agreement with the findings of the report. Perhaps knowing that the engineers were coming that day, Malik had not arrived at the office. Finally, a messenger was dispatched to Malik's house to secure a signature, but he came back empty-handed. Not knowing how to resolve the impasse, one of Malik's staff signed the document and put the seal of the BDO on the paper. The engineers told me that Malik was reluctant to sign the document because everyone was afraid of being implicated in inquiries into headmen. They attributed such fear not to the real political pressures he would have to encounter by doing so but on his lack of education. In other words, rather than seeing his reluctance to endorse a document that would have had a high political cost for him (much higher than for the engineers, who were relatively insulated) as a rational response to his structural position, it was interpreted as proof of his lack of ability and low level of education.

The connection between education and competence was so completely taken for granted that it occasioned comment only when there was a lack of fit. When an official saw a less educated subordinate doing a better job than a more educated one, she or he searched hard for explanations that might fit this seeming anomaly. Once when I accompanied Agarwal on an inspection trip, I was struck by her system of classifying anganwadi workers by their educational achievements. The first thing she told me about each of the four centers we visited that day was the anganwadi workers' educational qualifications. In the first village we visited both of the anganwadi workers were upper-caste women. Agarwal informed me that the worker at the first center we visited was "only high school pass." The teacher at the second center in the same village had a master of arts degree. As we were heading out of the village Agarwal commented on the contrast between the two centers. The children at the center run by the worker who only had a high school degree seemed better taught, and the teacher appeared more enthusiastic than the teacher with the higher degree. Agarwal seemed troubled by this discrepancy. She told me that in the past she had found the teacher who had a master's to be very good, and she was therefore surprised that we had found that the children in her center appeared to be so underprepared. Rather than straightforwardly attributing the positive results of the first center to the hard work and enthusiasm of the teacher, Agarwal was troubled by the anomaly that a less educated worker appeared to have obtained better results with her pupils.

The first center we visited in the next village was poorly run: the teacher was unenthusiastic, and the children did not seem to know the alphabet or any songs. When we left, Agarwal expressed surprise at the poor performance of the pupils. She told me that previously this had been one of the best centers in the entire block. The center was run by a scheduled-caste woman with a bachelor of arts degree who had applied for the post of supervisor in the department, a post just below that which Agarwal, the CDPO, occupied. The worker attributed the children's performance to the fact that a number of them had recently left the center to join the primary school in the village. Thus she had a new batch of students who had not yet learned much. Agarwal appeared to accept this explanation. When we went to the second center in that village Agarwal informed me that the older, higher-caste woman who ran it was "high school pass." Here the children presented a refreshing contrast to the other center in the same village: they were enthusiastic, knew the number table and the alphabet very well, and were enjoying the experience of being in school, despite the fact that their classroom was in a cowshed, literally cheek by jowl with several cows and buffaloes tethered there.

On our way out of this village there followed a very interesting discussion between Agarwal and one of the subordinates who had accompanied us on the trip. They talked of the pros and cons of hiring people who were overqualified for the job of anganwadi worker. Agarwal commented that of the four centers we had seen that day, the two that were functioning well were operated by workers with high school degrees, whereas the two poorly run ones were supervised by workers with higher educational qualifications. Agarwal speculated that anganwadi workers whose qualifications exceeded the minimum—a high school degree—felt that the job was below their dignity.[27] They were always on the lookout for a better job that would give them a real salary, perhaps as a teacher in a government-certified school; they accepted the job of anganwadi worker solely because of the lack of other opportunities for employment. Agarwal concluded that it was a mistake to hire overqualified people because they always felt underappreciated.

What was interesting to me about the discussion between Agarwal and her subordinate was how they framed the problem for which they were searching for an explanation. Rather than posing the question in terms of how the success or failure of centers could be attributed to a range of explanatory factors—the experience of the teacher; the workers' level of enthusiasm; the age of the children; how hardworking the teacher was; how convenient the anganwadi was for its target population; and the like—they instead focused almost entirely on the teachers' educational qualifications. Why did they assume that was the critical factor? The relationship between educational qualifications and competence was so strongly inscribed in their minds that when they ran into facts that appeared to contradict this assumption they were genuinely puzzled. What need not be said because it was a part of the common sense of bureaucrats then explicitly became an object of discourse. Although not obvious from the example of the two villages presented above, associating competence with education level was significant because most of the less educated anganwadi workers were lower caste and tended to be poorer than those with higher educational qualifications.

It is in this sense that one can say the reverence for degrees was irrational. It did not rest on any logical, reasoned argument that deduced competence from specific features of the educational process. One could argue, for example, that in order to obtain higher degrees people needed to cultivate qualities like discipline, the ability to work hard and to meet deadlines, the ability to apply existing knowledge to new situations, and so on. Someone with such a degree might therefore be expected to do a better job than someone who did not demonstrate such qualities or did not have the opportunity to develop these qualities, as evidenced from their previous record. But I never once heard such arguments being articulated. For state officials it could truly be said that degrees were something irrationally reverenced. Yet degrees could also be seen as a fetish in the Marxist sense: as the products of alienated labor—characterized by rote learning and the mass production of graduates and dependent on the production of answer sheets under time pressure in exams—that stood as objects that had power over their producers, that is, the real power to determine their prospects and life chances.

If degrees were treated as fetish objects by state officials, documents produced by the state were invested with magical powers by the clients of state programs. Although subaltern and illiterate people were especially likely to treat written documents as objects with inherent powers, to some degree that view was held by all the subjects of the state.[28] Such documents were invested with the aura of the state. I found that a villager, particularly an illiterate one, would carefully keep every written communication from a bureaucratic office as if it were a sacred object. It would be wrapped in paper, then perhaps in cloth, and the cloth would then be carefully placed in a metal trunk, along with other precious commodities, and kept inside the sole room in the village house that was protected from the elements. Dust was the greatest enemy. Dust would get inside every little nook and cranny in the house, and paper, particularly if it was not of high quality (and usually it was not), disintegrated quickly once it was exposed to dust. And village homes for the most part were exposed to the elements. People spent the larger part of their lives in the open; most families had neither a compelling need nor the resources to build brick-enclosed rooms. Even well-to-do rural residents built several small rooms within a large open courtyard surrounded by high walls. Of these rooms, one might be completely enclosed with a door that could be locked. The other rooms were typically made of thatched roofs and lacked doors. All the household's valuables, including jewelry and cash, were hidden away in large locked metal boxes in the closed room. It is here that documents were usually stashed away, like so many hidden treasures, protected from the depredations of dust (see also Steedman 2001).

At first, this attitude toward documents might appear to stress the unusual importance given to state writing by people at the margins of literacy. But how different is it from our own practices of putting presumed valuable documents in safe deposit boxes in banks? After all, documents like a birth certificate, a title deed, or a passport are not originals in the sense that a record of them exists in the appropriate bureaucratic office and a new copy can theoretically be made. What makes these documents valuable is that, in practice, obtaining copies even in this information age is quite expensive in terms of time and effort. Perhaps bureaucratic offices make the retrieval of such information difficult for their clients precisely because the authority of these offices is inversely related to the ease with which they part with such materials.

Like genies, such texts, produced at the right moments, can have magical effects. Goody (1986: 17) explains that texts such as "'The Book of Magic' flourished in situations of restricted literacy partly because its interpretation was a specialized task."[29] In such a context the written word attains a charismatic power in and of itself, a process that Goody terms "grapholatry" (1986: 16). The place where this is most explicit is Tibet: "The illiterate cannot use a book in his praying, except to hold it in his hands and raise it to his forehead to 'rub off the blessing' as he intones the syllable OHm" (Ekvall in Goody 1986: 15). The prayer wheel of Tibetan Buddhism combined rotary motion with the power of the printed or written word "to enable illiterates to gain the merit that comes from reading the scriptures" (Ekvall in Goody 1986: 16). The spell that writing has on illiterate people cannot be interpreted apart from its use as an instrument of domination by religious and bureaucratic elites (two groups that are closely related in a theocratic state like Tibet). It is not surprising that one of the first actions of those involved in peasant movements, particularly millenarian ones, is to destroy state records dealing with land and taxes (Guha 1983). Lest one think of this as an archaic practice, recent incidents point to the contrary. When farmers in the southern Indian state of Karnataka attacked the offices of Monsanto as part of a protest against globalization, they ransacked its offices, threw all the files onto the street five floors below, and set them on fire (Gupta 1998).[30]

The power possessed by the documents of modern bureaucracies has little to do with the aura of their creators (see also Das 2004; Tarlo 2003). This is in sharp contrast to the officials described by Messick, whose social standing, depending upon their personal qualities of uprightness and moral probity, invested a document with authenticity and was unlike the "sensuously curved" seals that registered an official's unique imprint (1993: 224, 242). However, as we shall presently see, the authenticity of documents continues to be an important problem: the loss of the aura of the object did not eliminate the problem of authenticity.[31] State documents were continually shadowed by their doubles, the counterfeit, or duplicate in local parlance in western U.P., and the illegitimate copy. The counterfeit represented but one strategy by which subaltern groups contested the dominance of bureaucratic writing.

Weapons of the Weak?

If one believes that writing is the medium by which bureaucrats perpetuate structural violence on poor, rural people, then it makes sense to focus on literacy as the chief weapon in the fight against such violence. This is one reason that literacy, and writing in particular, is often seen as an essential element in subaltern struggles for liberation and empowerment. But is the degree of faith shown in such a prescription justified? I complicate this picture of the empowering effects of literacy by considering the links between writing, democracy, and liberation.

I first examine the possibilities and limits of an approach that emphasizes the emancipatory promise of literacy because it is often presumed that the best way for subaltern groups to oppose the domination exercised by literate elites is to become literate, to use the master's tools. I then discuss not just writing in a narrow sense, but the broader connections and disjunctures between democratic participation and literacy. I explore the ambivalences and contradictions of structural violence based on literacy in a political situation in which illiterate people are, for the most part, enthusiastic participants in democratic processes. In other words, what conflicts are engendered by the discrepancy between a high degree of political literacy and a low level of functional literacy? Last, I look at the production and circulation of illegitimate forms of writing that mimic and copy official bureaucratic writing. The term *duplicate* in rural U.P. connotes, as noted, both copy and counterfeit. Duplicate writing is to be found wherever state documents are necessary and requires a theory of the counterfeit that sees it as not merely a response to domination, but as coeval with state writing. Put together, these three themes will illuminate how exactly literacy is implicated in structural violence.

WRITING BACK

I argued above that the procedures of the Indian state, like those of modern states in general, privilege writing and devalue oral forms of communication. Oral forms were treated with suspicion, as being unreliable and untrustworthy, whereas written communication was perceived to be stable in its expression and meaning.[32] Given the importance of writing in state procedures, literacy is essential if subaltern peoples are to prevent exploitation at the hands of bureaucratic elites. Hence becoming literate is one very important strategy of empowerment for poor, semiliterate, and illiterate populations. Almost all the illiterate people I knew in rural U.P. were acutely aware of how much they were disadvantaged by not knowing how to read and write and were fully committed to preventing their children from sharing such a fate. For the same reason, lower-class and lower-caste people who were literate and who had perhaps even attained a school education were much more comfortable in dealing with state officials and better at safeguarding their interests against such officials. Given this fact, it is ironic that states often mount adult literacy campaigns in order to protect the poor from exploitation by moneylenders and other rapacious groups. State elites almost never consider that an important use of literacy might be to empower the poor against the state.[33]

If writing was not employed in exploitation, literacy would not become a tool of empowerment against structural violence. However, the belief in the liberating potential of literacy is not confined to situations such as this. Literacy campaigns have often been the first major actions undertaken by popular socialist revolutionary governments, such as those in Cuba and China. Efforts to achieve full literacy share a teleological narrative about civilizations that posits a historical evolution from near-complete illiteracy to complete literacy. Within India such a narrative is used to distinguish the southern states, which have high literacy rates, exemplified by Kerala, and the so-called Bimaru states of the north, which generally have much lower rates of literacy and, overall, much lower rates of economic growth.[34] Even in the West such a narrative came to fruition only with the imposition of compulsory schooling in the early nineteenth century (Boyd and King 1995). Historians have often interpreted the degree of literacy of a society as "an essential mark of civilization" (Clanchy 1979: 7).[35] However, such a view assumes that situations of restricted literacy, a term in which the teleology of complete literacy is already present, are somehow anomalous and that movement toward complete and full literacy is the natural progression of societies. In the modern world, one might say that the assumption of full literacy shapes everything from the design of road signs to that of computers.[36] Even when icons are employed, they are accompanied by letters, and very often written signs are used exclusively even when icons would have been more effective.

If one resists such a teleology and recognizes that in the past two thousand years the vast majority of people in the world lived in situations in which only a small group of individuals knew how to read and write (Goody 1986: 4–5), then the narrative of literacy as liberation becomes problematic. So widely held and so naturalized has this relationship become that it seems almost reactionary to argue that literacy is not essential to liberation and empowerment. Yet I argue that there are at least three good reasons to resist this comfortable assumption.

The first reason has to do with the unraveling of the binary encoding of literacy. It is difficult to establish definitively whether someone with low levels of proficiency in reading and writing is literate or illiterate; for a population, it is almost never the case that it is fully literate or fully illiterate. Combined, these two problems demonstrate that the idea of a fully literate population is a mirage masking situations that may be closer to restricted literacy and propagating an ideology by which countries in the North continue to assert their fully modern status vis-à-vis the global South. Rather, literacy should be thought of as a gradient, both for an individual and for a population (Collins and Blot 2003). One can begin with an elementary distinction between the capacity to read and the capacity to write.[37] Would we say that a person who can read is literate if he cannot write? Is it enough to consider a minimal definition of literacy in terms of reading or writing ability, or should one really be thinking of their degree of functional literacy? Is someone who knows how to read and sign his or her name literate? Would one classify an individual who can write but not do basic mathematics as literate? In an advanced capitalist nation-state, is an individual who cannot compose a letter or memo literate? How would one characterize the literacy of a person who does not know how to operate an automated bank teller machine or a computer? Paulo Freire, in his pioneering work The Pedagogy of the Oppressed (1970), emphasized how much literacy depends on political context. Teaching someone to read and write is not what leads to liberation; rather, liberation is gained by how he or she is taught to read and write and what uses are made of that literacy. In Freire's understanding of literacy, the pedagogical and the political are inextricably linked. A fully literate population, in this view, would be one that is mobilized against oppression and exploitation.

This brings me to the second point that bears on the relationship between literacy and resistance. Literacy in the sense of being lettered is not by itself a guarantee that subaltern peoples will be able to improve their life situation, either by being better able to fight oppression or by finding avenues for upward mobility. It might be true that literacy enables both of these consequences, at least for some people, so that a small proportion of newly literate subalterns are affected, but the ability to read and write may also have the opposite consequence. The ability to read, especially, can lead to new possibilities of co-optation and incorporation into hegemonic projects. Literary forms as disparate as the novel, the newspaper, and the popular magazine are then able to interpellate subaltern subjects into hegemonic projects. Clanchy (1979: 8) recognizes this when he says there is "little sociological evidence to suggest that a minimal ability to read and write has released proletariats in modern societies from mental confinement." Such an understanding is caught up in a telos in which literacy is seen as having opened up worlds of possibilities for upper-class people. This is often what provides the pedagogic justification for fiction: reading fiction, it is said, broadens one's mental horizons.[38] Disregarding the class prejudices implicit in Clanchy's statement, one can only note that in the United States nonfiction consistently outsells fiction in the bestseller lists.

My third and final reason for resisting the easy equation of literacy with liberation follows from a new emphasis on the oral in the postmodern world. In the standard narrative, as societies become modern they move from illiteracy to partial literacy to full literacy. In this rendering, as societies move to full literacy, writing achieves dominance over orality. Communication theorists are now positing a new epoch of orality in which telephones, televisual media, and soundscapes are becoming more important culturally and socially than the written word. This is the lesson sometimes deduced from the decline of newspaper subscriptions and from survey data showing that in the contemporary United States more people get their news from television than from newspapers. Following the conventions of popular history, the rise or revaluation of the oral is accompanied by prophecies of an epoch of orality replacing a now-superannuated epoch of writing. Clanchy (1979: 8) appears to subscribe to such a view when he writes that the technology of writing "may be entering its final century." If, on the contrary, we view the history of literacy not as one in which written modes have replaced oral ones but one in which the two have comfortably coexisted for at least two millennia (see, for instance, Messick 1993: 21–30), then we should expect not that the new forms of orality will necessarily replace the written word but that they will create a new configuration of the communicative field. However, there are profound political implications of this new epoch of orality for societies in which only a small proportion of people is literate. The spectacle and the performative achieve a new prominence when technologies for disseminating oral performance, for example, television, radio, and sound recording, become dominant.

A critical difference exists, however, between the technology of oral transmission in the presence of a speaker and the televisual or telephonic transmission of that person's speech. Therefore, in thinking about the political consequences of orality we should distinguish between various technologies of orality, just as we need to make a distinction between handwritten letters and e-mail. Orality when the speaker is present in the same space as the hearer is not the same thing as when she or he is present on the television screen: what matters here is not the presence or absence of orality as the mediation of the voice. The new age of orality is not a return to a previous situation or even simply an extension of it, but constitutes a completely different situation, one in which politics cannot be equated with modes of oral communication mediated by face-to-face presence. That said, these new technologies of oral communication offer a new way for politicians to reach and create their formally illiterate constituents, which, in turn, has profound implications for the nature of democracy.

A closer examination of the ideas of literacy and literate societies does not clearly lead us to the conclusion that literacy has a central role to play in empowering the poor to mitigate the effects of structural violence or that it has the kind of efficacy often ascribed to it by romantic ideas that focus on its role in mobilizing subaltern consciousness. For literacy to be effective in the fight against structural violence, one needs to pay attention not just to the fact of literacy itself but to the political contexts in which literacy develops. Literacy opens up new possibilities of hegemonic incorporation as much as it does novel avenues of subaltern resistance. Furthermore, the possibilities of political empowerment opened up by oral media such as television and mobile telephony have made the link between structural violence and state writing less decisive for the lives and livelihoods of the poor.

If literacy is taken as a precondition for empowerment in general, it is considered even more essential in republican forms of government. Can a democratic politics survive without literate citizens? How can illiterates exercise a responsible vote? These questions loomed large for Indian leaders at the time of Independence in 1947. Under colonialism, even in the context of the limited opportunities for self-rule, the franchise had been far from universal.[39] Nor were there good examples to draw upon from the Western historical experience, in which disenfranchised groups had to wage a protracted struggle for the rights to suffrage. The struggle for women to attain the right to vote is well known, as is the continuing difficulty that African Americans and other minorities face in order to exercise their voting rights. In most of the debates about the extension of suffrage, literacy was not the primary reason for denying these groups the right to vote. There was almost no historical precedent when the Indian state decided after Independence to conduct the experiment of universal suffrage in a country where literacy rates hovered around 30 percent.[40]

Literacy rates are uniformly lower in rural areas, and they continue to be highly correlated to class and gender. At least in north India, poor, rural women are the least likely to be literate.[41] Universal suffrage did not just constitute an experiment in giving illiterate people the ability to participate in governance: it simultaneously sought to empower the poor through the ballot box. The central leadership, particularly Nehru, firmly believed that poverty in the countryside was owing to institutional inequalities rather than poor productivity. The leadership hoped that giving poor people the vote would help reverse inequalities of power in the countryside peacefully. China served as India's main competitor in the race for development, and the leadership in India was anxious to avoid the Chinese example of agrarian change through violent revolution. Universal suffrage, it was believed, would allow the poor majority to vote their class position and elect to office representatives who would look after their interests.

Given that India's population constituted one-third that of the non-Western world, the decision to grant universal suffrage to all adults dramatically increased the proportion of the world's population living in a democracy. To appreciate how radical a decision universal suffrage constituted in India shortly after Independence in 1947, one need only remember that universal suffrage was obtained in Great Britain as recently as 1928, with the granting of voting rights to women after a lengthy struggle. Less than two decades separated full voting rights for all citizens in a long-established democracy and in the first of the new nation-states from which the yoke of colonial rule had just been lifted.

In this context, one has to think about the exact relationship between literacy and democracy. What does one mean by democracy? Much of the discussion about whether illiterate people can be responsible citizens centers on the procedures for voting. Literacy is taken as the necessary condition of democratic politics because it is assumed that illiterate citizens would find it hard to be informed voters. How would they read campaign materials and party platforms? how would they learn about individuals if they could not read newspapers or pamphlets and flyers describing what candidates stood for? Even something like reading the names on a ballot becomes a challenge not only for the voter but also for election officials, who have to design the ballot to accommodate voters who are illiterate. Furthermore, there were questions about whether literacy would have to be a requirement for elected officials. How could elected officials represent their constituency if they could not read the bills on which they had to vote and if they could not write legislation themselves? And would such politicians lower the quality of democracy because they were untutored in the conventions of parliamentary procedure and debate on the floor of the house? Like the ballot, parliamentary procedure itself had to be altered to accommodate representatives who were on the margins of literacy.

The Indian experience demonstrates that the procedures of democracy do not require literacy and that a vigorous democracy can flourish in the absence of formal literacy. What is far more essential is political literacy, and my point here is that political literacy does not depend on formal literacy as a precondition.[42] A fully or largely literate population is neither necessary nor sufficient for political literacy. If it were necessary, then flourishing democracies like India could not exist without a functionally literate population. If it were sufficient, then we would find functioning democracies everywhere that literate populations are to be found, and we know from the histories of dictatorships that this is often not the case.[43]

My point is that arguments positing literacy as a requirement for democracy operate under a notion of democracy that is largely formal instead of substantive.[44] The excitement in scholarly as well as political circles over the rapid expansion of democracy in the wake of the Cold War is largely limited to the institution of formal democracy. This includes, most importantly, the conduct of free and fair elections. But it also emphasizes universal suffrage for all adults, including ethnic, linguistic, and religious minorities, and the commitment to a competitive electoral system of government with at least two parties. The emphasis here is on procedural fairness and transparency. When one begins to ask about the connection between literacy and substantive democracy as political and economic empowerment, the questions raised become even more acute. By substantive democracy I mean what Kaviraj (2003: 146) describes as "an alternative, Tocquevillean reading of democracy's success—which is not just a continuation of a system of [elected] government, but the capacity of this government to produce long-term egalitarian effects." Is it possible to think about upward mobility of the most disenfranchised segments of a nation-state's population without the benefit of literacy? How, exactly, can empowerment and enfranchisement occur among groups that are illiterate or on the margins of functional literacy?[45] Also, is it not ironic that multilateral institutions are urging Third World governments to cut expenditures on elementary schooling in the name of fiscal discipline while heavily promoting formal democracy and voter education in those very countries? The appearance of democracy seems to be increasing in symbolic significance at the same time that the conditionalities imposed by multilateral institutions and foreign aid undermine governments' ability to determine their own economic and financial future.

One should be careful, however, not to dismiss formal democracy. Ideally, the rule of law and the creation of a space for public discussion and debate enable citizens to live without fear of arbitrary state violence (Habermas 1989). Stripped of its utopian possibilities, such a space of public debate emerges with its dual properties of publicness and stratification. Language hierarchies, for instance, may make debates among elites in fora like newspapers and television simultaneously public and yet inaccessible to the majority of the population. In the Indian public sphere, for instance, debates among educated elites on English-language television channels have this property of being public and yet incomprehensible to most of the nation's population.[46] In this regard, it behooves one to pay attention to the terms in which *democracy* is understood and negotiated in different languages: what are the words and concepts through which people participate in democracy (Nugent 2009; Schaffer 2000; West 2009)?[47] The importance of deepening democracy was one important reason the leadership of the postcolonial Indian state reorganized regional states along linguistic lines. Kaviraj (1992: 56–57) comments sardonically that "Nehru agreed to linguistic reorganization because of the undeniable force of the argument of democracy—that use of the vernacular in administration would bring government closer to the people, because that was the language they were illiterate in."

Unlike Western nation-states, which have witnessed a rolling back of substantive democracy over the past few decades under neoliberal regimes, India over the past fifty years has seen formal democracy metamorphose into an expansive state-led project that is ideologically committed to equality. Kaviraj (2003: 159) argues that such an egalitarian commitment has not taken the form of equalizing incomes, but of "a real redistribution of dignity." He is referring to a fundamental shift in formal politics in which lower-caste parties have successfully pressed for recognition and representation.[48] It is in this context that the violence of poverty described in this book has to be situated. If the state in India were ideologically opposed to redistributive measures or uninterested in redressing deep-seated historical inequities, it would make the lack of urgency in eradicating poverty much easier to understand. It is this commitment to equality, to the redistribution of dignity, and to the inclusion of the formerly marginal in the national project that makes the continued violence enacted on the poor so paradoxical.

One of the chief forms in which demands for dignity are pursued is in the sphere of employment.[49] Although the Indian Constitution does not allow private firms to be required to hire a certain percentage of lower-caste workers, this is not the case with government agencies and the entire publicly funded higher education system. Quotas arouse some of the same ire among upper classes and conservatives in India as in the United States, but quotas are an important and enduring feature of government policy. What makes the Indian case unique is that no major political party—not even the right wing, conservative Hindu nationalists who have become such important players on the national political scene—has publicly opposed the system of quotas. For any major party to come out openly against them would be political suicide; it would have to face potentially massive retaliation at the ballot box. Instead, the strategy has been to pursue a neoliberal agenda in which cutting the size of government and making government jobs less attractive compared with the private sector makes the quantity and quality of these positions less important. Similarly, by allowing private higher educational institutions to exist, the significance of a reserved quota of seats for admission into government colleges declines. These processes are slow, however: setting up a high-quality, prestigious new college or slashing the number of government employees is difficult. Therefore, for the medium run, quotas will continue to play a central economic and political role.

In the public sphere there is little contestation of quotas, but in everyday conversation quotas for lower castes are the object of the articulation of acute class and caste antagonisms.[50] Every government job has specified minimum educational qualifications and maximum-age requirements. If a job is reserved for a lower-caste person, then the minimum educational requirements are usually lower and the maximum age usually higher than they are for a general position for which eligibility is not restricted to lower-caste candidates. The quota system put in place to remedy extensive, deep-seated, and continuing discrimination against lower-caste people runs up squarely against the conceptions of meritocracy referred to earlier, in which exams are so central. So much are the two sets of prejudices conjoined that when upper-caste officials see evidence of supposed incompetence, they automatically assume that the incompetent person must be lower caste and must have obtained his position illegitimately, by meeting lowered standards of competence. So, for example, one of the engineers mentioned earlier who was scornfully ascribing the BDO's incompetence to his low educational qualifications then went on to say, "An additional problem is that the reservation system has brought in many people who are simply incompetent. They don't understand what is to be done and don't have the capability to carry out their tasks." Since neither the BDO nor any of his staff (to the engineers' knowledge) was lower caste, such a statement was neither relevant to their concerns nor had any basis in their experience with the field staff. It was a general prejudice that gained its efficacy from endless repetition rather than from its correspondence with any empirical reality.

Historically, it is unclear whether the ubiquity of meritocratic discourse among upper-caste bureaucrats first arose with the system of quotas for lower-caste groups; however, it has certainly intensified since there have been enough lower-caste people whose educational qualifications enable them to meet the quotas left unfilled for many years. In my experience, even lower-caste people rarely contested the idea that selection for state jobs should be meritocratic. Very few people argued that a commitment to the principles of justice or of equality required one to support the granting of positions to oppressed groups in society, no matter what the merit of the applicant.[51] Oddly enough, the debate did not hinge on how merit was to be ascertained: almost everyone agreed that grades and educational qualifications were appropriate guides to merit. The only difference between opposing positions depended on whether one thought it appropriate to lower the educational qualifications necessary to obtain jobs in the reserved quota. That debate did bring questions of justice and equality to the table but in a limited framework.

If one were to translate the views of bureaucrats in order to situate them in the history of academic theorizing on bureaucracy, there would appear to be widespread consensus in India that a bureaucracy ought to be Weberian: recruitment ought to be done on the basis of "specialized examinations or tests of expertise" (Weber 1968: 999). And although most people believed that this should be the primary criterion and that people were, on the whole, selected on the basis of their performance in competitive exams, it was also the case that everyone recognized that the system could be manipulated and that with political connections and "pull," one could sometimes subvert the purported criteria.[52]

Such subversion could occur in a number of ways. First, there was the time-honored technique of cheating in the exams (see below). One official told me that an acquaintance of his had boasted that he helped his son pass the school exams by cheating. Once the son got his diploma, the father paid a bribe to get him a job in the police. In his new uniform, the son earned an unofficial monthly income that was more than the total amount he paid to secure the job in the first place, indicating that the bribe had constituted an excellent return on investment. Second, one can use a combination of political advantage and money to ensure that one is chosen ahead of other candidates. Typically, many candidates meet the minimum qualifications for any job. Educational qualifications are thus necessary but rarely sufficient for selection, especially in positions for which no established precedent exists to automatically choose the candidate with the highest grades.

Against Weber's assumption—that bureaucratic selection is meritocratic if it accords with the results of exams and respects educational qualifications—is the view that educational achievement effectively reproduces class hierarchies rather than reflect fairly the distribution of talent and ability. Success in competitive exams depends not only on access to schooling, but also, more important, on the quality of schooling, both of which are heavily dependent on class and on social and geographic location. And then there is the so-called invisible curriculum shaped by teachers and by the cultural capital of the family to which the child belongs (Bourdieu 1996). Finally, there is the ability to translate capital in money form (to pay bribes, for example) into educational capital (a diploma obtained by cheating) and social capital (a job on the police force) (Bourdieu 1986). Far from being meritocratic, Bourdieu argues, educational achievement largely reproduces existing social hierarchies of different forms of capital, allowing for some upward mobility but mainly reflecting conversions from one type of capital to another. A system that depends on success in educational achievement militates against the democratic aspirations of subaltern and lower-caste people. The emphasis on written documents in bureaucratic procedure helps prevent the sweeping changes brought about by democratic processes from radically altering the relations of inequality reproduced by the actions of bureaucratic offices, including caste and class relations within the bureaucracy itself.[53]

In sum, two large social processes are moving in opposite directions, and conflict is inevitable. On the one side is a renewal of democratic politics enabled by the charismatic qualities of the spectacle and oral performance. Television, audio- and video-cassettes, and cable television enable the reproduction of the spectacle, which does not rely as much on the mediation of written language. Political events are now increasingly produced with an eye toward their televisual transmission.[54] The technologies enabling a second epoch of orality in the West have a very different role to play in a social setting in which literacy was never widespread. No longer restricted to an audience that can be reached through writing, a vigorous popular democracy is unleashed in a public sphere marked by competitive politics (Reddy 2005). Although there is much to celebrate in such a situation, one must be wary of its vulnerability to demagoguery, to co-optation by a "passive revolution," or to the real dangers posed by a consolidation of ownership as domestic and global monopoly capitalists eye an increasingly lucrative market.[55]

On the other side stands the fetish of educational qualifications and degrees, which has received a fresh impetus from India's emergence as a world power in coding and back-office work. All that stands in the way of access to global consumer goods is an education that has market value with the corporations, both Indian and multinational, involved in that economy. For those people whose aspiration is that their children participate in this new global economy, writing and literacy are more important than ever before. The lure of degrees, documents, and the written word therefore shows no signs of abating.

What implications does this conflict have for the poor? Will structural violence carried out on the poorest intensify? Or will the new forms of inclusion engendered by a populist politics that is not mediated by literacy enable the amelioration of chronic poverty?[56] Although the evidence is mixed, it does suggest that the pressure of democratic politics, which has seen the election of many lower-caste parties in the poorest states in the north, increases the likelihood that redistributive policies will be enacted. The election of lower-caste legislators in greater numbers has given many poor, lower-caste people the kind of access to the politically powerful they could not have before. At the same time, the high growth rates that have resulted from India's insertion into the global service economy have provided the government with the tax revenues to underwrite redistributive policies. However, the service economy has been built not just on literacy but on a whole system of higher degrees in technical fields. The growth of this economy has also increased the exclusion of the poor because a greater cultural and educational gap now separates them from participation in this sector. Poor people, especially the poor in rural areas, cannot hope to have access to the kind of education that might prepare them for jobs in the new global service economy, especially since it often requires an English education.

The value of degrees and documents is ultimately guaranteed by the state (Bourdieu 1996: 376). Even when such institutions as private universities and schools issue certificates of educational achievement, the state ultimately ensures their authenticity. Private institutions may mimic the state in using elaborate seals, watermarks, and signatures to mark degrees, official transcripts, and other records of educational achievement, but the state's ability to prosecute and incarcerate people who use forged documents underlines private institutions' dependence on the state as the guarantor of symbolic credit. Unlike the theft of personal property, in which the criminal's gain is someone else's loss, producing a fake degree is not a zero-sum game. The person who gains a fake certificate does not thereby take away the certificate of someone else; the action becomes a crime entirely because of its potential impact in devaluing certification as symbolic property.

COUNTERFEIT WRITING

Given the potential consequences of producing illegitimate documents, processes of writing that mimic and copy official writing in another register therefore are extremely important. This is the register of the fake, the forged, and the counterfeit. The chief argument I develop here is that the counterfeit is not to the authentic as the copy is to the original. Not every original work of art or fiction begets a copy. By contrast, every official device that marks a document as authentic begets its shadowy double, the counterfeit. The counterfeit and the authentic are coeval; like Saleem Sinai of *Midnight's Children* (Rushdie 1981), every authentic document brings into the world a shadowy, illegal, and usually subaltern twin. Forgery, Clanchy (1979: 2) notes, is probably as old as writing itself. According to Marc Bloch, forgery flourished in Europe in the eighth century and the ninth (1961: 91–92); forgers of official documents found themselves in the tenth stage of the eighth circle of hell in Dante's inferno (Radnóti 1999: 165). Coins, seals, and religious relics were the objects most often forged in this period, indicating that forgery was always closely associated with state inscription.[57]

Forgery is a creative, positive act (one forges ahead) that challenges the right of the state to authenticate, to adjudicate between the true and the false. Forgery can be a subaltern strategy to undermine the authority of state writing.[58] Perhaps not surprisingly, its etymology leads back to artisanship, with the same connotations of skill and lower-class location (Radnóti 1999: 6). Bourdieu (1996: 376) writes that the certification or validation of educational degrees is one of the ways in which the state acts as "the central bank of symbolic credit." Whether in the form of currency notes, diplomas, or driver's licenses, the counterfeit challenges this symbolic credit.[59] There is no originality in currency notes, which, after all, gain their currency by being exactly like other notes (with identical watermarks, seals, inserted metal, and signatures) except for their serial number. Mwangi (n.d.: 116) points out that fake money differs from real currency in that it is an exact duplicate, with an identical serial number. What makes the copy fake is who authorizes its production rather than any intrinsic property it might possess. Radnóti (1999: 14) observes that "forgery is the democratic satire and parody of the aristocracy of art"; not until the Renaissance was forgery seen to be a moral sin. Even so, forgers have been largely seen as rogues, rascals, and imposters rather than as criminals, and stories about forgers correspondingly stress the picaresque rather than the illegal.[60]

In the case of the programs I studied, it was the "illegibility" of village society in the eyes of state officials that created the conditions for the success of the duplicate document (Scott 1998). In the monthly meeting of anganwadi workers at the main office in Mandi, several women talked about going to their centers. This suggested that, contrary to official policy, some of them were commuting to their centers and did not actually live in the villages where they worked. The head of the ICDS office was telling me about the difficulties she encountered in determining the residency status of prospective anganwadi workers. Proof of residence consisted of getting a certificate from the headman testifying to that fact. The result of this policy was that many women managed to obtain certificates for villages where a position of anganwadi worker had opened up but where they did not, in fact, live. Headmen would provide such certificates of residence in exchange for cash or as a favor to a relative. Recognizing this problem, a new GO had made such certificates of residence harder to obtain. According to the new policy, not only the headman had to certify that a woman was resident in a village, but also another, higher official (the tehsildar). The result, from the standpoint of potential job applicants, was to require them to make many additional trips to the tehsildar's office and bribe two officials instead of one. I found it incomprehensible why the solution to a problem caused by a lack of information about the details of village life (did an applicant actually live in the village she claimed to be from?) was thought to be best resolved by involving an official who was further removed, institutionally and geographically, from the village.

There was a vigorous trade in the production of true documents that was critically mediated by money.[61] The ability to create putatively authentic certificates—for example, of residence, educational achievement, physical fitness for military service—depended on access to money. But money was not enough; one often needed personal connections to get the attention of the relevant official who would agree to produce a fake document on short notice.[62] In this way, symbolic capital, money capital, and social capital in the form of connections and kinship were all tightly linked together.

The counterfeit document flourished in that space of indeterminacy created by the illegibility of rural society in official circles. Even when such information was officially collected, it was not always retrievable nor could it always be trusted. For example, to figure out whether claims to residency were authentic, it might have been possible to use census data or the information collected to ensure the accuracy of electoral rolls. But such data were not easily available to officials such as the CDPO and even if they were, that it would have been of much use, given the unreliability of the collection techniques, was unclear. Women and children were especially scarce in the official record, a situation that the ICDS program was quickly changing (see chapter 7). However, the absence of women and children from the official record furnished the background for duplicate certification to flourish.

The biopolitical project of managing the population depends on good, that is, reliable, trustworthy, accurate statistical data on the population that is to be managed. In the absence of such data, it is doubtful if it makes sense to even talk about biopolitics. As we will see, one of the chief functions of anganwadi workers was to collect such data on women and children, the segment of the population least well documented in the official record (see chapter 7). It is therefore not a little ironic that state officials knew so little about anganwadi workers, including the basic fact of whether they lived in the village where they worked. The counterfeit flourished precisely in the space opened up by the incompleteness of the biopolitical project, a space that the anganwadi workers had been hired to fill. Although their primary job description was that of crèche manager, responsible for bringing benevolent interventions in health, nutrition, and education to poor girls under five years of age, part of the hidden curriculum of the ICDS program was to collect better statistics on poor children (see chapter 7). In the absence of such data, the biopolitical project of taking care of the most vulnerable parts of the population could not be operationalized.

Asha Agarwal was telling me how she checked whether the school certificates that potential job applicants brought to her were genuine. The educational requirements to become an anganwadi worker had been recently raised, and now even Dalit women needed at least a junior high school certificate. The problem, according to Agarwal, was that almost anyone could get a forged certificate from a junior high school and that determining its authenticity was impossible. She was concerned about this: Could a woman with a counterfeit degree shoulder her responsibilities as an anganwadi worker? "For if a person is not educated," Agarwal asked, "how is she going to teach others? And how will she understand what she is told?"

Agarwal asked all prospective applicants to write out sentences for her on a sheet of paper and to perform basic arithmetical tasks. She took a sheet of paper out of her purse and showed me the writing samples of eight candidates who had applied in response to a recent advertisement. She was sympathetic to women who complained of being out of practice; despite obvious differences in their abilities, she felt that all the candidates met the basic requirements for the job. This informal test of Agarwal's had no official standing, and candidates who would have otherwise passed such a test still had to attach a copy of their junior high school certificates to the application. The fear of forgery, therefore, created its own parallel economy of unofficial procedures employed by officials.

Even if the job applicants whom Agarwal was screening had completed junior high school as required, it was highly unlikely they had been given a certificate of completion or had managed to preserve it and carry it with them to the village where they moved after getting married.[63] Because such certification was necessary to be hired as an anganwadi worker, they were likely to obtain a counterfeit document that could be submitted with their application.[64] The fake document attested to an achievement (finishing junior high) that was very likely to be true: what was being forged here was not the underlying property, ability or merit, but the documentary evidence attesting to that ability. Mwangi (n.d.: 115) makes an acute observation in this regard when she says, "Forgeries, confusingly, are real until they are not." In other words, only at the moment of unmasking, of the revelation of falsity, does it become a forgery; until then, it functions like the real thing. In this case, the forgery attested to an ability that was real, so there was no fear that it would be unmasked.[65]

It is often assumed that the counterfeit functions to undermine the legitimacy of state writing. But Das (2004: 245) proposes a radically different way of thinking about forgery. She argues that forgery and mimicry should not be seen as enfeebling the state; rather, they are necessary to the state's legitimacy. Iterability "becomes not a sign of vulnerability but a mode of circulation through which power is produced." She offers examples of community groups and NGOs producing and employing documents that mimic the processes of the Indian state, ironically, often to commute, mitigate, or reverse the ill effects produced by that very state, such as police participation in riots against minorities. Similarly, Tarlo (2003: 74) demonstrates how the mimicry of official writing operates in a field where the lines between the unofficial and the official become blurred. Tarlo shows that the Slum Department officially recognized people as "unauthorized occupants," which gave them certain rights belied by the category. In order to be so recognized, the supplicant had to produce papers drafted by an attorney that offered official proof that they had paid for the plot in question, a purchase that was illegal.

The counterfeit thus shadows the authenticating procedures of the state. While doing fieldwork, I found that the fear of the counterfeit profoundly influenced the modes of operation in the bureaucracies I studied. Malik, the BDO, signed documents with a looping flourish that was more art than signature. He was pleased that it was extremely difficult to copy. He told me very proudly that he had a special signature for drawing money from the treasury, one which could be executed only by holding a fountain pen at a particular angle and which was even more artistic than his normal signature. "This special signature," he boasted, "makes it almost impossible for people to copy [it]."

To the extent that stamp papers, degrees from certified educational institutions, signatures of notaries, government seals, and watermarks authenticate, they create a parallel economy of the inauthentic: the forged and the counterfeit, which constantly threaten, simultaneously, to undermine the authoritativeness of state writing and to multiply its effects and effectiveness. From their vantage point, officials were habituated to see this parallel, often subaltern economy as a threat to the value of official writing. Therefore, the search for ever-more elaborate strategies of authentication, whether these took the form of informal (and, strictly speaking, illegal) tests or consciously elaborated signatures, which functioned in the same manner as the elaborately carved calligraphic seals described by Messick (1993: 241–46). Such strategies of inscription acknowledged the ambivalent authority of state writing. From the perspective of subaltern peoples, duplicate certificates were merely ways to circumvent the arbitrariness of state procedures. Counterfeiting was one more device in a series of measures that enable subaltern resistance to bureaucratic domination. Educating children and participating in the political system to influence people and programs were other strategies effectively employed at the same time.

Conclusion

I complicate a straightforward narrative of bureaucrats using literacy to perpetuate violence on the poor. It is true that the Indian bureaucracy places an inordinate emphasis on the written word. In the context of widespread illiteracy among the poor, such an emphasis appears excessive and can only reinforce the suspicion that it is in place because it enables bureaucrats to control their poor subjects and clients more easily. However, it is useful to reconsider carefully the role of literacy in structural violence in the Indian context.

Regnant views hold that written procedure is essential to institutions such as bureaucracies because written documents preserve and record events and actions, transmit meanings in a more stable, reliable manner across time and space, are less liable to corruption and contradiction, and, in general, are less prone to interpretive error and play. But to what extent are these purported properties of the written defensible? Are such evaluations of the superiority of the written word not the outcome of a teleological view of history in which societies gradually move from illiteracy to full literacy, from barbarism to civilization, from primitive to modern? Taking the example of societies in which restricted literacy has always been the norm, can one reconsider the relationship between the oral and the written such that the first is not merely an inferior version of the second?

The consequences of assuming the superiority of the written over the oral are that the economies of exchange between the written and the oral are overlooked, resulting in the construction of a somewhat simplistic picture of the role of writing in structural violence. I argue strenuously against such an assumption: structural violence is not the straightforward result of literate bureaucrats having access to writing and illiterate villagers not having it. This result partly owes to the fact that, as normally used, the concepts of literacy and illiteracy are inchoate and messily unspecific, and partly because it is simply incorrect to posit that power flows out of the nib of a bureaucrat's pen. Literacy is important, but the rise of populist politics predicated on a new age of orality is reconfiguring the relationship between poor people and legislative and bureaucratic power on the one hand and between writing and orality on the other.

Far from finding radical differences in their attitudes toward the written, I have argued that the irrational reverence bureaucrats had for formal educational achievements was not less magical than the powers attributed by poor, illiterate villagers to official written documents. At least poor people had good reason to correlate those documents with powerful effects; by contrast, state officials' expectation that educational achievement should automatically result in superior performance had no logical explanation. Ironically, state officials were perhaps more likely than villagers to treat a certain kind of literacy, indexed by educational degrees, as possessing inexplicable powers. The fetishization of a certain type of literacy, indexed by degrees of higher education, was much more likely to exist among literate people than among illiterate villagers.

Poor people, in fact, contested the power of literate bureaucrats in a number of ways that were not mutually exclusive. First, almost all poor villagers were extremely keen that their children learn to read and write so that they would be better able to negotiate the world of bureaucratic institutions and perhaps even obtain a government job. Second, participation in the political sphere, facilitated by the new possibilities unleashed by televisual and telecommunication technologies, enabled subaltern rural peoples to put pressure on recalcitrant bureaucracies to act in their favor. Finally, when all else failed, there was always the recourse to mimic state writing by producing counterfeit certificates and affidavits in order to receive benefits and services. The emphasis on writing by bureaucracies was thus combated through mimicry, subversion, and counterdomination through the political process.

The relationship between literacy and structural violence was therefore a complex one. Poor people's ability to obtain a grant for a house or a loan for milch cattle was mediated not so much by their ability to sign their own name or to know the procedures of bureaucracy, but by their access to politically powerful people, whether it was the headman or someone more important in the hierarchy. The biopolitical project of managing and caring for the population did not happen only through bureaucrats but also through elected officials. Elected officials bartered benefits for political support and risked failing to be reelected if they were not seen as doing enough for their constituents. But the ability of poor people to access goods and services through politically powerful people was always uncertain and limited. Poor people could not count on elected officials for support that was either systematic or consistent. On the other hand, since the bureaucracy lacked basic information about village communities—and it was irrelevant whether such information was transmitted in written or oral form—it always bestowed a degree of arbitrariness to the biopolitical project. Some poor people were helped whereas others, equally poor or poorer, were not. What is important is that the production of such arbitrariness was not in any critical way mediated by literacy, by whether the poor person in question knew how to read and write.

What I have argued in chapter 5 and in this one, therefore, is that literacy is complexly articulated with structural violence. One needs to pay attention to how it mediates and structures such violence, but the relationship between them has turned out to be anything but straightforward and certainly belies the easy certainties of a politics that sees literacy as an end in itself.

PART FOUR   **GOVERNMENTALITY**

POPULATION AND NEOLIBERAL GOVERNMENTALITY 7

In this chapter, I investigate the relation between changing forms of the care of the population on the one hand and shifts in political economy on the other. For social democratic states in the industrial world, the transition from a sovereign welfare state to a neoliberal market economy has meant the rolling back of government expenditures on the care of the population. However, what does this transition mean for a nation-state like India, which never had a welfare state that guaranteed a minimal degree of security to its citizens? How does one think about the changing contours of violence enacted against the poor with the arrival of market reforms? I compare two programs aimed at poor women to investigate the links between governmentality and neoliberalism. I contrast the Integrated Child Development Services (ICDS) program, in some ways a classic welfare scheme that aimed to deliver tangible benefits to poor women and vulnerable children, with the Mahila Samakhya program, whose goal was to empower women to improve their life situations but not to deliver anything to them by way of goods and services. All references to Mahila Samakhya in this chapter rely on the primary research done by Sharma (2008).

In the introductory chapter I introduced the paradox of a state that intervened vigorously to better the condition of the poorest and most vulnerable part of its population but still ended up managing not to avoid the death of a massive number of people. In the intervening chapters, I suggested several explanations for this outcome, ranging from corruption to the bureaucracy's demand for educational and cultural capital. Here, I want to look at another dimension of the everyday practices of specific programs aimed at the most vulnerable sections of the population—techniques of regulation, enumeration, and accountability—that may help one understand how bare life is constituted through programs that aim to include the economically and socially marginal into the sovereign body of the nation-state through development (Greenhalgh 2003a).[1] With the advent of neoliberal agendas there is a shift in the types of programs aimed at vulnerable populations. What implications does such a change have for the populations targeted by these policies? Is there a corresponding transformation in forms of governmentality, and, if so, to what end?

Foucault (2007: 105) argued that starting in the eighteenth century population became the object of sovereign power and discipline in a new way in that the growth of the welfare of the population within a given territory and the optimization of its capabilities and productivity became the goal of government. The goal of good government became not simply the exercise of authority over the people within a territory or the ability to discipline and regulate them but to foster their prosperity and happiness. Thanks to the rise of the science of statistics, population became an independent realm and force in social life separate from the state and the family. As an aggregate statistic, the population had its own intrinsic rhythms and regularities and exerted its own effects on the economy and on the nation. Population became the new field of state action: an object whose control, regulation, welfare, and conduct become the main goal of government.[2]

An example of governmentality can be seen in family planning. There may be state policies that promote or regulate an optimal family size through tax incentives, advertising campaigns, public health policies, zoning laws, and so on. In addition, corporate policies may promote a fixed family size in the form of leave policies, the provision of insurance, and the like; women's magazines and popular culture may influence how many children a couple might desire or want; the comments of neighbors, coworkers, and teachers might draw attention to those who violate societal norms by having too many children or not enough children, and so forth. All of these are forces of governmentality; and between the concern with population—its health, longevity, productivity, resources—that is so central to state policy, think tanks, and private agencies and the desires that inform and regulate the sexual behavior and intimate relations within the private and domestic realms of heteronormative families and marriages are a series of relays that transmit and translate ideas, practices, and policies from one realm to the other. Governmentality allows one to bring under a single analytical lens the entire domain, showing the operation and role of state agencies within a wider field of action and intervention made possible by a range of social actors and discourses.

What is interesting in this discussion of governmentality is that the welfare of populations within territorial states is so often discussed in isolation from the wider context in which those states exist. In particular, if one is thinking of European states in the eighteenth century, as Foucault was, the welfare of the population within those states was intimately linked with the welfare of those other populations who were the object of their state's actions: their colonial subjects. Yet, despite his political sympathies, nowhere do colonial rule or colonial subjects make their appearance in Foucault's discussion of governmentality (Spivak 1988; Stoler 2002). Similarly, in Miller and Rose (1990, 1992), Rose (1996), and Rose and Miller (1992), the wider, transnational linkages, even when they are acknowledged, drop out of the picture analytically. In practice, governmentality remains a concept deeply tied to the conduct of populations within the boundaries of the nation-state. I use the term *global governmentality* to index a different approach to the question of the regulation of populations, one that acknowledges that transnational linkages in the movement of ideas, material resources, technologies, and personnel are critical to the care of populations. The construction of the poor as a category of people is itself deeply imbricated in international and transnational discourses of development that came into being after the Second World War. Institutions such as the World Bank have made the poor a global category at the same time they have insisted that national governments are responsible for the solution to poverty.

Governmentality does not name a negative relationship of power, one characterized entirely by discipline and regulation. The emphasis, rather, is on its productive dimension: governmentality is about a concern with the population, with its health, longevity, happiness, productivity, and size (Gal and Kligman 2000: 15–36; Greenhalgh and Winckler 2005). However, managing a population involves an immersion in the details and minutiae of people's lives. Here mechanisms of discipline and regulation are important not merely as repressive measures but as facilitators of new modes of accountability and enumeration. If one takes governmentality not as a system set in place once and for all during the Enlightenment but as an ever-renewing and ever-deepening process, one has to consider how it is itself a conjunctural and crisis-ridden enterprise, how it engenders its own modes of resistance, and makes, meets, molds, or is contested by new subjects.

Moreover, one has to ask whether the concept of governmentality helps us understand the violence of poverty, and if so, how. Why should care and concern for the population or for optimizing its productivity lead to the production of bare life? Are the deaths of the poor an unintended consequence of the management of the population? Alternatively, are they the result of the fact that the desperately poor are left out of the project of "improving the condition of the population" that is the hallmark of governmentality (Foucault 2007: 105)?

The two programs examined here are very similar in terms of their objectives but quite distinct in terms of philosophy and plan. The ICDS program was started in 1975. It fits the classic mold of a welfare program run by a paternalist state for indigent women and children. The other program, the Mahila Samakhya, began a decade and a half later and in many ways exemplifies the concerns with empowerment and self-help characteristic of neoliberal governmentality (Sharma 2008). The contrasts between these programs enable a conversation about how postcolonial developmentalist states are being reshaped in the context of global neoliberalism. Rather than beginning with the a priori assumption that neoliberal regimes represent a revolutionary transformation in forms of government, the material presented here allows me to ask if there are continuities between welfare programs before and after neoliberal policies, and, if there are, where exactly they lie. This enables me to elaborate on the particularities of state reformation under neoliberalism by using the example of the postcolonial Indian state. Doing so allows me to arrive at a much more nuanced interpretation of the modalities and effects of neoliberal globalization on forms of governmentality than would be possible otherwise. Is the widespread assumption that neoliberal transformations lead to the abandonment of the poor to the vicissitudes of the market justified? Is the orientation to rapid growth accompanied by a trickle-down approach to questions of income distribution? If so, how does the care of the poor change with the emergence of this new regime?

The market-friendly reforms of 1991, implemented by the Indian government under pressure from the IMF, are widely interpreted as opening up the Indian economy to the forces of globalization (Corbridge and Harriss 2000; Khilnani 1999). Choosing two programs situated on either side of this temporal divide may serve to isolate the effects of globalization on the Indian state's antipoverty measures. There are at least two reasons why such a hypothesis may be mistaken, however. First, I will demonstrate that the ICDS program from its very start was part of a transnational set of ideas and policies that were global in their reach and effects. It would be a mistake to argue that before the market reforms of 1991 the state in India was not already involved in forms of transnational governmentality. I argue instead that the form of globalization changed after liberalization, and I therefore refer to the post-1991 period as one of neoliberal globalization. Reformulated, the question becomes one about the shifts that occurred in antipoverty programs after neoliberal reforms within an already transnational state.

Second, while market reforms may have had a great impact on some bureaus of the state at the federal level, their influence on lower levels of government and on agencies not directly connected to sectors such as large industries or consumer goods is much less obvious. An approach to the state that sees it in a disaggregated frame is cautious about the inferences it draws from some of the large policy shifts at the federal level. It should not be assumed that the effect was equally momentous at lower levels of the bureaucracy. Once again, this observation draws us into the importance of studying everyday actions of particular branches of the state to understand what has in fact changed and at which levels and to identify the conditions in which discrepant representations of the state circulate. The actions of lower levels of the developmental state were critical to the poor, and I will suggest that neoliberal policies did not result in big changes there.

Whereas globalization points to the need for a new theoretical vocabulary to respond adequately to changes in the world, a transnational approach to the state (Ferguson and Gupta 2002; Khagram and Levitt 2004; Trouillot 2003) signals the need to go further. A transnational analytical frame can be usefully distinguished from neoliberal globalization as a phenomenon in that it can be used as much to study the high-sovereign nation-state as it can to understand a state that is thoroughly embedded in neoliberal globalization. Development planning in India, for instance, has been the hallmark of the postcolonial sovereign national state and yet has always been inflected by transnational processes and ideologies. Whereas centralized, socialist planning like that under Nehru dominated roughly the first four decades of independent India, the post-liberalization Indian state's development planning agenda is shaped by global neoliberal ideas and policies.[3] Taking a transnational approach to studying the state not only can reveal the extent to which the high-sovereign national state is always already transnational but also can help uncover the shifts and overlaps in the nature of national state formation across disparate moments of globalization. Poverty-reduction initiatives in the Nehruvian era were no less a part of transnational circuits of ideas, knowledges, personnel, and institutions than those that followed in the era of neoliberal reform. However, neoliberalism was accompanied by a new set of antipoverty initiatives that stressed self-help and emphasized that the poor could take the initiative and use the market to help themselves rather than rely on government assistance and handouts. The new buzzwords were *empowerment*, *microcredit*, and *entrepreneurialism* (Sharma 2008).

A comparison of the ICDS program with Mahila Samakhya serves well to illustrate these points about the state and globalization for several reasons. ICDS had many of the hallmarks of a classic welfare program run by a sovereign nation-state; by contrast, Mahila Samakhya exemplified the concern with empowerment and self-actualization associated with neoliberal governmentality (Sharma 2008). Not surprisingly, ICDS was started and fully developed well before the sea change in economic policy, whereas Mahila Samakhya came into being in a world context dominated by neoliberal policies and shortly before a program of liberalization was enforced in India. In other words, the question of the relationship of the state to globalization is put into acute relief by juxtaposing the two programs. Does Mahila Samakhya represent the retreat of the state as compared to ICDS, or does it represent the reconstruction of the state to make it compatible with market forces and the requirements of global capitalism? Perhaps it is something else entirely—a response to the felt need for reforming the state in light of its failure to deliver goods and services to the poorest?

I will first provide a detailed description of the ICDS and Mahila Samakhya programs and then consider three aspects of the programs to demonstrate how bare life was produced through the management of the population and through discipline and surveillance. Foucault insists that these technologies of rule are not successive but simultaneous (2007). I look closely at three such technologies: inspection trips, techniques of enumeration, and struggles over the definition of work in the two programs. Finally, I argue for a new understanding of the relation between neoliberalism and structural violence.

Welfare versus Empowerment

Comparing the ICDS program with Mahila Samakhya proves apt for a variety of reasons. Both had a very similar target group, that is, poor, rural women. Both relied on their rural clients to provide so-called altruistic labor for the betterment of themselves and their communities; in addition, Mahila Samakhya was dependent on a small staff of nongovernmental employees to do empowerment work. Moreover, both programs actively recruited indigent women—separated, widowed, abandoned, divorced, or never married—who were head of households to be workers (Sharma 2008). Finally, the programs had similar unintended effects in that they brought women into state and transnational projects of governmentality through enumeration and classification and through their recruitment as workers and targets of these programs. If we want to understand how violence on the poor is exercised through their inclusion in programs of development, these two programs serve as ideal case studies.

The similarities made the contrasts between the two programs even sharper. The chief contrast I highlight here is that the programs were the product of two periods in the history of India's post-Independence development, with their respectively divergent philosophies. ICDS had the goal of reducing population growth rates and speeding up the nation's development; it aimed to deliver entitlements to a group of recipients, poor women and children, who had hitherto been ignored by the biases built into implicitly androcentric development interventions. Mahila Samakhya, while relying on a philosophy of community development and radical social change, was much more skeptical of the utility of delivering entitlements and was built instead around the idea that poor women's own agency had to be mobilized through empowerment to make long-lasting change. The differences between ICDS and Mahila Samakhya lay not only in the fact that ICDS had its genesis in a period when the model of the sovereign national state was paramount, and Mahila Samakhya was launched in a period when neoliberalism was the dominant global ideology, but also in that the two programs embodied correspondingly different ideas in their basic design, structure, strategies, and goals.

LIBERAL WELFARE AND GOVERNMENTALITY: THE ICDS PROGRAM

The ICDS program was launched, as noted, in 1975, soon after the formulation of the National Policy for Children. It was spurred by awareness that India exhibited some of the world's highest rates of infant mortality, morbidity, and malnutrition and extremely high rates of maternal mortality during birth. In 2010 the infant mortality rate was 53 per thousand and the under-five mortality rate was 69 per thousand, and the maternal mortality rate stood at 450 per 100,000 live births.[4] The more pertinent statistic concerns the poorest 20 percent of the population, and the figures there tell a much more troublesome story: the infant mortality rate and under-five mortality rate for the poorest part of the population soars to 97 and 141 per thousand, respectively (Human Development Report 2007: 255).[5] For purposes of comparison, the report of the United Nations Development Programme puts the infant mortality rate in 1960 at 165 per thousand live births, indicating that it has been more than halved in the past forty years.

The Ministry of Women and Child Development (MWCD) operates ICDS.[6] The goal of the program is to provide a set of services that consist of supplementary nutrition for pregnant women and young children as well as education, immunizations, and preventive medicine for poor and lower-caste children. The immunization program is run by the Ministry of Health and Family Welfare, which also manages the Primary Health Centers (PHCs). It takes advantage of the presence of a large number of children and at-risk women in the anganwadis to inoculate children, pregnant women, and nursing mothers against the most common diseases.[7] After experimenting with supplementary nutrition programs that produced generally poor results (Tandon, Ramachandran, and Bhatnagar 1981: 382), the ICDS program was initiated to provide a package of well-integrated services that combined nutrition, health, education, and day care for children under six years of age and nutrition and health for pregnant women (Heaver 1989; Sharma 1986; Tandon, Ramachandran, and Bhatnagar 1981).[8]

The program is interesting for a number of reasons. Launched with only 33 projects in 1975, ICDS expanded to 1,356 projects in the next ten years, and to 7,073 projects by 2009 (http://wcd.nic.in/icds.htm; accessed 17 May 2011; Government of India 1985: 4; National Institute of Public Cooperation and Child Development 1997: 3), ICDS has been one of the fastest growing development programs ever run by the Indian state. The ICDS program has grown even when the Indian government started reining in expenditures on other budget items in the post-liberalization era. In fact, allocations for ICDS in the Tenth Plan (2002–7) went up by 458 percent as compared to the Eighth Plan (1992–97) (Government of India 2005).[9] The government of India went even further in the budget of 2005, making ICDS into a universal program covering all 5,380 blocks of the country (http://indiabudget.nic.in; accessed 15 December 2008).

The ICDS program is also important because it initiated an approach to control population growth rates by paying attention to the quality of the population (Anagnost 1995; Chatterjee and Riley 2001; Dasgupta 1990; Greenhalgh and Winckler 2005). It is one of the first large-scale examples of population planning that, after the UN-sponsored conference in Cairo in 1994, has attained the status of official dogma.[10] From a theoretical perspective, ICDS is a nearly perfect example of the regulation, care, and documentation of the population, especially those parts of the population (women and children) that are poorly represented in official statistics. If biopower is about the management of the population, then its basis lies in knowledge about that population (Gal and Kligman 2000: 15–36). Programs like ICDS not only included new groups of people under the care of the state, but also exponentially increased data about so-called vulnerable populations.

The origins of ICDS are not to be found simply in transnational discourses and strategies of population control but have to be situated in a historical context in which other national efforts to control population had failed (see especially Chatterjee and Riley 2001). In Indian policy circles, controlling the growth of population has always been high on the agenda. India's population was 442 million in 1960, 884 million in 1992, and 1,029 million by 2001 (Government of India 2001). Rapid population growth created fears over the adequacy of the food supply, dissipated the gains of development, as the growth rate had to be that much higher to outpace the increased number of citizens, and created the potential to impose huge new demands on state services. When the ICDS program was launched the Indian government already had substantial experience with an aggressive birth control campaign. It had used a modernization theory model, according to which exposing people to information would change their attitudes, which in turn could change people's practices: this was called the knowledge-attitude-practices model. When I was growing up in India in the sixties and seventies, it was impossible to miss the inverted red triangle that was a symbol of birth control. It was accompanied by the slogan, *Hum do, hamaare do* (Us two, our two). Sometimes there was an additional graphic displaying a man, a woman, a boy, and a girl.

When it became clear that methods of population control built on modernization theory were proving ineffective, so that better knowledge of contraception and the inculcation of modern attitudes failed to alter birth control practices, a sense of frustration set in among policymakers. That frustration was reflected in the adoption of strong-arm tactics to control population during the Emergency of 1975–77. By all accounts, the methods used during the Emergency—forced sterilizations of men, especially among the poor and politically weak segments of the population—only helped create suspicion toward all government efforts to control population and proved no more effective than the policies of the previous era. Sanjay Gandhi's followers often invoked China as an example of successful population control and held democracy to be the chief reason for India's failure.[11] The overwhelming defeat of the Congress (I) in the elections that followed, leading to the formation of a non-Congress government for the first time in India's post-Independence history, has been attributed by most political observers to the coercive tactics used in birth control during the Emergency.

In the post-Emergency period there was a lull in family planning campaigns. It was in this context that the ICDS program, which had already been started as a strategy to control population during the Emergency, emerged as the only credible population program remaining. The ICDS program took over as a technology of birth control that sought to reduce gross birth rates by focusing on maternal mortality and on the quality of life for those children already born, that is, by reducing the mortality and morbidity rates for infants. At the same time, transnational organizations began promoting similar policies that focused on all aspects of the health of children and pregnant women. The idea was that if child mortality could be decreased, it would reduce the incentives for people to have more children as a form of insurance. This is why immunizations for pregnant women and children were supplemented by preventive medicine and supplementary nutrition. The logic simply states that lower birth rates are highly correlated with higher status for women and are accompanied by better nutrition, education, and health care for them and their children (Chatterjee and Riley 2001; Cliquet and Thienpont 1995; Sen 1994).

As far as the Indian government was concerned, investment in the development of human resources or human capital was expected to pay high dividends, especially when targeted at women and children. This was, in fact, the explicit language in which the "ICDS Experience" was summarized in a government brochure: "The experience of ICDS during its first decade (1975–1985) indicates that it has the potential of becoming a silent revolution: a profound instrument of community development and human resource development" (Government of India 1985: 24).

In fact, if one does not frame the population question narrowly, one can appreciate how the ICDS brings forth an explicit conjunction between the development of human resources, communities, and the nation. The relationship between population, political economy, and sovereignty so central to governmentality is revealed quite clearly. In a country like India children under fourteen constitute a large proportion of the population (42 percent according to the 1971 census and 35.3 percent in 2001) (http://www.censusin dia.gov.in; accessed 15 December 2008). More than 80 percent of all children live in rural areas and have poorer access to government services than their urban counterparts (Dasgupta 1990: 1302). It is estimated that 2.1 million Indian children die before reaching the age of five every year, mostly because they contract common illnesses like diarrhea, typhoid, malaria, measles, and pneumonia. The Government of India's National Policy for Children proposed fifteen measures to achieve the goals of fulfilling children's needs. It stated, "The nation's children are a supremely important *asset*. . . . Children's programmes should find a prominent part in our national plans for the development of human resources, so that our children grow up to become robust citizens, physically fit, mentally alert and normally healthy, endowed with the skills and motivations *needed* by society. . . . It shall be the policy of the State to provide adequate services to children, both before and after birth and through the period of growth, to ensure their full physical, mental and social development" (Baig 1979: 339–41; emphasis added).[12]

Such a statement reinforced directives in the Constitution of India that provided for, among other things, free and compulsory education for all children up to the age of fourteen. The authors of the Constitution directed the government to attempt the provisioning of educational services to all children within ten years of the commencement of the Constitution (Dasgupta 1990: 1304). The point I wish to make here is that concerns with the needs of national development were not incidental to programs aimed at children. In fact, the National Policy for Children explicitly conceived of the ICDS scheme as a response to its first three directives, which proposed a comprehensive health program, supplementary nutrition to remove deficiencies, and the care and nutrition of expectant and nursing mothers (Baig 1979: 340). These themes were spelled out even more explicitly in a memorandum attached to the national policy by the Indian Council for Child Welfare, which argued that "the child is an investment in the future of the nation and must, therefore, be an integral part of economic planning" (Baig 1979: 334–35).[13]

The relationship between ICDS and other development goals of the nation-state is thrown into relief by the supplementary nutrition supplied to ICDS centers. In Mandi Block the program had switched in the late eighties to a wheat-based program. What was significant about this shift was that the wheat allocated to it came from the Food Corporation of India (FCI). The FCI was the body that purchased wheat from farmers in the area at support prices set by the government. The policy of buying all the wheat that farmers could sell at preannounced prices was one of the cornerstones of the green revolution and had led to the accumulation of large surpluses in government warehouses. The state's use of this surplus wheat for ICDS thus took the results of agricultural development policies and quite literally fed them into its welfare policies. The development of agriculture and the development of human resources, in other words, were placed in a synergistic relationship that would lead to the development of national sovereignty. The wealth of the nation was tied to the welfare of its population.

I have called the ICDS a welfare program, but that term needs qualification given its connotations for most people in northern, industrial countries. What a welfare program means in a Third World context has to be qualified by the knowledge that the state that runs such a program is not a welfare state. The logic of the program was never one of providing a security blanket for the poorest segments of the population. Rather, the justification for the program arose from the need to invest in human capital for the development of the nation-state. The idea was that investing in the reduction of child mortality, improving the life chances of infants and young children, especially girls, and providing them with a basic education would help to improve the quality of human capital in the nation. Especially if such a program helped bring down the birth rate, it could contribute more to the development of the nation-state than any other government intervention. Nowhere in the design and implementation of the ICDS were there justifications that relied on a logic of the market. The program was entirely about strengthening the sovereign nation-state. The exercise of sovereignty was not built on exclusion; on the contrary, it was predicated on including the poor in the nation-state. It is easy to see why children were targeted by the program: investing in them would pay off in that they would become productive workers who would safeguard the future of the nation-state. However, it would be hard to extend this logic to the indigent and vulnerable women who were recruited by the program as workers. It is difficult to explain their inclusion entirely with reference to market rationality.

NEOLIBERAL GOVERNMENTALITY AND EMPOWERMENT: THE MAHILA SAMAKHYA PROGRAM

Mahila Samakhya is a rural women's empowerment program that was launched as a pilot project in three Indian states, U.P., Karnataka, and Gujarat, by the Department of Education of the Ministry of Human Resources Development in 1988–89 with Dutch government funds. The program now covers 9,000 villages and 60 districts in ten states (Jandhyala 2005). Mahila Samakhya views social inequalities and women's lack of awareness of their rights and of knowledge of government programs as barriers to gender equitable development. The program works by organizing women into village-level collectives (*sanghas*), raising awareness, and mobilizing them for social development (Sharma 2008).[14]

Mahila Samakhya differs from other development initiatives, such as ICDS, in that it does not seek to deliver material goods to beneficiaries. It also differs from ICDS and other programs targeted at women in not being within the Ministry of Women and Child Development. Before its budget increased and it was elevated to a ministry, the Department of Women and Child Development was perceived to be weak and underbudgeted (Gupta and Sharma 2006). It was criticized for seeing women as vulnerable, for focusing on single women and widows, and for being a department that doled out favors to its recipients. By contrast, Mahila Samakhya's location in the Department of Education signaled not only that women's issues would not be ghettoized but also that there was no natural link between the development agendas pertaining to women and children.

The biggest difference from the ICDS, which is directly implemented by MWCD, is that Mahila Samakhya is a government-organized nongovernmental organization. While the national Mahila Samakhya office is a part of the Department of Education, the program is implemented through registered societies or NGOs in each state where it operates. Each state office, or Mahila Samakhya Society, is responsible for managing various district-level program offices, which in turn oversee the work of several block-level Mahila Samakhya offices. Although a government-appointed bureaucrat heads Mahila Samakhya's national office in New Delhi, the staff at the state, district, and block levels is drawn from the nongovernmental sector (Sharma 2008).

The Mahila Samakhya program resulted from the confluence of several translocal processes: national policy priorities; the Indian women's movement; transnational shifts in development discourse; and interventions in the economy by supranational regulatory bodies like the World Bank and IMF (Sharma 2008). Feminist engagements with state structure and development thinking contributed to centering empowerment as a development goal and method. At the national level the critical engagements by activists from the Indian women's movement with Indian state agencies during the 1970s and 1980s around women's marginalization and oppression laid the groundwork for tackling gender inequalities through alternative means like empowerment. These activists highlighted the failure of the government's modernization policies to address women's needs and to reduce poverty (Government of India 1974) and struggled to make laws relating to dowry, custodial rape, and domestic violence and development policies more amenable to women (Agnihotri and Mazumdar 1995; Gandhi and Shah 1992). By the late 1980s the Gender and Development perspective played an important role in focusing attention on gender and empowerment issues within the development world (Kabeer 1994). Since the UN-sponsored conference in Cairo in 1994, empowerment has become firmly entrenched as a mainstream strategy of development (Gupta and Sharma 2006; Sharma 2008).

It is not entirely surprising that the rise of empowerment strategies has occurred during the era of neoliberal governmentality. On the one hand, supranational regulatory bodies like the World Bank are promoting empowerment as a crucial aspect of development; on the other hand, these same institutions are demanding austerity measures that reduce welfare provisioning. That those institutions whose structural adjustment policies have had intensely disempowering effects on the livelihoods of marginalized people across the globe are encouraging and funding grass-roots empowerment efforts begins to make sense when one sees empowerment through the lens of neoliberal governmentality. Empowerment fits with the neoliberal agenda of small government, participatory governance, and market-based competitiveness (Sharma 2008).

While empowerment-based development strategies in India and the Mahila Samakhya program are not products of neoliberal thinking, the coincidence of the government's promotion of empowerment with its implementation of liberalization policies offers a striking example of how empowerment has come to function as a key axis of neoliberal governance (Dean 1999; Hindess 2004).[15] As compared to welfare-based programs like ICDS that distribute material resources to particular groups, empowerment programs like Mahila Samakhya are inexpensive because they do not deliver any goods. Implementing programs that empower marginalized populations to meet their own needs through intangible means facilitates the neoliberal goal of leaner, more efficient government. Furthermore, the project of self-governance and self-development makes rule more decentered and diffused throughout society and thus more participatory. Under such a regime, if individuals are unable to lift themselves out of poverty they have only themselves to blame (Sharma 2008).

Rather than being a provider of welfare the postcolonial developmentalist Indian state is being reframed as a facilitator of development and an empowering agent. The Indian state cannot renege on its welfare duties since its identity is deeply tied with the project of national development. However, the neoliberal state can now legitimately farm out its welfare tasks to empowered agents and communities, who are expected to secure their own livelihoods through competitive market strategies.

Mahila Samakhya and ICDS both work with similar groups of poor women, but they belong to different moments of globalization, represent different national policy agendas, and have dissimilar organizational structures, strategies, and goals. One program, as noted, delivers goods and services to the most vulnerable populations of poor children and women in the form of immunizations, supplementary nutrition, and income supplements for workers. Since sickness is the leading cause for why people become poor, these goods and services are critically important (Jeffery and Jeffery 2010; Krishna 2010; Pinto 2004). However, as we have seen, a lack of educational and cultural capital enables the poor to be subjected to great structural violence. Empowerment, although an essential step toward addressing such violence, may not by itself provide the poor with nutrition, clothing, housing, and medical care. The complex relation between empowerment and the provision of goods and services can best be understood by looking closely at some concrete examples of the everyday functioning of these programs.

Governmentality, Surveillance, and Structural Violence

Close ethnographic observation of the ICDS and Mahila Samakhya programs reveals how specific practices of surveillance, enumeration, and struggles over the definition of work resulted in bureaucratic indifference and structural violence. The connections between welfare, neoliberalism, and biopolitics vary enormously in different sociohistorical circumstances, and I want to demonstrate the sometimes surprising contours of their articulation in the Indian context. My argument is that, as different as ICDS and Mahila Samakhya were in their ideology, they exhibited many similarities in their daily operation. Ultimately, these similarities proved to be much more important in producing bureaucratic indifference and exercising structural violence on the poor. An analysis centered on ideology would be at a loss to explain the rather similar biopolitical impetus of both programs and would overstate the importance of the transition from welfare to neoliberalism.

The concern with the size and quality of the population embodied in the ICDS program was exhibited in techniques of regulation, enumeration, and accountability. The numerous procedures and rules regulating the daily functioning of the anganwadis made little sense when viewed from a bottom-line perspective of gains in health and nutrition.[16] Yet such regulations were not incidental to the ICDS. As important as the goals of the program were—reducing infant and maternal mortality, increasing educational achievements for girls, providing supplementary nutrition to decrease morbidity—the methods aimed at achieving those goals were equally important. The size of the population was being controlled, but, perhaps more important, new subjects were being created.

The ICDS office in Mandi was located in one of the side streets that led off the busy road that served as the major shopping center of the modern part of town. When I tried to find the ICDS office I walked right past it; this happened on more than one occasion. I had been told to look for the blue UNICEF jeep that served as the unofficial mascot of the ICDS program. I missed the office because the jeep was missing, and, unlike other government offices, which displayed large signs, this one had no outward indication that an office existed in that building. It was a nondescript space consisting of a small driveway barely large enough for a vehicle and a narrow flight of stairs to one side. One went up the stairs and arrived at a terrace no wider than eight feet that had a series of doors opening up to it on the left. There were three rooms: the first housed the main office, where two clerks had their desks and where the peon usually stood; the second was used primarily as a storage space; the third, furthest from the stairs, belonged to the dynamic, articulate CDPO of Mandi Block, Asha Agarwal. Agarwal, who was in her thirties, sat behind a large desk in a sparsely furnished, minimally decorated room, and, like other officers, she had a buzzer on her desk that she pressed whenever she needed to get the attention of the peon.

As the head of the office, Agarwal's daily routine consisted of tasks devoted to keeping anganwadi centers open and functioning smoothly. To that end, her most effective instrument of discipline was the surprise inspection. Surprise inspections, along with the practices of collecting statistics and the struggles waged by anganwadi workers over who they were and what they did, illuminate how techniques of regulation, enumeration, and accountability functioned to perpetuate structural violence even when the overt goal was to bring welfare to vulnerable parts of the population.

INSPECTION TRIPS

The chief instrument of bureaucratic surveillance was the surprise inspection, which functioned to ensure that the goals of regulation, enumeration, and accountability were met. Regulation took the form of ensuring that the anganwadi centers functioned at regular days and times, that the workers and children were obeying instructions about how the day care center ought to be run, how the schooling was to be accomplished, and how the facilities had to be maintained. Enumeration was important in that one of the officers' primary responsibilities was to monitor the degree to which the anganwadi workers collected data, especially information about women and children who were the targets of the ICDS program. In this sense, the object of the officers' surveillance was the degree to which the anganwadi worker monitored her client population. As we will see, in practice this model worked quite unevenly. Accountability was accomplished by a series of checks that ensured that the data recorded by the anganwadi worker matched what could be observed during the inspection. For example, if the anganwadi worker claimed that forty children regularly attended the center and ate their meals there, she might be asked to explain why only twenty students were there during a surprise inspection; or the claims of the anganwadi worker about what she had taught the students might be tested by giving the students an impromptu test in recitation, counting, or spelling.

One of the greatest challenges facing the bureaucrats was to ensure that the village women who had been hired to run the anganwadis were in fact operating them. Agarwal would often impress upon me, in her confident, engaging tone of voice, the importance of inspections for ensuring the proper operation of anganwadi centers in her block. She reinforced her point by relating the following anecdote to me. When she had taken over the Mandi office it had been without a head for several months. The government had appointed one of the previous supervisors to be a temporary head. Agarwal pointed out that appointing a junior official to monitor the functioning of anganwadis was doomed to failure because in-charges, as the temporary CDPOs were termed, were at the same level in the official hierarchy as those they were to supervise and hence lacked the authority to discipline (khainch-naa, "pull") them. In addition, the office jeep had not been operating for a year because the money to repair it had not been sanctioned by the state government. The temporary head had used the lack of a vehicle to justify the fact that she had not made any inspection trips. This in turn had enabled those working under her to slack off, and the clerks too felt they could get away with not fulfilling their responsibilities. Once supervisors stopped making inspection trips, anganwadi workers felt they had nothing to fear, and they ceased to operate the centers. Agarwal claimed that because inspections had not been conducted the whole system stopped functioning.

During Agarwal's first few months in Mandi the office jeep was still inoperable, so she, too, had not conducted any inspection trips. When it appeared that the vehicle would not be repaired in the near future she started taking public transportation to pay surprise visits to the centers. She went to four centers and found none of them functioning. She felt that there was no point in visiting other centers because she would end up giving warnings to all the workers under her. At the next monthly meeting of anganwadi workers she announced that if she did not find the centers functioning she would take disciplinary action against the workers concerned. Following that warning, she resumed her inspections. At first she found attendance at the centers spotty. However, once word spread that she had started issuing warnings and docking anganwadi workers' pay the centers started operating again. Even in the absence of an official vehicle Agarwal managed to use inspection trips effectively.

Agarwal invited me on several inspection trips. She had carefully planned our itinerary so that we would visit centers that had a record of good performance. But the fact that these were surprise visits meant they could not serve as public relations exercises. The first trip we took was on a cold, overcast day soon after the office had received a fresh disbursement of funds for purchasing petrol. The blue ICDS jeep, which had been lying idle because of insufficient funds for repairs and for petrol, was coaxed into life by the driver. Since anganwadis were supposed to operate from nine in the morning to one in the afternoon, we left the Mandi office just before nine. Agarwal and I sat alongside the driver in front, while the supervisor responsible for the areas we were visiting was in the back. Our first stop was the petrol station. Agarwal informed me that the state government had requested all offices to cut their expenditures by 20 percent. Since the office's annual report was due at the end of the following month they had to run around even more than usual. She wondered aloud: How did the state government expect her to cut expenditures so drastically and still get all the work done for the annual report?

The first village we stopped in was Kalanda. The two anganwadis in Kalanda had been operating since 1985, when the ICDS project began in Mandi Block. I was told that it was a primarily Muslim village, and we encountered an impressive mosque at the entrance to the village rather than the temple often seen in Hindu-majority villages. The village was most unusual for the well-maintained quality of its streets and the complete absence of sewage water and garbage on them. I was told that many men in the village were masons and had volunteered their labor to lay the roads and the drains. Some of them had gone to work as laborers in the Middle East and had come back with small fortunes, which accounted both for the relative grandeur of the mosque and the neat-looking houses.

The first anganwadi we went to inspect was housed in a dark room that served as the storage area for a farm family. A huge pile of lentils occupied half the room, completely covering one wall and a good proportion of the floor space. The anganwadi worker, a pleasant, energetic woman, quickly sent the helper to round up additional children to add to the fourteen who were already there. Agarwal asked the children to count numbers and to recite the alphabet, which they did with practiced ease. One child in particular, who was a little older than the rest, had written down numbers all the way to one hundred on his slate and had also memorized all the poems and songs they had been taught. While we were at this center a number of children came in looking washed and scrubbed. Agarwal told me that the teacher had only a high school degree but seemed to be doing a good job with the children. She castigated the anganwadi worker for not removing the charts, which functioned as teaching aids, from the wall where the lentils had been piled. "It is your job to look after the charts," she told her. "When you knew that the crop was going to be stored there, why didn't you remove the charts beforehand?" After inspecting the attendance registers and writing a brief report in the inspection register, which noted when the inspection took place, how many children were there, and what the children had demonstrated, we left the center and headed for the second one.

The second center in Kalanda was in the porch of a house. When we reached it the anganwadi worker was nowhere to be seen. There were a handful of very young children present, along with the helper. When asked where the anganwadi worker was, the helper claimed not to know. Agarwal attempted to coax some of the children to stand up and recite the number table or identify objects on an alphabet chart; however, none of them opened their mouths. It was hard to tell whether this was out of shyness and fear of the visitors or because of their unfamiliarity with the task. We waited for a few minutes and then headed back to the jeep. As we were leaving, the anganwadi worker came hurrying toward us. She apologized profusely and blamed her delay on the fact that the bus she was traveling on had broken down. Agarwal chastised her in no uncertain terms. Even if her bus had broken down, she said, this was no excuse for reaching the center at 11:15 instead of 9 A.M. The anganwadi worker lamented her bad luck, saying that we happened to visit on the only day she had arrived late. She tried to persuade us to come back to the anganwadi for a few minutes, but Agarwal wanted to see centers in other villages that day, and it was fast approaching closing time. On our way to the jeep, Agarwal noted wryly how much better the center operated by the woman who was only "high-school pass" seemed compared to the second one, despite the fact that the second anganwadi worker had a master's degree. Agarwal observed that the children at the first center seemed better taught and the teacher displayed more enthusiasm (see chapter 6).

During her inspection trips Agarwal referred to the attendance registers, in which anganwadi workers had to record the number of children who came to the center, in order to evaluate the performance of an anganwadi. If she did not find a center open or functioning properly during a surprise visit she docked the worker's pay for that day and left a note requesting an explanation (*spashtikaran*) of why the worker was not there. Repeated absences or delays in responding to the CDPO's demand for an explanation resulted in extended pay cuts; however, a decision to terminate employment required a great deal of documentation and careful groundwork on the part of the CDPO.

One example of repeated abstention from duty was provided by Sona Devi, an older, widowed woman with three children who lived in a large village called Hamirpur, which had three anganwadi centers. Agarwal told me she had found Sona Devi's center closed during her last three inspection visits. Agarwal opened her inspection ledger and showed it to me as evidence: it indicated that she had reached the center at 12:30 P.M. and found it closed. When asked why there were no children at her center, Sona Devi replied that they had all gone to see a play being performed in the village. But when Agarwal checked with workers at the other centers in the same village they claimed to be unaware of any play being performed at that time. Yet despite Sona Devi's poor record Agarwal so far had resisted firing her. All she had done was cut her pay for not performing her job. Sona Devi's case is especially interesting because it illustrates some of the contradictions in the objectives of the ICDS program. The women who were recruited as workers were also the subjects of the welfare goals of the program. As a widow and mother of three children, Sona Devi was an ideal worker and subject. However, to the workers, ICDS was more akin to workfare than welfare. Recalcitrant workers like Sona Devi brought into the open the conflict embedded in the program between providing welfare to someone who was vulnerable and in need and demanding that women give back to the nation in order to receive benefits.

Agarwal proceeded to give me more examples of how difficult it was for her to fire and therefore discipline anganwadi workers, even when she knew they were not doing their jobs. Balvanti, an anganwadi worker, used to manage a center in her natal village. When she married and left for her husband's village, her father requested that his younger daughter be made the anganwadi worker in her place. Agarwal told him she was required to advertise the position, and, furthermore, all new positions were reserved only for scheduled-caste applicants.[17] Agarwal waited for Balvanti's letter of resignation, but it never arrived. After her marriage Balvanti returned to her natal village for a few months before she moved permanently to her new home.[18] During the time she was back in her parents' home she resumed operating the anganwadi. Agarwal added that Balvanti had been a conscientious worker and had done a very good job of running the anganwadi. However, eventually

Balvanti had left for her husband's village. Whenever she returned to her parents' home for brief periods during the year she would reopen the center and operate it for a few days. As a result, the anganwadi remained closed for most of the year. Once when Agarwal had gone on an inspection tour and found the center closed she went to Balvanti's house to verify her whereabouts. She was told that Balvanti had just left for the fields on some urgent business. A small child standing nearby piped up, "She hasn't gone to the field; she has gone to her own home!" Her family members' lie was exposed. During previous inspection visits, Agarwal had tried to persuade Balvanti's family that she would be better off resigning rather than being fired. She told them, "This is a government department. By resigning, she leaves with her self-respect intact. By getting fired, she brings disrespect to herself." Yet eighteen months after that incident, Agarwal had not received a resignation letter. She added that it was imperative that she fire Balvanti before a new consignment of food was allocated to the ICDS program because if she waited until after the food had been supplied Balvanti, knowing she would have to resign soon, might appropriate the food for her own use. Agarwal also knew that Balvanti would come back to her parents' home for Holi, the spring harvest festival, and was afraid she might restart the anganwadi for a few days. Agarwal would then have to conduct three more inspections before she could fire her. Agarwal underlined the difficulty of her task by noting that the two registered letters she had sent to Balvanti were not returned to the office, and there was no evidence that they had been delivered. Agarwal surmised that Balvanti's family probably knew the village postal worker and had cajoled him into handing the letter over to them without signing a receipt. She had drafted another letter terminating Balvanti's employment and was about to send it to her boss, who would have it signed and delivered officially. Balvanti's case demonstrates how someone who was upper caste and belonged to a relatively wealthy family could obtain a job as an anganwadi worker through social connections despite the fact that she did not fit the profile of the targeted worker. Moreover, using her cultural capital and contacts in the bureaucracy (in this case, the postal worker), she could collect a paycheck without doing her job because she knew how to do just enough to keep from getting fired.

Agarwal showed me examples of letters in which she had put two anganwadi workers on notice and had demanded a written explanation of why they were absent from their centers. Both women responded within a day, saying that they could not be at the anganwadi because their children had suddenly taken ill. Agarwal told me she heard this excuse frequently. If she found a center that was not functioning during a surprise visit, she would visit it again in a few days, usually within a fortnight. If she found that the center was still not operating, she would leave a warning and would dock the worker's pay for yet another day. Shortly thereafter, she would visit the same anganwadi for a third time; if it was still not operating she would leave a third warning and thereby prepare the way for suspending the worker. Unlike government employees, who could almost never be fired, anganwadi workers could be terminated after the third warning. However, Agarwal usually gave them another chance. "When we go to higher officials to get rid of someone," she explained, "they tell us, 'First make the file thicker.'" In other words, get more material, more paperwork, before taking any action. The thicker the file, the easier it is to get a decision to fire someone.[19] The bureaucratic requirement for paperwork disadvantaged poor and lower-caste women as compared to their richer and upper-caste sisters. The latter were more likely to have the educational and cultural capital to negotiate the demands for paperwork and, more important, to be familiar with bureaucratic process. New positions not reserved for lower-caste women were more likely to go to candidates from upper castes and richer households. For the same reason, if they were not doing their job adequately women from such backgrounds were better able to resist being fired. This is precisely the disadvantage that Mahila Samakhya had been initiated to overcome.

The arbitrariness built into officials' discretionary power could be employed in a compassionate manner as well. This was brought home to me on a warm winter day when the staff at the ICDS office had pulled the desks and chairs onto the narrow porch to take advantage of the sunny weather. While I was talking to Agarwal a man came up the stairs and headed into the office. After consulting with the clerk he came and handed a slip of paper to Agarwal. It was an application for leave on behalf of his wife, who was an anganwadi worker. The application requested leave for a few days because she was ill. Accompanying the application was an impressive stack of papers, including an x-ray, which the man plopped down in front of Agarwal. He said that if she did not believe him, she could look at the medical papers and convince herself that his wife was telling the truth. Agarwal categorically refused to believe the man. She said she had made surprise visits to that center on two occasions and found it closed both times. What was more, many villagers had come to her, complaining that the center did not function. She told the man that if his wife could not operate the center because she was ill, she should have applied for medical leave, and Agarwal would have been happy to endorse such an application. Alternatively, his wife could have applied for casual leave (which, however, was limited to twenty days a year). Agarwal emphasized, however, that the worker could not keep the anganwadi closed indefinitely because she was ill and continue drawing a salary. She added that she had not yet received an explanation (*spashtikaran*) to the letters she had left at the center. She demanded to know why, if the worker was ill, the center was not being run by her helper: "If your wife cannot make it to the anganwadi on certain days, why is the helper absent? I should find the helper [at the center] even if the anganwadi worker is not there." The man defended his wife, saying she could not force the helper to show up. However, Agarwal did not give up her line of questioning. If his wife went to the anganwadi regularly, why did the attendance registers not demonstrate that fact by listing the names of the children who were present? "When I went there," Agarwal said, "none of the registers had been filled." That charge finally broke the man's resistance. He then switched tactics and claimed that it was hard to entice children to come to the anganwadi when there was no food (*poshtahaar*) provided to them. Agarwal responded by saying that by that logic none of the anganwadis in Mandi should have been operating since there was no food being distributed at any of them. Defeated by such a battery of arguments, the man left. When he had gone, I asked Agarwal if she intended to fire that particular anganwadi worker. To my surprise, she said she did not think it necessary to resort to such a drastic step. "This was only my second warning to her," she said. "We have to allow for the possibility that there are often genuine reasons why the center is not open." Anganwadi workers sometimes came back on track after repeated warnings, and in that particular case she would wait a little longer. Despite being rule-bound, or perhaps because of it, bureaucrats often had a great deal of discretionary power, especially in matters of discipline. As this example shows very clearly, bureaucratic discretion as much as indifference could make a difference to the lives of workers and clients. Agarwal could have proceeded to fire this worker, as she had obviously been drawing a salary without operating her center. However, she had decided not to do so because she recognized that the woman had been quite sick and probably needed the money for treatment.

Agarwal proceeded to tell me about other anganwadi centers that were in trouble, drawing on the cases of Balvanti and Sona Devi referred to earlier, and emphasized the difficulties she had in doing anything to remedy the situation. Agarwal had already been to Balvanti's village twice, a supervisor had visited once, and they had both found the anganwadi closed. In addition, when Agarwal went to inspect the center, villagers complained that it no longer functioned properly. However, oral complaints were of little use, and

Agarwal was frustrated in her efforts to persuade villagers to write down what they told her. "The problem," she said, "is that when you ask someone to give you a complaint in writing, they at once withdraw what is otherwise vociferous criticism. With government work, unless you have something in writing, you cannot build a case and take any action."[20]

Political capital was an important resource for anganwadi workers, not only to get the job but also to keep it in case they were in trouble. Sona Devi, whose pay had been docked by Agarwal, had decided to put political pressure on Agarwal to restore her stipend. One day five men came to talk to Agarwal and told her she had no right to speak to Sona Devi in an "insulting tone." Agarwal presented her case to them and asked them what they wanted her to do given the fact that Sona Devi's anganwadi was found not to be functioning on three occasions. Ignoring her question, the men said they were not asking her to do anything; they just wanted to warn her to not "misbehave" with her workers. Agarwal became enraged as she recounted what had happened: "First, she [Sona Devi] does something wrong, and then she tries to put [political] pressure on me! That makes me even angrier." Despite her anger, however, Agarwal realized that Sona Devi had political support, and she would have to be extra careful before dismissing her.

Surprise inspections and registers were two methods by which regulation and accountability were pursued. It was not only that superior officers at higher levels traveled in jeeps; it was also that they traveled in order to conduct inspections, to discipline, reward, encourage, and punish. Registers helped them do just that, since registers enabled them to check their observations against what had been noted. For example, Agarwal complained that workers who ran anganwadi centers in their homes often brought in additional children when they saw the dust of the jeep in the distance. By the time the CDPO actually reached the center, there were many children there even if the anganwadi had not been operating. However, she managed to catch the worker's deception in such cases by checking the names of the children present against the names (if any) entered in the attendance register. The CDPO's ability to swoop down on the space of the anganwadi worker was thus mediated by the semiotic of dust; a smoke signal delivered by that very device, the jeep, that enabled her to suddenly enter the space of the anganwadi worker.

The surveillance exercised by superior officers over their subordinates was part of the routine functioning of the Indian state. Again, this kind of monitoring did not easily translate into control and discipline. The authority of the CDPO, like that of any superior officer in the hierarchy, could be subverted, deferred, or denied through a range of tactics. The workers who were the objects of surveillance by their superiors did not merely conform and police themselves as expected. Rather than simply regulating and normalizing, the power of superior officers to exercise surveillance over their workers sometimes provoked disruptive reactions that threatened the hierarchical assumptions of bureaucratic order. Government by state bureaucracies did not smoothly translate into self-government by anganwadi workers; there were significant points of tension and friction in the art of government. An analysis of the state bureaus and levels enables one to appreciate that bureaucratic indifference to the poor is always a contingent and contested outcome, not simply the result of the actions or attitudes of particular bureaucrats. In Foucault's (2007: 87–114) idea of governmentality, a critical idea is that of relays that transmit modalities of government that connect seemingly unrelated domains and practices. But in such a model does one lose a sense of the friction that impedes or defers this orientation of diverse domains toward each other? How does the idea of governmentality allow one to understand the process that leads to such a convergence?

The relationship between anganwadi workers and villagers was also often a contested one. As part of their job anganwadi workers were required to collect vast amounts of data, particularly about women and children, segments of the population that had not been as extensively surveyed, counted, classified, measured, injected, or schooled in the past. The monitoring of anganwadi workers by superior officers was meant partially to ensure that, in turn, the anganwadi workers were conscientiously monitoring the population they were serving.

ENUMERATION: A NUMBERS GAME?

I have discussed the importance of numbers to the writing practices of states (see chapter 5). The biopolitical management of the population depends upon statistical enumeration: means, medians, and standard deviations allow one to gauge what is normal and which behavior needs modification because it is thought to be deviant. Even the Agambenian idea of bare life depends on modes of classification and enumeration. It is clear from Agamben's examples of Nazi Germany that it is not individuals but classes of people who become homo sacer. However, in order to determine who belongs to this class, categorization, enumeration, and documentation are essential. Those who can be killed must first be known, codified, recorded, and enumerated, and, very importantly, separated from the rest of the population. How does this process work in conditions of extreme poverty? We will see some of these mechanisms at work.

Enumeration was not a stated goal of the ICDS program, but it ended up being an important function for several reasons. Data collection was built into the everyday procedures of the program, although the quality of the data appeared unimportant and its utility unclear. A second reason may have been that, unlike other government programs, ICDS was incessantly evaluated. Literally hundreds of evaluation reports of ICDS were prepared for different blocks and regions, quite out of proportion to the resources invested in the program. Such over-appraising may have been the result of the heavy involvement of transnational actors, for whom evaluation was a critical tool in their development portfolio. A vital index of performance for such evaluations was provided by the number of beneficiaries. Therefore, the Indian government required anganwadi workers to maintain an impressive array of registers in which everything was recorded. They also had to document that they were indeed meeting the targets specified in terms of numbers of beneficiaries served, number of children immunized, amount of supplementary nutrition distributed, number of anganwadi workers operating in a block, and so forth. Finally, since women and children were poorly represented in official statistics, village surveys helped determine whether a new center was needed and also provided better information about local residents.

Although they were not government employees, anganwadi workers were expected to behave like them in one important regard. They had the crucial responsibility of generating official statistics for the state. In an appropriate image, Hacking (1982) has characterized the activities of the modern state as generating an "avalanche of numbers."[21] In the anganwadi program record keeping often appeared to be an end in itself; it also had far-reaching effects in mapping, surveying, and tabulating the population and, most importantly, in potentially monitoring the lives of women and children.

Enumeration is a critical modality of governmentality; it is through the collection of statistics that the conduct of conduct can be affected. What kinds of statistics are collected, who collects them, and how they are used all affect the regulation of populations, techniques of accountability, and the formation of group identities. Foucault (2007: 100–101) has pointed out the family resemblance between statistics and the state and that the rise of statistics is integral to the science of the state that developed in Europe at the end of the sixteenth century. Kaviraj (1994) links enumeration to a specifically modern form of community identity, which he opposes to "fuzzy" communities. It is through the purposeful counting of peoples as members of certain kinds of groups that arguments about representativeness, about majorities and minorities, about who is falling behind and who is ahead in income data, educational achievements, and so on can be made. Statistics are not collected just by the state; and they are certainly not always collected or employed in the interests of the state.[22] Aggrieved groups can quite effectively marshal statistics against the state to justify a range of actions. My argument is that statistics function to gauge things like activity levels or health, monitor the actions of social agents, and regulate the behavior of populations. All these functions extend beyond the state and belong to the realm of government more generally. It is difficult to imagine biopolitics without the aid of statistical enumeration and classification. However, the political functions of statistical representation are necessarily open-ended. I have already suggested that statistical classification is essential to the constitution of bare life: determining who can be killed already presumes operations of enumeration and classification. The urgency of enumeration derives from the state's need to know who is vulnerable because people who are not part of the official record cannot possibly be saved. However, when women and children move from the statistical nonspace of the unrecorded to the surveyed and targeted group who become the object of benevolent intervention, do their life chances improve? Nobody knows the answer to this question. What one can say for sure, however, is that structural violence attains a qualitatively different form when the state recognizes populations as vulnerable but still does not help them.

One of the chief functions of anganwadi workers, and by far their most time-consuming activity, consisted of documenting and generating statistics. A plethora of registers recorded various aspects of the anganwadi: for example, an attendance register noted such things as how many children were in the center each day and the child's name, father's name, and caste; a nutrition register recorded how much food and fuel was consumed; a third register was used to record the birth dates of each child born in the village and its parents' names, ages, and castes. Similar records were kept of all deaths. The name, age, and caste of each pregnant woman and a record of the outcome of the pregnancy were recorded in another register. A travel log maintained a record of when and why an anganwadi worker was missing from a center. An inspection register was maintained in which supervisors, the CDPO, and other visitors recorded their impressions about the functioning of the anganwadi. Registers were devices for self-monitoring, technologies of self-discipline that were simultaneously portfolios for recording the effectiveness of the care of the population on the one hand and for enabling the surveillance and control of the worker on the other.

Maintaining all these records posed a daunting challenge to most anganwadi workers, particularly those who lacked the requisite cultural capital in the form of mathematical skills. Sharda Devi was an anganwadi worker in the village of Bhaipur, a few miles from Mandi. Her husband was a self-taught "doctor" who was also the community health worker for the village. When I visited her center she complained about the mathematics involved in the supplementary nutrition program. Different quantities of food, measured in grams, had to be given to children, pregnant women, and nursing mothers. Then the totals had to be added up for each category and for all groups for each day. The totals were next tallied against the amount of food actually left in the center. When the CDPO came on her inspection trips, one of the things she looked for were discrepancies in the registers and the actual amount of food remaining at the center. Sharda Devi's husband asked pointedly, "How do they expect a person with an eighth-grade education to do all this? If I didn't help her, she would never be able to manage the books." However, everyone, including the CDPO, understood that the object of the exercise was not so much to detect corruption as to keep the record straight, so that no aspersions of corruption could reasonably be made. Thick files and carefully totaled numbers were more important than action because the logic of bureaucratic justification demanded written evidence, a fact often lost on semiliterate or illiterate people in rural areas. It mattered less that a worker appropriated supplementary nutrition meant for the poor children and pregnant mothers for whom it was intended than that she entered amounts in the nutrition register such that the figures all added up and tallied with the amount of food left.

There was more to the functioning of anganwadis than generating numbers so that tables and columns totaled up correctly. A silent revolution was indeed taking place through this program, and it was not just in the development of human resources. Perhaps for the first time in the history of the nation-state records were being kept on births and deaths in rural areas. Anyone who has attempted to do a census of an Indian village knows how difficult it is to record precise ages and dates of birth, as the techniques of the modern, Western imaginary of the nation and its population is (mis)translated into incommensurable modes and methods of recording the passage of time as it intersects with life histories. I looked at several registers in anganwadis that recorded information about births. The mothers' ages, which may have been as low as fifteen years, were all carefully recorded as being over the legal age of marriage: eighteen years and six months, nineteen years, or twenty-two years. However, the births of children in the village since the anganwadi program began in Mandi were recorded accurately to the day, sometimes to the hour. The registers contained similar, relatively accurate information about deaths. In other registers were data on inoculations, the weight of infants and pregnant women, attendance at the anganwadi, and so forth. The anganwadi program had resulted in a quantum leap in data on women and children, particularly in the areas of fertility and infant mortality. One cannot speak of biopolitics in the absence of such data; however, the mere fact that data were collected did not necessarily mean they were used for biopolitical ends. Unlike other data collected by state workers, the incessant monitoring of ICDS by state and transnational agencies ensured that data were aggregated and used.

It may be objected that since anganwadi workers were not trained census takers, the quality of the data they collected was suspect. Indeed, since there were no mechanisms to check whether an anganwadi worker had recorded all the births and deaths in a village or had accurately noted down the exact birth dates of individuals, it would have been impossible to tell if a birth or death had been recorded correctly. What needs to be pointed out, though, is that, unlike census takers, anganwadi workers either lived in the village in which they worked or went daily to the village to operate the anganwadi. They could gather a great deal of information from the children who came to the anganwadi. Further, births and deaths were major public occasions in villages in western U.P. and could go undetected only with great difficulty. Finally, anganwadi workers had no incentive not to record such events or to misrecord them. Although there were few mechanisms to double-check the records kept by anganwadi workers, there was little reason to be suspicious of the figures that had been entered in the registers.

The broader point I wish to make here is that a seeming by-product of the functioning of the anganwadi program was a series of numbers, modes of enumeration, classification, and recording that applied mainly to women and children. This was a segment of the population whose low level of literacy and lack of participation in the formal economy had kept it relatively insulated from the chronotope of state surveillance. What differentiated the anganwadi worker from the census taker was precisely the degree of familiarity with the village that no outsider could ever obtain. Even when the anganwadi worker kept her distance from the social life of the village, from its politics and divisions, she still knew a lot more about individuals and families than any other state official. More important, the anganwadi worker learned a great deal about women in the village, a segment of the population relatively insulated from the gaze of other state officials, especially male officials.[23] In exchange for the services offered by the ICDS program, village women had to provide information about themselves and their children (that such an exchange was on the minds of villagers will become clear from the examples below). In extending a helping hand to the most vulnerable segments of its population, however, did the program manage to fulfill its mission of lowering infant mortality and morbidity rates and of improving the life chances of young girls? The evaluation studies were ambivalent, one of the reasons the Indian government had not released its own comprehensive evaluation report.[24] What is interesting for my argument, though, is the violence that was enacted on the scene of care. The ICDS program promised a comprehensive program of medical, educational, and nutritional inputs, but it failed to deliver one critical component. The supplementary nutrition provided by the program was erratic and did not reach children at the time just before harvest, when household stocks of food were likely to be at their lowest. That supplementary nutrition was the most important aspect of the program for villagers was clear from the fact that attendance at anganwadis doubled when food was available. One can speak about violence here in the sense of the gap between the promise of care and the lack of funding for the program that would have made that care a reality. One can also speak of arbitrariness in the provision of care in that, in the absence of any comprehensive map of the population, it was impossible for anyone to know if the program was in fact serving its target population. The children who attended an anganwadi were well documented, but the ones who did not were outside the ambit of surveillance and care, beyond the ambivalent embrace of biopolitics.

Whether or not the state's role in rural life was increased by the anganwadi program, new modes of governmentality were definitely being introduced by the program, techniques of enumeration and data gathering and novel technologies of regulation and accountability. Despite the best efforts of anganwadi workers, villagers often resisted any attempt to collect statistics. At one of the monthly meetings I attended several anganwadi workers stood up to document the difficulties they had experienced in collecting the information they were required to enter in the registers. One worker said that villagers refused to allow their children's weight to be measured. One day, as part of her duties, she had weighed some children, and the next day a little boy fell ill. His sibling told the rest of the family that the child had been weighed the previous day. Measuring children's weights and pronouncing them healthy was considered reason enough to attract envy, the evil eye (buri nazar) so feared by people in western U.P.[25] After that, none of the households in the village would allow their children to attend the anganwadi. They told the anganwadi worker, "When you don't feed the children, why do you weigh them?" She could not convince them that no harm would come to children by weighing them.

Similarly, some anganwadi workers reported that when they went from door to door to do a survey of the population, people often refused to cooperate with them. "Why do you come to our house to do the survey when we have to come to you for inoculations and injections?" the anganwadi workers were asked with impeccable logic. "You should just sit at the center and do the survey there." Anganwadi workers also described their difficulties in asking questions about all members of a family. Villagers challenged them with the words, "When you feed only the children, why do you want to take a survey that includes everyone? Why do you want to find out who has died? Are you going to feed the dead too?" The workers said they had no good responses to such questions and were sometimes unable to persuade villagers to cooperate with them.

For the agencies funding and supporting ICDS, monitoring the weight of children was important both because it helped provide the justification for the program in areas where a large proportion of children were malnourished and because it could demonstrate the effectiveness of supplementary nutrition as an essential component of the program. Similarly, surveying the entire population could yield helpful data on what proportion of the population was composed of children under five, of sex ratios, and of the size and composition of families. Yet such surveys provided no tangible benefits to recipients, who may have had good reason to be wary of knowledge collected about them that appeared to be unrelated to the services offered.

When analysts use the concept of the state, the impression conveyed is of a unitary and cohesive institution that has potentially great capacities for controlling, monitoring, and manipulating its population. However, when one disaggregates the state and analyzes the workings of individual bureaucracies and programs like the ICDS, it becomes more difficult to conceptualize a coordinated, systematic institution that can exploit the data collected by its various apparatuses. In fact, the level of coordination between agencies and bureaucracies of the state implied by the term *surveillance*, with its connotation of linkages between data collection and repression, suggests capabilities that the state may not possess. The ICDS staff at the block level diligently accumulated the data collected by the anganwadi workers and passed it on to the district level, where it was fed into national statistics on the program. It was not apparent if anyone at the district level was processing the data or using it in any way. I was told of mountains of data sitting there waiting to be processed. Hacking's image of an "avalanche of numbers" is appropriate: it suggests an undirected, undisciplined flow, triggered by the smallest disturbance—a mountain of numbers threatening to cascade down without being directed to any end. If biopolitics depends upon knowledge of the population, its tendencies and fluctuations, then it would be hard to characterize the relationship between the Indian state and poor women and children, the most vulnerable section of its population, as a biopolitical one. The reason simply was that no single agency, inside or outside the state, had the knowledge to make biopolitics possible.

Although Mahila Samakhya differed from ICDS in emphasizing shifts in consciousness rather than in meeting quantitative targets, it too depended upon a form of biopolitics for its operation. Collecting data became an important function of Mahila Samakhya, one aimed at raising the consciousness of its women clients. Mahila Samakhya's field staff compiled narrative reports that detailed their work with various collectives and critically evaluated such efforts. These documents were consolidated into quarterly and annual reports that sought to document the empowering effects of Mahila Samakhya on the participants in the program. However, targets were beginning to creep into the program. Some bureaucrats, for instance, wanted hard evidence of Mahila Samakhya's literacy efforts. For instance, they wanted to know how many women and adolescent girls trained by Mahila Samakhya had passed the state examinations. The program's staff felt uncomfortable with such an exercise, which did not highlight the more meaningful, unquantifiable changes that participation in Mahila Samakhya had brought to their clients' lives (Sharma 2008).

Paradoxically, the qualitative focus of the Mahila Samakhya program depended on techniques such as census surveys and participatory rural appraisals.[26] Mahila Samakhya's staff periodically conducted baseline household surveys in villages in order to understand the issues faced by potential clients and to make strategic interventions in women's lives. Surveys covered general indicators such as poverty, literacy, and family size as well as specific questions about women's socioeconomic status. When the Mahila Samakhya staff tried to get information from villagers, they inquired what they would get in return. Would they be given tangible benefits? Would the officials advance their own careers by administering the surveys, leaving the villagers to lives of drudgery and servitude? Some villagers refused to participate because they said they had received no benefits from being part of previous surveys. Others who did participate identified themselves as belonging to the below poverty line category.

One can see the importance of enumeration as a critical modality of biopolitics and governmentality. Although ICDS and Mahila Samakhya were entirely different in philosophy and implementation, they shared the conviction that improving the life chances of the poor required a certain type of statistical knowledge about the population. Establishing a baseline was important if the effectiveness of the change they were bringing about was to be measured and documented, even when the change itself was not, as in the Mahila Samakhya program, quantifiable. Another area where the two programs converged was in the ambivalent status of their workers.

WORKERS' SELF-PERCEPTION

One of the interesting parallels between ICDS and Mahila Samakhya lay in the status of their workers. Both programs selected workers who were themselves seen as welfare beneficiaries. Women who were widowed, abandoned by their husbands, or divorced were preferred as workers (or volunteers, as they were called). In the patriarchal and virilocal village societies of north India, these women were rightly considered most vulnerable and literally as those who had no place in the social and spatial order, no place they could depend on for economic and physical security. The programs employed a model of workfare rather than welfare, and the work expected of their employees was to build social capital. Anganwadi workers distributed nutrition and provided educational and health services to hard-to-reach populations; Mahila Samakhya workers provided information about underutilized government resources so that poor people could take advantage of the many schemes already in place for their benefit. At the same time, perhaps unwittingly, both sets of workers aided in the biopolitical project of mapping the population so that it could be managed and disciplined better. For my purposes, it is important to understand how these workers saw themselves and how they interpreted what they were doing as quasi-state functionaries. Lacking such a perspective, one cannot understand how they acted and to what ends and how the impact of their actions differed from their intentions.

Nowhere was the struggle over the meaning of work in the ICDS program more manifest than in the component of schooling. Contrary to the state's efforts to portray them as voluntary workers, most anganwadi workers that I interviewed referred to themselves as teachers, consciously eliding the difference between themselves and schoolteachers. The state, on the other hand, employed the discourse of motherhood in representing the efforts of anganwadi workers as being voluntary. By this logic, what anganwadi workers did in the crèches was deemed an extension of what a good mother would have done at home: the only difference was that the anganwadi workers performed that function for more children than would normally be found in a household. By the state's logic, therefore, the work done by an anganwadi worker differed in scope from what she did at home but was qualitatively equivalent to mothering. In contrast, by referring to themselves as teachers, anganwadi workers emphasized how similar their work was to that performed by teachers in elementary schools. Anganwadi workers, in effect, chose to emphasize the qualitatively different nature of work in the anganwadi as compared to that in the home.

Anganwadi workers were proud of those students who had either refused to leave their centers to go to a "Montessori" (the name for any school that charged tuition and claimed to teach English as a subject) or returned to the anganwadi because they had learned so much there. Once, I dropped in to visit the anganwadi in Alipur. Sharmila, the Brahmin woman who was the anganwadi worker, pointed to one of the girls in her class. Before she joined the anganwadi the girl used to walk a fair distance to a Montessori in an adjacent village. When she started attending the anganwadi regularly she discovered that her classmates knew more than she did. Sharmila commented that, because the Montessori charged Rs. 15 a month as tuition and the anganwadi school taught children for free, people in the village assumed that the education students received at the Montessori was better. "They don't value this education because it is free," Sharmila concluded.

At one of their monthly meetings anganwadi workers complained that, ironically, the superior education provided at the anganwadis actually created problems. The workers claimed that as soon as the children learned a little bit at the anganwadi their parents felt they were too bright to stay there and would transfer them to a Montessori or a government-run primary school. This resulted in high turnover, and many children left the anganwadis soon after beginning their education. The anganwadi workers added that this was bad for the children because in the government schools they were packed eighty to a class, and the teachers were usually found sipping tea in the courtyard instead of teaching. They pointed out that teachers in the government schools were paid thousands of rupees for their efforts, whereas anganwadi workers were compensated little for giving children individual attention.

The tension between voluntary worker and teacher was symptomatic of a more general contradiction that underlay the design of the anganwadi program. On the one hand, the anganwadi program was built on the notion that women, as the supposed natural caregivers for children, would be best suited to bring health and educational interventions to young children and to pregnant women and nursing mothers. On the other hand, anganwadi workers were expected to be professional in carrying out their duties and were bound to an even more impressive array of bureaucratic procedures and record keeping than their better-paid counterparts in government service.

The struggle over the definition of their occupation as teaching rather than voluntary work must be interpreted in the context of the struggle waged by anganwadi workers, particularly those who did not have the support of a male partner, to secure a livelihood. The stipends paid to anganwadi workers were so low that it was not possible for them to subsist on them alone. The position of anganwadi workers was not analogous to female welfare recipients whose position was theorized by Nancy Fraser as moving from dependence on a male partner to dependence on the state (seen as masculine). The effort by anganwadi workers to recast themselves as teachers was not only about acquiring symbolic capital, but also about staking claims to a real salary in the future, to an income sufficient to give them a measure of financial independence.

Mahila Samakhya functionaries were also paid an honorarium and did not have the job security, status, employment benefits, and incomes of government workers. Mahila Samakhya workers were seen as providing altruistic, voluntary service in helping move their disadvantaged sisters forward. Like the work of anganwadi workers, this was considered a naturalized extension of women's reproductive work, which is typically within the ambit of the family and remains mostly unremunerated in market economies (Sharma 2008).

Mahila Samakhya employees shared with anganwadi workers a feeling that what they did as professionals was qualitatively different from their tasks at home. Organizing women in villages drew them into a public sphere where they had previously little experience. They learned to write reports, to talk in public settings with men and women, to lead training workshops, to ride bicycles, to understand and use bureaucratic procedures, and to deal with government officials. Their work not only helped empower women to exercise their rights, but also was crucial to the success of other government development projects. They taught rural women how to monitor development projects and how to hold bureaucrats accountable. Mahila Samakhya workers contrasted themselves to government employees in emphasizing their dedication to the job, as seen in their willingness to work diligently for a fraction of the pay government employees received (Sharma 2008).

I have looked at three sets of governmental practices to think about the relationship between neoliberalism and biopolitics through an examination of two programs, the ICDS and the Mahila Samakhya. While there is much to distinguish the two programs, an ethnographic examination reveals surprising similarities in the operation of the programs. Both were heavily invested in the biopolitical goal of mapping the population so that it could be better served, managed, and controlled. Both depended upon the exploitation of underemployed women who were disadvantaged by patriarchal social structures in the first place. It is cruelly ironic that, by not paying these women a living wage, the state perpetuated the structural violence that it was employing these women to help their sisters overcome.

Conclusion: Neoliberalism and Structural Violence

In investigating the links between neoliberalism and welfare here, I argue that a focus on the everyday practices of programs that are ideologically and conceptually on different sides of the neoliberal agenda enables one to understand continuities in forms of structural violence. Much work on contemporary state reform in India has in fact focused on tracking changes in trade and finance regimes, the deregulation of markets, and the dismantling of subsidies and of the license raj, and so forth. Many scholars have quite rightly commented on the dangers of the retreat of the state to the lives and survival of marginalized populations like rural women. Few have conducted detailed investigations of precisely how neoliberal globalization is transforming the redistributive functions of the Indian state or affecting its legitimacy and identity as an agency of social welfare. Does neoliberalism usher in a new era of violence on the rural poor? Is it complicit with an expansion of the production of bare life? These questions lie at the forefront of my analysis. The answers I arrive at take one away from where most of the controversy about neoliberalism is focused: on ideology and the formulation of policy. Instead, by concentrating on the specific modalities by which programs are implemented, I demonstrate that there are substantial continuities in biopolitics and violence across the period that divides neoliberal governance from earlier forms of rule.

In addition, by juxtaposing the everyday practices of state agencies at different levels against the broad shifts in national policy I further complicate the notion of state reform. Changes at the national level may or may not be reflected in the everyday practices of government officials and agencies at the level of the regional state, district, or subdistrict. My analysis shows how neoliberalism impacts various state sectors and levels differently and thereby marks the specificity of global neoliberal processes. My intention is to complicate overarching notions of state reform that are in fact based largely or exclusively on Western liberal democratic state policies. For example, the commonplace that neoliberalism results in cutbacks to welfare is hard to generalize for states that have never been welfare states. The now-well-accepted story that neoliberal reform results in a war on the poor, extending and deepening existing inequalities, requires careful rethinking in such a context. Mahila Samakhya could easily be interpreted as a program with a classic neoliberal agenda of creating subjects who are responsible for their own welfare. However, does it matter that Mahila Samakhya is working to empower its subjects so that they can better utilize government programs already in place for poor people? Since it is not the market but the state that is being appealed to here, how does one think of the articulations between neoliberalism and welfare in this context? The broader goal is to illustrate a mode of analysis that, when applied to disparate contexts, may yield important insights into the nature, extent, spatial location, and contradictions of neoliberal transformation of rule and states. It might help reveal the unevenness of neoliberal transformation and perhaps point to unexpected overlaps across contexts, through which a more nuanced picture of global neoliberalism can be reached.

The two programs I have analyzed are separated by a vast gap in terms of institutional design, policy objectives, the respective ideologies embedded in them, and the global political-economic context in which they were conceived. However much they differed in these important dimensions, they were also uncannily similar in many of their daily practices, from techniques of enumeration to their positioning of workers. While this does not mean that the two programs look exactly alike at the level of daily practice, it does show the overlaps between the programs that complicate a picture of clean breaks. In the eyes of villagers such continuities were often more important than the large structural and ideological distinctions that lay behind the scenes. Ignoring such facts, analysts might well conclude that epochal changes were taking place when they were not perceived as such by the targets and beneficiaries of such programs and perhaps even by some government officials. For this reason the articulation of everyday practices and representations with political economy, social structure, and institutional design offers a wider lens through which to examine and understand the continuities and discontinuities in states. In particular, if we seek to understand the production of violence against the poor, we are ill served by the metanarratives of globalization and neoliberalism. What we need, instead, is a much more nuanced appreciation of the manner in which such large trends articulate with particular contexts to produce forms of structural violence.

By disaggregating the state into its various levels and bureaus and by drawing attention to the routine, everyday practices of state bureaucracies, I am arguing that it is through such practices that the state becomes a material force in people's lives and domination is legitimized. For example, when Mahila Samakhya workers rebuffed demands for entitlements by saying they were merely an NGO and not a government organization, they were endorsing and perpetuating the belief that it is the government's job to distribute entitlements and to take care of the indigent. In other words, in the very act of distinguishing their activities from those of state employees, Mahila Samakhya workers were creating an image and expectation of legitimate state action. The Indian state differs from neoliberal states in the West that have slowly withdrawn the expectation that it is their job to look after the needy: market reforms in India have not been accompanied by the belief that poor people's lack of resources is the result of their internal mental and moral deficiencies. However, I might argue that it is precisely the consistent failure of the Indian state to deliver entitlements to the poorest that has been the distinguishing feature of the post-Independence state in India. The paradox I noted in chapter 1 should now be clear: the Indian state continues to base its legitimacy on its efforts to bring development to the poorest parts of its population and yet regularly fails to deliver on that promise.

Disaggregating the state shows us that disagreement and dissension characterize development bureaucracies. For example, some politicians and bureaucrats viewed Mahila Samakhya's aim of empowering women as a threat. Mahila Samakhya personnel often criticized the suspicion or overt hostility they encountered from local officials. Bureaucrats sometimes expressed their distrust by asking Mahila Samakhya workers if they intended to break up families (Sharma 2008). To a man (and I use *man* intentionally), officials in the block office told me that the ICDS program was a waste of the government's money and that it made no sense to fritter away scarce resources on women and children. Such reactions demonstrate that policy agendas set at the national level are not necessarily endorsed or supported by lower levels of the bureaucracy. Some initiatives, in fact, are actively subverted and never properly implemented; others are creatively reinterpreted to fit local conditions. These inconsistencies, conflicts, and corruptions, revealed through careful ethnographic analysis, are not incidental to how states function but lie at the heart of the institutional organization and reproduction of states. At the same time, it would be a great mistake to blame lower levels of the bureaucracy for the generally poor results of antipoverty programs. Thanatopolitics, I argue, is built into the design of government programs to the extent that the "difficulty" of removing poverty is normalized in the discourses of political and bureaucratic elites. This lack of urgency is encoded into the design of poverty alleviation programs and leads to a bureaucratic culture in which failures of implementation are not merely tolerated but expected.

However, we cannot see this lack of urgency as a problem just for the national state. Thinking about the levels, sites, and scales of the state also directs us to the role of transnational ideologies, institutions, and processes of governance in the management of poverty. In this regard, the lack of urgency on the part of transnational agencies and financial and political elites in the First World in preventing the deaths of poor people worldwide is on a par with the situation inside India. One could point to the abysmally low figures of foreign aid from rich nation-states or to the fact that the misdirection of what little aid is provided is deliberately ignored. Similarly, when faced with a choice between making marginal improvements in their own economy or enormous changes for the lives of the poor, policymakers in the North consistently choose to sacrifice the lives of the poor (I am thinking here of agricultural subsidies, among other things). Finally, through encouraging reckless consumption and environmental pollution in their own countries, political and economic leaders in the North actively collaborate to reduce the life chances of the poor.[27] Another reason for paying attention to transnational ideologies and the agendas of transnational institutions is that national policies and programs have historically emerged in articulation with them. For example, one could ask to what degree support for the rapid expansion of the ICDS program was dependent on the emergence of the Cairo consensus on population policy. Similarly, what does one make of the coincidence of the timing of the start of the Mahila Samakhya program with the global promotion of neoliberal ideologies by multilateral institutions that are dominated by powerful Western states such as the United States and the United Kingdom?

Even as one examines the articulation of transnational ideologies with national policymaking processes, however, one should also be wary of arguments that appear to "read off" trends in India from dominant global processes. However much transnational institutions and ideologies may have influenced the Indian experience, it would be a mistake to assume that welfare and empowerment programs in India simply reflect global trends. The two programs I have examined almost stereotypically represent two separate moments of globalization and modes of government. ICDS is a classic welfare program in which a paternalist state promises to look after indigent women; by contrast, Mahila Samakhya seems to exemplify the neoliberal emphasis on self-government and self-actualization. Yet a closer look reveals paradoxical and contradictory processes at work within each program and across them. For example, Mahila Samakhya explicitly draws upon the ideas of the Brazilian educator Paulo Freire as well as on national and transnational feminist movements, which problematized welfarist approaches to women's development that saw women as passive recipients of charity and promoted dependent relations between women and the state. Empowerment as a goal is thus the result of specific historical conjunctures with many different and unlikely partners.

One argument proposing to explain the rise of empowerment programs is that they function to transform the state in a neoliberal direction. In neoliberalism, large-scale redistributive programs such as ICDS are seen as unproductive because they increase recipients' dependency on the state and do not help make the state leaner and more efficient. By contrast, empowerment programs that do not deliver any goods and services to various client groups cost very little. Further, they help reduce social sector spending and therefore enable the state to shrink. The movement to neoliberal governmentality in the West has seen the dismantling of "welfare as we know it" and its replacement with programs that emphasize empowerment, such as workfare (Clarke 2004: 21–25). In the West neoliberal policies have replaced welfare programs —these constitute modes of governmentality that are sequential.

In the Indian case, these two modes of governmentality do not constitute sequential phases; instead, they are propagated simultaneously. For instance, the focus on empowerment encoded in such programs as Mahila Samakhya was supposed to have replaced welfare approaches to women's development like ICDS. Yet ICDS was not scaled down after the introduction of Mahila Samakhya; on the contrary, it has been made a universal program operating in all 5,380 blocks in the country. Counterintuitive as this may seem in the framework of neoliberalization, the growth of such welfare programs makes more sense once situated in the political and economic context of contemporary India. Populist democratic politics have ensured the growth of ICDS ever since ruling coalitions have struggled to build and maintain legitimacy after the opening of the Indian economy to global markets. For the vast majority of India's poor who live in rural areas, liberalization has been largely interpreted as a project by urban elites for urban elites. There is an ever more visible and growing gap between those hooked into global circuits of exchange and employment and those outside it. The ones outside this global circuit constitute a majority of the population, and they are unable to benefit from liberalization because of a lack of global markets for what they produce or because they lack the appropriate education or because of their lack of familiarity with English.[28] Politically, there are strong democratic pressures on the government to intervene in favor of those being left behind by market liberalization.[29] Distributive programs are perceived to contribute in important ways to the legitimacy of governments.[30] Instead of replacing welfare, empowerment programs help increase the efficiency of the delivery of essential goods for the survival of poor women (Gupta and Sharma 2006). Empowerment is seen as a means to enhance the ability of poor women to access services and programs already in place. Welfare services can be improved by the mechanism of empowerment, as one of the big problems with entitlements has been the inability of potential recipients to exert pressure on the bureaucracy to make sure that it delivers planned benefits.

Apart from delivering electoral support to politicians and popular support to the bureaucracy, entitlement programs are important to political and bureaucratic elites for another reason. Large programs with huge budgets allow avenues of patronage that prove essential in a democratic political system.[31] The distribution of goods and services allows politicians and bureaucrats to do favors to their supporters by providing them with jobs and material resources. Therefore, the prestige of a government program is directly correlated to its budget. Empowerment programs, with their low budgets and low overheads, are unlikely to get much political support in legislative and administrative circles. Another very important aspect of large programs is that they allow a percentage to be skimmed off to support the political projects of politicians and bureaucrats and enable their conspicuous lifestyles. Among the many considerations that go into the support of an entitlement program, the needs of the poor are nowhere near the top of the agenda. Some of the poorest may benefit from the distribution of favors to supporters, but such an agenda does not often reach the people who most need the resources. Not only corruption but also the supposedly normal operation of democracy often militates against the life chances of the poorest.

I have so far emphasized some of the reasons the state in India has not attempted to dismantle its welfare programs and bureaucracy. In fact, the relationship between welfare and neoliberalism is even more counterintuitive than I have suggested. The government's continued implementation of welfare interventions like ICDS might not have been possible without the transformation of the economy after liberalization. Because liberalization has led to higher rates of growth, government revenues have been increasing despite cuts in tariffs and taxes. This has made more resources available for redistributive purposes. Once again, we see contradictory forces at work to create this conjuncture: the ideology of neoliberal governmentality supports cutting back welfare programs, not increasing their reach. However, the pressures of securing legitimacy in a democratic politics and the growing economic resources that allow for this possibility have resulted in an expansion of ICDS.[32] A simplistic understanding of neoliberalism's impact on the poor would miss the multiple ironies at play here, ironies that demand us to pay close attention to social processes rather than rehearsing well-intentioned political slogans.

There is no definitive evidence whether neoliberal economic policies in India have left the poor more vulnerable to disease, malnutrition, and unemployment through, respectively, the breakdown of the public medical infrastructure, higher prices for food grains, and the lack of employment opportunities, particularly in rural areas and among unskilled laborers. Such outcomes are very likely. However, we do know that liberalization has been accompanied by the universalization of ICDS and the launching of a massively ambitious program of employment generation, the Mahatma Gandhi National Rural Employment Guarantee Act. Under this new scheme, every household, no matter what its economic status, will receive wages equivalent to a hundred days of employment a year.[33] What remains to be seen is whether such ambitious measures to care for the poor will end up making a dramatic difference to their life chances. Will the poor continue to be "targets" of programs intended to shore up the legitimacy of ruling regimes but that make little difference to whether they live or die? Are the programs to care for the poor in place precisely to inoculate us to the political possibility of their death becoming a scandal? Questions like these need to be at the forefront of any investigation of the relation between the state and poverty in India.

The fundamental question raised in this book is why a state dedicated to development appears to be incapable of doing more to combat the violence of chronic poverty. Given that the past two decades have seen rapid rates of growth in India this question becomes even more acute. Poverty rates have fallen—but why have they not fallen faster? Why do so many of India's citizens continue to live in such appalling conditions? And why does their death not constitute a scandal that delegitimizes ruling regimes? Referring to Foucault and Agamben, I have tried to demonstrate how biopolitics operates through "normal" bureaucratic procedures in a manner that depoliticizes the killing of the poor.

Here I seek to trace the implications for the poor of the political economy of India since liberalization. What implications does the peculiar pattern of growth in India, with services being the leading sector, have for the poor? How does one explain the paradox of high rates of growth in the past twenty years coexisting with persistent and tenacious poverty? Why has the decline in poverty not been more rapid, given the greater emphasis being paid by the state to welfare schemes and redistributive programs? Finally, at a time when ambitious new schemes of social development are being announced regularly, why is the Indian state faced with an armed insurgency from its poorest and most disenfranchised citizens?

I begin with the changing nature of the Indian state. In his landmark analysis of the postcolonial state Pranab Bardhan (1984) argued that three blocs or dominant proprietary classes—industrial capitalists, rich farmers, and the "salariat"[1]—were bargaining for power and dividing the resources mobilized by the state among themselves. The danger of a state that was formed by the relative bargaining power of this tripartite coalition was that resources, rather than being expended on productive investment, were often frittered away on current consumption through subsidies and handouts to keep each bloc happy.

Liberalization signaled the breakup of this precarious balance between dominant classes and also signaled the decisive movement of the state machinery in favor of industrial capitalists. The Indian economy after liberalization has not followed the classical model of development. According to this story—the dominant story of economic history—a nation-state develops by first employing surpluses from agriculture to fund manufacturing industries and then, as wage rates and levels of expertise rise and the economy grows more information centered, by shifting the center of gravity from manufacturing to services.

By contrast, India's economic development is somewhat anomalous in that services have not risen after a prolonged period of growth in manufacturing. The manufacturing sector has gone from being a distant second to agriculture to a distant second to services. Any story of India's development trajectory has to consider the importance of the fact that services make up 55 percent of India's GDP and employ 28 percent of the workforce, as compared to industry, which makes up 29 percent of GDP and only 12 percent of total employment. The situation in agriculture is quite dismal: agricultural growth has consistently been lower than growth rates in services and industry, particularly in the two decades after the Indian economy was liberalized. I want to first trace the implications of this fact for the patterns of accumulation in the Indian economy and for its effects on poverty in particular.

Any long-range plan for combating acute poverty has to begin with the generation of employment and income for the vast majority of poor people, with a safety net to help ensure that those who are unable to work can survive on the basis of transfer payments. It is here that the particular pattern of economic growth in India after economic reforms is especially discouraging in regard to the prospects of the poor.

The Implications of Growth Patterns for the Poor

It is now clear that rapid growth in India has not generated a correspondingly high growth in employment. This is primarily for two reasons: first, manufacturing technology employed in the growth of industry has been quite capital-intensive and thus has not generated as much employment as more labor-intensive technology might have done;[2] and, second, high growth in the service-led sectors has led to a selective investment in human capital because of the manner in which the sector is tied to the global economy. The consequences of these two developments are that the benefits of growth have not spread widely through the rapid absorption of the unemployed and underemployed.

The importance of the service sector has not significantly improved the employment prospects of those who do not have the educational capital to link into the global economy of services. Here, the divide between the person who went to a rural or semiurban high school and studied in a vernacular language and a person who went to an elite, English-speaking school in a large city is enormous and unbridgeable. The effects of the dual economy (Lewis 1954) become visible in the labor market: on one side are the people who have high-status jobs because they work for large companies in the formal sector; on the other are those who are condemned to work in the informal sector. Few people have the prospect of moving from the low-status side of this divide to the other because of the investments in educational capital required. The poorest people have little hope of securing employment in the formal service sector because they are often illiterate and because their children are rarely able to access the quality of schooling that would catapult them into the formal sector employment market.

The success in services has created a dual economy characterized by sharp income disparities. The people who have benefited most from the growing connection with the global economy are those in the knowledge industries, who were, in any case, the most privileged in terms of cultural and educational capital. The service economy creates sharp divisions in any society in which literacy rates are low for the simple reason that only a few people can hope to join that economy, with its attendant benefits. Given India's low investment in higher education and even lower investment in primary education, there is no time in the foreseeable future when the majority of Indian workers will be able to join the globally connected service sector, except in ancillary jobs such as drivers, peons, food service workers, and janitorial staff. Even there employment will be limited to those who have significant educational and cultural capital compared to the mass of available workers. This all but rules out employment prospects in this sector for the poorest parts of the population.

If the broad base of workers is to be employed by industry, then it is more likely to happen by exploiting labor arbitrage in the manufacturing sector. Despite the fact that there is and always has been a labor elite in manufacturing, educational and cultural barriers to joining this elite are few. One needs good contacts to get such a job but, depending on the nature of the job, not a lot more else by way of skills and knowledge. There are two caveats here: first, that global competition in this sector is much more intense, especially from countries like China, which have the advantage of relatively good infrastructure and a reasonably well-educated workforce; second, given the capital intensity of most industries today, the employment effect of new capital investment is relatively weak. In other words, given the massive numbers of underemployed and unemployed people in India, the amount of capital needed to employ most or all of them in manufacturing industries would be immense. This would have to be accompanied by huge investments in infrastructure in order to attract manufacturing capital. Nobody knows where those investments will come from, so it is likely that the country will see incremental growth in this sector rather than phenomenal changes.

There are two exceptions to what I have said so far, and they both concern the informal sector. The rise of services, and with it a middle-class with large sums of disposable income, has given rise to a boom in construction. Most of these construction projects can be classified into three categories: infrastructure projects; office buildings, shopping malls, and similar buildings; and, finally, housing for the middle class in the form of high-rise buildings and single-family homes. All of these construction projects use unskilled laborers, many of whom migrate to work in such projects from rural areas in other states. Such laborers are almost never provided with housing and therefore have to eke out an existence in slums and shantytowns in urban areas or at the construction sites themselves. Children can often be seen working at these construction sites, which are almost never regulated to ensure that they meet existing guidelines for safety and the employment of child labor. This is one of the ways in which the poor "benefit" from economic growth, by obtaining ancillary, often dangerous jobs at the margins of such growth.

The second exception has to do with the wide variety of informal manufacturing that arises to support formal manufacturing units. Unskilled workers, who cannot obtain jobs in the formal sector, sometimes find employment in these small, unregulated firms that are set up to manufacture spare parts for larger firms and that also produce unofficial replacement parts for industries and for the vast array of consumer goods flooding the market. The size of this informal industrial sector is unknown, but it is likely that its employment effects on poor, illiterate people are considerably more significant than those of industries in the formal sector.

Finally, this leaves agriculture and nonfarm agro-based industries as the last resort for absorbing the vast numbers of rural unemployed and under-employed. When liberalization was introduced, agriculture accounted for 32 percent of GDP; within two decades that figure has almost been halved. This is not because of negative growth rates but because growth rates of other sectors have increased much more rapidly. Although agriculture now represents less than 16 percent of GDP (2009–10 figures), officially it still accounts for 52 percent of all employment. Actually, that is a misleading statistic because it very likely confuses rural residence with agricultural employment.

Rural areas continue to house the majority of the population. However, many rural people—about a quarter, according to Dipankar Gupta (2005: 752)—are now employed primarily in nonagricultural work, so the traditional equation between agricultural and rural assumed in the statistic above no longer holds. Another way of putting it is to state that the importance of agriculture in the Indian economy is receding but the importance of rural populations is not. Yet even today when people talk of the countryside it is almost exclusively in terms of peasants and farming rather than of people who live there and do nonagricultural tasks such as craft work, weaving, sericulture, and brick manufacture. There is a very substantial and probably severely undercounted rural population that subsists by seasonal migration. Finally, because there are now better roads connecting the countryside with cities, many people commute from villages to jobs in nearby towns and cities. Given that most poor, rural people lack such assets as agricultural land and milch cattle, they are more likely to engage in nonagricultural work in rural areas and to migrate seasonally for jobs in cities.

Why did liberalization not cause growth rates in the agricultural sector to jump, as in services and manufacturing? Why has the impact of trade liberalization on agriculture been so weak? Agricultural goods have encountered stiffer resistance partly because of trade protectionism in the North, particularly in Europe and the United States. Agricultural goods have not found markets (and high profits) in international trade, and growth rates of exports have been slow. The government was very slow to support agri-food processing and value addition by setting up cold chains, road infrastructure, the development of ports, export incentives, and marketing support for the Fresh Fruits and Vegetables sector, which includes horticulture, with its high margins—the steps that might have resulted in a booming agricultural sector. Even the growing demand from the large cities did not generate enough upstream demand for agricultural products to lead to fast rates of growth and employment in rural areas. Perhaps the sole exception here is the story of milk, butter, and fresh cheese (*paneer*) production, but that process started well before liberalization. It was left to private firms to advance crop loans to farmers to grow cotton and oilseeds, and this was done without any system of crop insurance. The suicides of farmers that have resulted, apart from their human tragedy, serve as a grim lesson to young people in rural areas: stay away from this job or you may end up like this.[3] Is it any wonder, then, that young people do not want to stay in agriculture, that they would rather work in a nonagricultural job, preferably in a nonrural setting (D. Gupta 2005)?

Why did liberalization not benefit agriculture? At the time that liberalization was introduced there were in fact several strong peasant movements, of which the best known were the Bharatiya Kisan Union (BKU) in U.P., Shetkari Sangathan, Sharad Joshi's movement in Maharashtra, and the Karnataka Rajya Raitha Sangha (KRRS), led by Professor Nanjundaswamy. Although led by rich peasants and primarily benefiting them, all these movements had built multiclass rural coalitions that sought to bring people together along sectoral and geographical lines (rural and Bharat versus urban and India). However, they were sharply divided among themselves in terms of opening the economy to global trade in agricultural commodities. Some of them favored doing so, seeing it as an opportunity to reap large profits. For example, the onion growers of Joshi's coalition favored the opening of markets in agricultural commodities because of the new possibilities of exporting their crop; others, however, like the BKU, that had built their central platform on input subsidies feared this move because profits on the crops they were primarily growing (wheat, sugar cane) would be undercut by international competition. KRRS also agitated against the entry of trading and seed-selling multinationals like Cargill into the Indian market. Unlike the federations of Indian industry (FICCI and FII), which, despite differences among their members, quickly resolved to support liberalization and then used government policy to favor industry as a sector, the peasant movements were hopelessly divided and failed to come up with a unified set of demands for the agricultural sector.

The result has been that agriculture has recorded the slowest growth rates of the sectors in the Indian economy. Agriculture is the only place where the vast majority of the unemployed and underemployed population can find employment in the short and medium term, but that will not happen if there is slow growth in this sector (Eswaran, Kotwal, Ramaswami, and Wadhwa

2009). Without significantly increasing growth rates in agriculture, there is little chance that the poor will see a growth in their employment prospects or wages.[4] In the absence of employment opportunities, any effort to combat poverty will have to continue to depend on transfer payments, and the role of the state in mediating those payments will continue to be central.

Proponents of liberalization sometimes assume that if growth rates are high enough, the problem of poverty will automatically be solved because wealth will trickle down and create income opportunities for all groups. But if high growth rates have a narrow population base and depend on high levels of skill and educational capital, very likely the benefits of high growth in the economy as a whole will not reach the majority of the nation's population. The most probable result of this skewed pattern of growth is that it will only increase inequalities between people in urban and rural areas and between educated workers in the service sector and others. Poor people in rural areas in particular find that there is little room in the new economy for those who do not have high levels of cultural and educational capital.

If one thinks about poverty, it is not just the widening economic distance created by the conjunction of class and sectoral differences that is of concern. Equally important is the fact that the lives and experiences of many people who are part of the new global economy are increasingly cut off from those of the urban and, especially, rural poor. For most of the urban middle-class there is no possibility of understanding, let alone sympathizing, with the struggles faced by poor people. An upper-middle-class child growing up in a large city in neoliberal India, a child who has never been outside an air-conditioned space, will find it difficult to even imagine the life of a rural child who has never had access to such basic necessities as adequate quantities of food, running water, and good schools and textbooks, let alone feel some degree of solidarity with such a person. Although such class divisions are not new, the gap between those who have tapped into the global economy and those who have not is increasing rapidly in contemporary India, and this has mostly negative implications for the type and intensity of structural violence that one is likely to see emerging in the future. Already, middle-class citizen groups clamoring for clean cities are crowding out their poorer neighbors by encouraging the demolition of shantytowns, and middle-class demand for services often proceeds on the assumption that poor people's access to small quantities of free water and electricity should be stopped in order to provide a more regular supply for those consumers who can afford to pay. Citizens whose incomes have gone up now demand a Western lifestyle, often pitting them against the poor in an unequal competition for scarce resources.

Nevertheless, despite the fact that the urban poor and the rural poor in agricultural areas have been adversely affected by the skewed pattern of growth in India, they are not as badly off as the poorest citizens of the nation-state. I am referring to the indigenous, tribal population, which is facing an unprecedented threat not only to its livelihood, but also to its very existence.

Armed Violence and Structural Violence

In the middle of September 2009 Prime Minister Manmohan Singh surprised a number of people by declaring that Naxalite violence was India's "gravest internal security threat" (The Hindu, 16 September 2009, 1). The term "Naxalite," originating from the name of a village in West Bengal where a peasant insurgency began in the 1960s, is used to refer to a disparate group of left-wing Maoists who are affiliated with the Communist Party of India-Marxist-Leninist (CPI-ML). Manmohan Singh could have chosen many likely candidates for such an honor: the separatist movements in Kashmir and Assam that have been threatening to tear apart the country; Islamic terrorists who were collaborating with the Pakistani secret service to destabilize India; Hindu fanatics who were undermining Indian democracy by waging a majoritarian war against Muslims; the Shiv Sena, who was murdering people from other states working in Maharashtra. Why, one wondered, did the prime minister choose the Maoists as the target of his government's ire? Manmohan Singh admitted that the government had not been successful in containing this menace and that the level of violence attributable to left-wing extremism continued to rise in the affected states (Deccan Herald, 16 September 2009, 1). The prime minister went on to say that Naxalism "manages to retain the support of a section of the tribal communities and the poorest of the poor in many affected areas" (Deccan Herald, 16 September 2009, 1). Home Minister Palaniappan Chidambaram claimed even that the number of people who had died because of the Maoist menace far exceeded those who had died of other causes and that that fact therefore justified putting the threat posed by Maoism at the top of the government's security agenda. "They have declared a war on the Indian state," he said. "They are anti-development. They do not want the poor to be emancipated or become economically free" (http://www.timesonline.co.uk, 12 March 2010; accessed 19 July 2010).

The official consensus on why poor tribal people are rebelling seems to be that it is the outcome of ineffective government programs aimed at development and redistribution.[5] By this logic, poor tribals are registering their protest at the inadequacy of developmental interventions in their lives. The fact that they are taking up arms implies that the government has failed in its developmental mission. The two central assumptions of this discourse are that armed struggle is a form of protest against the poor implementation of development programs to provide schools, hospitals, roads, production loans, and so on to tribals and that, like everyone else, tribal people are really looking for such interventions to help better their lives. Such an explanation comes with its own agendas for action, which target lower-level officials for their failures to implement the programs already in place. It also propagates the idea that tribal people really share in this developmental vision and reinforces the state's developmental agenda. But, as commonsensical and comforting as this proposition might be, it fails to explain why tribal people are rebelling now. After all, the nonimplementation of the state's developmental agenda is not new: since Independence most of these interventions have not reached tribal peoples, and they have not protested before. What has changed recently to give the rebel movement a boost?

The problem of interpreting what is now a civil war led by radical left groups and supported by tribal populations as a protest against developmental failures is that it turns a blind eye to the larger issues brought about by the particular developmental agenda of the state in India. Two issues are notably salient here. The first is that India's tribal populations have been heavily impacted by large infrastructure projects such as big dams, whose goal is to provide electricity to urban residents and water to farmers. Although the Sardar Sarovar project drew international attention for its impact on poor tribal populations, it is only one very visible symbol of a far-reaching program to build several big dams. The ambitious plan to link India's four major cities with highways—National Highway Development Project—cuts through many areas inhabited by tribal groups, as does the proposed project on the linking of rivers—National River Linking Project.[6]

Second, the emphasis on growth has led to a renewed interest in areas where mineral resources are concentrated. Infrastructure projects like large steel plants and thermal power plants are being set up in areas that have iron ore and coal, respectively. It turns out that most of India's untapped mineral resources lie in areas where tribal populations live. Since liberalization, the rights to mine these minerals have been sold to multinational corporations of Indian and foreign origin. Tribal people do not for the most part have title to their land partly because nonagrarian modes of production are poorly served by procedures of land titling. Large chunks of tribal territory, which are owned by the state, have been leased to mining companies. Once mining operations begin in these territories, they will forcibly displace the tribal people who inhabit them. This is the immediate cause for alarm among tribal peoples; they are faced with the prospect of eviction from their traditional lands by the pressures of industrialization and infrastructure development. It would be hard to explain some of the nation-state's poorest citizens' enthusiasm for armed insurrection on the grounds that they were protesting the failure of development. That is not new: they have never had schools and schoolteachers, hospitals and doctors, or banks and microcredit. Similarly, they have always had to deal with the rapaciousness of forest officials and timber contractors, the brutality of policemen, and the arbitrariness of local government officials.

What is new is that they are now facing the prospect of being evicted from their traditional lands. In response to the threat posed by Maoists, the government has launched a high-profile police action in India's tribal belt. A radical left-wing guerrilla movement has long flourished in the forested areas of India's tribal belt, seeking to redress the appalling conditions of exploitation of India's indigenous peoples and finding protection in terrain that is difficult for police and army forces to traverse. This movement is quite small in terms of numbers and fighting ability, but it is seen as a grave danger by the Indian state. As tribal people are increasingly displaced by infrastructure projects and mining companies, the possibility exists that this movement will converge with tribal uprisings, and that would render those areas unsafe for corporate and governmental activity. To preempt such a possibility, the Indian government has started a massive police action to flush out the Maoists from these territories. Whether or not government forces are successful in their efforts, one thing is clear: the vast majority of poor tribals, who are not connected to the Maoist movement in any sense, are likely to flee their homes as a consequence of being caught in the deadly crossfire between government forces and the Maoists. Such a clearing of the territory is precisely the result that would allow mining companies unfettered access to the land, and those with a bent for conspiracy see a hidden agenda in the state's sudden interest in escalating the fight against Maoists.

The eviction of tribals from their land is facilitated by the lack of legal protection for their rights to land. Even when tribal people have occupied certain territories for many generations, they are essentially considered squatters on state land and have no legal claims to it. When the state auctions off mineral rights on that land, tribal people have no legal basis on which to assert their rights to stay on that property and receive no compensation that may aid them when they are displaced. Unlike property owners, they are not eligible for compensation since their land is not seized under eminent domain. Tribal groups are not only the most marginal of India's poor, but also legally liminal, since they, unlike indigenous groups in the United States and Canada, have not been granted any sovereign rights under the Indian Constitution.

Confronted with a form of enclosure movement created by the trajectory of development being pursued in India, tribal people are faced with the prospect of being displaced from the forests that have not only given them sustenance but also represent the meaningful landscape in which they live. Displacement for tribals means separation not just from economic livelihoods but from the cultural and spiritual resources that give meaning to their lives. Fleeing from the conflict between government forces and the Maoists, the nation-state's poorest citizens will be exposed to physical hardship and social death. They will be robbed of the forest resources that sustained them physically and of the spiritual and community resources that sustained them socially. India's indigenous population constitute what Agamben means by homo sacer, people whose deaths will not even be considered a sacrifice on the altar of development. Unlike those who are recognized as projected affected persons owing to their displacement from big dams and other infrastructure development projects, the tribals who flee from the armed conflict will have no special status that entitles them to compensation or to resettlement aid. This is one of the ways in which people are not simply exposed to death but are killed by an unofficial displacement that does not even allow them recognition as victims of development.

Structural violence and armed violence come together here to lead to the death of the poor. Small peasants have successfully resisted the appropriation of their land under eminent domain because they have a secure legal entitlement, and they can decide whether they wish to sell their land when manufacturing industries want to set up a base, as we have seen from the recent examples of Singur and Nandigram, where peasant groups foiled attempts by their state governments to expropriate farming land for industrial development. By contrast, indigenous groups have a much more tenuous legal entitlement to the land on which they have historically lived. Most of the land on which they live is legally owned by the state, and the government could move forward on the sale of mineral rights on these lands without seeking the approval of these communities or obtaining their consent. Indigenous groups are thus faced with the prospect of being evicted from their lands without consultation or compensation. Fearing that the Maoists will be able to capitalize on this fact and convert a small guerrilla movement into a mass tribal uprising, the government has taken action to preempt such an eventuality. The result has been nothing but an intensification of forms of violence against the poorest citizens of the nation-state. Caught between the direct violence of paramilitary units and the Maoists, many poor tribal people will have no choice but to flee their home villages. Because such flight will be seen as voluntary, that is, not required by the government, the displaced, who will already have experienced a social death in being separated from their homes, will be exposed to death anew by being plunged into a situation in which they lack the knowledge, resources, and infrastructure to earn a living or to benefit from welfare programs.

Given this background, one can see why official explanations of the success of Naxalites in tribal areas are so inaccurate. It is difficult to believe that tribal dissatisfaction with the failure of government programs to reach them lies at the root of the insurgency. However important this fact may be, it pales in comparison to the wholesale threat to the lifestyle and livelihoods of tribals posed by infrastructure and industrial development. The Maoist insurgency needs to be theorized not as a protest against the failures of the welfare state, but as a desperate struggle against the failures of a developmental vision in which tribals, even more so than other poor people, are seen as expendable—as homo sacer, those who can be killed without sacrifice, inside and outside the law.

One cannot generalize from the condition of poor tribals to all of the poor. With tribal groups one sees the logic of primitive accumulation—which depends on the dispossession and displacement of people already living on mining lands—with sharp clarity. However, the violence against tribals does not help one in understanding the position of other groups of poor people. It does not explain, for example, the paradox of neoliberal state policies accompanied with a growing emphasis and increased investment in social services.

Competitive Populism and the Poor

In the standard narrative of neoliberalism, the emphasis has always been on the slashing of public expenditure by cost-conscious governments, not on increasing public outlays to enable people to meet their basic needs. One of the puzzles of contemporary neoliberal India is how one explains the increase in social investment aimed at the poor. One could argue that this is a peculiar outcome of Indian democracy because voter participation for poor, subaltern, and rural populations is often higher than that of urban, middle-class people and because poor and rural groups form a preponderant part of the electorate. The increasing visibility of new programs of social welfare could be seen as a form of competitive populism, in which regimes attempt to cement their popularity by starting programs to appeal to indigent voters.

Another explanation for the rise of welfare programs has been offered by Chatterjee (2008), who emphasizes elites' fear of class war. He argues that if the effects on the poor and those displaced from their land and livelihoods by primitive accumulation are not reversed by government policies, it might turn them into "dangerous classes." I think there is altogether too little evidence to suggest that current social programs are intended to reach or actually do reach those who are being displaced from their lands and livelihoods by current patterns of capitalist development. But this hypothesis does suggest something important about the role played by interpretive frameworks in shaping government policy. The dominant interpretive framework among ruling elites appears to be that poor people take up violence only when social welfare programs fail to provide them with the resources necessary to survive. Therefore, when faced with violent social upheavals like the Naxalite movement in tribal areas, policymakers respond by ratcheting up spending on social welfare and improving the implementation of existing government programs. As part of the war against the Maoists, a tenfold increase in social spending on Naxal-affected areas of India is being proposed (TNN, 8 July 2010).[7]

The broad support enjoyed by policies of inclusive growth that form the cornerstone of the ruling regime's economic policies may also be motivated by this fear of violence if the needs of the poor are ignored. In practice, "inclusive growth" has not meant including the poor in growth. What it has meant is taking the higher government revenues obtained from rapid growth in sectors of the economy tied to the global market and redistributing them to indigent sections of the population. It is fair to say that the growth of the rural economy has not been a central concern of government policy and that without involving the rural economy inclusive growth is not possible because that is where the majority of the population lives.

I think one can adequately explain the enthusiasm for ramping up government schemes to help poor people by the politics of democracy rather than by the fear of class war. The lesson learned from successive elections is that parties are punished for ignoring the needs of rural voters: the lesson often taken from the Bharatiya Janata Party's (BJP's) "India Shining" fiasco in 2004 is that the party failed to pay attention to rural voters (although there were probably other reasons for that defeat having to do with the failure to build a good electoral coalition). Similarly, the lesson taken from the Congress's reelection in 2009 is that rural sops paid off handsomely. In states, midday meals and free electricity appeared to be the chief vote getters. The success of the late Y. S. Rajasekhara Reddy, popularly known as YSR, in Andhra Pradesh in kicking out the tech-savvy and entrepreneurial former chief minister Chandrababu Naidu from power illustrates this process of electoral populism.

In the initial period after the advent of neoliberal policies there were indeed cutbacks in government expenditures on social services. Yet in the past few years incredibly ambitious new social programs like the Mahatma Gandhi National Rural Employment Guarantee Scheme have been launched. This scheme is the most expensive social program ever launched in India and one of the most expensive such programs in the developing world. The budget for 2009–10 allocated Rs. 39,000 crores ($8.4 billion) to this program. Other programs have also been planned, launched, or extended. These include the programs for basic education (Sarv Shiksha Abhiyan), with an allocation of Rs. 13,100 crores ($2.8 billion), a program to provide midday meals in schools, with an allocation of Rs. 8,000 crores ($1.7 billion), extending the ICDS program to make it universal, that is, extended to every block in the country, with a budget of Rs. 6,700 crores ($1.5 billion); Bharat Nirman, a program for building rural infrastructure at Rs. 40,900 crores ($8.8 billion), the National Rural Health Mission, funded at Rs. 12,070 crores ($2.6 billion), a rural drinking water mission funded at Rs. 7,400 crores ($1.6 billion), Total Rural Sanitation Program at Rs. 1,200 crores ($250 million), a slum eradication program called the Jawaharlal Nehru National Urban Renewal Mission, with a budget of Rs. 11,842 crores ($2.5 billion). In addition, the creation of an official category of below poverty line status comes with a host of subsidies and grants; and the latest budgets have also seen a jump in the expenditure on health services, to almost 10 percent of the total budget.

What is interesting about these programs is not merely that they go against the grain of received wisdom about neoliberal cutbacks to welfare, but that their scope and scale have been so dramatically extended as the central and state governments have become friendlier to corporate capitalist interests. There is no doubt that the fear of a backlash against the urban capitalist class by those who have been left out of the rapid growth of India's economy provides the legitimacy for such programs, which for the most part are seen as necessary even by those groups.

Electoral democracy might help explain why these programs are introduced, but it does not help one understand how they are financed. This is where the role of industrial capital becomes central. The ability of central and state governments to fund these programs has a lot to do with the increases in tax collections that have been registered in recent years. Most of the increased tax revenue comes from large companies and salaried employees. Agriculturalists are not taxed, no matter how wealthy and, de facto, neither are small traders, merchants, and owners of businesses in the unorganized sector. Independent professionals like builders, doctors, lawyers, and accountants typically pay only a small fraction of the tax they owe. However, the advantage for state governments of having large corporate enterprises in manufacturing, services, and retail is that tax revenues are much more reliable. With the rapid growth of the manufacturing and services sector tax revenues have climbed, and it is these resources that enable the large social programs demanded by the needs of democratic politics.[8] This is a very important reason industrial capitalists have succeeded in taking control of the state apparatus.

Democracy has created a situation in which the funding for electoral politics and for redistributive social programs comes increasingly from capitalists, but the popular vote comes mainly from rural populations and the urban underclass, the denizens of political society (Chatterjee 2008). To bridge this contradiction, programs like the Employment Guarantee Scheme and ICDS are necessary, as are the school lunch program and free electricity for farmers. On the other hand, it is also important for the state to allow capitalists increasingly greater access to decision making and central authority, to create tax holidays, new export schemes, Special Economic Zones, allow agricultural land to be converted to industrial use, and so on. Regimes have to balance the demands made by those who have not benefited from India's high growth rates and its immersion into the global economy for services on the one hand, and on the other the demands of corporate capital and the urban middle classes to create a good investment climate and world-class facilities in terms of infrastructure, and services such as hospitals, schools, universities, and so forth. There may very well come a point when these competing demands cannot be reconciled, but for the moment they lie in an uneasy compromise.

I have tried to explain how the tripartite coalition of industrialists, agriculturists, and bureaucrats that formed the dominant coalition in the license-permit raj has been replaced by different fractions of industrial capital. Despite this ascendancy of an urban, industrial class, with its attendant expansion of middle-class, salaried people living in cities and towns, the state has expanded its welfare functions in rural areas and among the poorest parts of the population. I argue that this is best explained by the articulation of popular democracy and decentralization with a form of capitalism with a narrow population base. I also suggest that unless growth rates in agriculture go up sharply, especially in its labor-intensive modes, aggregate employment in the country is unlikely to rise and inequalities will continue to widen.

Welfare programs may be able to paper over the cracks in the social orders of the nation-state, but it is not clear how long such a strategy can be effectively maintained. India still has the world's largest population of acutely poor people (from 250 to 450 million people live under one dollar per day), and the challenge facing the Indian state is to provide basic nutrition, education, healthcare, housing, sanitation, and clothing to all its population. Although growth has been rapid, the patterns of growth are such that they have left out and will continue to leave out the majority of the nation's poor population. The prospect that higher growth rates will bring about a significant and sharp reduction in absolute poverty is not good. The poor will continue to die from preventable causes, and the biopolitical task of managing the population will proceed apace with the self-satisfied air of a job done well against long odds. The pattern of growth after liberal "reforms," in other words, will ensure that the poor continue to be killed against the backdrop of a shining India.

1. Poverty as Biopolitics

1. I prefer the more cumbersome locution the "state in India" to the "Indian state" because, as argued below, the study of the state should not be confused with, or confined to, the nation-state. My study of the state in India is not just about the national state, but the state at the regional or provincial level, as well as at the levels of the district, sub-district, and Block. These levels are linked to each other but are not reducible to the "Indian state."

2. The lower number, 250 million, is based on National Sample Survey (NSS) data that estimate the percentage below the poverty line in 2004–5 as 22.15 percent and a population estimated at 1.115 billion. The higher figure, 427 million, comes from Chen's and Ravallion's (2007) estimate of the population living under $1/day in 2004. Using different methods of measurement, Chen and Ravallion (2007: 21–23) estimate the total number of people in India living below $1/day as anywhere from 371 million to 427 million. I realize that a head-count measure of poverty is a crude way to estimate levels and intensities of poverty (Sen 1982: 10–11). My point is that one does not need a sophisticated measure of poverty to be struck by the immensity of the problem.

3. India's position as the world's fourth largest economy is true if the GDP is calculated in terms of purchasing power parity; in nominal terms, India's position is twelfth. The first three positions are held by the United States, China, and Japan (World Bank 2008).

4. The data on infant mortality are from 2005. However, for the poorest 20 percent of the population the data are from the Human Development Report 2009: 201.

5. The figures for Mumbai come from Appadurai (2000: 646); the data for Kolkata are from Kundu (2003: 4). Kolkata also has a high proportion of people who sleep on the sidewalks.

6. The exact figures are 6 percent for education and 3 percent for health (http://www

.medindia.net/news). For changes over the 1980s and 1990s, see Dev and Mooij (2002), and Mooij and Dev (2004).

7. I take the evocative phrase "the scandal of the state" from the title of Rajeswari Sunder Rajan's book (2003). It will become clear that there are many overlaps between her concerns in that book and mine.

8. I have employed a very simple metric to come up with these figures. If everyone in India lived as long as they do in Kerala, there would be 12 percent more people in the nation-state. That gives us the total number. Divided by the average lifespan of 65 years, we can get a crude annual estimate. Demographer Shripad Tuljapurkar estimates that my figures would need to be revised upward by at least 20 percent and perhaps as much as 50 percent. In other words, actual annual mortality rates may be closer to 3 million (e-mail communication, August 19, 2007).

9. I am not arguing that the best way to theorize poverty is as an emergency. Calhoun (2004) makes a powerful case for reinterpreting global emergencies outside the framework of global humanitarianism. He contends that conceptualizing disasters and other emergencies as unpredictable, abnormal, and brief prevents one from seeing that they are a normal part of the global order rather than an exception (2004: 375). By emphasizing that so-called natural disasters are never simply natural, Calhoun points to the role of human agency and social inequity in creating such disasters, which makes them more akin to poverty than may be apparent at first glance. The analogy I draw with natural disasters is for the limited goal of emphasizing the lack of urgency in the response to poverty deaths as compared to the response to earthquakes or cyclones.

10. I am drawing here on the pioneering work on social suffering by Kleinman, Das, and Lock not only in emphasizing "what political, economic, and institutional power does to people" (1997: ix) but also in underlining the blindness in moral sensibility that enables people not to acknowledge the pain of others (1997: xiii). Calhoun (2004: 392–93) cautions us about the depoliticizing effects of the use of humanitarian aid to manage global instability. One such effect is to convince people that in normal circumstances poor people do not need help.

11. I am inspired by Scheper-Hughes's original intervention about the "routinization of human suffering . . . and the 'normal' violence of everyday life" (1992: 16). As Kleinman, Das, and Lock put it, "Much of routinized misery is invisible" (1997: xiii).

12. A closely related point is made by Kohrman (2007: 90) when he considers the depoliticization of tobacco deaths in China. A different critique of Agamben is offered by Fassin (2005: 381), who argues that the camp and the polis are the two sides of contemporary Western democracies.

13. One can reasonably surmise that the share of officials with such attitudes is roughly similar to other urban, middle-class Indians.

14. Elsewhere, Agamben (2000: 44) says that the camp is "the new biopolitical nomos of the planet" and "the fundamental biopolitical paradigm of the West."

15. The Emergency was, in Agamben's terms, a "state of exception." The prime minister, Indira Gandhi, declared a national emergency in 1975 and suspended the rule of law. The Emergency was characterized by the large-scale violation of human rights and the

arbitrary detention and torture of citizens. It was also the time when forced sterilizations were carried out in large camps; hundreds of operations were conducted daily in a desperate attempt to slow down population growth rates (see chapter 7).

16. The importance of paying attention to the differences between the refugee camp and the Nazi death camp has been emphasized in Redfield (2005: 341). Feldman's (2008) work on bureaucratic practice in Gaza, which was transformed into a giant refugee camp after 1948, helps illuminate the importance of bureaucratic practices in politically unstable places. Feldman's understanding of bureaucracy resonates most closely with my approach in this book.

17. Another, more permanent type of camp is the prison. The production of bare life in maximum security prison is explored by Rhodes (2005).

18. Marx comments in the Eighteenth Brumaire that "Hegel remarks somewhere that all great world-historic facts and personages appear, so to speak, twice. He forgot to add: the first time as tragedy, the second time as farce."

19. At prevailing exchange rates, that would be approximately equal to two dollars a month.

20. By contrast, *aurat* means "woman" but not "human." The Hindi words thus have analogous meanings as "man" and "woman," where *man* is often used as a substitute for *human* whereas *woman* is almost never employed in that manner.

21. I cannot detail the different connotations of man, human, and citizen and the relationship between them here. However, this relationship will perhaps be clearer from the descriptions of the interactions between bureaucrats and their clients provided in the rest of the book. I am grateful to Miriam Ticktin for emphasizing the importance of these issues to me.

22. The categories of care and concern refer to the policy facts of reaching out to provide welfare. I do not imply that policy directives translated into phenomenological outcomes and that state officials were compassionate or respectful of their clients.

23. Apropos to this section's epigraph, Morris claims that the suffering of groups and large populations is extremely hard to experience, represent, and grasp: "We see but in another sense do not see—do not truly experience—the suffering of multitudes" (1997: 39).

24. These ideas are most fully developed at the end of Foucault's lectures in the academic year of 1976 (2003).

25. Mbembe's (2003) term for this violence is "necropolitics." Banerjee (2006) qualifies this argument by bringing it into conversation with neoliberalism and neocolonialism, preferring to use the locution "necrocapitalism."

26. The only example Foucault is able to summon for this kind of violence is Nazism, which he explains as the fear that allowing someone else to live will dilute or weaken one's own population. He suggests that this obsession with eugenics and the fear of miscegenation is what enables the singular violence of Nazi biopolitics (Foucault 2003: 258–63).

27. Even when the law is blatantly violated, as when the Bollywood star Salman Khan ran his jeep over people sleeping on the sidewalk, nothing ever came of it: those people were beyond the principle of sacrifice.

28. The notion of sovereignty is insightfully explored in Hansen and Stepputat (2006).

29. This relation is perfectly illustrated in Farquhar's and Zhang's description of Maoist China (2005: 318–22).

30. Although Agamben goes on to suggest that the state of exception is now the norm, the ethical power of his analysis—its normative critique—depends upon a relation between "nonexceptional" states and normal life in which a sovereign ban does not operate for citizens.

31. Agamben's point would apply better to economic refugees from Bangladesh and Nepal in India.

32. This situation is analogous to the one reported by Biehl for Brazil. However, one difference is that the poor in India are not blamed for their own deaths because they have moral or civic deficiencies (see Biehl 2004: 120). One cannot study the violence of poverty without at the same time drawing attention to the social silence surrounding that violence (Das 1997; Cavell 1997: 95).

33. For a similar point regarding China, see Kohrman (2007: 108–9). Despite the fact that China's developmental indices are much stronger than India's, Kohrman argues that tobacco deaths constitute precisely a state of exception that does not generate public protest or condemnation.

34. Elden (2007) argues that the very forces of governmentality that were creating the population as an object were also creating territory as an object. Territory is not thus that which is displaced by a concern with the population but a property of states that is coproduced and coeval with population.

35. The relation between biopower and the nation-state has been emphasized in Farquhar and Zhang (2005).

36. Interestingly, Foucault identifies racism as such a sodality but nowhere mentions nationalism (2003: 255–58). Morris (1997: 39–40) argues that suffering is recognized only within a moral community. The nation functions as a moral community when it does not allow its members to be exposed to death. However, the violence of poverty in India and the relative indifference to its eradication indicate that the moral community is drawn in such a manner that not all of its citizens are included.

37. For example, such a discourse is mobilized in India to discuss Bangladeshi migrants.

38. Perhaps the only case in which such a sovereign right is challenged is in the case of civil war, particularly in regions that have natural resources. There are many examples of global humanitarian aid being mobilized when there is large-scale disaster such as famine, earthquake, tsunami, etc., but these examples only reinforce the argument about sovereignty as such aid is invited by the nation-state and has to be accepted by the government in power.

39. Galtung says, "It will soon be clear why we are rejecting the narrow concept of violence—according to which violence is somatic incapacitation, or deprivation of health, alone (with killing as the extreme form), at the hands of an actor who intends this to be the consequence" (1969: 168).

40. Galtung goes on to specify what he means: "Thus, the potential level of realization is that which is possible with a given level of insight and resources. If insight and/or

resources are monopolized by a group or class or are used for other purposes, then the actual level falls below the potential level, and violence is present in the system" (1969: 169).

41. Readers will be aware that the reference to capabilities points to Amartya Sen's work (1999: 19–20).

42. Farmer (2005: 9) criticizes an approach to structural violence that focuses entirely on legal protections to civil and political rights and instead draws attention to situations in which actions could have been taken to protect the vulnerable but are not taken.

43. Gledhill (1999) argues that the demands imposed on Third World states by global capitalist enterprises, along with the geopolitical agendas of northern states, sometimes results in the creation of states that kill their own citizens.

44. Another modality by which structural violence is effaced is by technocratic neutrality (Farmer 2005: 10).

45. In his work on Médecins Sans Frontiers, Redfield argues that the decision over life and death can be exercised by organizations other than states (2005: 344).

46. This point bears similarity with Ticktin's (2006) argument that humanitarianism functions as a means of violence and exclusion.

47. In an insightful article Nuijten (2004) demonstrates how systematic policy produces arbitrary outcomes in an agrarian community in Jalisco, Mexico. Although Nuijten's concern with arbitrariness is not identical to mine, her work does provide a good example of such processes in another part of the world.

48. For a more careful exploration of the many ways in which the state systematically discriminates against women, see Sunder Rajan (2003).

49. In fact, Veena Das (2007) offers an exemplary model of how to do this. The people she worked with were in fact the victims of extreme somatic violence and had lost family members to violence. Nevertheless, Das focuses on their agency in not forgetting and in not allowing others to forget the violence, while also attempting to stitch together a semblance of normal life.

50. I am calling not for a pure space in which subaltern subjectivity finds expression but for a mediated, translated, politically compromised space (Spivak 1988).

51. I have used the pseudonym Mandi for both the subdistrict and the district.

52. The IAS is an elite cadre of officials chosen through an extremely competitive nationwide exam. In its self-image, method of selecting officers, and style of operation it follows in the footsteps of the Indian Civil Service, the "steel frame" of the British colonial government.

53. Since the time I began this research, a new state, Uttarakhand, has been carved out of U.P., and new districts have been created in the remaining area.

54. The exact date of Singh's speech presenting the new reforms was 24 July 1991. Singh was appointed India's prime minister on 22 May 2004.

55. I am by no means suggesting that there have been no changes in these other sectors, levels, and branches of the state or that there have been no important changes in U.P. However, it is unclear to what extent these changes can be causally connected to liberalization in particular.

56. The agencies that did have some essential continuities with the colonial state and

perhaps even with precolonial states had to do with the keeping of land records (and hence rural taxation) and with policing.

57. One could not connect the genealogy of the activities of the Irrigation Department to the range of programs being run by the block office. Irrigation was only peripherally connected to the functions of the block office since it was a separate department with its own agenda.

58. For an overview of the changing nature of the tasks that central bureaucracies have to deal with and the often conflicting demands placed upon them see Krishnan and Somanathan (2005).

59. The work of Bardhan (1997, 2006) has been particularly important in advancing the scholarly understanding of corruption.

60. Stoler has made a persuasive case for considering such affective relations to be central (2004: 4–20). The distinction made by Massumi (2002) between affect and emotion offers an important direction for studying affective relations between the state and the poor.

61. See Feldman's (2008: 12) parallel description of governmentality in Gaza, in which techniques of rule are emphasized.

2. The State and the Politics of Poverty

1. Fuller and Harriss (2000: 1–2) argue that until recently anthropology paid scant attention to the cultural dynamics of modern states. This does not rule out an extensive anthropological literature on the state in general (see note 2).

2. The literature on this topic is by now quite extensive and includes Abrams 1988; Alexander 1997; Althusser 1971; Anagnost 1995, 1997; Ashforth 1990; Bayart 1993; Bourdieu 1999; Brow 1988; Brubaker 1992; Clarke 2004; Cohn 1987a, 1987b, 1996; Coronil 1997; Corrigan and Sayer 1985; Coutin 2003; Enloe 2000; Eyal 2003; Feldman 2008; Gal and Kligman 2000; Geertz 1980; Handelman 1978, 1981; Hansen and Stepputat 2001; Herzfeld 1992; Joseph and Nugent 1994; Kasaba 1994; Mann 1986; Mbembe 1992; Mitchell 1989, 1991; Mukerji 1997; Navaro-Yashin 2002; Nelson 1999; Nugent 1994, 1997; Scott 1998; Sharma and Gupta 2006; Steinmetz 1993; Stoler 2002, 2004; Taussig 1992, 1997; Urla 1993; Verdery 1996, 2004; and Yang 1989.

3. Nielsen (2007: 695) presents a fascinating example of a context in which the state idea is produced and acted upon even in the absence of the state.

4. Some of the propositions forwarded here overlap with the existing literature. However, taken together, the propositions presented in this chapter represent a unique and coherent theory of the state. The distinctiveness of the approach I advocate lies not only in the connections made between the different propositions, but in the emphasis I place on different aspects of the theory of the state, including methodological ones.

5. I have more to say about this point later in this chapter. Disaggregating the poor is important precisely because distinct segments of poor people are impacted very differently by state programs and policies. However, whenever one uses a category such as "the poor," one ends up homogenizing and collectivizing a group that cannot be so ordered, and I merely wish to underline this in order to keep our critical

antennae up as we read texts in which the poor are invoked. I wish to thank Gail Kligman for emphasizing this point (personal communication, Monday, 13 December 2010).

6. Peter Taylor (1994: 151–52) suggests that the reason for the persistence of such unitary conceptions of the state may lie in its unique ability to organize social relations through territoriality.

7. While Kantola (2007) advances an argument that is similar to Gal and Kligman, her focus is on the notion of sovereignty in international relations theory. Kantola argues that looking at different levels of the state from a gendered perspective allows her to critique one of the main assumptions of international relations theory, namely, the unity of the state.

8. One measure of the proliferation of development programs was that even the person chiefly responsible for implementing them did not have an exact number at his fingertips.

9. The language and ideology of targets underlines the top-down, hierarchical, militarist, and masculinist discourse of state programs. A target is to be shot at, attacked, invaded, and penetrated.

10. *Shaasan* can stand for any level of the administrative hierarchy, from the central or federal government down to the local level.

11. An ethnography of government statistics—how they are generated, how they are verified, and how they circulate—might make for a fascinating research project. Apart from the question of the quality of the statistics generated, there is the issue of who produces knowledge about the social and what kind of knowledge is produced in the collection and circulation of statistics.

12. If one tries to map some of the important work on the modern state done in anthropology and India and focus on just one fact, namely, the level of the state being studied, some interesting observations result. Many important scholarly monographs on the state have focused largely or solely at the federal level. Here, I would include the historical ethnographies of Fernando Coronil (1997) on the Venezuelan state and Andrew Apter (2005) on the Nigerian state. This is also the case with pioneering work on the Indian state, such as Pranab Bardhan's *The Political Economy of Development in India* (1984). On the other hand, works that focus on regional states in India include books by Atul Kohli (1987), John Echeverri-Gent (1993), and Thomas Hansen (2001). Clifford Geertz's fascinating study (1980) explores the relations between the central Balinese state and regional ones.

13. In the case of the scholarship on India, Bardhan (1999) and Kohli (1987) focus on administrative and legislative divisions; Hansen (2001) concentrates on the legislative dimension in his focus on one political party; and Rajeswari Sunder Rajan (2003) deals most extensively with the judicial system.

14. The phrase "the state" is rarely used in popular discourse in a country like the United States, where one is more likely to hear criticisms or praise of "the government." In nation-states where socialist political parties and leftist thought have been more important, such as France and Britain, the state is more likely to be part of everyday discourse. I am grateful to Keith Baker for suggesting this to me.

15. The topic of state effects created by micro-markers has barely been mined in the existing scholarly literature.

16. This is not intended to be a panhistorical argument. For example, an event such as a riot might shape the perception of people who experienced violence very profoundly. But even in such cases, as Das (2007) has argued, it is the encounter with various forms of bureaucracy *after* the riots, from the police to politicians and riot-relief agencies, that may be of greater importance in determining people's ideas of the state.

17. Holmes and Marcus (2006) have termed such forms of knowledge production "para-ethnography." For more on this process, see part 3 of the book, "Inscription."

18. I am grateful to Sean Cubitt of the University of Melbourne for stimulating questions that led to this formulation (13 September 2007).

19. I am aware that not all subaltern people are poor. Here, I am talking of those people who are both poor and subaltern.

20. Although I take the phrase from Machiavelli, the earliest writing in this genre is generally attributed to Chanakya's *Arthashastra*. I would include in this genre white papers and a great deal of the academic work on development.

21. Much has been made about the similarity of institutional forms of states in the work of sociologists like Meyer (1980), and Meyer, Boli, Thomas and Ramirez (1997).

22. Gal and Kligman (2000) have emphasized this point in their study of reproduction and family in East Central Europe.

3. Corruption, Politics, and the Imagined State

An earlier version of this chapter was published in the *American Ethnologist* (Gupta 1995).

1. Nuijten (2003) makes a very similar argument about the relationship between Mexican peasants and the state.

2. The term *retail corruption* is taken from Parry (2000).

3. Since the terms *narrative*, *discourse*, and *representation* have been used to mean such divergent things, this definitional foray, which carries the risk of appearing overly simple for literary analysts, is important for purposes of clarity for readers in the social sciences.

4. Steinmetz has summarized it well: "Narrative thus has a beginning, a middle, and an end, and the movement toward the end is accounted for by conflicts, causal explanations, and the sequence of events" (1992: 497). There is a great need for scholars trained in literary analysis to direct their attention to corruption narratives as a genre of folklore (see chapter 4).

5. Ironically, an earlier version of this chapter (Gupta 1995) has been criticized for employing *discourse* to cover practice and action (Fuller and Harriss 2000: 13).

6. Hegel had proposed a triangle, but the third leg—the family—has often dropped out of the analysis of the public sphere. This is a problematic move because so many spheres of state action like the census, the registration of land, laws on inheritance, etc. depend upon a notion of a household and a family.

7. Daniel Jordan Smith (2007) makes a similar point in his incisive study of corruption in Nigeria.

8. Herzfeld remarks, "Thus anthropology, with its propensity to focus on the exotic and the remarkable, has largely ignored the practices of bureaucracy. . . . Yet this silence is, as Handelman has observed, a remarkable omission" (1992b: 45). Handelman's work (1978, 1981) attempts to do for bureaucracies what ethnographers such as Rohlen (1974, 1983) have done for institutions such as banks and schools. Recent work that focuses on bureaucracies includes Riles (2000, 2006) and Hull (2003).

9. An interesting discussion of the problem posed by such stereotypes is found in the introduction to Smith (2007). Pierce (2006: 888) raises similar questions in his study of Nigeria. Shore and Haller (2005: 3) emphasize this point as well.

10. The term *Third World* encapsulates and homogenizes what are in fact diverse and heterogeneous realities (Mohanty 1988). It implies further that First and Third worlds exist as separate and separable spaces (Ahmad 1987). I will thus capitalize it to highlight its problematic status. In a similar manner, the West is obviously not a homogenous and unified entity. I use it to refer to the effects of hegemonic representations of the West rather than its subjugated traditions. I therefore use the term simply to refer not to a geographical space but to a particular historical conjuncture of place, power, and knowledge.

11. A phenomenon that Johannes Fabian (1983) calls "allochronism."

12. This point was first made by Partha Chatterjee (1990) in response to Charles Taylor (1990). Chatterjee's book (1993) restates the argument and develops it further.

13. I am grateful to Dipesh Chakrabarty for first bringing this to my attention. See the excellent concluding chapter of his monograph of the working class in Bengal (1989).

14. Scholarly and popular definitions sometimes overlap. However, at times they may diverge quite sharply. An excellent review of the problems of definition has been provided by Williams (1999). A comprehensive overview of the literature on corruption in economics is provided in Bardhan (1997) and Jain (2001). Similarly, a review of the literature for anthropology is to be found in Shore and Haller (2005) and for development and politics is provided by Doig and McIvor (1999). Rose-Ackerman's pioneering work (1978, 1999) has provided the most detailed and thoughtful analysis of corruption in its many forms.

15. Rose-Ackerman (1999: 91) points out that while this definition is widely accepted, it fails to recognize that the distinction between private and public roles is not found in all societies. I would qualify this by saying that at the very least one can say that this distinction does not have the same meaning in different societies. See Shore and Haller (2005: 2) for a trenchant critique of this definition.

16. The causes of corruption identified in the literature are far too varied to reconstruct here (Bardhan 1997, 2006; Heidenheimer and Johnston 2002; Hellman, Jones, Kaufmann, and Schankerman 2000; Gillespie and Okruhlik 1991; Husted 1999). Heidenheimer and Johnston (2002) is still probably the most exhaustive resource for the definition, causes, and consequences of corruption. Hellman et al. (2000) point out that corruption is fundamentally seen as a problem of governance and is found where states are too weak to control their bureaucrats, to protect property and contract rights, and to provide institutions that result in the effective rule of law.

Hellman et al. (2000: 4) choose, instead, to emphasize "state capture," the effort by corporations to change state rules by making private payments to public officials.

17. Ades and di Tella (2000: 19–22) refute this idea on the basis of existing data.

18. This point is made in Jain's survey of the literature (2001: 97), in which he notes that only one study has focused on the relation between corruption and income distribution. That study noted that high levels of corruption adversely affected the poor, causing both poverty and increased income inequality.

19. The word itself is derivative of the Sanskrit *bhransh*, which means "to fall or drop down." *Falling* connotes much the same as in English, namely, to stray from or deviate from a prescribed path. In turn, straying from the right path implies a normative vision of right conduct that may draw upon notions of *dharma*. Bodily gestures and moral orientations are thus brought together in both cases. I am grateful to Vasudha Dalmia for helping me locate this derivation.

20. Smith (2007: 53–87) gives several examples of similar actions in Nigeria, where illegal or immoral actions in support of kin were not considered corrupt, even when similar actions by other people were denounced as corrupt.

21. The failure of social scientists to problematize modern imagination has been underlined by Scott (1998), who demonstrates the violence that has attended the implementation of "schemes to improve the human condition" through what he calls "state simplifications." These are techniques of imposing order and organization on what are considered chaotic and disorderly traditional systems.

22. In her work on Ghana, Hasty (2005) emphasizes the relations between discourses of corruption and affectively engaged social desires.

23. The headman is an official elected by all the registered voters of a village. Political parties rarely participate in village elections in the sense that candidates do not represent national or regional parties when contesting these elections. Although they may play important roles in representing the village to bureaucratic and party institutions, headmen are considered neither part of the administration nor the grass-roots embodiment of political parties.

24. Since the word *federal* is rarely used in India, I will refer to it by its Indian equivalent, that is, *central*.

25. I use the term *hold court* because Sharmaji's mode of operation is reminiscent of an Indian *darbar*, a royal court (a novel that exploits precisely this meaning of the term, *Raag Darbari*, is analyzed in chapter 4).

26. At the exchange rate prevailing at the time of the incident in 1989, $1 = Rs. 18, the client in effect handed Verma the equivalent of $0.56. That figure is misleading, however, since it does not indicate purchasing power. Ten rupees would be enough to buy a hearty nonvegetarian lunch at a roadside restaurant for one person or one kilogram of high-quality mangoes but not enough for a pair of rubber slippers.

27. Following the pioneering work of Judith Butler (1990), I could employ the vast body of work on performativity here. However, in the context of the state, performativity has more often been deployed to think about performances by the state rather than the more mundane interactions between officials and clients (see Taylor 1997;

Navaro-Yashin 2002; and especially Sharma 2008). I am grateful to Don Moore for first bringing this point to my attention.

28. This was not always the case. In most instances, the amount that had to be given was common knowledge and was often baldly stated by the concerned officials. Thus, there was considerable variability in the way that rents were extracted. Some rents were firmly set while others had to be negotiated around a modal amount. In general, when the amount that had to be funneled to higher officers was indexed to the total cost of the transaction (say, at 1 percent of the value of a house), then the rent was more likely to be a fixed, well-known percentage.

29. At prevailing rates of exchange, that was approximately $215.

30. The village development worker is a functionary of the regional government responsible for the implementation of development programs in a small circle of villages, the number in the circle varying from three to a dozen depending on their populations. Like other government officials, the village development worker is subject to frequent transfers, at least once every three years.

31. Sripal claimed to know the exact amount by consulting "people who can read and write." The officials at the block office told me, however, that a sum of Rs. 8,000 was allocated for such projects.

32. The relationship between literacy and bureaucracy is explored at greater length in chapter 6. Sripal's actions serve as a useful example of the arguments advanced in that chapter.

33. I later learned that Rs. 3,000 of the total cost is given as a loan that has to be paid back in twenty installments stretching across ten years.

34. Fuller and Harriss (2000: 25) support this observation in their own synthesis of the anthropology of the modern Indian state when they say, "It is also notable that even the poor, low-status and weak can sometimes benefit from their own adequately competent manipulation of political and administrative systems."

35. I would like to thank Joel Migdal for pointing this out to me.

36. The symbolic representation of the state has been explored by several scholars. Bernard Cohn (1987b: 658), for instance, has demonstrated how the Imperial Assemblage of 1877 enabled the British colonial state to represent its authority over India at the same time as it made "manifest and compelling the [colonial] sociology of India." See also Geertz 1980; Dirks 1987. Recent work includes, among a large set, D. Taylor 1997; Apter 1999, 2005; Navaro-Yashin 2002; and Özürek 2004a, b.

37. I have deliberately avoided use of the term *public sphere*. As Habermas (1989) makes clear, the public sphere is the space where civil society emerges with the rise of bourgeois social formations. It is there that critical, rational debate among bourgeois subjects could take place about a variety of topics, including the state, and it is there that checks on state power emerge through the force of literate public opinion (Peters 1993). Since the argument that follows raises doubts about the wholesale import of these categories to the particular context being analyzed, the notion of the public sphere is not particularly helpful. I should hasten to add that I am by no means implying that the West is unique in possessing a space for public debate and

discussion. The notion of the public sphere, however, denotes a particular historical and cultural formation shaped by feudalism, kingly rule, and the rise of capitalism, the importance of urban centers, and the dominant role of the church as an institution that is not replicated in the same form elsewhere in the world.

38. Whereas radio and television were strictly controlled by the government in India until the early 1990s, the press was and continues to be relatively autonomous and frequently critical of the state. The only other important source of news in rural areas, transnational radio, remained limited in its coverage of India in that it focused on major stories and lacked the detail and specificity of newspaper accounts.

39. Riles (2000: 2) emphasizes the importance of documents to all anthropological work and draws attention to the low evidentiary and conceptual status of documents in anthropology.

40. This is not to imply that anthropologists have not incorporated newspapers into their analysis in the past (see, for example, Benedict 1946). Herzfeld (1992a: 94) explains the marginal role of newspapers very clearly: "Journalism is treated as not authentically ethnographic, since it is both externally derived and rhetorically factual. . . . In consequence, the intrusion of media language into village discourse has largely been ignored." Herzfeld makes a strong case for scrutiny of newspapers even when the unit of analysis is the village; others, like Benedict Anderson (1983) and Achille Mbembe (1992), have stressed the theoretical importance of newspapers in the construction of the nation and for the analysis of the state, respectively.

41. My analysis of newspapers looks at connections between local and transnational discourses of corruption but not at the links between transnational capital and local newspapers. For example, although none of the locally distributed newspapers (English-language or vernacular) is even partially owned by transnational corporations, many of them depend on multinational wire service bureaus for international news. A detailed study would also have to account for the complex relationship between domestic and international capital accumulation. Further, the connection between the ownership and content of newspapers is an incredibly difficult one to establish and is quite beyond the scope of this chapter. I wish to thank an anonymous reviewer for raising these stimulating questions.

42. Herzfeld has issued a warning one would do well to heed: "We cannot usefully make any hard-and-fast distinctions between rural and urban, illiterate and learned (or at least journalistic), local and national. These terms—urbanity, literacy, the national interest, and their antonyms—appear in the villagers' discourse, and they are part of that discourse . . . the larger discourses about Greece's place in the world both feed and draw nourishment from the opinions expressed in the tiniest village" (1992a: 117). "Attacking 'the state' and 'bureaucracy' (often further reified as 'the system') is a tactic of social life, not an analytical strategy. Failure to recognize this is to essentialize essentialism. Ethnographically, it would lead us to ignore the multiplicity of sins covered by the monolithic stereotypes of 'the bureaucracy' and 'the state'" (1992b: 45).

43. Although literacy rates were relatively low throughout the region, the impact of newspapers went far beyond the literate population, as news reports were orally

transmitted across a wide range of groups. For this reason, researchers have to be careful about drawing political implications from low rates of literacy (chapter 6 explores this question in detail). Political news on state-run television, Doordarshan, by contrast, was met with a high degree of skepticism because everyone concerned knew that it was the mouthpiece of the government.

44. *India Today* is published in a number of Indian languages and has a large audience in small towns and villages. Corruption also figures prominently in the vernacular press, and in what follows I will compare the coverage there with magazines like *India Today*.

45. At prevailing exchange rates, Rs. 64 crores = $36 million. Therefore, 64 paise was equal to 3.6 cents, less than the cost of a cup of tea.

46. The program in question was the Integrated Rural Development Programme (IRDP).

47. This fact should dispel the myth that the discourse of corruption is to be found only among the urban middle class of so-called Westernized Indians.

48. To warm one's pockets is a metaphor for taking a bribe. I have translated all the titles from the Hindi original.

49. The sweet in question is a regionally famous one—*pedaas* from Mathura.

50. It would perhaps be more accurate to talk of subject-positions rather than subjects here.

51. My analysis here is limited to Hindi newspapers that publish local news of the Mandi region.

52. For the importance of rumors in the countryside, see especially Guha 1983 and Amin 1984, 1995.

53. It is in this sense of violation of norms that the term is often extended to moral life quite removed from the state, to mean debasement, dishonesty, immorality, vice, impurity, decay, and contamination. The literature on corruption has been bedeviled by the effort to find a set of culturally universal, invariable norms that would help decide if certain actions are to be classified as corrupt. The only reason I have chosen not to spend too much space here discussing the classic corruption literature is that it had very little to say about the chief concerns of this chapter, namely, the ethnographic analysis of the everyday functioning of the state and the discursive construction of the state in public culture. A representative sample of the viewpoints in the corruption literature can be obtained from Clarke 1983; Huntington 1968; Heidenheimer and Johnston 2002; Klitgaard 1988; Leff 1964; Leys 1965; Monteiro 1970; Rose-Ackerman 1978; Scott 1969, 1972; Tilman 1968; and Wade 1982, 1984, 1985. A spate of ethnographic accounts of corruption is shedding new light on the topic: see, for example, Pavarala 1996; de Sardan 1999; Parry 2000; Smith 2001; Bähre 2005; Haller and Shore 2005; and Hasty 2005.

54. I am grateful to Lata Mani for stressing this point to me.

55. For example, a highly placed official who fails to help a close relative or fellow villager obtain a government position is often roundly criticized by people for not fulfilling his obligations to his relatives and village brothers. On the other hand, the same people often roundly condemn any official of another caste or village who has done precisely that as being corrupt and guilty of encouraging nepotism.

56. Focusing on issues like corruption allowed the Kisan Union to build a multiclass alliance of which the poor were a part. Most of the other concerns of this farmer's organization reflected its base among the better-off residents of the countryside.

57. Interestingly, although the rhetoric of the Kisan Union predicates its opposition to the state in terms of the state's antifarmer policies, most of its grass-roots protests are organized around local instances of corruption. The behavior of corrupt officials then becomes further evidence of the state's exploitation of farmers.

58. If one were to analyze the discourse of corruption in a region where dominant landed groups and lower levels of the state were more overtly complicit, one would probably find that it attains a very different texture.

59. De Vries (2002) makes an important argument about how the imagination of the state is mediated by particular kinds of representations and performances. In western Mexico the figure of the cacique is central to imaginations and representations of the state.

60. At the time this interview took place, Rajiv Gandhi was the prime minister of India.

61. One *lakh* = 100,000. At the time of the interview, Rs. 1 *lakh* was approximately equal to $6,000.

62. I am grateful to an anonymous reviewer for raising this important question.

63. Other peasants who believe that lower, but not upper, levels of government are corrupt may not hold that belief for the same reasons as Ram Singh.

64. All government positions have reservations or quotas for the scheduled castes—a certain percentage of jobs at any given rank are kept aside for people from the lowest castes.

65. Sometimes the word *shaasan*, which is closer to "administration," is also employed.

66. I am by no means implying that the viewing of television explains why Ram Singh holds this opinion about the corrupt middle levels of the state. He may very well believe in it for other reasons as well. Television, however, seems to have influenced his views on this matter: "We get a little more worldly."

67. His reference to "illiteracy" must not be taken literally—he was referring to his perceived lack of cultural capital.

68. This point has been emphasized by Herzfeld (1992a: 99) in his discussion of the Greek village of Glendi and the provincial town of Rethemnos: "There has never been any serious doubt about the importance of the media in connecting villagers with larger national and international events. Like the folklore of earlier times, the media spawn an extraordinarily homogenous as well as pervasive set of political clichés. Much less well-explored, however, is how this discourse is manipulated." Herzfeld's use of the term "manipulation" should not be taken to imply the presence of a deep intention working toward particular goals; rather, one should think of employability, that is, the diverse ways in which such discourse can be used in different circumstances.

69. There may be an important element of fantasy in poor people's construction of the state with a capital S: as a coherent, coordinated, and powerful entity whose locus of authority rests at the pinnacle of political power. Ram Singh's faith in the central

government has echoes of such a fantasmatic construction (see also Nuijten 2004: 223; Taussig 1992).

70. It might be objected that this kind of statement involves an analytical circularity: constructions of the state are contextual and situated; yet any attempt to define context and situation involves the use of discourses that may themselves have been shaped by, among other things, constructions of the state. Following Foucault and especially Haraway (1988), I want to argue that the search to escape the mutual determination of larger sociopolitical contexts and discursive positions is untenable. The analyst, too, is part of this discursive formation and cannot hope to arrive at a description of situatedness that stands above, beyond, or apart from the context being analyzed. I am grateful to an anonymous reviewer at *American Ethnologist* for forcing me to clarify this point.

71. Frustrated with the reification of the state and convinced that it was just a source of mystification, Radcliffe-Brown (1940: xxiii) argued that the state be eliminated from social analysis! One of the most thoughtful discussions on this topic is to be found in Abrams (1988).

72. Fuller and Harriss (2000: 23) argue along similar lines but they offer the opinion that "The state can and often does appear to people in India as a sovereign entity set apart from society by an internal boundary that seems to be as real as its external boundary." I have deliberately left my conclusions more open-ended because I do not think we have the ethnographic evidence to back up such a claim with any degree of confidence.

73. See also Smith (2007: 88–137), where the articulation of foreign donors, NGOs, and the Nigerian state is presented in some detail.

74. See also chapter 4.

75. See Hansen (1998) for an example from Mexico. Harrison (2006) makes the point that international discourses of corruption profoundly influence local ones without determining their content or meaning.

76. Elyachar (2005: 113) makes much the same argument, emphasizing the distinctiveness of corruption in a neoliberal context as opposed to others. Her argument forces one to think about the historical discontinuities and disjunctures hidden in the term *corruption*.

77. The relationship between local, national, and international contexts vis-à-vis the meaning of corruption is explored in Harrison (2006).

78. Amartya Sen's study of famines (1982) employs a theory of entitlements to explain who suffers in a famine and why. See also Appadurai (1984).

79. I am not suggesting that it is only here where possibilities for intervention exist.

80. The source is *A Tract on Monetary Reform* (Keynes 1971).

4. Narratives of Corruption

1. Film, television, and radio are other extremely important media for the circulation of such narratives, but the analysis of these texts is beyond the scope of this chapter.

2. One of the most common stories involved the edict that all officials had to be at their

office. The story went that officials were too scared to stay away from their offices illegitimately, but when they all turned up for work they discovered there were not enough chairs in the office to seat everyone. Since there had never been a day when all government servants actually attended their offices, the office had never made provisions to seat everybody!

3. Smith (2007: xii–xiii) makes a similar point about why he started working on corruption in Nigeria. A broader argument for the importance of fiction to development studies is made in a very interesting article by Lewis, Rodgers, and Woolcock (2008).

4. I use *stories* and *narratives* as synonymous terms.

5. Bhatti's television show *Ulta-Pulta* (1987) proved to be enormously popular. It showed an ordinary character who has to deal with corruption in different arenas of everyday life. Such depictions of what Parry (2000) has called "retail corruption" struck a chord with viewers. Bhatti (2001) followed up this show with a series satirizing the higher education system. Closer to Bhatti's original series is *Office Office*, a series of vignettes about corruption in which an ordinary person is caught in the web of corrupt officials. Each episode has the same actors in different bureaucratic institutions, ranging from the railways to the police to the municipal office. It shows wily bureaucrats who efficiently and ruthlessly extract resources from a hapless and simple-minded client and usually do not deliver the services he desires.

6. A very thoughtful exploration of the relation between narrative and violence is to be found in Briggs 2007.

7. For example, the number of people who claim to have personally delivered sacks of rupee notes to the prime minister's or chief minister's house is likely to be very small. However, the number of people who can relate stories about "someone they know" who has indulged in such a practice is much higher; the circulation of such stories depends in part on their plausibility and in part on their unverifiability.

8. For these ideas on the iterability of social practices, I draw especially on the work of Butler (1993) and Bourdieu (1977: 78–95; 1990). The intertwining of linguistic and social iterability is central to their understanding of the reproduction of relations of inequality, which are always contingent (see in particular Bourdieu 1993). Despite the very significant advances made by their work, much remains to be explored for an understanding of "the imagined state" (see chapter 3) and its narratives, particularly in terms of corruption.

9. In my opinion this complexity has been insufficiently appreciated in the scholarly literature on corruption, which pays almost no attention to narratives or to their relation to actions.

10. Bardhan (2006: 341) points to the difference between the manner in which economists approach the problem of corruption, emphasizing incentives and punishments, from that of anthropologists and sociologists, who put the stress on values and ethics. Staying within the bounds of this division for the moment, I do not see these as mutually exclusive approaches. In fact, I will argue that one cannot reset incentives and punishments without addressing values and ethics, and vice versa.

11. After all, there are other features of social life that are just as ubiquitous as corruption but that draw little comment from people who live in those social worlds.

12. In posing this question I do not mean to imply that people in urban India or elsewhere in the world may not be equally fascinated by corruption or that there is something peculiarly Indian in this response. I have limited myself to rural north India so that I do not imply that a fascination with corruption is somehow inherent to the phenomenon rather than a historically and culturally situated reaction. Starting from what I empirically observed, I hope to generate some insights that other scholars can employ in their own investigations of urban India and elsewhere in the world.

13. Among the scholars who have made promising interventions in this direction are Wade (1982, 1984, 1985), Pavarala (1996), Guhan and Samuel (1997), Visvanathan and Sethi (1998), Parry (2000), and Gould (2010).

14. Bähre (2005: 112) argues that scholars "need to embrace the anger, frustration, and actions of those who suffer from these [corrupt] practices." He is making a case for a particular kind of scholarly positioning.

15. Ahmad and Massumi distinguish affect from emotion. Although I use the terms interchangeably here, my analysis partakes more of the circulation of affect. For the affective charge of corruption, see also Hasty (2005).

16. Lomnitz (1995) suggests something similar in his analysis of political ritual in Mexico.

17. Such a reading practice brackets a more literary analysis of the form of corruption narratives, a task that lies beyond my competence.

18. The Jawahar Employment Scheme combined previous programs such as the National Rural Employment Programme and the Rural Landless Employment Guarantee Program. In August 2005 the JRY was, in turn, replaced by the National Rural Employment Guarantee Act, which was in 2009 renamed the Mahatma Gandhi National Rural Employment Guarantee Act.

19. Rajiv Gandhi's charges were not without support in the writings of social scientists. Wade (1982, 1985), for example, recounts how the "market" for public office, combined with a systematic bureaucratic appropriation of illegal revenue, has slowed developmental efforts in India. The problem for anyone who seeks to establish the exact extent of corruption is that the practices may be well known but remain for the most part undocumented and unobservable.

20. Such projects, which attempted to leave the state's impression on the landscape, have been an essential part of territorial states, as Mukerji (1997) has argued in her fascinating study of the gardens of Versailles.

21. Each ward elected two or three members to the village council depending on its population. After the 73d Amendment to the Indian constitution set up a formal structure for Panchayati Raj in 1993, one-third of the seats in the village council were reserved for women. In most villages in U.P. particular castes occupy a contiguous space or neighborhood in a village. The election of the village council by ward thereby ensured a fair representation of different castes on the village council. This did not say anything about political factions, since lower-caste and upper-caste groups could be split into factions, allied with each other. A powerful headman could have supporters of different castes elected from different wards.

22. Officials like Das complained that even if a road was half complete, no one cared as long as the money allocated for the project had been spent.

23. The method by which such statistics were generated or cited was never made explicit. Rajiv Gandhi's estimate was not based on any careful study of the inefficiencies of the bureaucracy. The figures of 90 percent given to me by the official and the 5 percent cited by the head of the block office were not based on any systematic data collection or published report.

24. The secretary is appointed for a Nyaya Panchayat, a unit that exists in purely administrative space and has no real presence on the ground. The Nyaya Panchayat typically consists of seven or eight villages.

25. Scheduled castes are untouchable castes; Muslims are technically outside the caste system but, depending on their occupation, are often placed within the caste hierarchy by being positioned between the three upper castes and the untouchables. If they work with leather or other so-called polluting occupations, Muslims are treated on a par with the scheduled castes.

26. This was not a very large outlay of resources (roughly US $233), approximating the money needed to build a one-room brick (*pucca*) house. Since funds were tied to population, bigger villages often received much higher allocations. When the program began in the late 1980s, the total sum allocated for the entire block was between Rs. 150,000 and Rs. 200,000, less than Rs. 2 per person in the block (approximately US $0.07). By 1992 the funds allocated for the program had increased substantially.

27. It is difficult to render an exact translation of the Hindi phrase he used: *jitnaa padhlikh laytaa hai, utna hee usmay swarth badh jata hai.*

28. As far as I am aware, there has been little written about the Indian state that seeks to understand this paradox.

29. Although he was legally required to do so, the secretary indicated that it was not fair of Das to expect him to have to come to these villages on a regular basis from his home, which was far away. In other words, there was a gap between their mutual understandings of what constituted normal practice as opposed to what was written down in the rules of procedure.

30. Monies that were now going to headmen had previously flowed through the bureaucracy and had constituted a substantial portion of these very bureaucrats' unofficial earnings.

31. Examples might include a road that was only partially completed or that washed away after the monsoon rains. Incompetence and mismanagement intensified and concentrated suspicions and allegations of corruption.

32. There were rules about how the funds were supposed to be distributed. In the old system, however, such rules were rarely observed.

33. I am not commenting here on its literary properties. I am concerned rather with the ethnographic insights it offers into the postcolonial Indian state.

34. An English translation by Gillian Wright was published by Penguin India in 1992, and it is from this version that I quote here.

35. In chapter 3 I described Sharmaji's office in the same terms because of the mix of counselors, courtiers, and favor-seekers to be found there.

36. It is significant that Vaidyaji is seldom depicted treating a patient in the novel! His medical expertise is clearly incidental to his vocation, which is politics.

37. Villages were often considered healthy environments compared to towns because they were perceived to be open and relatively unpolluted.

38. Jonathan Spencer (1997) has stressed this point in an important article.

39. By the time I did my fieldwork, it would have been almost impossible to find a police station where the constables were completely illiterate. The distinction between a literate bureaucracy and its largely illiterate clients forms the substance for chapter 6.

40. In a recent essay focusing on the middleman, Khanna and Johnston (2007) argue that brokers play a key role in affirming the status of officials and giving the bureaucracy a human face for clients.

41. The irony of this image can be appreciated only by keeping in mind that most villagers were illiterate even in Hindi and hence would be unable to read the advertisement ostensibly painted for their benefit.

42. Shukla does not say whether the "great man" is a politician or a senior bureaucrat.

43. In discussing high-ranking state officials, it makes sense to talk about their social separation from villagers and village life. However, such a gap would scarcely be visible at the lowest levels of officialdom. Many officials, like the secretary in the story above, continue to live in their home villages; they are state officials, but they are also themselves villagers. I am grateful to Stanley Tambiah for emphasizing this point (personal communication, 28 April 2003).

44. Compared to the complete dominance of economists in planning today, anthropologists and political scientists played a much more important role in the period after Independence. For example, Oscar Lewis's work (1954) on village politics was sponsored and published by the Planning Commission of India.

45. Incidentally, Nehru himself is often blamed for tolerating corruption and not coming down harder on corrupt officials, leading to a soft state (Myrdal 1968) and the institutionalization of forms of bribery that are considered the bane of Indian bureaucracies today.

46. In spite of massive new state interventions in the countryside, for example, through the Employment Guarantee Scheme and the universal elementary education program (Sarva Shiksha Abhiyan), very little new anthropological work in India appears to be focused on rural areas.

47. A similar argument about the importance of narrative to development is made by Rodney Hall (2003).

48. Anna Hazare's movement mobilized this anger against everyday forms of corruption among the urban, middle class. Had it built class coalitions with the rural poor, it would have proved to be a truly transformatory project. Hans Hansen's (1998) work on corruption in Yucatán demonstrates how moral critique of corruption can be mobilized and how it changes the manner in which the state is imagined.

49. Bardhan (2006: 347) goes on to say, "In general, by tireless and sustained public

campaigns to raise the social and political penalties of malfeasance, a critical mass of opportunist officials and politicians have to be convinced over a long enough period that corruption is not cost effective. This is a long and uphill battle, but well worth fighting."

5. Bureaucratic Writing as State Practice

1. In addition to Goody's pioneering work (1968, 1986, 1987), there have been other important anthropological studies of bureaucratic writing. See, for example, Messick (1993), Riles (2000), Tarlo (2003), Hull (2003, 2008), Das (2004), Gordillo (2006), Navaro-Yashin (2007), and Feldman (2008).

2. Heimer (2000: 95–126), Hull (2008), and Navaro-Yashin (2008) all emphasize the uses of documents by different groups of people.

3. Weber places great importance on writing as one of the constitutive conditions of modern bureaucracies (1968: 957).

4. Some of the requirements of paperwork in private bureaucracies are also owing to government regulations and hence can be traced back to government bureaucracies. However, a great deal of paperwork is internally generated and cannot be directly attributed to the impositions of the state.

5. The same forms of writing are to be found in bureaucracies of other states as well. As Weber pointed out a long time ago (1968: 956–57), there is more than a family resemblance between state bureaucracies and those found in modern corporations, nonprofit organizations, and neighborhood voluntary associations. For the different types of bureaucratic writing, see Orlikowski and Yates (1994).

6. Messick (1993: 231–50) reports that texts in Yemen, unlike other parts of the Arab world, were often written in the form of a spiral. In more recent, modern documents, by contrast, writing is constrained to straight lines, as in Western documents (Messick 1993: 234). This was connected to the loss of the centrality of the private notary as author and witness and the extension of state control (Messick 1993: 236), features that emphasize replicability and anonymity.

7. The form might include a question about a person's profession or place of residence, allowing status hierarchies to enter into consideration.

8. This feature of stripping away context has been stressed by Hargadon and Sutton (1997).

9. I borrow the concept of enframing from Mitchell (1988: 44–45); Malkki (1995) has also written about forms of categorical thinking.

10. Another kind of performance enacted by the form has been stressed by Aho (1985) and Brenneis (2000): its neutrality, transparency, and instrumentality. Forms insulate themselves from critical scrutiny by adopting a rhetoric of instrumentality.

11. Riles (2000: 5) says, "The ability to create and maintain files is the emblem of modern bureaucracy."

12. One fascinating version of this statement is to be found in the construction of the "file self." See Chatterji (1998) for a wonderful demonstration of this concept.

13. Tarlo (2003: 70–79) offers a detailed description of how files are put together in an urban bureaucracy.

14. The third copy was called the foot of the fine, and its purpose was to create a record that could be deposited in the treasury for archival purposes. In this way, private citizens could have transactions permanently recorded in the royal treasury (Clanchy 1979: 48). However, the practice of making copies of government dispatches was not an English invention. It forms a recorded part of bureaucratic procedure even in the ancient kingdom of Ebla (2400–2250 BC) (Goody 1986: 97). Goody points out that in West Africa the quantity of paperwork and the size of the bureaucracy underwent a drastic shift under colonialism (1986: 113–14), so one should be careful of reading this as a universal feature of bureaucracies.

15. The secretary's job was to be the official record keeper of the proceedings of the Kisan Seva Kendra as well as of the various village councils (panchayats) that had been assigned to him.

16. Appadurai remarks of the British colonial state that "statistics were generated in amounts that far defeated any unified bureaucratic purpose. . . . There is ample evidence that the significance of these numbers was often either nonexistent or self-fulfilling, rather than principally referential with regard to a complex reality external to the activities of the colonial state" (1993: 316–17).

17. Later, Clanchy remarks, "It would be rash to assume that such archives brought a return of information to the government which balanced the worry and expense of making them. . . . The making of such records is an indicator of the efficiency of the government rather than its cause. . . . The royal archives constituted a vast potential source of information, which could not be thoroughly consulted in the medieval period itself. Historians today are better equipped to search the rolls than the king's clerks were in the thirteenth century" (1979: 50).

18. Goody provides a very similar account of the growth of bureaucracy in northern Ghana from the colonial to the postcolonial period: "Over the eighty years that have elapsed since the [colonial] conquest, the lateral and vertical differentiation of the administrative set-up has grown enormously" (1986: 115).

19. The contrast being drawn here is with a person who is treated as an individual, that is, as someone who has a distinct life narrative.

20. Snow (1959) has posed this distinction as a problem for the modern university and for modern life.

21. One can think of these reports as supplying their readers with news of the state.

22. Further details can be found in chapter 2. Goody (1986: 95) observes that control over time through numbers was as important to politics as the controlling of space. In this regard, the role of the mass-manufactured watch was central, as it democratized an objective, mechanical calculation of time.

23. Since biogas plants required a substantial capital investment, poor people could not afford them. Therefore, although caste was a factor in the selection of recipients, class seldom played a role. Almost all the recipients were relatively wealthy households with agricultural land. In turn, the success of the plants had a lot to do with this narrowing of available households, as will become clearer in what follows.

24. The reference here is not to women in general, since there were plenty of *jat* women in Mandi as well. Rather, the subject of this sentence is women of the dominant

landowning group of *thakurs*. Partly because of status considerations and partly because of stronger patriarchal controls over their movement, thakur women did not work in the fields. However, they did a substantial amount of agricultural labor, such as the processing of various foods, in the courtyards of their homes.

25. Appadurai says, "Illustrating literally the power of the textual 'supplement,' . . . numerical tables, figures, and charts allowed the contingency, the sheer narrative clutter of prose descriptions of the colonial landscape, to be domesticated into the abstract, precise, complete, and cool idiom of number" (1993: 323). Numbers come with their own version of clutter; that is why presentations of numbers need narrative that focuses one's attention on the most important numbers in a table, the bottom line.

26. This is sometimes seen as the difference between records and reports (Smith 1985). Appadurai comments of the colonial bureaucracy in India that "numbers in reports provided more of a normalizing frame, balancing the contestatory and polyphonic aspects of the narrative portions of these reports" (1993: 326).

27. In its own language, this process is about reducing the number of variables to facilitate comparison. The numbers of statistics that could potentially be generated from cases that have many variables are very large; the reduction to a single variable is often a political act rather than merely a technical one. The simple tasks of bureaucratic accounting may thus conceal the depoliticization that goes on in such work.

28. In an insightful discussion Asad (1994) meditates on a similar process in the social sciences, comparing ethnographic work to statistical modes of representation.

29. Appadurai notes, "By the end of the eighteenth century, 'number,' like 'landscape,' 'heritage,' and the 'people,' had become part of the language of the British political imagination, and the idea had become firmly implanted that a powerful state could not survive without making enumeration a central technique of social control" (1993: 317).

30. The degree to which the census has become a baseline for understanding can be gauged from the fact that in his remarkably novelistic and self-reflexive text *Tristes Tropiques*, Lévi-Strauss struggles to determine the exact numbers for the Nambikwara population (1967: 286). It is a truly quixotic endeavor because he has little primary or secondary data, and, furthermore, the number he estimates has no role to play in his (or his readers') understanding of the Nambikwara.

31. Appadurai points out, for example, that the Mughal state did not conduct a census of persons and that the enumeration of group identities was not important to the Mughal state (1993: 329). To appreciate the political role of statistics, he argues, one must see that "colonial bureaucratic practice . . . helped to create a special and powerful relationship between essentialization, discipline, surveillance, objectification, and group-consciousness, by the last decades of the nineteenth century" (1993: 328). Kaviraj contrasts such enumerated communities with the "fuzzy communities" of premodern political formations (1992: 25–26).

32. Another argument proceeds from the distinction between higher-order or second-order needs and basic or primary needs. In this way of thinking, one first attends to the basic needs of food, clothing, housing, and good health and only then to higher-

order needs. Such a view implicitly constructs a Maslowian hierarchy of needs, ignoring issues of path dependence and directionality. In other words, how one fulfills basic needs will have profound implications in whether people live meaningful and rewarding lives. Conversely, the goals that a political and social formation aspires to will shape how it goes about meeting the basic needs of its citizens and what priority it gives to those needs.

33. The Human Development Index is part of the Human Development Reports issued by the United Nations Development Program (UNDP) (http://hdr.undp.org/en/).

34. In this regard, see in particular Ranajit Guha (1983: 251–77).

35. Kapur and Mehta (2005) draw attention to the rule-bound procedures of Indian state bureaucracies as well as to the lack of incentives for improving performance.

36. This program was intended for those poor and scheduled-caste people whose annual income was below Rs. 4,800 in 1991–92. People who did not have adequate housing, that is, who lived in houses that were falling apart or were *kaccha* (impermanent mud houses), were chosen as beneficiaries.

37. A beneficiary was sanctioned a number of bricks that would have been sufficient for a dwelling that was thirteen feet by eight feet. Almost all the houses constructed under this program were one-room dwellings.

38. By *intra-bureaucratic* I mean a process that does not involve members of the public as informants, witnesses, or spectators.

39. Weber (1968: 957) identifies the ability to appeal decisions in a highly regulated manner as a hallmark of modern bureaucracy.

40. The language of submission of a complaint—to register or to file—refers once again to the centrality of the register and the file in bureaucratic procedures. The complaint will become another entry in a register, a new file will be constituted because of the complaint.

41. Examples of how such paper trails were constructed are found in chapter 7.

42. The secretary was supposed to reside in one of the villages under his jurisdiction.

43. Jenkins and Goetz (1999) give an account of the pioneering organization in the state of Rajasthan, the Mazdoor Kisan Shakti Sangathan, which first demonstrated the power of the right to information.

44. The reluctance to get involved is similar to that found in the context of criminal cases in the United States: eyewitnesses often do not come forward for fear of retaliation by the criminals or the danger of having their lives exposed to public scrutiny because of media coverage or because of the ensuing police investigation or legal proceedings or both.

45. At prevailing exchange rates, this meant that a little over ten dollars was at stake for the labor costs.

46. By this, I mean that, by granting all the funds directly to the headman, the JRY invited complaints and criticism from his political opponents. Very often the opponents had good reason to complain. My point is that the very structure of the program made complaints more likely to be filed than other such programs.

47. Being sent to a difficult post was the harshest punishment possible in a system where one did not have the fear of being fired.

48. A break in service annuls one's seniority. Since all promotions are made strictly in order of seniority, a break in service can prove to be extremely detrimental to one's career.

49. This incident bears some similarity to the incident from the novel *Raag Darbari*, described in chapter 4. The only difference is that here the supervisor of the farm was not complicit in the corrupt scheme.

6. Literacy, Domination, and Democracy

1. Notable exceptions are Goody (1968, 1986) and Messick (1993).

2. The implications of Derrida's thought for anthropology are explored in a fascinating and insightful article by Morris (2007).

3. I am limiting these remarks to what Derrida calls writing "in the colloquial sense" rather than "writing in general" (1976: 125).

4. Goody (1986: 20) cites a Chinese commentary on the *Book of Changes* that says, "The holy men of a later age introduced written documents . . . as a means of governing the various officials and supervising the people." Notice that the function of governing lower-level officials comes before that of the supervision of laypeople.

5. Such an argument about the superiority of writing as extending the capabilities of oral communication across time and space—long familiar in Eurocentric accounts of the rise of the West—can be criticized on many grounds: for reinstating a logo-centrism in which speech comes first and writing functions as a means to extend speech (Derrida 1976); for overlooking the fact that large empires that relied largely on oral modes of communication existed in non-Western contexts (Kaviraj 1992b: 29); and, finally, for ignoring the hierarchy of languages and writing skills among officials.

6. By opposing class interests within an elite, I am pointing to the tensions between different fractions of capital (Marx 1977 vol. 3).

7. I am grateful to Dan Segal for suggesting this term to me (comments on talk at Pitzer College, 12 September 2005).

8. This point is made very well by Brian Stock (1983: 3–11).

9. I owe this formulation to Lawrence Cohen.

10. Tarlo (2003: 77–79) reports, for instance, that the illiterate and semiliterate people who filed petitions with the Slum Department did so in an archaic English, with the mediation of professional letter writers.

11. Tarlo (2003: 75) goes on to say, "For 'paper truths', despite their flimsiness and elasticity, despite their potential to be forged or destroyed, none the less have authority, belonging as they do to the world of the modern state where the written word reigns supreme."

12. I am not suggesting that such a process will result in greater access or justice, but it places the onus of responsibility on officials. Das (2004: 227–29) has convincingly demonstrated that when state officials are complicit in perpetrating violence on citizens or exploiting clients, such a process hides as much as it reveals. For instance, riot victims who came to report crimes against them were forced to include a formulaic paragraph enframing their complaint in a way that mitigated the act of violence.

13. This practice does not differ much from that of the Islamic courts in Yemen described by Messick (1993: 209), in which oral testimony lay at the center of court processes, which otherwise relied heavily on the written word.

14. As we shall see, the charge of logocentrism or phonocentrism makes more than a little sense here. The motif of presence, the metaphysics of presence, as authorizing the truth of oral testimony is central and does, in fact, trace directly to the Greek sources Derrida critiques in *Of Grammatology* (1976). Speech is seen as offering an unmediated, or less mediated, access to truth.

15. I put these terms in quotation marks to indicate the difficulty and insufficiency of translating *sharia* into either of these categories.

16. I am using the term *prejudice* here not in its colloquial sense, but in its literal meaning as "prejudgment."

17. Given that e-mail is written, one would have expected the opposite response, namely, that what may be forgotten or misrepresented in speech can be set down unambiguously in writing. Indeed, sometimes people do take this position, but it is surprising how often the skepticism of writing in this context hinges on the uncertainty of whether the reader's interpretation will follow the writer's intent.

18. It is no small irony that the term *religions of the book* is used for teachings that were orally transmitted by their founders and written down only later by others. One would expect that people who follow these texts as the literal truth would find this fact disturbing since they cannot be sure that what was written down was in fact the exact words of the founders; the only way to be sure of that would have been if the prophets had written the words themselves.

19. That is why companies so jealously guard their reputations and trademarks. As the service economy has expanded, it is these commodities that have become the most important property of a business.

20. Such a position on the hierarchy of written and oral materials also reinforced European self-consciousness of their superiority, as possessors of a written history based on written documents, vis-à-vis people in Africa and Asia, who, as people lacking such a history, were the objects of discovery and colonization. When the Europeans found strong literate traditions and forms of record keeping in places such as India they attempted to derive law and custom from such sources.

21. For example, speech is broken down into five stages, of which the first three are internal to the speaker and have no shape in the form of words or sentences.

22. The details of this case are presented in chapter 7 on managing the population.

23. It might appear that humans are now moving toward a worldwide situation of universal adult literacy. However, progress toward this goal is by no means guaranteed, as many poor countries have had to slash their budgets for elementary education under pressure from multilateral institutions such as the IMF that require them to reduce the fiscal deficit in the name of supposed good governance. In any case, one might argue that the important benchmark in today's world is computer literacy, and there the digital divide will ensure that a condition of restricted literacy will continue to exist for a long time to come.

24. A clear case in which the connection between structural violence and survival is

linked to papers is immigrants in the West who lack papers and hence have to live a precarious existence. See, in particular, the fascinating work of Ticktin (2006) on the *sans papiere* in France and also the work of Didier Fassin (2005).

25. Competitive exams for professionalization are found even in fields that Weber does not mention explicitly, such as accounting, architecture, business, and engineering. In the United States the whole process of creating meritocracy through exams begins with school-leaving tests (SATS) that greatly influence a student's prospects for college admission. That such exams have become an endemic feature of the educational system rather than a particular mechanism of selection for bureaucratic office reinstates Weber's point about the increasingly bureaucratic nature of modern society.

26. A small number of positions at higher levels were kept for individuals who were promoted in the hierarchy rather than recruited directly for those positions. For example, an IAS officer was normally given the position of a district magistrate (DM) as his first posting. However, there were a small number of district magistrates in every state who were promoted from senior sub-district magistrates (SDM) even though these officers did not belong to the elite cadre of the IAS. The IAS exams are probably one of the most competitive examinations held anywhere in the world: of two hundred thousand applicants, four hundred to five hundred are chosen for the service, a success rate of 0.2–0.25 percent.

27. Weber (1968: 1000) comments on bureaucrats' demands for a "status-appropriate" salary rather than a wage according to performance. Anganwadi workers definitely occupied a low status as compared to primary school teachers or other white-collar jobs that would have been appropriate for someone with a college degree or higher qualification.

28. Das (2004: 225) has argued that one needs to see the state "as neither a purely rational-bureaucratic organization nor simply a fetish, but as a form of regulation that oscillates between a rational mode and a magical mode of being." She sees writing technologies as embodying this double aspect of the state.

29. Magical texts dealt with particular problems: how to concoct a potion to win back a mistress, or how to compose a spell to bring back a runaway servant: "This tradition of magical texts goes back to the beginnings of writing itself, stemming as it does from the Mesopotamian world where writing itself developed" (Goody 1986: 16).

30. These were, for the most part, literate farmers protesting the threat to their livelihoods posed by multinational corporations.

31. Since Benjamin connects the loss of the aura of the object with the ability to make reproductions, this statement might appear to represent a refutation of Benjamin. However, what he was suggesting by the term *authenticity* was something entirely different (Benjamin 1968: 221).

32. This is by no means a modern prejudice. Citing the virtues of writing, Henry III in 1247 stressed its indelibility and its ability to preserve the memory of events for posterity (Clanchy 1979: 79).

33. I am grateful to Raka Ray for bringing this point to my attention.

34. Amita Baviskar has pointed out to me that literacy projects often emphasize reading rather than writing. Literacy rates are thereby indexed to reading abilities and rudi-

mentary skills such as being able to produce a signature, rather than focusing on writing skills, which are more complex.

35. "It is constantly worth asking whether we are right in wishing to contrast at any price spoken language and written language as agents of civilization, considering the first as an obstacle to progress and the second as its active promoter" (I. Hajnal quoted in Clanchy 1979: 7).

36. I am referring to the fact that working with computers requires people to be literate in the usual sense. Computer literacy means a different level of functional skills needed to use computers effectively. Many people who are literate may not be computer literate in this sense, but literacy is a necessary condition for being computer literate.

37. I am grateful to Virginia Dominguez for bringing this point to my attention.

38. Other justifications of fiction's pedagogic functions include the following: it allows one to travel to other places without leaving home; it allows empathy for people whose life situations one might not otherwise share; in the case of historical novels, it allows one to experience history from the inside in all its immediacy; and, finally, it allows one to think about and resolve moral dilemmas in one's own life through vicarious participation in someone else's life.

39. Kaviraj (2003: 157) claims that "the electorate at the last election under colonial administration was about 14 percent of the adult population."

40. If we were to subtract the urban literate from this number, the rates of literacy would be even lower. The majority of the population lived in the countryside, and in 1950 the overwhelming proportion of this population was illiterate.

41. For an excellent overview of literacy achievements, see Jean Drèze (2004). Nussbaum (2003) focuses on female literacy across the world.

42. Nussbaum (2003: 333) recognizes this point while arguing that literacy increases the bargaining power of women in elected offices such as village councils. Nussbaum argues that greater political participation by women sometimes drives the demand for female literacy rather than the reverse (2003: 334). In her study of the rise of Dalit politics in the state of U.P., Pai (2001) points to the central role of the electoral process and of education.

43. I am grateful to Saba Mahmood and Anjali Arondekar for suggesting these points to me.

44. Kaviraj (2003) calls it a minimal interpretation of democracy and contrasts it to an expansive interpretation.

45. It is unclear what literacy rates really measure, as noted above. If someone can sign their name they are considered literate and counted as such in the Indian data. This says almost nothing of a person's ability to negotiate more complex demands.

46. Kaviraj (1992: 31) offers the example of bilingual Brahmins who jealously guarded access to Sanskrit. They could engage in public discussion that was inaccessible to the majority, whose linguistic skills extended to one or more vernaculars.

47. For example, Bubandt (2006) argues that corruption and sorcery are central to the conceptualization and operation of democracy in Indonesia.

48. Mendelsohn (1993) argues that it is the combination of competitive electoral pro-

cesses and the rise of alternative sources of employment for subaltern groups outside villages that has brought about a transformation of authority in rural India,
loosening the grip of dominant castes and of the model that posited political authority as arising from landownership alone.

49. It might appear contradictory that dignity is pursued through the quest for government jobs, which as much as anything are about redressing income inequality.
However, at least at lower levels in the hierarchy, government jobs carry a special,
high status that jobs in private corporations do not.

50. Although I will primarily talk of jobs in what follows, the same discourses and
debates are to be found with regard to admission to government colleges and universities.

51. In this context one should not forget that the state is the largest employer in the
formal sector. Therefore, a state position did not just mean the chance for a secure,
relatively prestigious career: it often represented the only avenue for a decent job.
Alternative sources of employment in the formal, organized sector of the economy,
that is, private corporations, were small, and self-employment or a job in the informal sector offered much smaller monetary rewards and correspondingly higher
risks.

52. Manipulating the system requires capital, both monetary and symbolic. On the
whole, upper-caste and upper-class people are better able to use this strategy than
lower-class and lower-caste people.

53. One of the first actions of Dalit-led governments in U.P. has been the transfer en
masse of senior officials whom they consider unsympathetic to their cause. Although such actions cause great upheavals in the bureaucracy because they violate
systematic procedure deemed essential to modern bureaucracies (Weber 1968), the
leaders see them as necessary to the successful implementation of pro-poor and
pro-Dalit social programs. However, shifting personnel so that more committed
bureaucrats are in charge of implementation may demonstrate limited success in the
absence of changes in bureaucratic procedure, such as the emphasis on written
documents.

54. I am thinking, for example, of the Rath Yatra, led by the leader of the BJP, L. K.
Advani.

55. Shah (2001) strikes a cautionary note when he points to the possibility that Dalit
politicians may be co-opted by the dominant class.

56. Examples of such new forms of inclusion are the reserved seats on the bodies of
village governance (panchayats) and programs such as the District Poverty Initiatives
Project (DPIP). However, as Gaiha and Kulkarni (2006) point out with reference to
the DPIP, the evidence about whether inclusion results in empowerment is in-
conclusive.

57. Two of the three items on this list—coins and seals—were directly associated with
the state, and, given that church and state were not separate as in the modern world,
religious relics may have had some ties to the state as well.

58. It can also be a strategy used by an underground parallel government such as a
resistance movement, an independence movement, or the Mafia.

59. See the wonderful discussion of counterfeit money in the context of colonial Africa in Mwangi (n.d.).

60. For a fuller discussion, see Radnóti (1999: 9–12). Forgery of currency by criminal gangs and competing nation-states is a completely different matter.

61. See Tarlo's (2003) fascinating description of the market for sterilization certificates in the Emergency.

62. This reference to an official producing fake documents needs explanation. The most common form of forgery I encountered was not of private individuals producing replicas of state documents, but officials who, in exchange for cash, created a document that may not have truly attested to the facts. For example, a doctor, with an appropriate payment, would provide a shortsighted applicant a certificate of good vision so that he could get a driver's license or be able to apply for a post in the army.

63. Because all marriages in this area were exogamous, women's homes after marriage were always in a different place from where they grew up and went to junior high school.

64. In this case, one might ask why they did not just get a certificate from their junior high school. The difficulties of such a task cannot be underestimated: the place could have been far away from their new homes and the journey hard to make at short notice (women could not travel alone safely); the junior high school was unlikely to have preserved older records; even if such records existed, officials in the junior high school were unlikely to take the trouble to dig them up and, in any case, would have been happy to produce a certificate in exchange for money. It was therefore simpler, cheaper, and more efficient to have such a document produced locally.

65. The situation is not unlike the famous story of Michelangelo's so-called forgery of antiques. He would borrow old masters' works from people who owned them, then copy them and, instead of returning the originals to their owners, give them his copy instead. They did not realize they had received a copy because it was so perfect. But, then again, did it really matter that the work they had was not the original? (Radnóti 1999: 2).

7. Population and Neoliberal Governmentality

Mahila Samakhya was studied intensively by my collaborator, Aradhana Sharma, and I will draw upon our jointly published work for the details about that program that follow (Gupta and Sharma 2006). However, this is not a reproduction of our joint work. I have drawn extensively on our article but have used it for my own purposes here.

1. Looking at the one child policy in China, Greenhalgh (2003b) provides a powerful account of how bare life is produced by concerns about the "quality" of the population. Planned population growth turns "unplanned" births into "black" persons who are systematically discriminated against in state policy and who may not even be enumerated in official statistics.

2. See in particular Foucault's lectures of 25 January and 1 February 1978 (2007). Gal and Kligman have an excellent presentation of the evolution of thought about the population in Europe (2000: 15–36).

3. The reliance on five-year plans for national self-sufficiency was modeled on the Soviet strategy of planned development.

4. The infant mortality data come from World Bank statistics (accessed through Google public data on 17 May 2011); the data for under-five mortality and maternal mortality comes from the Human Development Index: http://hdrstats.undp.org; accessed 17 May 2011).

5. The latest year for which I was able to find data for the poorest quintile was 2007.

6. Before it became a ministry, Women and Child Development was a department housed in the Ministry of Human Resource Development.

7. The health component for children included the administration of large doses of Vitamin A, iron and folic acid tablets, DPT and BCG immunization shots, and the monitoring of malnutrition by weighing or measuring midarm circumference; for pregnant women, measures included iron and folic acid tablets and tetanus shots.

8. In a survey conducted in twenty-seven of the thirty-three blocks in which the ICDS program began, Tandon et al. (1981: 380) reported that 76 percent of children under three years of age in rural areas and 78 percent of those under six were malnourished. Severe malnutrition was found in 21 percent of rural children under three and in 26 percent of tribal children in the same age group.

9. The exact amounts were as follows: expenditures in 1990–91 were Rs. 268 crores vs. Rs. 603 crores in 1998–99 (approximately $151 million). In the Eighth Plan, the expenditures were Rs. 2,271 crores vs. Rs. 10,392 crores in the Tenth Plan (approximately US $2,165 million over five years). Since then, expenditures have ramped up even more sharply: Rs. 6,300 crores (US $1260 million) was allocated for the program in the budget of 2008–9. The Eleventh Plan saw the allocation for ICDS jump to Rs. 44,400 crores (approximately US $9.87 billion) (http://wcd.nic.in/icds.htm; accessed 17 May 2011).

10. The official name of the conference was "International Conference on Population and Development" and it was held on 5–13 September 1994.

11. For a fascinating analysis of China's efforts in this field, see Greenhalgh (2003a, b).

12. That such concerns are by no means limited to India or developing countries can be seen from the history of babies (and their mothers) and the state in the West (Jenson 1986).

13. Such a statement immediately raises concerns about the status of indigent people who could not be seen as an investment. It also brings up statements about the unnecessary, even dangerous reproduction of poor people and minorities. Elite discourses, although almost never based in fact, posit that such groups endanger the welfare of all by reproducing recklessly (see Gal and Kligman 2000: 23).

14. For further details about Mahila Samakhya, see the excellent ethnography by Sharma (2008).

15. Various NGOs of different ideological bents, including Gandhian, Marxist, and feminist, have been involved in empowerment-based initiatives in postcolonial India. However, empowerment as a state project is a relatively recent trend. It began with the implementation of the Women's Development Programme (WDP) in 1984

in the north Indian state of Rajasthan. Mahila Samakhya built on WDP's visions and strengths while mitigating the program's weaknesses (Sharma 2008).

16. My concern is not to answer the question of whether ICDS succeeded in its stated objectives, but to ask what its unintended effects have been. Evaluations of ICDS have been mixed, some studies emphasizing that it has resulted in reducing infant mortality and maternal mortality and others questioning that conclusion (Ghosh 2004; Chandrasekhar and Ghosh 2007).

17. Scheduled castes (SCs in official terminology) are the lowest castes in the caste hierarchy.

18. This custom is known as *gaunaa* in west U.P.

19. See chapter 5 on practices of bureaucratic writing and the construction of files.

20. See also the discussion in chapter 5.

21. See also the work of Cohn (1987) and Appadurai (1993) on the Indian state. Appadurai (1993: 316) states the problem particularly well when he says, "Statistics were generated in amounts that far defeated any unified bureaucratic purpose."

22. I have earlier argued against the notion that the state can have a singular interest (see chapter 2).

23. This was not only because the ICDS program was a femocracy—staffed by women at all levels—but also because it was one of the few state agencies that employed women workers in rural settings. The only other women state officials were the auxiliary nurse and midwife in the Health Department. The Mahila Samakhya program later introduced other women working in official capacities in rural U.P.

24. I learned later that the difficulties I experienced in obtaining a research visa for this project might have had something to do with the ambivalent evaluations. The government, ever aware of the bad press it had obtained internationally for sex discrimination, was extremely reluctant to have researchers investigating the program.

25. The belief in the evil eye is not limited to people in western U.P., but is common in large parts of the South Asian subcontinent.

26. The following information summarizes some of the details presented in Gupta and Sharma (2006).

27. One does not need to posit a highly complex chain of causation here: the trees being cut down in Indonesia and Brazil deprive poor people not only of fuel wood but also of the food and fauna on which their daily lives depend; similarly, the rise of industrial shrimp farming is leading to the destruction of the environment which provided poor people in coastal communities with much-needed nutrients in the form of crops and fish.

28. Even if and when such people benefit from faster overall growth rates, the income and wealth gap between them and people like software engineers and call-center workers is growing very fast.

29. The present government has been especially attentive to these issues, as it is widely perceived that the previous coalition government was defeated at the polls because it did not pay enough attention to distributive concerns. The poster boy for the political cost of neglecting the unwired majority was Chandrababu Naidu, the computer-

savvy chief minister of Andhra Pradesh. Naidu achieved a high profile on the national and international stages by championing the information technology sector, the fastest growing sector of the Indian economy. Despite this and despite the fact that his state achieved some of the highest growth rates in the country, his party was soundly defeated in the elections.

30. I am careful to say that such programs are perceived to confer legitimacy because it is clear that leaders of political parties and opinion makers think this to be the case. As far as I am aware, there has been no systematic study investigating this phenomenon.

31. In the United States such programs are derisively referred to as pork barrel projects (from the image of pigs feeding at a trough), but the importance of pork shows no signs of decreasing and may have increased massively with the growth of secrecy and militarization in the years since the Reagan presidency.

32. In fact, the current government has implemented an enormous expansion of welfare through the Mahatma Gandhi National Rural Employment Guarantee Act (MNREGA).

33. The act is the most expensive welfare program ever launched in India. Rs. 40,000 crores were spent on it in 2010–11. That is roughly the outlay for ICDS for the entire Eleventh Five-Year Plan.

Epilogue

1. By the "salariat" Bardhan is referring to those in the bureaucracy and middle-class professionals who earned a relatively comfortable living through white-collar work.

2. There has been a vigorous discussion among economists about the phenomenon of "jobless growth" (Harriss 2009).

3. Farmers' suicides have not affected the poorest people as much insofar as the poorest parts of the rural population do not own any land and cannot get agricultural loans.

4. It is entirely possible for growth rates in agriculture to increase rapidly without a corresponding increase in employment, if growth is attained by capital-intensive technologies. However, such a scenario is hard to imagine in India. High growth rates will inevitably increase the employment opportunities for unskilled agricultural labor.

5. See statement by Rahul Gandhi to this effect (http://www.indianexpress.com/news/naxalism-connected-to-govts-inability-to-reach-out-rahul/526179/, 7 October 2009; accessed 19 July 2010). Sonia Gandhi and Home Minister Chidambaram have made almost identical statements.

6. For the National Highway Development Project, see the National Highways Authority of India website: http://www.nhai.org. Details about the National River Linking Project can be found at http://nrlp.iwmi.org.

7. This story is available at http://timesofindia.indiatimes.com/City/Mangalore/Centre-considering-Rs-1000-cr-package-cor-Naxal-affected-areas/articleshow/6144347.cms; accessed 14 July 2010. The Hindu quotes unnamed officials as saying that "issues of good governance, development, regular functioning of critical field institutions and public awareness are essential in dealing with naxalite activities" (http://www.hindu.com/2010/07/14/stories/2010071454111400.htm; accessed 14 July 2010). The same

story also quoted sources in the government as saying that Naxalites "tried to derive benefit from overall underdevelopment and from sub-normal functioning of field institutions like police stations, tehsils, development blocks, schools, primary health centres and anganwadi centres, which administered and provided services at the ground level and also reflected the State presence and writ."

8. Software exports are tax exempt. Therefore, most IT and ITES companies pay little, if any, corporate tax.

REFERENCES CITED

Aaj. 1989a. "Mob Carries Away Six Transformers from Electricity Station." 11 August.
——. 1989b. "Police Busy Warming Own Pockets." 18 July.
——. 1989c. "Blackmarketeering in Sugar and Kerosene." 22 July.
——. 1989d. "Farmers Harassed by Land Consolidation Official." 22 July.
——. 1989e. "To Get Telephone to Work, Feed Them Sweets." 22 July.
——. 1989f. "Plunder in T.B. Hospital." 25 July.
Abrams, Philip. 1988. "Notes on the Difficulty of Studying the State." *Journal of Historical Sociology* 1(1), 58–89.
Abu-Lughod, Lila. 1990. "The Romance of Resistance: Tracing Transformations of Power through Bedouin Women." *American Ethnologist* 17(1), 43–55.
Ades, Alberto, and Rafael di Tella. 2000. "The New Economics of Corruption: A Survey and Some New Results." *Combating Corruption in Latin America*, ed. Joseph S. Tulchin and Ralph H. Espach, 15–52. Washington: Woodrow Wilson Center Press.
Agamben, Giorgio. 1998. *Homo Sacer: Sovereign Power and Bare Life*. Translated by Daniel Heller-Roazen. Stanford: Stanford University Press.
——. 2000. *Means without End: Notes on Politics*. Translated by Vincenzo Binetti and Cesare Casarino. Minneapolis: University of Minnesota Press.
——. 2005. *State of Exception*. Translated by Kevin Attell. Chicago: University of Chicago Press.
Agnihotri, Indu, and Vina Mazumdar. 1995. "Changing Terms of Political Discourse: Women's Movement in India, 1970s–1990s." *Economic and Political Weekly* 30(29), 1869–78.
Ahmad, Aijaz. 1987. "Jameson's Rhetoric of Otherness and the 'National Allegory.'" *Social Text* 17, 3–25.
Aho, James A. 1985. "Rhetoric and the Invention of Double Entry Bookkeeping." *Rhetorica* 3(1), 21–43.

Alexander, M. Jacqui. 1997. "Erotic Autonomy as a Politics of Decolonization: An Anatomy of Feminist and State Practice in the Bahamas Tourist Economy." *Feminist Genealogies, Colonial Legacies, Democratic Futures*, ed. M. Jacqui Alexander and Chandra T. Mohanty, 63–100. New York: Routledge.

Almond, Gabriel A., Taylor Cole, and Roy C. Macridis. 1955. "A Suggested Research Strategy in Western European Government and Politics." *American Political Science Review* 49, 1042–44.

Almond, Gabriel A., and James Coleman. 1960. *The Politics of the Developing Areas.* Princeton: Princeton University Press.

Alsop, Ruth J., Anirudh Krishna, and Disa Sjoblom. 2001. *Inclusion and Local Elected Governments: The Panchayat Raj System in India.* Washington: World Bank Social Development Unit.

Althusser, Louis. 1971. "Ideology and Ideological State Apparatuses (Notes towards an Investigation)." *Lenin and Philosophy and Other Essays*, 127–86. New York: Monthly Review Press.

Amin, Shahid. 1984. "Gandhi as Mahatma: Gorakhpur District, Eastern UP, 1921–1922." *Subaltern Studies III: Writings on South Asian History and Society*, ed. Ranajit Guha, 1–61. Delhi: Oxford University Press.

——. 1995. *Event, Metaphor, Memory: Chauri Chaura 1922–1992.* Berkeley: University of California Press.

Anagnost, Ann. 1994. "The Politicized Body." *Body, Subject, and Power in China*, ed. Tani Barlow and Angela Zito, 131–56. Chicago: University of Chicago Press.

——. 1995. "A Surfeit of Bodies: Population and the Rationality of the State in Post-Mao China." *Conceiving the New World Order: The Global Politics of Reproduction*, ed. Faye D. Ginsburg and Rayna Rapp, 22–41. Berkeley: University of California Press.

——. 1997. *National Past-Times: Narrative, Representation, and Power in Modern China.* Durham: Duke University Press.

Anderson, Benedict. 1991. *Imagined Communities: Reflections on the Origins and Spread of Nationalism.* 2d edn. New York: Verso.

Appadurai, Arjun. 1984. "How Moral Is South Asia's Economy?—A Review Article." *Journal of Asian Studies* 43(3), 481–97.

——. 1986. "Theory in Anthropology: Center and Periphery." *Comparative Studies in Society and History* 28(1), 356–61.

——. 1990. "Disjuncture and Difference in the Global Political Economy." *Public Culture* 2(2), 1–24.

——. 1993. "Number in the Colonial Imagination." *Orientalism and the Postcolonial Predicament*, ed. Carol A. Breckenridge and Peter van der Veer, 314–39. Philadelphia: University of Pennsylvania Press.

——. 1996. *Modernity at Large: Cultural Dimensions of Globalization.* Minneapolis: University of Minnesota Press.

——. 2000. "Spectral Housing and Urban Cleansing: Notes on Millennial Mumbai." *Public Culture* 12(3), 627–51.

Appadurai, Arjun, and Carol A. Breckenridge. 1988. "Why Public Culture?" *Public Culture* 1(1), 5–9.

Apter, Andrew H. 1999. "The Subvention of Tradition: A Genealogy of the Nigerian Durbar." *State/Culture: State-Formation after the Cultural Turn*, ed. George Steinmetz, 213–52. Ithaca: Cornell University Press.

———. 2005. *The Pan-African Nation: Oil and the Spectacle of Culture in Nigeria*. Chicago: University of Chicago Press.

Aretxaga, Begoña. 2000. "Playing Terrorist: Ghastly Plots and the Ghostly State." *Journal of Spanish Cultural Studies* 1(1), 43–58.

———. 2003. "Maddening States." *Annual Review of Anthropology* 32, 393–410.

Asad, Talal. 1994. "Ethnographic Representation, Statistics and Modern Power." *Social Research* 61(1), 55–88.

Ashforth, Adam. 1990. *The Politics of Official Discourse in Twentieth-Century South Africa*. Oxford: Clarendon Press.

Bähre, Erik. 2005. "How to Ignore Corruption: Reporting the Shortcomings of Development in South Africa." *Current Anthropology* 46(1), 107–20.

Baig, Tara Ali. 1979. *Our Children*. New Delhi: Government of India, Ministry of Information and Broadcasting, Publications Division.

Bailey, F. G. 1963. *Politics and Social Change: Orissa in 1959*. Berkeley: University of California Press.

Balibar, Etienne. 2003. *We, the People of Europe? Reflections on Transnational Citizenship*. Translated by James Swenson. Princeton: Princeton University Press.

Banerjee, Subhabrata Bobby. 2006. "Live and Let Die: Colonial Sovereignties and the Death Worlds of Necrocapitalism." *Borderlands E-Journal* 5(1).

Bardhan, Pranab. 1984. *The Political Economy of Development in India*. New York: Basil Blackwell.

———. 1997. "Corruption and Development: A Review of Issues." *Journal of Economic Literature* 35(3), 1320–46.

———. 1999. *The Political Economy of Reform in India*. New Delhi: National Council of Applied Economic Research.

———. 2006. "The Economist's Approach to the Problem of Corruption." *World Development* 34(2), 341–48.

Bardhan, Pranab, and Dilip Mookherjee. 2005. "Decentralizing Antipoverty Program Delivery in Developing Countries." *Journal of Public Economics* 89(4), 675–704.

Barry, Andrew, Thomas Osborne, and Nikolas Rose. 1996. "Introduction." *Foucault and Political Reason: Liberalism, Neo-Liberalism, and Rationalities of Government*, ed. Andrew Barry, Thomas Osborne, and Nikolas Rose, 1–18. Chicago: University of Chicago Press.

Basch, Linda Green, Nina Glick Schiller, and Cristina Szanton Blanc, eds. 1994. *Nations Unbound: Transnational Projects, Postcolonial Predicaments, and Deterritorialized Nation-States*. Langhorne, Penn.: Gordon and Breach.

Basu, Amrita, and Atul Kohli, eds. 1998. *Community Conflicts and the State in India*. New York: Oxford University Press.

Bate, J. Bernard. 2002. "Political Praise in Tamil Newspapers: The Poetry and Iconography of Democratic Power." *Everyday Life in South Asia*, ed. Diane P. Mines and Sarah Lamb, 308–25. Bloomington: Indiana University Press.

Batliwala, Srilatha. 1997. "What Is Female Empowerment?" Paper presented in Stockholm, 25 April. http://www.qweb.kvinnoforum.se/papers/FRSU1.htm (accessed 3 August 2005).

Baviskar, Amita. 1995. *In the Belly of the River: Tribal Conflicts over Development in the Narmada Valley*. New Delhi: Oxford University Press.

Bayart, Jean-François. 1993. *The State in Africa: The Politics of the Belly*. Translated by Mary Harper, Christopher Harrison, and Elizabeth Harrison. New York: Longman.

BBC. 2007. "Indian Finance Minister: Full Text." http://news.bbc.co.uk/2/hi/business/6330691.stm, 3–4 February 2007.

Benedict, Ruth. 1946. *The Chrysanthemum and the Sword: Patterns of Japanese Culture*. Boston: Houghton Mifflin.

Benjamin, Walter. 1968. *Illuminations: Essays and Reflections*. Translated by Harry Zohn. New York: Schocken Books.

Bennett, Tony, Martin Graham, and Bernard Waites, eds. 1982. *Popular Culture, Past and Present*. London: Open University Press.

Berlant, Lauren. 1993. "The Theory of Infantile Citizenship." *Public Culture* 5, 395–410.

Bernstein, Richard. 1985. *Beyond Objectivism and Relativism: Science, Hermeneutics and Praxis*. Philadelphia: University of Pennsylvania Press.

Bhattacharjee, Ananya. 1997. "The Public/Private Mirage: Mapping Homes and Undomesticating Violence Work in the South Asian Immigrant Community." *Feminist Genealogies, Colonial Legacies, Democratic Futures*, ed. M. Jacqui Alexander and Chandra T. Mohanty, 308–29. New York: Routledge.

Bhatti, Jaspal. 1987. *Ulta-Pulta* (television series). Mumbai: Doordarshan.

——. 2001. *Professor Money Tree*. Mumbai: Alpha Punjabi.

Bidwai, Praful. 2003. "The Rise of the Cyber-Coolies." *New Statesman* 132(4663), 32–33.

Biehl, João. 2004. "The Activist State: Global Pharmaceuticals, AIDS, and Citizenship in Brazil." *Social Text* 22(3), 105–32.

Bloch, Marc. 1961. *Feudal Society*. Volume 1. Translated by L. A. Manyon. Chicago: University of Chicago Press.

Borneman, John. 1993. "Uniting the German Nation: Law, Narrative and Historicity." *American Ethnologist* 20(2), 288–311.

——. 1998. *Subversions of International Order: Studies in the Political Anthropology of Culture*. Albany: State University Press of New York.

Bornstein, Erica. 2005. *The Spirit of Development: Protestant NGOs, Morality, and Economics in Zimbabwe*. Stanford: Stanford University Press.

Bourdieu, Pierre. 1977. *Outline of a Theory of Practice*. Translated by Richard Nice. Cambridge: Cambridge University Press.

——. 1985. "The Social Space and the Genesis of Groups." *Theory and Society* 14(6), 723–44.

——. 1986. "The Forms of Capital." *Handbook of Theory and Research for the Sociology of Education*, ed. John G. Richardson, 241–58. New York: Greenwood Press.

——. 1990. *The Logic of Practice*. Stanford: Stanford University Press.

——. 1993. *Language and Symbolic Power*. Cambridge: Harvard University Press.

——. 1996. *The State Nobility: Elite Schools in the Field of Power*. Translated by Loretta C. Clough. Cambridge: Polity Press.

——. 1999. "Rethinking the State: Genesis and Structure of the Bureaucratic Field." *State/Culture: State Formation after the Cultural Turn*, ed. George Steinmetz, trans. Loic Wacquant and Samar Farage, 53–75. Ithaca: Cornell University Press.

Boyd, William, and Edmund J. King. 1995. *The History of Western Education*. 12th edn. Lanham, Md.: Barnes and Noble Books.

Bradsher, Keith. 2005. "Poverty and Superstition Hinder Drive to Block Bird Flu at Source." *New York Times*, 3 November, A1, A16.

Brahmbhatt, Milan, T. G. Srinivasan, and Kim Murrell. 1996. *India in the Global Economy*. Washington: World Bank Policy Research Working Paper Series 1681.

Brass, Paul. 1997. *Theft of an Idol: Text and Context in the Representation of Collective Violence*. Princeton: Princeton University Press.

——. 2003. *The Production of Hindu–Muslim Violence in Contemporary India*. Seattle: University of Washington Press.

Brenneis, Don. 2000. "Reforming Promise." *Documents: Artifacts of Modern Knowledge*, ed. Annelise Riles, 41–70. Ann Arbor: University of Michigan Press.

Briggs, Charles L. 2007. "Mediating Infanticide: Theorizing Relations between Narrative and Violence." *Cultural Anthropology* 22(3), 315–56.

Broch-Due, Vigdis. 1995. "Poverty Paradoxes: The Economy of Engendered Needs." *Occasional Paper Series*, no. 4: Poverty and Prosperity. Uppsala: Nordic Africa Institute.

Brow, James. 1988. "In Pursuit of Hegemony: Representations of Authority and Justice in a Sri Lankan Village." *American Ethnologist* 15(2), 311–27.

——. 1996. *Demons and Development: The Struggle for Community in a Sri Lankan Village*. Tucson: University of Arizona Press.

Brown, Ed, and Jonathan Cloke. 2004. "Neoliberal Reform, Governance and Corruption in the South: Assessing the International Anti-Corruption Crusade." *Antipode* 36(2), 272–94.

Brown, Wendy. 1995. "Finding the Man in the State." *States of Inquiry: Power and Freedom in Late Modernity*, 166–96. Princeton: Princeton University Press.

Brubaker, Rogers. 1992. *Citizenship and Nationhood in France and Germany*. Cambridge: Harvard University Press.

Bubandt, Nils. 2006. "Sorcery, Corruption, and the Dangers of Democracy in Indonesia." *Journal of the Royal Anthropological Institute* 12(2), 413–31.

Burawoy, Michael, and Katherine Verdery, eds. 1999. *Uncertain Transition: Ethnographies of Change in the Postsocialist World*. New York: Rowman and Littlefield.

Burchell, Graham. 1996. "Liberal Government and the Techniques of the Self." *Foucault and Political Reason: Liberalism, Neo-Liberalism and Rationalities of Government*, ed. Andrew Barry, Thomas Osborne, and Nikolas Rose, 19–36. Chicago: University of Chicago Press.

Burchell, Graham, Colin Gordon, and Peter Miller, eds. 1991. *The Foucault Effect: Studies in Governmentality (With Two Lectures by and an Interview with Michel Foucault)*. Chicago: University of Chicago Press.

Butler, Judith. 1990. *Gender Trouble: Feminism and the Subversion of Identity*. New York: Routledge.

———. 1993a. *Bodies That Matter: On the Discursive Limits of "Sex."* New York: Routledge.

———. 1993b. *Excitable Speech: A Politics of the Performative.* New York: Routledge.

Calhoun, Craig. 1989. "Tiananmen, Television and the Public Sphere: Internationalization of Culture and the Beijing Spring of 1989." *Public Culture* 2(1), 54–71.

———. 2004. "A World of Emergencies: Fear, Intervention, and the Limits of Cosmopolitan Order." CRSA/RCSA 41(4), 373–95.

Cavell, Stanley. 1997. "Comments on Veena Das's Essay 'Language and Body': Transactions in the Construction of Pain." *Social Suffering*, ed. Arthur Kleinman, Veena Das, and Margaret Lock, 93–98. Berkeley: University of California Press.

Chaitanya, Krishna V. 2004. "Growth of Foreign Direct Investment in India." *Economic Research* 17(1), 74–97.

Chakrabarty, Dipesh. 1989. *Rethinking Working-Class History.* Princeton: Princeton University Press.

———. 1991. "History as Critique and Critique(s) of History." *Economic and Political Weekly* 26(37), 2162–66.

———. 2000. *Provincializing Europe: Postcolonial Thought and Historical Difference.* Princeton: Princeton University Press.

Chalfin, Brenda. 2006. "Global Customs Regimes and the Traffic in Sovereignty: Enlarging the Anthropology of the State." *Current Anthropology* 47(2), 243–76.

Chandra, Kanchan. 2004. *Why Ethnic Parties Succeed: Patronage and Ethnic Head Counts in India.* New York: Cambridge University Press.

Chandrasekhar, C. P., and Jayati Ghosh. 2005. "Integrated Child Development Services Scheme—The Unfulfilled Potential." *Hindu Business Line*, Tuesday, 22 March.

Chatterjee, Nilanjana, and Nancy E. Riley. 2001. "Planning an Indian Modernity: The Gendered Politics of Fertility Control." *Signs* 26(3), 811–45.

Chatterjee, Partha. 1986. *Nationalist Thought and the Colonial World: A Derivative Discourse?* London: Zed Press.

———. 1990. "A Response to Taylor's 'Modes of Civil Society.'" *Public Culture* 3(1), 119–32.

———. 1993. *The Nation and Its Fragments: Colonial and Postcolonial Histories.* Princeton: Princeton University Press.

———. 1998. "Development Planning and the Indian State." *State and Politics in India*, ed. Partha Chatterjee, 271–97. Delhi: Oxford University Press.

———. 2004. *The Politics of the Governed: Reflections on Popular Politics in Most of the World.* New York: Columbia University Press.

Chatterjee, Partha, ed. 1998. *State and Politics in India.* Delhi: Oxford University Press.

Chatterji, Roma. 1998. "An Ethnography of Dementia: A Case Study of an Alzheimer's Disease Patient in the Netherlands." *Culture, Medicine and Psychiatry* 22, 355–82.

Chawla, Prabhu. 1990. "The '80 Politics." *India Today*, International Edition, 15 January, 18–25.

Chen, Shaohua, and Martin Ravallion. 2007. *Absolute Poverty Measures for the Developing World, 1981–2004.* Washington: World Bank Policy Research Working Paper 4211.

Clanchy, M. T. 1979. *From Memory to Written Record: England 1066–1307.* London: Edward Arnold.

Clarke, John. 2004. *Changing Welfare, Changing States: New Directions in Social Policy*. Thousand Oaks, Calif.: Sage.

Clarke, Michael, ed. 1983. *Corruption: Causes, Consequences, and Control*. London: Francis Pinter.

Cliquet, Robert, and Kristiaan Thienpont. 1995. *Population and Development: A Message from the Cairo Conference*. Boston: Kluwer Academic.

Cohen, Lawrence. 2001. "The Other Kidney: Biopolitics beyond Recognition." *Body and Society* 7(2–3), 9–29.

———. 2004. "Operability: Surgery at the Margin of the State." *Anthropology in the Margins of the State*, ed. Veena Das and Deborah Poole, 165–90. Santa Fe: School of American Research Press.

Cohn, Bernard S. 1987a. "The Census, Social Structure and Objectification in South Asia." *An Anthropologist among the Historians and Other Essays*, 224–54. Delhi: Oxford University Press.

———. 1987b. "Representing Authority in Victorian India." *An Anthropologist among the Historians and Other Essays*, ed. Bernard S. Cohn, 632–82. Delhi: Oxford University Press.

———. 1996. *Colonialism and Its Forms of Knowledge: The British in India*. Princeton: Princeton University Press.

Collier, Jane F., Bill Maurer, and Liliana Suarez-Navaz. 1995. "Sanctioned Identities: Legal Constructions of Modern Personhood." *Identities* 2(1–2), 1–27.

Collins, James, and Richard K. Blot. 2003. *Literacy and Literacies: Texts, Power, and Identity*. New York: Cambridge University Press.

Coombe, Rosemary J. 1993. "Tactics of Appropriation and the Politics of Recognition in Late Modern Democracies." *Political Theory* 21(3), 411–33.

Corbridge, Stuart, and John Harriss. 2000. *Reinventing India: Liberalization, Hindu Nationalism, and Popular Democracy*. Malden, Mass.: Blackwell.

Corbridge, Stuart, Glyn Williams, Manoj Srivastava, and René Véron. 2005. *Seeing the State: Governance and Governmentality in Rural India*. New York: Cambridge University Press.

Coronil, Fernando. 1997. *The Magical State: Nature, Money, and Modernity in Venezuela*. Chicago: University of Chicago Press.

Corrigan, Philip, and Derek Sayer. 1985. *The Great Arch: English State Formation as Cultural Revolution*. Oxford: Blackwell.

Coutin, Susan Bibler. 2003. "Cultural Logics of Belonging and Movement: Transnationalism, Naturalization, and U.S. Immigration Politics." *American Ethnologist* 30(4), 508–26.

Creed, Gerald. 1998. *Domesticating Revolution: From Socialist Reform to Ambivalent Transition in a Bulgarian Village*. University Park: Pennsylvania State University Press.

Cruikshank, Barbara. 1999. *The Will to Empower: Democratic Citizens and Other Subjects*. Ithaca: Cornell University Press.

Daniel, E. Valentine. 1997. "Suffering Nation and Alienation." *Social Suffering*, ed. Arthur Kleinman, Veena Das, and Margaret Lock, 309–58. Berkeley: University of California Press.

Darian-Smith, Eve, and Peter Fitzpatrick. 1999. *Laws of the Postcolonial*. Ann Arbor: University of Michigan Press.

Das, Veena. 1997. "Language and Body: Transactions in the Construction of Pain." *Social Suffering*, ed. Arthur Kleinman, Veena Das, and Margaret Lock, 67–91. Berkeley: University of California Press.

———. 2004. "The Signature of the State: The Paradox of Illegibility." *Anthropology in the Margins of the State*, ed. Veena Das and Deborah Poole, 225–52. Santa Fe: School of American Research Press.

———. 2007. *Life and Words: Violence and the Descent into the Ordinary*. Berkeley: University of California Press.

Das, Veena, and Deborah Poole, eds. 2004. *Anthropology in the Margins of the State*. Santa Fe: School of American Research Press.

Dasgupta, Shahana. 1990. "Child Welfare Legislation in India: Will Indian Children Benefit from the United Nations Convention on the Rights of the Child?" *Michigan Journal of International Law* 11, 1301–16.

Dean, Mitchell. 1999. *Governmentality: Power and Rule in Modern Society*. London: Sage.

Derrida, Jacques. 1976. *Of Grammatology*. Translated by Gayatri Chakravorty Spivak. Baltimore: Johns Hopkins University Press.

de Sardan, J. P. Olivier. 1999. "A Moral Economy of Corruption in Africa?" *Journal of Modern African Studies* 37(1), 25–52.

Dev, S. Mahendra, and Jos Mooij. 2002. "Social Sector Expenditures in the 1990s: Analysis of Central and State Budgets." *Economic and Political Weekly* 37(9), 853–66.

de Vries, Pieter. 2002. "Vanishing Mediators: Enjoyment as a Political Factor in Western Mexico." *American Ethnologist* 29(4), 901–27.

DiCarlo, Lisa. 2003. "Face of the Year." *Forbes* online. http://www.forbes.com/. 19 December.

Dirks, Nicholas. 1987. *The Hollow Crown: Ethnohistory of an Indian Kingdom*. Cambridge: Cambridge University Press.

Doig, Alan, and Stephanie McIvor. 1999. "Corruption and Its Control in the Developmental Context: An Analysis and Selective Review of the Literature." *Third World Quarterly* 20(3), 657–76.

Drèze, Jean. 2004. "Patterns of Literacy and Their Social Context." *Handbook of Indian Sociology*, ed. Veena Das, 345–61. Delhi: Oxford University Press.

Dube, Shyama Charan. 1958. *India's Changing Villages*. London: Routledge and Paul.

Easton, David. 1953. *The Political System: An Inquiry into the State of Political Science*. New York: Knopf.

———. 1957. "An Approach to the Analysis of Political Systems." *World Politics* 9, 383–400.

Echeverri-Gent, John. 1993. *The State and the Poor: Public Policy and Political Development in India and the United States*. Berkeley: University of California Press.

Elden, Stuart. 2007. "Governmentality, Calculation, Territory." *Environment and Planning D: Society and Space* 25, 562–80.

Elyachar, Julia. 2005. *Markets of Dispossession: NGOs, Economic Development, and the State in Cairo*. Durham: Duke University Press.

Engels, Friedrich. 1939. *Herr Eugen Dühring's Revolution in Science (Anti-Dühring)*. Edited by C. P. Dutt. Translated by Emile Burns. New York: International Publishers.

Enloe, Cynthia. 2000. *Maneuvers: The International Politics of Militarizing Women's Lives*. Berkeley: University of California Press.

Escobar, Arturo. 1984. "Discourse and Power in Development: Michel Foucault and the Relevance of His Work to the Third World." *Alternatives* 10, 377–400.

———. 1988. "Power and Visibility: Development and the Invention and Management of the Third World." *Cultural Anthropology* 3(4), 428–43.

———. 1992. "Imagining a Post-Development Era? Critical Thought, Development and Social Movements." *Social Text* 31/32, 20–56.

———. 1995. *Encountering Development: The Making and Unmaking of the Third World*. Princeton: Princeton University Press.

Esteva, Gustavo. 1992. "Development." *The Development Dictionary: A Guide to Knowledge as Power*, ed. Wolfgang Sachs, 6–25. Atlantic Highlands, N.J.: Zed Books.

Eswaran, Mukesh, Ashok Kotwal, Bharat Ramaswami, and Wilima Wadhwa. 2009. "Sectoral Labour Flows and Agricultural Wages in India, 1983–2004: Has Growth Trickled Down?" *Economic and Political Weekly* 44(2), 46–55.

Evans, Peter, Dietrich Rueschemeyer, and Theda Skocpol, eds. 1985. *Bringing the State Back In*. Cambridge: Cambridge University Press.

Eyal, Gil. 2003. *The Origins of Postcommunist Elites: From Prague Spring to the Breakup of Czechoslovakia*. Minneapolis: University of Minnesota Press.

Fabian, Johannes. 1983. *Time and the Other: How Anthropology Makes Its Object*. New York: Columbia University Press.

Farmer, Paul. 2005. *Pathologies of Power: Health, Human Rights, and the New War on the Poor*. Berkeley: University of California Press.

Farquhar, Judith, and Qicheng Zhang. 2005. "Biopolitical Beijing: Pleasure, Sovereignty, and Self-Cultivation in China's Capital." *Cultural Anthropology* 20(3), 303–27.

Fassin, Didier. 2005. "Compassion and Repression: The Moral Economy of Immigration Policies in France." *Cultural Anthropology* 20(3), 362–87.

Feldman, Ilana. 2008. *Governing Gaza: Bureaucracy, Authority, and the Work of Rule, 1917–1967*. Durham: Duke University Press.

Ferguson, James. 1994. *The Anti-Politics Machine: "Development," Depoliticization and Bureaucratic Power in Lesotho*. Minneapolis: University of Minnesota Press.

Ferguson, James, and Akhil Gupta. 2002. "Spatializing States: Toward an Ethnography of Neoliberal Governmentality." *American Ethnologist* 29(4), 981–1002.

Ferguson, Kathy E. 1984. *The Feminist Case against Bureaucracy*. Philadelphia: Temple University Press.

Foucault, Michel. 1979. *Discipline and Punish: The Birth of a Prison*. New York: Random House.

———. 1980. *Power/Knowledge: Selected Interviews and Other Writings, 1972–1977*, ed. Colin Gordon. New York: Pantheon Books.

———. 1982. *The Archaeology of Knowledge and the Discourse on Language*. Translated by A. M. Sheridan Smith. New York: Pantheon Books.

———. 1990. *The History of Sexuality.* Vol. 1. Translated by Robert Hurley. New York: Vintage.

———. 1991. "Governmentality." *The Foucault Effect: Studies in Governmentality,* ed. Graham Burchell, Colin Gordon, and Peter Miller, 87–104. Chicago: University of Chicago Press.

———. 2003. *"Society Must Be Defended": Lectures at the Collège de France, 1975–76.* Translated by David Macey. New York: Picador.

———. 2007. *Security, Territory, Population: Lectures at the Collège de France, 1977–78.* Translated by Graham Burchell. New York: Palgrave Macmillan.

Fox, Richard. 1985. *Lions of the Punjab: Culture in the Making.* Berkeley: University of California Press.

Frank, David John. 1994. *Global Environmentalism: International Treaties in World Society.* Ph.D. diss., Department of Sociology, Stanford University.

———. 1997. "Science, Nature, and the Globalization of the Environment, 1870–1990." *Social Forces* 76, 409–35.

Fraser, Nancy. 1989. "Women, Welfare, and the Politics of Need Interpretation." *Unruly Practices: Power, Discourse and Gender in Contemporary Social Theory,* 144–60. Minneapolis: University of Minnesota Press.

Freeman, Carla. 2002. "Designing Women: Corporate Discipline and Barbados's Off-Shore Pink-Collar Sector." *The Anthropology of Globalization: A Reader,* ed. Jonathan X. Inda and Renato Rosaldo Jr., 83–99. Malden, Mass.: Blackwell.

Freire, Paulo. 1970. *Pedagogy of the Oppressed.* Translated by Myra Bergman Ramos. New York: Seabury Press.

Friedman, Thomas L. 1999. *The Lexus and the Olive Tree.* New York: Farrar, Straus and Giroux.

———. 2004. "Will India Seize the Moment?" *Seattle Post-Intelligencer,* 1924, March, B7.

Fuller, C. J., and Véronique Bénéï, eds. 2000. *The Everyday State and Society in Modern India.* New Delhi: Social Science Press.

Fuller, C. J., and John Harriss. 2000. "For an Anthropology of the Modern Indian State." *The Everyday State and Society in Modern India,* ed. C. J. Fuller and Véronique Bénéï, 1–30. New Delhi: Social Science Press.

Gaiha, Raghav, and Vani S. Kulkarni. 2006. "Common Interest Groups, Village Institutions and the Rural Poor in India: A Review of the District Poverty Initiatives Project." *Contemporary South Asia* 15(1), 15–34.

Gal, Susan, and Gail Kligman. 2000. *The Politics of Gender after Socialism.* Princeton: Princeton University Press.

Galtung, Johan. 1969. "Violence, Peace, and Peace Research." *Journal of Peace Research* 6(3), 167–91.

Gandhi, Nandita, and Nandita Shah. 1992. *The Issues at Stake: Theory and Practice in the Contemporary Women's Movement in India.* New Delhi: Kali for Women.

Gardiner, John. 2002. "Defining Corruption." *Political Corruption: Concepts and Contexts,* 3d edn., ed. Arnold J. Heidenheimer and Michael Johnston, 25–40. New Brunswick: Transaction Publishers.

Geertz, Clifford. 1980. *Negara: The Theatre State in Nineteenth-Century Bali.* Princeton: Princeton University Press.

Ghosh, Shanti. 2004. "Child Malnutrition." *Economic and Political Weekly* 39(40), 4412–13.

Gillespie, Kate, and Gwenn Okruhlik. 1991. "The Political Dimensions of Corruption Cleanups: A Framework for Analysis." *Comparative Politics* 24(1), 77–95.

Gilroy, Paul. 1987. *"There Ain't No Black in the Union Jack": The Cultural Politics of Race and Nation*. London: Hutchinson.

Gledhill, John. 1999. "Official Masks and Shadow Powers: Towards an Anthropology of the Dark Side of the State." *Urban Anthropology* 28(2), 199–251.

Glick Schiller, Nina, Linda Basch, and Cristina Szanton Blanc, eds. 1992. *Towards a Transnational Perspective on Migration: Race, Class, Ethnicity, and Nationalism Reconsidered*. New York: New York Academy of Sciences.

Goody, Jack. 1968. "Introduction." *Literacy in Traditional Societies*, 1–26. Cambridge: Cambridge University Press.

——. 1986. *The Logic of Writing and the Organization of Society*. Cambridge: Cambridge University Press.

——. 1987. *The Interface between the Written and the Oral*. Cambridge: Cambridge University Press.

Gordillo, Gastón. 2006. "The Crucible of Citizenship: ID-paper Fetishism in the Argentinean Chaco." *American Ethnologist* 33(2), 162–76.

Gould, William. 2007. "The Dual State: The Unruly 'Subordinate,' Caste, Community and Civil Service Recruitment in North India, 1930–1955." *Journal of Historical Sociology* 20(1–2), 13–43.

——. 2010. *Bureaucracy, Community and Influence in India: Society and the State, 1930s–1960s*. London: Routledge.

Government of India. 1974. *Towards Equality: Report of the Committee on the Status of Women in India*. Delhi: Department of Social Welfare.

——. 1985. *A Decade of ICDS: Integrated Child Development Services*. New Delhi: Ministry of Human Resources Development. Department of Women's Welfare.

——. 2001. Census of India. Office of the Registrar General. http://www.censusindia .net; accessed 7 November 2008.

——. 2005. Planning Commission, Tenth Plan. http://planningcommission.nic.in; accessed 7 November 2008.

Gramsci, Antonio. 1971. *Selections from the Prison Notebooks*. Translated by Q. Hoare and G. N. Smith. New York: International Publishers.

Green, M. W. 1981. "The Construction and Implementation of the Cuneiform Writing System." *Visible Language* 15(4), 345–72.

Greenhalgh, Susan. 2003a. "Planned Births, Unplanned Persons: 'Population' in the Making of Chinese Modernity." *American Ethnologist* 30(2), 196–215.

——. 2003b. "Science, Modernity, and the Making of China's One-Child Policy." *Population and Development Review* 29(2), 163–96.

Greenhalgh, Susan, and Edwin A. Winckler. 2005. *Governing China's Population: From Leninist to Neoliberal Biopolitics*. Stanford: Stanford University Press.

Greenhouse, Carol, Elizabeth Mertz, and Kay B. Warren, eds. 2002. *Ethnography in Unstable Places: Everyday Lives in Contexts of Dramatic Political Change*. Durham: Duke University Press.

Grewal, Inderpal. 1998. "On the New Global Feminism and the Family of Nations: Dilemmas of Transnational Feminist Practice." *Talking Visions: Multicultural Feminism in a Transnational Age*, ed. Ella Shohat, 501–30. Cambridge: MIT Press.

Grown, Caren, and Gita Sen. 1988. *Development, Crises, and Alternative Visions*. London: Earthscan Publications.

Guha, Ranajit. 1983. *Elementary Aspects of Peasant Insurgency in Colonial India*. Delhi: Oxford University Press.

Guha, Ranajit, and Gayatri Chakravorty Spivak. 1988. *Selected Subaltern Studies*. Delhi: Oxford University Press.

Guhan, Sanjivi, and Paul Samuel, eds. 1997. *Corruption in India: Agenda for Action*. New Delhi: Vision Books.

Gupta, Akhil. 1995. "Blurred Boundaries: The Discourse of Corruption, the Culture of Politics, and the Imagined State." *American Ethnologist* 22(2), 375–402.

———. 1998. *Postcolonial Developments: Agriculture in the Making of Modern India*. Durham: Duke University Press.

———. 2001. "Governing Population: The Integrated Child Development Services Program in India." *States of Imagination: Ethnographic Explorations of the Postcolonial State*, ed. Thomas Blom Hansen and Finn Stepputat, 65–96. Durham: Duke University Press.

Gupta, Akhil, and James Ferguson. 1992. "Beyond 'Culture': Space, Identity, and the Politics of Difference." *Cultural Anthropology* 7(1), 6–23.

———. 1997. "Beyond 'Culture': Space, Identity, and the Politics of Difference." *Culture, Power, Place: Explorations in Critical Anthropology*, ed. Akhil Gupta and James Ferguson, 33–51. Durham: Duke University Press.

Gupta, Akhil, and Aradhana Sharma. 2006. "Globalization and Postcolonial States." *Current Anthropology* 47(2), 277–307.

Gupta, Dipankar. 1997. *Rivalry and Brotherhood: Politics in the Life of Farmers in Northern India*. New York: Oxford University Press.

Gurevitch, Michael, Tony Bennett, James Curran, and Janet Woollacott, eds. 1982. *Culture, Society and the Media*. New York: Methuen.

Habermas, Jürgen. 1975. *Legitimation Crisis*. Translated by Thomas McCarthy. Boston: Beacon Press.

———. 1989. *The Structural Transformation of the Public Sphere: An Inquiry into a Category of Bourgeois Society*. Translated by Thomas Burger and Frederick Lawrence. Cambridge: MIT Press.

Hacking, Ian. 1982. "Biopower and the Avalanche of Printed Numbers." *Humanities in Society* 5(3, 4), 279–95.

———. 1991. "How Should We Do the History of Statistics?" *The Foucault Effect: Studies in Governmentality*, ed. G. Burchell, C. Gordon, and P. Miller, 181–96. Chicago: University of Chicago Press.

Hall, Rodney B. 2003. "The Discursive Demolition of the Asian Development Model." *International Studies Quarterly* 47(1), 71–99.

Hall, Stuart. 1981. "Notes on Deconstructing 'The Popular.'" *People's History and Socialist Theory*, ed. Raphael Samuel, 227–40. London: Routledge.

——. 1982. "Culture, the Media and the Ideological Effect." *Culture, Society and the Media*, ed. Tony Bennett, James Curran, Michael Gurevitch, and Janet Wollacott, 315–48. New York: Methuen.

——. 1986a. "Gramsci's Relevance for the Study of Race and Ethnicity." *Journal of Communication Inquiry* 10(2), 5–27.

——. 1986b. "Popular Culture and the State." *Popular Culture and Social Relations*, ed. Tony Bennett, Colin Mercer, and Janet Woollacott, 22–49. Milton Keynes: Open University Press.

——. 1997. "The Local and the Global: Globalization and Ethnicity." *Culture, Globalization and the World System: Contemporary Conditions for the Representation of Identity*, ed. A. King, 19–39. Minneapolis: University of Minnesota Press.

Haller, Dieter, and Cris Shore, eds. 2005. *Corruption: Anthropological Perspectives*. London: Pluto Press.

Handelman, Don. 1978. "Introduction: A Recognition of Bureaucracy." *Bureaucracy and World View: Studies in the Logic of Official Interpretation*, ed. Don Handelman and Elliott Leyton, 1–14. St. John's, Newfoundland: Institute of Social and Economic Research.

——. 1981. "Introduction: The Idea of Bureaucratic Organization." *Social Analysis* 9, 5–23.

Handler, Richard. 1985. "On Having a Culture: Nationalism and the Preservation of Quebec's Patrimoine." *Objects and Others: Essays on Museums and Material Culture*, George W. Stocking Jr., 192–217. Vol. 3 of *History of Anthropology*. Madison: University of Wisconsin Press.

Hann, Chris M., ed. 2002. *Postsocialism: Ideals, Ideologies and Practices in Eurasia*. New York: Routledge.

Hannerz, Ulf. 1986. "Theory in Anthropology: Small Is Beautiful?" *Comparative Studies in Society and History* 28(1), 362–67.

Hansen, Hans Krause. 1998. "Governmental Mismanagement and Symbolic Violence: Discourses on Corruption in the Yucatán of the 1990s." *Bulletin of Latin American Research* 17(3), 367–86.

Hansen, Thomas Blom. 2000. "Governance and Myths of State in Mumbai." *The Everyday State and Society in Modern India*, ed. C. J. Fuller and Véronique Bénéï, 31–67. New Delhi: Social Science Press.

——. 2001. *Wages of Violence: Naming and Identity in Postcolonial Bombay*. Princeton: Princeton University Press.

Hansen, Thomas Blom, and Finn Stepputat. 2006. "Sovereignty Revisited." *Annual Review of Anthropology* 35, 295–315.

Hansen, Thomas Blom, and Finn Stepputat, eds. 2001. *States of Imagination: Ethnographic Explorations of the Postcolonial State*. Durham: Duke University Press.

Haraway, Donna. 1988. "Situated Knowledges: The Science Question in Feminism and the Privilege of Partial Perspective." *Feminist Studies* 14(3), 575–99.

Hardt, Michael, and Antonio Negri. 2000. *Empire*. Cambridge: Harvard University Press.

Harrison, Elisabeth. 2006. "Unpacking the Anti-Corrupting Agenda: Dilemmas for Anthropologists." *Oxford Development Studies* 34(1), 15–29.

Harriss, John. 2009. "The 'Double Movement' in India: Social and Political Responses to Economic Liberalization and Its Consequences." Paper presented at the workshop "Neoliberal Crises in Post-Reform India." Max Planck Institute for Social Anthropology, Halle, 24–25 September.

Harvey, David. 1989. *The Condition of Postmodernity: An Enquiry into the Origins of Cultural Change.* New York: Blackwell.

——. 2007. *A Brief History of Neoliberalism.* New York: Oxford University Press.

Hasty, Jennifer. 2005. "The Pleasures of Corruption: Desire and Discipline in Ghanaian Political Culture." *Cultural Anthropology* 20(2), 271–301.

Heaver, Richard. 1989. *Improving Family Planning, Health, and Nutrition Outreach in India.* World Bank Discussion Papers no. 59. Washington: World Bank.

Heidenheimer, Arnold J., and Michael Johnston, eds. 2002. *Political Corruption: Concepts and Contexts.* New Brunswick: Transaction Publishers.

Heimer, Carol A. 2000. "Conceiving Children: How Documents Support Case versus Biographical Analyses." *Documents: Artifacts of Modern Knowledge*, ed. Annelise Riles, 95–126. Ann Arbor: University of Michigan Press.

Hellman, Joel S., Geraint Jones, Daniel Kaufmann, and Mark Schankerman. 2000. *Measuring Governance, Corruption, and State Capture: How Firms and Bureaucrats Shape the Business Environment in Transition Economies.* Washington: World Bank Policy Research Working Paper, WPS 2312.

Hemment, Julie. 1999. "Gendered Violence in Crisis: Russian NGOs Help Themselves to Liberal Feminist Discourse." *Anthropology of Eastern Europe Review* 17(1), 35–58.

Herzfeld, Michael. 1992a. "History in the Making: National and International Politics in a Rural Cretan Community." *Europe Observed*, ed. John Campbell and João de Pina-Cabral, 93–122. Houndsmills, England: Macmillan Press.

——. 1992b. *The Social Production of Indifference: Exploring the Symbolic Roots of Western Bureaucracy.* Chicago: University of Chicago Press.

Hevia, James. 1994. "Loot's Fate." *History and Anthropology* 6(4), 319–45.

Higgot, Richard A., Andreas Bieler, and Geoffrey R. D. Underhill. 2000. *Non-State Actors and Authority in the Global System.* London: Routledge.

Hindess, Barry. 2004. "Liberalism—What's in a Name?" *Global Governmentality: Governing International Spaces*, ed. Wendy Larner and William Walters, 23–39. London: Routledge.

Hobson, Dorothy, Stuart Hall, Andrew Lowe, and Andrew Willis, eds. 1980. *Culture, Media, Language.* London: Hutchinson.

Holmes, Douglas, and George E. Marcus. 2006. "Fast Capitalism: Para-Ethnography and the Rise of the Symbolic Analyst." *Frontiers of Capital: Ethnographic Reflections on the New Economy*, ed. Melissa Fisher and Greg Downey, 33–57. Durham: Duke University Press.

Holston, James, and Teresa P. R. Caldeira. 1998. "Democracy, Law, and Violence: Disjunctions of Brazilian Citizenship." *Fault Lines of Democracy in Post-Transition Latin America*, ed. F. Aguero and J. Stark, 263–96. Miami: North-South Center.

Hull, Matthew S. 2003. "The File: Agency, Authority, and Autography in an Islamabad Bureaucracy." *Language and Communication* 23(3–4), 287–314.

——. 2008. "Ruled by Records: The Expropriation of Land and the Misappropriation of Lists in Islamabad." *American Ethnologist* 35(4), 501–18.

Humphrey, Caroline. 2002. *The Unmaking of Soviet Life: Everyday Economies after Socialism*. Ithaca: Cornell University Press.

Huntington, Samuel P. 1968. *Political Order in Changing Societies*. New Haven: Yale University Press.

Husted, Bryan W. 1999. "Wealth, Culture, and Corruption." *Journal of International Business Studies* 30(2), 339–60.

India Today. 1989. "A Methodical Fraud: IRDP Loans," 74–77, 15 March.

Jaffrelot, Christophe. 1996. *The Hindu Nationalist Movement in India*. New York: Columbia University Press.

——. 2003. *India's Silent Revolution: The Rise of the Lower Castes in North India*. New York: Columbia University Press.

Jain, Arvind K. 2001. "Corruption: A Review." *Journal of Economic Surveys* 15(1), 71–121.

Jandhyala, Kameshwari. 2005. *Empowering Education: The Mahila Samakhya Experience*. Paper commissioned for the EFA Global Monitoring Report 2003/4, *The Leap to Equality*. World Bank website, http://www.worldbank.org; accessed 24 January 2012.

Jayal, Neerja Gopal. 1999. *Democracy and the State: Welfare, Secularism and Development in Contemporary India*. New Delhi: Oxford University Press.

Jean-Klein, Iris. 2000. "Mothercraft, Statecraft, and Subjectivity in the Palestinian Intifada." *American Ethnologist* 29(1), 100–127.

Jeffery, Patricia, and Roger Jeffery. 1998. "Gender, Community, and the Local State in Bijnor, India." *Appropriating Gender: Women's Activism and Politicized Religion in South Asia*, ed. Amrita Basu and Patricia Jeffery, 123–42. New York: Routledge.

——. 2010. "'Money Itself Discriminates': Obstetric Crises in the Time of Liberalization." *The State in India after Liberalization: Interdisciplinary Perspectives*, ed. Akhil Gupta and K. Sivaramakrishnan, 133–51. New York: Routledge.

Jeffrey, Craig, Patricia Jeffery, and Roger Jeffery. 2004. "'A Useless Thing' or 'Nectar of the Gods'? The Cultural Production of Education and Young Men's Struggles for Respect in Rural North India." *Annals of the Association of American Geographers* 94(4), 961–81.

Jeganathan, Pradeep. 2004. "Checkpoint: Anthropology, Identity, and the State." *Anthropology in the Margins of the State*, ed. Veena Das and Deborah Poole, 67–80. Santa Fe: School of American Research Press.

Jenkins, Rob. 1999. *Democratic Politics and Reform in India*. New York: Cambridge University Press.

Jenkins, Rob, and Anne Marie Goetz. 1999. "Accounts and Accountability: Theoretical Implications of the Right-to-Information Movement in India." *Third World Quarterly* 20(3), 603–22.

Jenson, Jane. 1986. "Gender and Reproduction: Or, Babies and the State." *Studies in Political Economy* (20), 9–46.

Jessop, Bob. 1982. *The Capitalist State*. New York: New York University Press.

——. 1990. "Anti-Marxist Reinstatement and Post-Marxist Deconstruction." *State Theory: Putting States in Their Place*, ed. Bob Jessop, 278–306. University Park: Pennsylvania State University Press.

——. 1999. "Narrating the Future of the National Economy and the National State: Remarks on Remapping Regulation and Reinventing Governance." *State/Culture: State Formation after the Cultural Turn*, ed. G. Steinmetz, 378–405. Ithaca: Cornell University Press.

Joseph, Gilbert M., and Daniel Nugent, eds. 1994. *Everyday Forms of State Formation: Revolution and the Negotiation of Rule in Rural Mexico*. Durham: Duke University Press.

Kabeer, Naila. 1994. *Reversed Realities: Gender Hierarchies in Development Thought*. New York: Verso.

Kamtekar, Indivar. 1988. "The End of the Colonial State in India, 1942–1947." Ph.D. diss., University of Cambridge.

Kantola, Johanna. 2007. "The Gendered Reproduction of the State in International Relations." *British Journal of Politics and International Relations* 9(2), 270–83.

Kapferer, Bruce. 1988. *Legends of People, Myths of State: Violence, Intolerance and Political Culture in Sri Lanka and Australia*. Washington: Smithsonian Institution Press.

——. 2005. "New Formations of Power, the Oligarchic-Corporate State, and Anthropological Ideological Discourse." *Anthropological Theory* 5(3), 285–99.

Kapur, Devesh, and Pratap Bhanu Mehta. 2005. "Introduction." *Public Institutions in India: Performance and Design*, ed. Devesh Kapur and Pratap Bhanu Mehta, 1–27. New Delhi: Oxford University Press.

Kasaba, Resat. 1994. "A Time and a Place for the Non-State: Social Change in the Ottoman Empire during the 'Long Nineteenth Century.' " *State Power and Social Forces*, ed. Joel Migdal, Atul Kohli, and Vivienne Shue, 207–30. Cambridge: Cambridge University Press.

Kaviraj, Sudipta. 1992a. "The Imaginary Institution of India." *Subaltern Studies VII*, ed. Partha Chatterjee and Gyanendra Pandey, 1–39. Delhi: Oxford University Press.

——. 1992b. "Writing, Speaking, Being: Language and the Historical Formation of Identities in India." *Nationalstaat und Sprachkonflikte in Süd- und Südostasien*, ed. Dagmar Hellmann-Rajanayagam and Dietmar Rothermund, 25–68. Stuttgart: Franz Steiner Verlag.

——. 1994. "On the Construction of Colonial Power: Structure, Discourse, Hegemony." *Contesting Colonial Hegemony*, ed. Dagmar Engels and Shula Marks, 19–54. London: British Academic Press.

——. 2003. "A State of Contradictions: The Post-Colonial State in India." *States and Citizens: History, Theory, Prospects*, ed. Quentin Skinner and Bo Strath, 145–63. New York: Cambridge University Press.

Keck, Margaret, and Kathryn Sikkink. 1998. *Activists beyond Borders: Advocacy Networks in International Politics*. Ithaca: Cornell University Press.

Keynes, John Maynard. 1971. *A Tract on Monetary Reform: The Collected Writings of John Maynard Keynes*. London: Macmillan.

Khagram, Sanjeev, and Peggy Levitt. 2004. "Towards a Field of Transnational Studies and a Sociological Transnationalism Research Program." Hauser Center for Nonprofit Organizations Working Paper no. 24. http://ssrn.com/abstract=556993.

Khanna, Jyoti, and Michael Johnston. 2007. "India's Middlemen: Connecting by Corrupting?" *Crime, Law, and Social Change* 48(3), 151–68.

Khilnani, Sunil. 1999. *The Idea of India*. New York: Farrar, Straus and Giroux.

Kittler, Friedrich A. 1999. *Gramophone, Film, Typewriter*. Translated by Geoffrey Winthrop-Young and Michael Wutz. Stanford: Stanford University Press.

Kleinman, Arthur, Veena Das, and Margaret Lock. 1997. "Introduction." *Social Suffering*, ed. Arthur Kleinman, Veena Das, and Margaret Lock, ix–xxv. Berkeley: University of California Press.

Kligman, Gail. 1990. "Reclaiming the Public: A Reflection on Creating Civil Society in Romania." *East European Politics and Societies* 4(3), 393–438.

Klitgaard, Robert. 1988. *Controlling Corruption*. Berkeley: University of California Press.

Kohli, Atul. 1987. *The State and Poverty in India: The Politics of Reform*. New York: Cambridge University Press.

———. 2006. "Politics of Economic Growth in India, 1980–2005." *Economic and Political Weekly*, Part I: 1 April:1251–59; Part II: 8 April:1361–70.

Kohrman, Matthew. 2007. "Depoliticizing Tobacco's Exceptionality: Male Sociality, Death and Memory-Making among Chinese Cigarette Smokers." *China Journal* 58, 85–109.

Kopytoff, Igor. 1986. "The Cultural Biography of Things: Commoditization as Process." *The Social Life of Things*, ed. Arjun Appadurai, 64–91. New York: Cambridge University Press.

Kothari, Rajni. 1995. "Globalization and 'New World Order': What Future for the United Nations?" *Economic and Political Weekly of India*, 2513–17.

Kothari, Smitu, and Harsh Sethi, eds. 1991. *Rethinking Human Rights*. Delhi: Lokayan.

Krasner, Stephen D. 1978. *Defending the National Interest: Raw Materials Investments and U.S. Foreign Policy*. Princeton: Princeton University Press.

Krishna, Anirudh. 2002. *Active Social Capital: Tracing the Roots of Development and Democracy*. New York: Columbia University Press.

———. 2009. "Why Don't 'The Poor' Make Common Cause? The Importance of Subgroups." *Journal of Development Studies*, 45(6), 947–65.

———. 2010. "Poverty Knowledge and Poverty Action in India." *The State in India after Liberalization: Interdisciplinary Perspectives*, ed. Akhil Gupta and K. Sivaramakrishnan, 111–32. New York: Routledge.

Krishnan, K. P., and T. V. Somanathan. 2005. "Civil Service: An Institutional Perspective." *Public Institutions in India: Performance and Design*, ed. Devesh Kapur and Pratap Bhanu Mehta, 258–319. New Delhi: Oxford University Press.

Kundu, Nitai. 2003. "Urban Slum Reports: The Case of Kolkata, India." *Understanding Slums: Case Studies for the Global Report on Human Settlements*. London: University College. Online at http://www.ucl.ac.uk; accessed on 11 November 2008.

Larner, Wendy, and William Walters, eds. 2004. *Global Governmentality: Governing International Spaces*. New York: Routledge.

Leff, Nathaniel H. 1964. "Economic Development through Bureaucratic Corruption." *American Behavioral Scientist* 8(3), 8–14.

Lenin, Vladimir Ilyich. 1943. *State and Revolution*. New York: International Publishers.

Leve, Lauren. 2002. "Between Jesse Helms and Ram Bahadur: Women, 'Participation,' and 'Empowerment' in Nepal." *PoLAR: Political and Legal Anthropology Review* 24(1), 108–28.

Lévi-Strauss, Claude. 1967. *Tristes Tropiques*. Translated by John Russell. New York: Atheneum.

———. 1969. *Conversations with Claude Lévi-Strauss*. Edited by G. Charbonnier. Translated by John Weightman and Doreen Weightman. London: Jonathan Cape.

Lewis, David, Dennis Rodgers, and Michael Woolcock. 2008. "The Fiction of Development: Literary Representation as a Source of Authoritative Knowledge." *Journal of Development Studies* 44(2), 198–216.

Lewis, Oscar. 1954. *Group Dynamics in a North Indian Village: A Study of Factions*. New Delhi: Programme Evaluation Organisation, Planning Commission, Government of India.

Lewis, W. Arthur. 1954. "Economic Development with Unlimited Supplies of Labour." *Manchester School* 22(2), 139–91.

Leys, Colin. 1965. "What Is the Problem about Corruption?" *Journal of Modern African Studies* 3(2), 215–30.

Lomnitz, Claudio. 1995. "Ritual, Rumor and Corruption in the Constitution of Polity in Modern Mexico." *Journal of Latin American Anthropology* 1(1), 20–47.

Ludden, David. 1992. "India's Development Regime." *Colonialism and Culture*, ed. N. B. Dirks, 247–87. Ann Arbor: University of Michigan Press.

Lutz, Catherine. 2002. "Making War at Home in the United States: Militarization and the Current Crisis." *American Anthropologist* 104(3), 723–35.

MacKinnon, Catharine A. 1989. *Toward a Feminist Theory of the State*. Cambridge: Harvard University Press.

Maddox, Richard. 1990. "Bombs, Bikinis, and the Popes of Rock 'n' Roll: Reflections on Resistance, the Play of Subordinations, and Cultural Liberalism in Andalusia and Academia." Paper delivered at the 87th Annual Meeting of the American Anthropological Association. Phoenix.

Malkki, Liisa. 1995. *Purity and Exile: Violence, Memory and National Cosmology among Hutu Refugees in Tanzania*. Chicago: University of Chicago Press.

Mandel, Ernest. 1975. *Late Capitalism*. Translated by Joris De Bres. New York: Verso.

Mani, Lata. 1990. "Multiple Mediations: Feminist Scholarship in the Age of Multinational Reception." *Feminist Review* 35, 24–41.

Mankekar, Purnima. 1993. "National Texts and Gendered Lives: An Ethnography of Television Viewers in a North Indian City." *American Ethnologist* 20(3), 543–63.

———. 1999. "Brides Who Travel: Gender, Transnationalism, and Nationalism in Hindi Films." *Positions* 7(3), 731–61.

Mann, Michael. 1986. *The Sources of Social Power*. New York: Cambridge University Press.

Marx, Karl. 1972. *The Eighteenth Brumaire of Louis Bonaparte*. Moscow: Progress Publishers.

———. 1977. *Capital: A Critique of Political Economy*. Vol. 3. Translated by Ben Fowkes. New York: Vintage Books.

Massumi, Brian. 2002. *Parables for the Virtual: Movement, Affect, Sensation*. Durham: Duke University Press.

Maurer, Bill. 1997. *Recharting the Caribbean: Land, Law, and Citizenship in the British Virgin Islands*. Ann Arbor: University of Michigan Press.

Mawdsley, Emma, Gina Porter, and Janet Townsend. 2004. "Creating Spaces of Re-

sistance: Development NGOs and Their Clients in Ghana, India and Mexico."
Antipode 36(5), 871–89.

Mayer, Adrian C. 1967. "Caste and Local Politics in India." *India and Ceylon: Unity and Diversity*, ed. Philip Mason, 121–41. London: Oxford University Press.

Mbembe, Achille. 1992a. "The Banality of Power and the Aesthetics of Vulgarity in the Postcolony." Translated by Janet Roitman. *Public Culture* 4(2), 1–30.

———. 1992b. "Provisional Notes on the Postcolony." *Africa: Journal of the International African Institute* 62(1), 3–37.

———. 2003. "Necropolitics." Translated by Libby Meintjes. *Public Culture* 15(1), 11–40.

Mehra, Rajiv. 2000–2002. *Office Office*. SABe Television Network.

Mendelsohn, Oliver. 1993. "The Transformation of Authority in Rural India." *Modern Asian Studies* 27(4), 805–42.

Menon, Ritu, and Kamla Bhasin. 1993. "Recovery, Rupture, Resistance: Indian State and Abduction of Women during Partition." *Economic and Political Weekly* 28(17), WS2–WS11.

Merry, Sally E. 2001. "Spatial Governmentality and the New Urban Social Order: Controlling Gender Violence through Law." *American Anthropologist* 103(1), 16–29.

Messick, Brinkley. 1993. *The Calligraphic State: Textual Domination and History in a Muslim Society*. Berkeley: University of California Press.

Meyer, John. 1980. "The World Polity and the Authority of the Nation-State." *Studies of the Modern World-System*, ed. Albert Bergsen, 109–37. New York: Academic Press.

Meyer, John, John Boli, George M. Thomas, and Francisco O. Ramirez. 1997. "World Society and the Nation State." *American Journal of Sociology* 103(1), 144–81.

Michelutti, Lucia. 2002. *Sons of Krishna: The Politics of Yadav Community Formation in a North Indian Town*. Ph.D. diss., London School of Economics and Political Science.

Migdal, Joel S. 1988. *Strong Societies and Weak States: State–Society Relations and State Capabilities in the Third World*. Princeton: Princeton University Press.

Miliband, Ralph. 1965. "Marx and the State." *The Socialist Register*, ed. R. Miliband and J. Saville, 278–96. New York: Monthly Review Press.

———. 1969. *The State in Capitalist Society*. New York: Basic Books.

Miller, D. F. 1965. "Factions in Indian Village Politics." *Pacific Affairs* 38(1), 17–31.

Miller, J. Hillis. 1990. "Narrative." *Critical Terms for Literary Study*, ed. Frank Lentricchia and Thomas McLaughlin, 66–79. Chicago: University of Chicago Press.

Miller, Peter, and Nikolas Rose. 1990. "Governing Economic Life." *Economy and Society* 19(1), 1–31.

———1992. "Political Power beyond the State: Problematics of Government." *British Journal of Sociology* 43(2), 173–205.

Mitchell, Timothy. 1988. *Colonizing Egypt*. New York: Cambridge University Press.

———. 1991a. "America's Egypt: Discourse of the Development Industry." *Middle East Report* 169, 18–36.

———. 1991b. "The Limits of the State: Beyond Statist Approaches and Their Critics." *American Political Science Review* 85(1), 77–96.

———. 1999. "Society, Economy, and the State Effect." *State/Culture: State Formation after the Cultural Turn*, ed. George Steinmetz, 76–97. Ithaca: Cornell University Press.

Mitra, Chandran. 1989. "Tikait as the Mini-Mahatma: Understanding the Rural Mind-Set." *Times of India*, 9 August.

Mitra, Chandran, and Rashmee Z. Ahmed. 1989. "It's Naiyma's Niche, Near the 'Nahar.'" *Times of India*, 8 August, 1–12.

Mohanty, Chandra. 1988. "Under Western Eyes: Feminist Scholarship and Colonial Discourses." *Feminist Review* 30, 61–88.

Monteiro, John B. 1970. "The Dimensions of Corruption in India." *Political Corruption*, ed. Arnold J. Heidenheimer, 220–28. New York: Holt, Rinehart & Winston.

Mooij, Jos, and S. Mahendra Dev. 2004. "Social Sector Priorities: An Analysis of Budgets and Expenditures in India in the 1990s." *Development Policy Review* 22(1), 97–120.

Morris, David B. 1997. "About Suffering: Voice, Genre, and Moral Community." *Social Suffering*, ed. Arthur Kleinman, Veena Das, and Margaret Lock, 25–46. Berkeley: University of California Press.

Morris, Rosalind. 2007. "Legacies of Derrida." *Annual Review of Anthropology* 36, 355–89.

Mukerji, Chandra. 1997. *Territorial Ambitions and the Gardens of Versailles*. New York: Cambridge University Press.

Mwangi, Wambui. 2003. *The Order of Money: Colonialism and the East African Currency Board*. Ph.D. diss., University of Pennsylvania.

——. n.d. "The Stutter of the Real: Counterfeit Currency and Colonialism in East Africa." Unpublished manuscript, 103–38.

Myrdal, Gunnar. 1968. *Asian Drama*. New York: Random House.

Nandy, Ashis. 1990. "The Politics of Secularism and the Recovery of Religious Tolerance." *Mirrors of Violence: Communities, Riots and Survivors in South Asia*, ed. Veena Das, 69–93. Delhi: Oxford University Press.

National Institute of Public Cooperation and Child Development (NIPCCD). 1997. *National Evaluation of Integrated Child Development Services*. New Delhi: NIPCCD.

Navaro-Yashin, Yael. 2002. *Faces of the State: Secularism and Public Life in Turkey*. Princeton: Princeton University Press.

——. 2008. "Make-Believe Papers, Legal Forms and the Counterfeit: Affective Interactions between Documents and People in Britain and Cyprus." *Anthropological Theory* 7(1), 79–98.

Nelson, Diane. 1999. *A Finger in the Wound: Body Politics in Quincentennial Guatemala*. Berkeley: University of California Press.

Nicholas, Ralph W. 1963. "Village Factions and Political Parties in Rural West Bengal." *Journal of Commonwealth Political Studies* 2(1), 17–32.

——. 1968. "Structures of Politics in the Village of Southern Asia." *Structure and Change in Indian Society*, ed. Milton Singer and Bernard S. Cohn, 243–84. Chicago: Aldine.

Nielsen, Morten. 2007. "Filling in the Blanks: The Potency of Fragmented Imageries of the State." *Review of African Political Economy* 34(114), 695–708.

Nugent, David. 1994. "Building the State, Making the Nation: The Bases and Limits of State Centralization in 'Modern' Peru." *American Anthropologist* 96(2), 333–69.

——. 1997. *Modernity at the Edge of Empire: State, Individual, and Nation in the Northern Peruvian Andes, 1885–1935*. Stanford: Stanford University Press.

——. 2009. "Democracy Otherwise: Struggles over Popular Rule in the Northern Peruvian Andes." *Democracy: Anthropological Approaches*, ed. Julia Paley, 21–62. Santa Fe: School of American Research Press.

Nuijten, Monique. 2003. *Power, Community and the State: The Political Anthropology of Organisation in Mexico*. Sterling, Va.: Pluto Press.

——. 2004. "Between Fear and Fantasy: Governmentality and the Working of Power in Mexico." *Critique of Anthropology* 24(2), 209–30.

Nussbaum, Martha C. 2003. "Women's Education: A Global Challenge." *Signs: Journal of Women in Culture and Society* 29(2), 325–55.

O'Brien, Robert, Anne Marie Goetz, Jan Aart Scholte, and Marc Williams. 2000. *Contesting Global Governance: Multilateral Economic Institutions and Global Social Movements*. Cambridge: Cambridge University Press.

Ohmae, Kenichi. 1990. *The Borderless World: Power and Strategy in the Interlinked Economy*. London: Collins.

——. 1995. *The End of the Nation State: The Rise of Regional Economies*. New York: Free Press.

Ong, Aihwa. 1999. *Flexible Citizenship: The Cultural Logics of Transnationality*. Durham: Duke University Press.

——. 2000. "Graduated Sovereignty in South-East Asia." *Theory, Culture and Society* 17(4), 55–75.

Opler, Morris, William L. Rowe, and Mildred L. Stroop. 1959. "Indian National and State Elections in a Village Context." *Human Organization* 18(1), 30–34.

Orlikowski, Wanda J., and JoAnne Yates. 1994. "Genre Repertoire: The Structuring of Communicative Practices in Organizations." *Administrative Science Quarterly* 39(4), 541–74.

Özürek, Esra. 2004a. "Miniaturizing Ataturk: Privatization of State Imagery and Ideology in Turkey." *American Ethnologist* 31(3), 374–91.

——. 2004b. "Wedded to the Republic: Public Intellectuals and Intimacy-Oriented Publics in Turkey." *Off Stage/On Display: Intimacy and Ethnography in the Age of Public Culture*, ed. Andrew Shryock, 101–30. Stanford: Stanford University Press.

Pai, Sudha. 2001. "From Harijans to Dalits: Identity Formation, Political Consciousness and Electoral Mobilization of the Scheduled Castes in Uttar Pradesh." *Dalit Identity and Politics: Cultural Subordination and the Dalit Challenge*, ed. Ghanshyam Shah, 2:258–87. New Delhi: Sage Publications.

Paley, Julia. 2001. *Marketing Democracy: Power and Social Movements in Post-Dictatorship Chile*. Berkeley: University of California Press.

——. 2002. "Toward an Anthropology of Democracy." *Annual Review of Anthropology* 31, 469–96.

Parry, Jonathan. 2000. "The 'Crisis of Corruption' and 'The Idea of India': A Worm's Eye View." *Morals of Legitimacy: Between Agency and System*, ed. Italo Pardo, 27–55. New York: Berghahn Books.

Patnaik, Utsa. 2003. "Global Capitalism, Deflation and Agrarian Crisis in Developing Countries." *Journal of Agrarian Change* 3(1–2), 33–66.

Pavarala, Vinod. 1996. *Interpreting Corruption: Elite Perspectives in India*. New Delhi: Sage.

Peters, John Durham. 1993. "Distrust of Representation: Habermas on the Public Sphere." *Media, Culture, and Society* 15, 541–71.

——. 1993. "Historical Tensions in the Concept of Public Opinion." *Public Opinion and the Communication of Consent*, ed. Theodore L. Glasser and Charles T. Salmon, 3–32. New York: Guilford Press.

——. 1997. "Seeing Bifocally: Media, Place, Culture." *Culture, Power, Place: Explorations in Critical Anthropology*, ed. Akhil Gupta and James Ferguson, 75–92. Durham: Duke University Press.

Pierce, Steven. 2006. "Looking Like a State: Colonialism and the Discourse of Corruption in Northern Nigeria." *Comparative Study of Society and History* 48(4), 887–914.

Pigg, Stacy Leigh. 1997. "Found in Most Traditional Societies: Traditional Medical Practitioners between Culture and Development." *International Development and the Social Sciences: Essays on the History and Politics of Knowledge*, ed. F. Cooper and R. Packard, 259–90. Berkeley: University of California Press.

Pinto, Sarah. 2004. "Development without Institutions: Ersatz Medicine and the Politics of Everyday Life in Rural North India." *Cultural Anthropology* 19(3), 337–64.

Plato. 1995. *Phaedrus*. Translated by Alexander Nehamas and Paul Woodruff. Indianapolis: Hackett.

Poulantzas, Nikos. 1973. *Political Power and Social Classes*. London: New Left Books.

Povinelli, Elizabeth A. 1998. "The State of Shame: Australian Multiculturalism and the Crisis of Indigenous Citizenship." *Critical Inquiry* 24(2), 575–610.

Radcliffe-Brown, A. R. 1940. "Preface." *African Political Systems*, ed. Meyer Fortes and E. E. Evans-Pritchard, xi–xxiii. London: Oxford University Press.

Radnóti, Sándor. 1999. *The Fake: Forgery and Its Place in Art*. New York: Rowman and Littlefield.

Ramachandran, Vimala. 1998. "Engendering Development: Lessons from Social Sector Programmes in India." *Indian Journal of Development Studies* 5(1).

Rancière, Jacques. 2004. *The Philosopher and His Poor*. Edited and with an introduction by Andrew Parker. Translated by John Drury, Corinne Oster, and Andrew Parker. Durham: Duke University Press.

Reddy, Sanjay G. 2005. "A Rising Tide of Demands: India's Public Institutions and the Democratic Revolution." *Public Institutions in India: Performance and Design*, ed. Devesh Kapur and Pratap Bhanu Mehta, 457–75. New Delhi: Oxford University Press.

Redfield, Peter. 2005. "Doctors, Borders, and Life in Crisis." *Cultural Anthropology* 20(3), 328–61.

Rhodes, Lorna. 2005. "Changing the Subject: Conversation in Supermax." *Cultural Anthropology* 20(3), 388–11.

Richards, John F. C. 1993. *The Mughal Empire*. New York: Cambridge University Press.

Riles, Annelise. 2000. *The Network Inside Out*. Ann Arbor: University of Michigan Press.

Riles, Annelise, ed. 2006. *Documents: Artifacts of Modern Knowledge*. Ann Arbor: University of Michigan Press.

Robertson, A. F. 2006. "Misunderstanding Corruption." *Anthropology Today* 22(2), 8–11.

Rohlen, Tom. 1974. *For Harmony and Strength: Japanese White-Collar Organization in Anthropological Perspective*. Berkeley: University of California Press.

——. 1983. *Japan's High Schools*. Berkeley: University of California Press.

Rose, Nikolas. 1996. "Governing 'Advanced' Liberal Democracies." *Foucault and Political*

Reason: Liberalism, Neo-Liberalism and Rationalities of Government, ed. Andrew Barry, Thomas Osborne, and Nikolas Rose, 37–64. Chicago: University of Chicago Press.

———. 1999. Governing the Soul: The Shaping of the Private Self. London: Free Association Books.

Rose, Nikolas, and Peter Miller. 1992. "Political Power beyond the State: Problematics of Government." British Journal of Sociology 43(2), 173–205.

Rose-Ackerman, Susan. 1978. Corruption: A Study in Political Economy. New York: Academic Press.

———. 1999. Corruption and Government: Causes, Consequences, and Reform. New York: Cambridge University Press.

———, ed. 2006. International Handbook on the Economics of Corruption. Northampton, Mass.: Edward Elgar.

Roseberry, William. 1989. Anthropologies and Histories: Essays in Political Culture, History, and Political Economy. New Brunswick: Rutgers University Press.

Ruggie, John Gerard. 1993. "Territoriality and Beyond: Problematizing Modernity in International Relations." International Organization 47(1), 139–74.

Rushdie, Salman. 1981. Midnight's Children: A Novel. New York: Knopf.

Sassen, Saskia. 1996. Losing Control: Sovereignty in an Age of Globalization. New York: Columbia University Press.

———. 1998. Globalization and Its Discontents. New York: New Press.

Schaffer, Frederic C. 2000. Democracy in Translation: Understanding Politics in an Unfamiliar Culture. Ithaca: Cornell University Press.

Scheper-Hughes, Nancy. 1992. Death without Weeping. Berkeley: University of California Press.

Schmitt, Carl. 2006. Political Theology: Four Chapters on the Concept of Sovereignty. Chicago: University of Chicago Press.

Scott, David. 1999a. Refashioning Futures: Criticism after Postcoloniality. Princeton: Princeton University Press.

———. 1999b. "Colonial Governmentality." Refashioning Futures: Criticism after Postcoloniality, 23–52. Princeton: Princeton University Press.

Scott, James C. 1969. "Corruption, Machine Politics, and Political Change." American Political Science Review 63(4), 1142–58.

———. 1972. Comparative Political Corruption. Englewood Cliffs: Prentice Hall.

———. 1998. Seeing Like a State: How Certain Schemes to Improve the Human Condition Have Failed. New Haven: Yale University Press.

Sen, Amartya K. 1983. Poverty and Famines: An Essay on Entitlement and Deprivation. Oxford: Clarendon Press.

———. 1990. "More Than 100 Million Women Are Missing." New York Review of Books, 20 December.

———. 1994. "Population: Delusion and Reality." New York Review of Books, 22 September.

———. 1999. Development as Freedom. New York: Anchor Books.

Shah, Ghanshyam. 2001. "Introduction: Dalit Politics." Dalit Identity and Politics: Cultural Subordination and the Dalit Challenge, ed. Ghanshyam Shah, 2:17–43. New Delhi: Sage Publications.

Shapiro, Michael. 1991. "Sovereignty and Exchange in the Orders of Modernity." *Alternatives* 16(4), 447–77.

Sharma, Aradhana. 2008. *Logics of Empowerment: Development, Gender, and Governance in Neoliberal India.* Minneapolis: University of Minnesota Press.

Sharma, Aradhana, and Akhil Gupta, eds. 2006. *The Anthropology of the State.* Malden, Mass.: Blackwell.

Sharma, Urmil. 1986. "A Critical Assessment of Monitoring and Evaluation in Integrated Child Development Services Programme and Profile of Suggested Indicators in the Social Components." *Indian Journal of Social Work* 47(3), 303–13.

Shore, Cris. 2000. *Building Europe: The Cultural Politics of European Integration.* New York: Routledge.

Shore, Cris, and Dieter Haller. 2005. "Introduction—Sharp Practice: Anthropology and the Study of Corruption." *Corruption: Anthropological Perspectives,* ed. Dieter Haller and Cris Shore, 1–26. London: Pluto Press.

Shukla, Shrilal. 1992. *Raag Darbari.* Translated by Gillian Wright. New Delhi: Penguin.

Sikkink, Kathryn. 1993. "Human Rights, Principled Issue-Networks, and Sovereignty in Latin America." *International Organization* 47(3), 411–41.

Sinha, Aseema. 2005. *The Regional Roots of Developmental Politics in India: A Divided Leviathan.* Bloomington: Indiana University Press.

Skocpol, Theda. 1979. *States and Social Revolutions: A Comparative Analysis of France, Russia, and China.* Cambridge: Cambridge University Press.

Smith, Daniel Jordan. 2001. "Kinship and Corruption in Contemporary Nigeria." *Ethnos* 66(3), 344–64.

——. 2007. *A Culture of Corruption: Everyday Deception and Popular Discontent in Nigeria.* Princeton: Princeton University Press.

Smith, Richard Saumarez. 1985. "Rule-by-Records and Rule-by-Reports: Complementary Aspects of British Imperial Rule of Law." *Contributions to Indian Sociology* 19(1), 153–76.

Snow, Charles P. 1959. *The Two Cultures and the Scientific Revolution.* New York: Cambridge University Press.

Spencer, Jonathan. 1997. "Post-Colonialism and the Political Imagination." *Journal of the Royal Anthropological Institute* 3(1), 1–19.

Spivak, Gayatri Chakravorty. 1988. "Can the Subaltern Speak?" *Marxism and the Interpretation of Culture,* ed. Cary Nelson and Lawrence Grossberg, 271–313. Urbana: University of Illinois Press.

Ståhlberg, Per. 2002. *Lucknow Daily: How a Hindi Newspaper Constructs Society.* Stockholm: Stockholm Studies in Social Anthropology.

Steedman, Carolyn. 2001. *Dust.* Manchester: Manchester University Press.

Steinmetz, George. 1992. "Reflections on the Role of Social Narratives in Working-Class Formation: Narrative Theory in the Social Sciences." *Social Science History* 16(3), 489–516.

——. 1993. *Regulating the Social: The Welfare State and Local Politics in Imperial Germany.* Princeton: Princeton University Press.

——, ed. 1999. *State/Culture: State-Formation after the Cultural Turn.* Ithaca: Cornell University Press.

Stiglitz, Joseph E. 2002. *Globalization and Its Discontents*. New York: W. W. Norton.

Stock, Brian. 1983. *The Implications of Literacy: Written Language and Models of Interpretation in the Eleventh and Twelfth Centuries*. Princeton: Princeton University Press.

Stoler, Ann L. 1995. *Race and the Education of Desire: Foucault's History of Sexuality and the Colonial Order of Things*. Durham: Duke University Press.

———. 2002. *Carnal Knowledge and Imperial Power: Race and the Intimate in Colonial Rule*. Berkeley: University of California Press.

———. 2004. "Affective States." *A Companion to the Anthropology of Politics*, ed. David Nugent and Joan Vincent, 4–20. Malden, Mass.: Blackwell.

Strange, Susan. 1996. *The Retreat of the State*. Cambridge: Cambridge University Press.

Sunder Rajan, Rajeswari. 2003. *The Scandal of the State: Women, Law, and Citizenship in Postcolonial India*. Durham: Duke University Press.

Tandon, B. N., K. Ramachandran, and S. Bhatnagar. 1980. "Integrated Child Development Services in India: Objectives, Organization and Baseline Survey of the Project Population." *Indian Journal of Medical Research* (73), 374–84.

Tarlo, Emma. 2003. *Unsettling Memories: Narratives of the Emergency in Delhi*. Berkeley: University of California Press.

Taussig, Michael T. 1992. "Maleficium: State Fetishism." *The Nervous System*, 111–40. New York: Routledge.

———. 1997. *The Magic of the State*. New York: Routledge.

Taylor, Charles. 1987. "Interpretation and the Sciences of Man." *Interpretive Social Science: A Second Look*, ed. Paul Rabinow and William M. Sullivan, 33–81. Berkeley: University of California Press.

———. 1990. "Modes of Civil Society." *Public Culture* 3(1), 95–118.

———. 2004. *Modern Social Imaginaries*. Durham: Duke University Press.

Taylor, Diana. 1997. *Disappearing Acts: Spectacles of Gender and Nationalism in Argentina's "Dirty War."* Durham: Duke University Press.

Taylor, Peter J. 1994. "The State as Container: Territoriality in the Modern World System." *Progress in Human Geography* 18(2), 151–62.

Tennekoon, N. Serena. 1988. "Rituals of Development: The Accelerated Mahaväli Development Program of Sri Lanka." *American Ethnologist* 15(2), 294–310.

Ticktin, Miriam. 2006. "Where Ethics and Politics Meet: The Violence of Humanitarianism in France." *American Ethnologist* 33(1), 33–49.

Tilly, Charles. 1975. *The Formation of National States in Western Europe*. Princeton: Princeton University Press.

Tilman, Robert O. 1968. "Emergence of Black-Market Bureaucracy: Administration, Development, and Corruption in New States." *Public Administration Review* 28(5), 437–44.

Times of India. 1989. "Bofors Is Not a Major Issue: Pre-Election Survey 4." 13 August, 1, 7.

Trouillot, Michel-Rolph. 2003. "The Anthropology of the State in the Age of Globalization: Close Encounters of the Deceptive Kind." *Global Transformations: Anthropology and the Modern World*, 79–96. New York: Palgrave Macmillan.

Tsing, Anna Lowenhaupt. 2004. *Friction: An Ethnography of Global Connection*. Princeton: Princeton University Press.

United Nations Development Program (UNDP). 2007. *Human Development Report.* http://hdr.undp.org/en/reports/.

——. 2009. *Human Development Report.* http://hdr.undp.org/en/reports/.

Urla, Jacqueline. 1993. "Cultural Politics in an Age of Statistics: Numbers, Nations, and the Making of Basque Identity." *American Ethnologist* 20 (4 November), 818–43.

Vajpeyi, Ananya. 2007. *Prolegomena to the Study of People and Places in Violent India.* New Delhi: WISCOMP Foundation.

Verdery, Katherine. 1996. *What Was Socialism, and What Comes Next?* Princeton: Princeton University Press.

——. 1998. "Transnationalism, Nationalism, Citizenship, and Property: Eastern Europe since 1989." *American Ethnologist* 25(2), 291–306.

——. 2004. "After Socialism." *A Companion to the Anthropology of Politics,* ed. David Nugent and Joan Vincent, 21–36. Malden, Mass.: Blackwell.

Virmani, Arvind. 2005. "India's Economic Growth History: Fluctuations, Trends, Break Points and Phases." Occasional Paper, Indian Council for Research on International Economic Relations, New Delhi.

Visvanathan, Shiv, and Harsh Sethi, eds. 1998. *Foul Play: Chronicles of Corruption in India 1947–1997.* New Delhi: Banyan Books.

Wade, Robert. 1982. "The System of Administrative and Political Corruption: Canal Irrigation in South India." *Journal of Development Studies* 18(3), 287–328.

——. 1984. "Irrigation Reform in Conditions of Populist Anarchy: An Indian Case." *Journal of Development Economics* 14(3), 285–303.

——. 1985. "The Market for Public Office: Why the Indian State Is Not Better at Development." *World Development* 13(4), 467–97.

Wadley, Susan S. 1994. *Struggling with Destiny in Karimpur, 1925–1984.* Berkeley: University of California Press.

Walker, R. B. J. 1993. *Inside/Outside: International Relations as Politics Theory.* Cambridge: Cambridge University Press.

Weber, Max. 1968. "Bureaucracy." *Economy and Society: An Outline of Interpretive Sociology,* ed. G. Roth and C. Wittich, 2:956–1005. New York: Bedminster Press.

West, Harry. 2009. "'Govern Yourselves': Democracy and Carnage in Northern Mozambique." *Democracy: Anthropological Approaches,* ed. Julia Paley, 97–122. Santa Fe: School of American Research Press.

Wheeler, Stanton, ed. 1969. *On Record: Files and Dossiers in American Life.* New York: Russell Sage Foundation.

Williams, Robert. 1999. "New Concepts for Old?" *Third World Quarterly* 20(3), 503–13.

Woost, Michael D. 1993. "Nationalizing the Local Past in Sri Lanka: Histories of Nation and Development in a Sinhalese Village." *American Ethnologist* 20(3), 502–21.

World Bank. 2008. "World Development Indicators Database." Revised 17 October 2008. World Bank website, http://www.worldbank.org; accessed 11 November 2008.

Yang, Mayfair Mei-hui. 1989. "The Gift Economy and State Power in China." *Comparative Studies in Society and History* 31 (1 January), 25–54.

Bardhan, Pranab, 79, 80, 138, 280, 300n59, 303n14, 310n10, 313n49, 326n1

bare life, production of: camps and, 6–7; China and, 323n1; classification, enumeration, and, 261, 263; neoliberal governmentality and, 238, 240, 272; population quality and, 323n1; prisons and, 297n17; sovereignty and, 17–18, 105, 142; statistical enumeration and, 263; structural violence and, 21

Baviskar, Amita, 320n34

BDO. *See* Block Development Officer (BDO) Satendra Malik (pseud.)

Below Poverty Line (BPL) as category, 58, 108, 156, 292

Benjamin, Walter, 320n31

Bharatiya Janata Party (BJP), 291

Bharatiya Kisan Union (BKU), 82, 89–90, 99, 284, 308nn56–57

Bharat Nirman program, 292

Bhatti, Jaspal, 112, 310n5

Biehl, João, 298n32

Bimaru states, 215

biogas projects, 154–55, 315n23

biopolitics and biopower: Agamben's *homo sacer* and, 16–18, 261–62; counterfeit data and, 228; disaggregated state and, 71–72; enumeration and, 261–69; Foucault's concept and Agamben's critique, 14–17; normalizing statistics and, 42; population knowledge and, 245; sovereignty, nationalism, and, 17–19; state theory and, 41–42; statistical data and classification and, 263, 265, 268; universality implicit in, 43. *See also* governmentality and neoliberalism; structural violence

birth records, 264–65

Bisipara, Orissa, 126

BKU (Bharatiya Kisan Union), 82, 89–90, 99, 284, 308nn56–57

Bloch, Marc, 226

Block Development Officer (BDO) Satendra Malik (pseud.): biogas projects and inscription, 154–55; camp for pensioners and, 8–9; complaints and, 175–78, 186; education and, 209–10; on political interference, 179; special signature of, 230; targets and, 47–48

block offices, 26, 114, 156

blocks: camp for pensioners and, 8; ICDS and, 276, 324n8; organizational structure, 27–28; progress reports and political interference, 48–49; statistics and, 157

Blot, Richard K., 196

Bofors affair, 94

Bourdieu, Pierre, 224, 227, 310n8

Brahmins, 321n46

branches. *See* levels, branches, and functions of the state

Brazil, 298n32, 325n27

bribery. *See* corruption and discourses of corruption

Briggs, Charles L., 310n6

British colonial state, 157–58

brokers, 130–32, 313n40

Bubandt, Nils, 321n47

Buddhism, Tibetan, 213

bureaucracy and bureaucrats: appeals to higher authority, 50, 87–88, 96; bending to unintended ends, by villagers, 134; breaks in service, 182, 318n48; bureaucratization of daily life, 32; contingency, bureaucratic, 9, 13–14; contingency and chaos vs. disciplinary rationality, 9, 13–14; educational qualifications, reverence for, 208–12, 225; elected officials, tensions with, 51–52; examinations, 209, 224–25, 320n25; imagined state from position of, 104; India's political/administrative structure, 26–29; indifference vs. arbitrariness and, 6, 23–25; intra-bureaucratic conflict and complaints, 180–87; meritocratic discourse, 81, 208–9, 223–24, 320n25; promotion vs. appointment, 320n26; public interaction around government offices, 82; public servant–private citizen distinction, collapsing, 90; regime vs., 102; respect, narratives of loss of, 120–21; rule manipulation, 50; status and, 320n27; subverted goals of, 23; targets, 47–48, 154, 301n9; transfers by Dalit government, 322n53. *See also* corruption and discourses of corruption; Integrated Child Development Services (ICDS) program; writing, bureaucratic; *specific positions*

Butler, Judith, 304n27, 310n8

Calhoun, Craig, 296nn9–10

camp as archetypal space, 7–8, 296n12, 296n14, 297n16

camp for pensioners, 8–14

capital, industrial, 292–93

caring: arbitrariness and, 23–24; economic rationality and, 13; paradox of death and, 14; uncaring as constitutive modality of the state, 23

castes, lower and scheduled: biopolitics and, 58; corruption, imagined state, and, 100–104; Dalit-led governments in U.P., 322n53; education and, 211; employment quotas for, 56, 222–24; hiring quotas, 178–79; house construction corruption case ("Sripal"), 86–88; housing programs for, 86; land allocation case ("Ramnarain"), 50–51; mass media, corruption narratives, and, 100–104; Muslims and, 312n25; postcolonial state and, 98–99; programs for lower-caste women, 32; village governance reform and, 137; in village population, 27

categorization and classification, 145, 155, 156–57

CDPOs. See Child Development Project Officer (CDPO) Asha Agarwal (pseud.); Child Development Project Officers

census data: collection methods, 42–43; Lévi-Strauss and, 316n30; Mahila Samakhya and, 268–69; narrative and statistics, 159

Chakrabarty, Dipesh, 303n13

Chanakya, 302n20

Chatterjee, Partha, 107, 291, 303n12

Chen, Shaohua, 295n2

Chidambaram, Palaniappan, 15–16, 286

Child Development Project Officer (CDPO) Asha Agarwal (pseud.): in bureaucratic structure, 26–27; complaints and, 170–72, 181–84, 207; education and, 210–12; inspections and, 164–66, 253–60; job applicants and, 229

Child Development Project Officers (CDPOs), 162–66, 181–84

China, 298n33

citizenship: camp for pensioners and assertion of, 12; literacy and democratic citizenship, 219–26; postcolonial state and, 98–99; refugees as outside, 19

civil society, 77–78, 107, 180

Clanchy, M. T., 148, 153, 205, 207, 217–18, 226, 315n17

classification and categorization, 145, 155, 156–57

class war, fear of, 291

Cohen, Lawrence, 7

Cohn, Bernard, 136, 159, 305n36

Collins, James, 196

colonial state, British, 157–58

Communist Party of India-Marxist-Leninist (CPI-ML), 286

competence, education associated with, 210–12

competitive populism, 290–94

complaints: appeals to higher authority, 50, 87–88, 96, 174; conflictual relations revealed in, 167; fabrication of, 185–86; files of, 146, 147; inspections and, 166; intra-bureaucratic conflicts, 180–87; language of submission, 317n40; lawsuits vs., 169, 170; number of, 179; oral vs. written, 168–69, 198–99, 200–201, 207; petitions vs., 167–68; reluctance to submit, 175, 179–81; structural violence and, 167, 173–74, 178, 184; transformation into statistics, 156; village feuds, 169–74; by villagers against state officials, 174–80

computer literacy, 321n36

Congress party, 101–3, 104, 245–46, 291

Constitution of India, 247

construction boom, 282. See also Jawahar Rojgaar Yojana (JRY)

contingency, bureaucratic, 9, 13–14

contract enforcement, 204

corruption and discourses of corruption, 80–81; overview and terminology, 75–77; accountability discourse and, 97–98, 99; BKU and, 82, 89–90; Bofors affair, 94; bribe giving as cultural practice, 85–86; causes of, in the literature, 303n16; civil society and, 77–78, 107; colonial vs. postcolonial, 98–99; complaints against headmen, 170–74; conceptual and methodological problems in, 104–10; definitions and meanings of, 79–80, 303nn14–

corruption and discourses (*cont.*)

15; development narratives, 114–25; documents for cash, 227, 323n62; in economics vs. anthropology and sociology, 310n10; examinations and, 224; as folklore, 302n4; house construction case ("Sripal"), 86–88; incentives and, 112; incompetence, mismanagement, and, 123, 312n31; land records case ("Sharmaji" and "Verma"), 82–86; mass media representations and the imagined state ("Ram Singh" case), 100–104; Nehru's social engineering and, 136–37; newspaper narratives, 92–97; policy implementation and, 91; political anthropology and, 136–38; poor, adverse impact on, 91–92; rumors and, 97; Shukla's *Raag Darbari* and Bailey's *Politics and Social Change*, 125–35; social engineering schemes and, 136–37; social judgment of, 80–81; state credibility, undermining of, 99–100; state-society and public-private distinction and, 90; structural violence and, 76, 109–10, 111, 138; Third World stereotypes of, 79

counterfeit writing, 214, 226–31

court systems, 135, 201

cultural capital: complaints and, 169, 175, 179–80; corruption case ("Ram Singh"), 100–104; exams and, 224; literacy and, 195–96; performance of lack of, 103

cultural struggle, 61–62, 108

currency, forged, 227

Cuttack, Orissa, 130

cynicism in Bailey's *Politics and Social Change*, 132

Dalits. *See* castes, lower and scheduled

dam projects, 287

darbar (royal court), 126–29, 304n25

Das, Veena: on agency, 299n49; on bureaucracy, 6; on forgery and mimicry, 230; *Life and Words*, 20; on magical-rational state, 320n28; on resettlement colonies, 7; on routinized misery, 296n11; on social suffering, 296n10; on structural violence, 20; on violence, 318n12

death. *See* mortality; structural violence

death records, 264–65

degrees, educational, 208–12, 225

democracy: Bubandt on, 321n47; citizenship and, 99, 219–26; competitive populism and the poor, 290–94; forgery and, 227; literacy and, 192, 200, 214–15; literacy and democratic citizenship, 219–26; malign neglect and, 138; neoliberalism and, 276–78; oral communication and, 218; poor, participation of, 18; population control and, 245; states of exception and, 6; universal suffrage, 219–20. *See also* village councils (*panchayats*)

Department of Education, 249

Derrida, Jacques, 193, 194, 318n3, 319n14

developmental rhetoric: Bailey's *Politics and Social Change*, Shukla's *Raag Darbari*, and, 132–33, 134–35; empowerment and, 250; in political anthropology, 128; transnational construction of the poor and, 239; tribal rebellion and, 286–87

development programs. *See* governmentality and neoliberalism; welfare, antipoverty, and subsidy programs; *specific programs*

de Vries, Pieter, 308n59

dignity, 222, 322n49

disaggregated state. *See* state, the

discourse, as term, 76–77. *See also* corruption and discourses of corruption

District Magistrate (DM): in bureaucratic structure, 27; camp for pensioners and, 8; complaints to, 87–88; coordination efforts of, 28; promotion vs. appointment, 320n26

District Poverty Initiatives Project (DPIP), 322n56

District Rural Redevelopment Authority (DRDA), 116

di Tella, Rafael, 304n17

documents as magical and revered, 212–14

Doig, Alan, 303n14

dominant classes, 280

domination: Abrams on, 43; counterfeiting and, 215, 231; cultural struggle and, 108; literacy and, 213–14; statistics and, 158; writing and, 142, 193–95, 199. *See also* structural violence

Doordarshan (state television), 103, 307n43

Dube, S. C., 136
duplicate, counterfeit writing, 214, 226–31
Durkheim, Emile, 153

economic growth. See growth patterns
education: anganwadi workers as teachers,
270–71; certification of, 229; fetishization of educational qualification, 208–12,
225; "Montessori" schools, 47, 270;
quotas and qualification levels, 223–24;
reform movement and educational
institutions, 129; Sarv Shiksha Abhiyan
program, 292; selfishness associated
with levels of, 120; service sector and, 281
efficiency, 25, 124, 138
egalitarian commitment of the Indian state,
222
Elden, Stuart, 298n34
elected officials: interference by, 48–50;
intra-bureaucratic conflict and, 186–87;
suspicion and tensions with bureaucrats,
50–52, 122. See also headmen
Electricity Board, 89–90
Elyachar, Julia, 309n76
e-mail, 202, 319n17
Emergency of 1975–77, India, 7, 111–12,
245, 296n15
employment: anganwadi workers as both
workers and clients of welfare state, 183–
84, 256; hiring decisions and caste, 178–
79; patterns, by sector, 280–86; quotas,
56, 222–24; work, struggle over meaning
of, 269–72
empowerment: corruption discourse and,
109; entitlement vs., 109; literacy and,
197–98, 214–21; NGOs and, 324–25n15;
transnational neoliberalism and, 250
empowerment programs. See governmentality and neoliberalism; Mahila
Samakhya
enframing, 145, 188
Engels, Friedrich, 156
engineering development, 114–25
English bureaucracy, 202, 315n14
entitlement vs. empowerment, 109
enumerated communities, 158, 316n31
enumeration. See statistics and
normalization

everyday practices and routines: meanings
constituted out of, 70; neoliberalism
globalization and, 272; state represented
in, 55–56, 58–60, 67–68
evil eye (buri nazar), 267, 325n25
examinations, 209, 224–25, 320n25
exception, states of, 6, 7, 17–18, 298n30
exploitation. See structural violence

Fabian, Johannes, 303n11
family, Hegel on, 302n6
family planning, 238
Farmer, Paul, 21
Fassin, Didier, 7, 296n12
federalism, Indian system of, 27–28
Feldman, Ilana, 297n16
feminist movements, 249, 276
Ferguson, James, 109
fiction, pedagogic function for, 217, 321n38
files: bureaucracy and creation of, 314n11,
314n14; categorization and, 156; complaints and, 317n40; contents of, 146;
destruction of, 214; the "file self,"
314n12; information retrieval and, 145–
46; life history of, 146–47; meanings of
states and, 70; misplaced, 200; negative
decisions in, 147; notations in, as bureaucratic activity, 150, 151; red tape and continuities with colonial practices, 147–48;
standardization and, 188; thickness of,
258, 264; transfers of officials and, 147
First Information Reports (FIRS), 200
Food Corporation of India (FCI), 247
foreign exchange crisis, 30
forged documents, 214, 226–31
forms: anonymity, 145, 188, 314n6; enframing, categorization, and, 145, 156; performativity and, 314n10; portability of, 145;
replicability, 24, 145, 188, 314n6; standardization and, 145, 188
Foucault, Michel: on biopower, 14–15; on
governmentality, 238, 239, 261; on governmentalization of the state, 46; on Nazi
biopolitics, 297n26; on security vs. sovereignty, 18; state theory underlying, 41–
42; on statistics, 262; on technologies of
rule, 242
Fraser, Nancy, 271

Ideological State Apparatuses (ISAs), 65

illiteracy. See literacy

Imperial Assemblage (1877), 305n36

imperialism, Western, vigilance toward, 106–7

inclusion: literacy and, 225–26; paradox of poverty and, 6, 18; violence, popular sovereignty, and, 18

income and wealth gap, 281, 325n28

incompetence and caste assumptions, 223

India: Constitution of, 247; federalism in, 27–28; liberalization program, history of, 29–32, 276–78; political/administrative structure, 26–29. See also specific topics and programs

Indian Administrative Service (IAS), 27, 299n52, 320n26

Indian Civil Service, 299n52

Indian Council for Child Welfare, 247

India Today, 95, 307n44

indifference vs. arbitrariness, 6, 24

indigenous, tribal population, 286–90

Indira Awaas Yojana (Indira Housing Program), 86, 161

Indonesia, 321n47, 325n27

industrial capital, 292–93

infant mortality rate, 3, 243–44, 324n4

informal sector, 282–83

infrastructure projects and tribal rebellion, 287

inscription: anticipatory, 161–63; e-mail, 202, 319n17; European superiority and, 319n20; forgery and authenticity, 226–31; future of, 205; publicity campaign in Shukla's Raag Darbari, 133–34; "religions of the book," 319n18; researcher complicity with reification and, 66–67. See also literacy; writing, bureaucratic

inspections, 160–66, 167, 173, 252–61

Integrated Child Development Services (ICDS) program: bureaucratic structure of, 26–27; data collection and enumeration and, 252–53, 262–68; data comparison and, 157; evaluation and overappraisal of, 262; expansion into universal program, 244, 292; goal of, 26; inscription in, 66–67; inspections and, 163; liberal welfare, governmentality, and, 243–48; Mahila Samakhya com-

pared to, 240, 242–43, 250–51; nation and, 62; residency requirements and counterfeit certificates, 227–29; surveillance and monitoring through inspection, 252–61; ubiquity of the state and, 65; village office, 251–52; work, struggle over meaning of, 269–71. See also anganwadi workers

Integrated Rural Development Programme (IRDP), 307n46

inventories, 195

involvement, reluctance of, 175, 317n44

Irrigation Department, 32, 300n57

Islamic sharia' and writing vs. orality, 201

Islamic terrorists, 286

Jain, Arvind K., 303n14, 304n18

Jats, 155

Jawaharlal Nehru National Urban Renewal Mission, 292

Jawahar Rojgaar Yojana (JRY): budget and, 31; complaints and, 172–73, 317n46; corruption narratives and, 114–25; history of, 311n18

Jenkins, Rob, 317n43

Johnston, Michael, 303n16, 313n40

Joshi, Sharad, 284

junior engineers of the Rural Employment Scheme, or JE (RES), 116–23, 161, 175–76

jurisdictions of Center vs. state governments, 27–28

Kalahandi, Orissa, 126

Kamtekar, Indivar, 23

Kantola, Johanna, 301n7

Kapur, Devesh, 317n35

Karnataka Rajya Raitha Sangha (KRRS), 284

Kashmir, 286

Kaviraj, Sudipta, 158, 203, 205, 221–22, 262–63, 316n31, 321n39, 321n44, 321n46

Kerala, 215, 296n8

Keynes, John Maynard, 109

Khan, Salman, 297n27

Khanna, Jyoti, 313n40

Kisan Seva Kendra (Farmers' service centers) program, 149–52, 162, 163, 198–99, 206–7

Kleinman, Arthur, 6, 296nn10–11

knowledge: biopower and, 245; knowledge claims and nature of the state, 53; situated, 53, 102, 104; subaltern knowledge of levels of state authority, 88

Kohrman, Matthew, 296n12, 298n33

Kopytoff, Igor, 146–47

Krishna, Raj, 4

Kulkarni, Vani S., 322n56

land: activism for reforms, 56; corruption case ("Sharmaji" and "Verma"), 82–86; eviction and displacement of tribal people, 287–90; interagency conflict case ("Ramnarain"), 50–52; redistribution programs, 208

land records officials. See patwaris

Latour, Bruno, 23

lawsuits vs. complaints, 169, 170

legitimacy, 60–61, 230

levels, branches, and functions of the state: in anthropological research, 301n12; biopolitics and, 42; disaggregated state and, 45–46, 52–53; policy tactics and, 69; situated constructions and, 102; subaltern knowledge of, 88. See also state, the

Lévi-Strauss, Claude, 192–95, 316n30

Lewis, Oscar, 136, 313n44

liberal welfare. See governmentality and neoliberalism; Integrated Child Development Services (ICDS) program

liberation, narrative of literacy as, 215–18

Life and Words (Das), 20

life threats, 87–88

literacy: overview, 191–92, 195–96; binary encoding vs. gradient of, 216; campaigns for, 215, 320n34; computer literacy, 321n36; democratic citizenship and, 219–26; dependency on writing, 203; documents as magical and revered, 212–14; educational qualifications and degrees, fetishization of, 208–12, 225; liberation, problematic teleology of, 215–18; multilingual context of, 197, 221; newspapers and, 306n43; orality and, 196–97, 198–208, 217–18; police and, 313n38; political context and, 216–17; rates of, 199, 219, 320n34, 321n45; reading vs. writing ability, 196, 320n34; restricted, 175, 194–201,

205, 207, 213, 216, 319n23; social anthropology and Lévi-Strauss on, 192–95; structural violence and, 218, 225–26, 232–33; universal, worldwide goal of, 319n23; women's political participation and, 321n42. See also inscription; writing, bureaucratic

Lock, Margaret, 6, 296nn10–11

logocentrism, 319n14

Lomnitz, Claudio, 311n16

Machiavelli, Niccolò, 302n20

Maharashtra, 284, 286

Mahatma Gandhi National Rural Employment Guarantee Act (2005), 31–32, 278, 292, 311n18, 326nn32–33

Mahila Samakhya: as empowerment program, 248–51; enumeration and, 268–69; ICDS compared to, 240, 242–43, 250–51; introduction of, 31; neoliberal transformation and, 273; work, struggle over meaning of, 271–72

malnutrition, 324n8

manufacturing sector, 282

Maoist insurgency, 286–90, 291

Marcus, George E., 302n17

market-friendly reforms (1991), 240–41

Marx, Karl, 194, 297n18

mass media. See media and mass media; television

Massumi, Brian, 300n60, 311n15

maternal mortality rate, 243

Mayer, Adrian, 136

Mazdoor Kisan Shakti Sangathan, 317n43

Mbembe, Achille, 16, 297n25, 306n40

McIvor, Stephanie, 303n14

media and mass media: autonomy of, 38; corruption narratives, imagined state, and, 100–104; Herzfeld on manipulation of, 308n68; "new age of orality" and, 205. See also newspapers; television

Meerut district, 155

Mehta, Pratap Bhanu, 317n35

Mendelsohn, Oliver, 321n48

meritocratic discourse, 81, 208–9, 223–24, 320n25

Messick, Brinkley, 201, 202–3, 214, 230, 314n6, 319n13

Michelangelo, 323n65
micro-markers, 59
middle class, 22, 25, 30, 98, 102, 282, 285, 293
Miller, D. F., 136
Miller, Peter, 239
mining, 287–88
Ministry of Health and Family Welfare, 244
Ministry of Women and Child Development (MWCD), 244, 249, 324n6
Mitchell, Timothy, 55
modernization, 135
modernization theory model, 245
Mohanpur, Orissa, 130–31
moral community, 298n36
moral norms and corruption, 80–81, 307n53
Morris, Rosalind, 297n23, 298n36
mortality: death records, 264–65; Foucault on biopower and, 14–15; poverty and excess deaths, 4–6; rates of infant, child, and maternal mortality, 3, 243–44, 246–47, 324n4. See also biopolitics and biopower
Mughal bureaucracy, 148, 157, 316n31
Mukerji, Chandra, 311n20
mukhya sevikas (supervisors), 27
Muslim-majority villages, 254
Muzzafarnagar district, 155
Mwangi, Wambui, 227, 229, 323n59

Naidu, Chandrababu, 292, 325–26n29
Nandigram, 289
narrative: of literacy as liberation, 215–18; statistics and, 153, 156–57, 159, 166; as term, 76–77, 302n4
narratives of corruption: action, relationship with, 122–23; alteration of, 138; analytical and ideological work performed by, 114; competing, 124; engineering development narratives, 114–25; as genre, 111; importance of, 111–13; Nehru's social engineering and, 136–37; political anthropology and, 128, 136–38; public officials caricatured for touring, 133–34; Shukla's Raag Darbari and Bailey's Politics and Social Change, 125–35; as storytelling form, 113; structural violence and, 111, 138; travel of, 113–14

National Highway Development Project, 287
nationalism: Bailey's Politics and Social Change and, 132; Foucauldian biopolitics and violence of, 19; political anthropology and, 128; Shukla's Raag Darbari and, 134–35
National Policy for Children, 243, 247
National River Linking Project, 287
nation-states: comparison between, 69–71; Foucauldian biopolitics and, 18–19; states vs., 295n1; struggle for the imagined state and, 61–62
natural disasters, state response to, 4
Naxalite movement, 286, 290, 291, 326n7
Nazi death camps, 7–8, 297n26
Nehru, Jawaharlal: corruption narratives and, 114, 313n45; literacy and, 219, 221; neoliberalism and, 241; reforms of, 136
neoliberalism. See governmentality and neoliberalism
newspapers: autonomy of, 30n38; corruption narratives, 92–97; English vs. Hindi, 94–95; literacy and, 306n43; local sections, 93; metropolitan, 95; transnational capital and, 306n41
Nicholas, Ralph, 136
Nielsen, Morten, 300n3
Nigeria, 304n20
Nirbal Varg Awaas Yojana (Weaker Sections Housing Program), 86
nongovernmental organizations (NGOs), 249
normalization. See statistics and normalization
norms, moral, 80–81, 307n53
NREGA. See Mahatma Gandhi National Rural Employment Guarantee Act (2005)
Nuijten, Monique, 302n1
Nussbaum, Martha C., 321nn41–42
nutrition, supplementary, 247–48, 264, 266
Nyaya Panchayat, 312n24

Of Grammatology (Derrida), 193, 319n14
Opler, Morris, 136
orality and literacy, 196–97, 198–208, 217–18
oral vs. written testimony, 168–69
Orissa, 125, 130–34

Pai, Sudha, 321n42

Panchayati Raj legislation, 31, 69, 311n21

panchayats. See village councils

para-ethnography, 302n17

Parry, Jonathan, 123, 310n5

patwaris (land records officials): in bureaucratic structure, 27; corruption case
("Sharmaji" and "Verma"), 82–86; interagency conflict and, 51; oral performance
of records, 206–7

peasant movements, 284. *See also* Bharatiya
Kisan Union (BKU)

performativity: bribes and, 84; forms and,
145, 314n10; lack of cultural capital and,
103; the state and, 304n27

petitions vs. complaints, 167–68

phonocentrism, 319n14

Pierce, Steven, 303n9

Planning Commission, 136

pluricenteredness as methodological challenge, 64

police: complaints against, 186; First Information Reports (FIRs), 200; literacy and,
313n38; in Shukla's *Raag Darbari*, 128–29;
writing by, 143

political action: collaboration-resistance
dichotomy and cultural struggle, 108; disaggregated state and policy intervention,
68–69; statistics as, 158

political anthropology and corruption narratives, 128, 136–38

political capital, 175, 176, 260

political society, Chatterjee on, 78

Politics and Social Change: Orissa in 1959
(Bailey), 125, 130–34

population as field of action, 238, 323n1. *See
also* governmentality and neoliberalism

population growth, 244

population-level analysis and normalization,
15

population planning, 244–47

populism, competitive, 290–94

postcolonial state: Bardhan on dominant
classes in, 280; development mission of,
22, 240, 241, 250; discourses of corruption and accountability in, 98–99; excess
deaths in, 5; Latour on, 23; literacy and,
200; Shukla's *Raag Darbari* and, 125–26;

statistics and, 158. *See also* governmentality and neoliberalism; state, the

poverty, violence of. *See* structural violence

poverty and the poor: Below Poverty Line
(BPL) as category, 58, 108, 156, 292;
bureaucratic writing and, 149, 187–88;
Chidambaram on wiping out, 15–16; construction of the poor as social class, 107–
8; disaggregation of, 44, 300n5; economic growth and, 279, 285; inclusion,
paradox of, 6, 18; intra-bureaucratic conflict and, 183–84, 187; literacy and teleology of liberation, 215–18; measures of,
58, 295n2; normalization of, 15–16; performance of, indexing lack of cultural
capital, 103; possible explanations for,
22–23; rates of, 3–4, 295n2; researcher
complicity and, 66; situated knowledge
and, 53; state legitimacy and, 60; statistics and, 158–59; as structural violence,
19–22; structural violence as lens on, 22;
thanatopolitics and, 5–6, 17, 275; transnational development discourses and
construction of, 239; tribal people, 286–
90. *See also* welfare, antipoverty, and subsidy programs

programs. *See* welfare, antipoverty, and subsidy programs

promotion vs. appointment, 320n26

protectionism, 283

public, construction of, 96–97

public culture: corruption, imagined state,
and, 100–105; ethnography of the state
and, 77; representations of corruption in,
92–100

Public Distribution System (PDS), 31

"public sphere," 305n37

punishment posts, 181, 317n47

Raag Darbari (Shukla), 125–36, 318n49

Radcliffe-Brown, A. R., 309n71

radio, transnational, 30n38

Radnóti, Sándor, 227, 323n60

Rajasthan, 324–25n15

Ramnarain (pseud.), 50–52

Ravallion, Martin, 295n2

Reddy, Y. S. Rajasekhara (YSR), 291–92

Redfield, Peter, 297n16

Spencer, Jonathan, 313n38

Sripal (pseud.), 86–88

state, the: Abrams's institutional-conceptual dichotomy, 43–44; anthropology, levels of the state in, 301n12; bureaucracy-regime distinction, 102; capacity and capability, assumptions in, 183; civil society and, 77–78; comparative study, implications for, 69–71; credibility, undermining, 99–100; discursive constitution of, through corruption, 78, 105–6; egalitarian commitment, 222; as employer, 322n51; epistemological uncertainty and, 52–53; everyday practice and discursive construction of, 77; as facilitator of development and empowering agent, 250; fantasy in construction of, 308n69; fieldwork examples of disaggregation, 47–52; Foucault on governmentalization of, 46; Foucault's biopolitics and, 41–42; hegemonic blocs and cultural struggle, 61; knowledge linked with state power, 192; legitimacy and, 60–61; liberalization program, history of, 29–32, 276–78; literacy and, 191; as magical-rational, 320n28; mass media and imagining, 100–104; methodological challenges of translocalism, pluricenteredness, ubiquity, and complicity with reification, 63–68; nation, the transnational, and the imagined state, 61–63; nation-state vs., 295n1; newspaper narratives and, 92–97; political implications of conceptions of, 68–69, 108; positioned imagining of, 104; practices, discourses, and representations of unified state, 55–60; scholarly and political gains and costs of unitary concept of, 53–55; as social imaginary, 56, 60–61; society vs., 90; sources of everyday instantiation of, 59; uncaring as constitutive modality of, 23; unitary conceptions vs. disaggregation of, 44–47; Weber on violence and, 19. See also bureaucracy and bureaucrats; corruption and discourses of corruption

statistics and normalization: "avalanche of numbers," 262, 268; biopolitics and, 14–15, 42–43, 49, 71–72; birth and death records, 264–65; block biogas projects and, 154–55; block progress reports and political interference, 48–49; as bureaucratic writing, 153–59; classification and, 156–57; comparison facilitated by, 157; counterfeit data and biopolitics, 228; forms and, 145; Foucault on, 262; governmentality and enumeration, 251, 252–53, 261–69; legibility and, 42; narrative and, 153, 156–57, 159, 166; as political intervention, 158; poverty and statistical representation, 58; registers and, 148; resistance to, 266–67

status in bureaucracy, 320n27

Steinmetz, George, 114, 302n4

Stock, Brian, 205

Stoler, Ann L., 113, 300n60

structural violence: arbitrariness and, 24–25; armed violence and, 286–90; class divisions and, 285; complaints and, 167, 173–74, 178, 184; corruption and, 76, 111, 138; corruption discourse and undermining, 109–10; defined, 19–21; disaggregated view of the state and, 47; egalitarian commitment and, 222; governmentality, neoliberalism, and, 251–52, 272–78; governmentality and, 251–52; international silence on, 63; intra-bureaucratic conflict and, 184; literacy, writing, and, 191–92, 196, 207–8, 218, 225–26, 232–33; mortality and, 21–22; neoliberalism and, 272–78; political anthropology and, 137–38; possible explanations for, 22–23, 25–26; poverty through lens of, 22; statistics and, 159, 263, 266; survival and, 319n24; transnational, 275; uncaring and, 23. See also biopolitics and biopower

subaltern knowledge, 88

subaltern resistance. See resistance, subaltern

Subdistrict Magistrate (SDM), 8

subsidy programs. See welfare, antipoverty, and subsidy programs

suffrage, universal, 219–20

suicides of farmers, 284, 326n3

Sunder Rajan, Rajeswari, 296n7

supplements, statistical, 155–56, 316n25

surveillance: disaggregated state and, 267–68; governmentality and, 252–61; inspections, 160–66, 167, 173, 252–61; registers and, 148–49

Tandon, B. N., 324n8
targets, 47–48, 154, 301n9
Tarlo, Emma, 200, 230, 314n13, 318nn10–11, 323n61
tax collections, increase in, 292–93
Taylor, Charles, 303n12
Taylor, Peter, 301n6
tehsildar (subdistrict officer), 8–13
television: corruption narratives, 101–3; democratic politics and, 225; *Doordarshan* (state television), 103, 307n43; English-language, 221; orality and, 218; *Raag Darbari* serialized on, 126; *Ulta-Pulta* show, 310n5
Thakurs, 155, 316n24
"Third World," 79, 303n10
Tibet, 213
Tikait, Mahendar Singh, 99
Times of India, 94
Total Rural Sanitation Program, 292
touring, public officials accused of, 133–34
translocality: corruption discourse and, 105; imagined state and, 62; Mahila Samkhya and, 249; as methodological challenge, 63–64
transnationalism and the interstate system: corruption narratives, migration of, 113; empowerment strategies and, 250; governmentality, global, 239; high-sovereign state as always already transnational, 241; local newspapers and transnational capital, 306n41; national policymaking articulated with, 275–76; silence on structural violence, 63; state imaginary and, 62–63; statistics and, 158–59; structural violence and, 275; tension between legitimacy and sovereignty, 106; universal literacy goal, 319n23; urgency, lack of, 275
transparency narratives, 138
tribal people, 286–90
triplicate, 148
Tristes Tropiques (Lévi-Strauss), 316n30
tubewells, 177–78
Tuljapurkar, Shripad, 296n8

ubiquity of the state as methodological challenge, 64–65
Ulta-Pulta (television show), 310n5
United States, 59, 202, 217, 283, 326n31
untouchable castes. *See* castes, lower and scheduled
Uttar Pradesh state government, 149–52, 322n53

Vajpeyi, Ananya, 7
Verma (pseud.), 82–86
village cooperatives, 129
village councils (*panchayats*): complaints against, 198–99; election of, 311n21; inclusion and, 322n56; Jawahar Rojgaar Yojana (JRY) and, 115–16; reform movement and, 129, 137, 311n21; secretaries, 117–21; in Shukla's *Raag Darbari*, 132; system of, 115
village development workers (VDWs), 86–88, 305n30
village feuds, 169–74
villages, romanticization of, 127–28
villagewide meetings, 115–16
violence: armed, 286–90, 291; biopower and, 16; direct vs. structural, 21; episodic, 20; Gandhian discourse, 127; invisible forms of, 5; life threats, 87–88; of nationalism, 19; popular sovereignty and, 18; refugees and, 19; Scott on state simplifications and, 304n21; in Shukla's *Raag Darbari*, 127. *See also* structural violence

Wade, Robert, 311n19
Weber, Max: on appeals, 317n39; on meritocracy, 224; on power in personalistic social world vs. bureaucratic, 24; on rationality in bureaucracy, 208–9; on salaries and status, 320n27; on state as monopoly of violence, 19; on writing, 314n3, 314n5
welfare, antipoverty, and subsidy programs: comparison and, 70; competitive populism and, 290–94; cutbacks in, 31; implementation, 25, 47–48, 91; neoliberal policies and, 32; proliferation of, 47, 301n8. *See also* governmentality and neoliberalism; Integrated Child Development Services (ICDS) program

West, as term, 303n10
Williams, Robert, 303n14
women, 155, 315n24, 325n23
Women's Development Programme (WDP), 324–25n15
work, struggle over meaning of, 269–72
workfare, 256, 269, 276
writing, bureaucratic: complaints, 166–87; constitutive function of, 143, 149–53; counterfeit, 214, 226–31; dependence on, 203–4; documents as magical and revered, 212–14; files, 145–48, 258, 314nn11–13, 317n40; forms, 144–45, 156, 314n10; importance of, and scholarship on, 141–44; inspections, 160–66, 167, 173; inventories, 195; letters of explanation, 165; movement of, 147, 203; orality and, 198–208; oral vs. written testimony, 168–69; proliferation of documents, 152–53; record destruction by peasant movements, 213–14; registers, 148–49, 164, 166, 259, 260, 263–65, 317n40; reports, 148; statistics and enumeration, 153–59; structural violence and, 196, 207–8. *See also* inscription; literacy

Yemen, 201, 202, 314n6, 319n13
YSR (Y. S. Rajasekhara Reddy), 291–92

Akhil Gupta is professor of anthropology at the University of California, Los Angeles. He is the author of *Postcolonial Developments: Agriculture in the Making of Modern India* and the editor, with K. Sivaramakrishnan, of *The State in India after Liberalization: Interdisciplinary Perspectives*.

Library of Congress Cataloging-in-Publication Data
Gupta, Akhil
Red tape : bureaucracy, structural violence, and poverty in India /
Akhil Gupta.
p. cm.—(A John Hope Franklin Center book)
Includes bibliographical references and index.
ISBN 978-0-8223-5098-9 (cloth : alk. paper)
ISBN 978-0-8223-5110-8 (pbk. : alk. paper)
1. Poverty—Government policy—India. 2. Public welfare—India.
3. Political corruption—India. 4. Bureaucracy—India. I. Title.
HC440.P6G858 2012
302.3'50954—dc23   2011053298

Made in the USA
Middletown, DE
16 January 2018